Unravelling unauthorized migrants' legal consciousness processes

Unravelling unauthorized migrants' legal consciousness processes

Mieke Kox

eleven

Published, sold and distributed by Eleven
P.O. Box 85576
2508 CG The Hague
The Netherlands
Tel.: +31 70 33 070 33
Fax: +31 70 33 070 30
e-mail: sales@elevenpub.nl
www.elevenpub.com

Sold and distributed in USA and Canada
Independent Publishers Group
814 N. Franklin Street
Chicago, IL 60610, USA
Order Placement: +1 800 888 4741
Fax: +1 312 337 5985
orders@ipgbook.com
www.ipgbook.com

Eleven is an imprint of Boom (The Hague).

Design cover: Textcetera, The Hague

ISBN 978-90-4730-209-4
ISBN 978-94-0011-399-2 (e-book)

Table of Contents

Abbreviations **ix**

1 Understanding unauthorized migrants' legal consciousness **1**
- 1.1 Why migrants' perspectives on the law matter 3
- 1.2 Guiding research questions 5
- 1.3 The Dutch legal context as a case of restricting unauthorized residence 7
- 1.4 Drawing upon legal consciousness 8
- 1.5 This book 12

2 Setting the scene: Regulating migration **17**
- 2.1 Regulating migration in a European context 17
- 2.2 Regulating migration in the Netherlands 23
  - 2.2.1 Protecting the Dutch external borders 23
  - 2.2.2 Using internal migration controls 25
- 2.3 To conclude 33

3 Methods: A multi-sited ethnography among unauthorized migrants **35**
- 3.1 Getting started: Accessing the research field 36
- 3.2 Collecting data: Being in the field 39
  - 3.2.1 Interviewing unauthorized migrants 39
  - 3.2.2 Participant observation with unauthorized migrants 41
  - 3.2.3 Participant observation within the immigration system 43
  - 3.2.4 Fieldwork with returned and deported migrants 45
  - 3.2.5 Leaving the research field 47
- 3.3 The research group 48
- 3.4 The analysis 49
- 3.5 Some reflections on my positionality, ethics and limitations 51
  - 3.5.1 Positionality 51
  - 3.5.2 Ethical considerations 54
  - 3.5.3 Limitations of the study 58
- 3.6 To conclude 59

4 'I call it a system.' Unauthorized migrants' understandings of the long reach of Dutch internal migration controls 61
4.1 Introduction 61
4.2 Internal migration controls, deportability and the Netherlands 63
4.3 Methodology 66
4.4 Deportability in the Netherlands: Confrontations with a multi-layered system 67
4.4.1 The first layer: Different controlling actors 69
4.4.2 The second layer: Policies and laws within and above migration management 71
4.4.3 The third layer: Dutch internal control mechanisms contributing to the EU's externalized control 73
4.5 To conclude 75

5 'If you don't have documents or a legal procedure, you are out!' Making humanitarian organizations partner in migration control 79
5.1 Introduction 79
5.2 The ambiguous roles of humanitarian organizations 81
5.3 Methodology 83
5.4 Local humanitarian organizations in the Netherlands 84
5.5 Incorporating support organizations for unauthorized migrants 86
5.6 Selection, exclusion, return and enforcement by humanitarian organizations 89
5.7 The changed character of humanitarian organizations 92
5.8 To conclude 93

6 The pains of being unauthorized in the Netherlands 97
6.1 Introduction 97
6.2 The pains of imprisonment 100
6.3 Methodology 101
6.4 The pains of being unauthorized in the Netherlands 102
6.4.1 Deprived of healthy and secure living conditions 103
6.4.2 Deprived of social and geographical mobility 105
6.4.3 Deprived of citizenship 107
6.4.4 Differences in experiences explained 108
6.5 To conclude 110

7	**'Where is the justice?' Unauthorized migrants' perceptions of the legitimacy of Dutch immigration system**	**113**
7.1	Introduction	113
7.2	The current understanding of legitimacy	116
7.3	Methods	117
7.4	Unauthorized migrants' legitimacy perceptions	119
7.4.1	Lawfulness	119
7.4.2	Justification based on shared beliefs	121
7.4.3	Consent	126
7.5	To conclude	128
8	**Reconceptualizing empirical legitimacy of situations of severely conflicting social interests**	**131**
8.1	Introduction	131
8.2	Methods	134
8.3	Unauthorized migrants' substantive needs	135
8.3.1	Security guarantees	136
8.3.2	The best interests of the child	138
8.3.3	The right to liberty	140
8.4	To conclude	143
9	**Pressured into a preference to leave? A study on the 'specific' deterrent effects and perceived legitimacy of immigration detention**	**147**
9.1	Introduction	147
9.2	The Dutch immigration detention regime	151
9.3	Conditional deterrence?	153
9.4	Data and method	155
9.5	Results: Pressured to depart?	158
9.5.1	Quantitative overview	158
9.5.2	The voice of the detainee	163
9.6	To conclude	171
10	**'I am so tired of the law.' Understanding the shaping of unauthorized migrants' legal consciousness over time**	**177**
10.1	Introduction	177
10.2	Drawing on legal consciousness	180
10.3	Methods	182
10.4	The Dutch immigration system over time	183
10.5	Unauthorized migrants' legal consciousness over time	185

10.5.1 A first legal consciousness process: aspiring better living conditions, staying away from the law 186
10.5.2 A second legal consciousness process: aspiring to legalization, actively engaging with the law 192
10.6 To conclude 198

11 To conclude: The limits of the law 203
11.1 The law as a comprehensive, multi-layered system 204
11.2 The law as a powerful force 207
11.3 The law's powerlessness 211
11.4 Understanding the powerful and powerless functioning of the law 213
11.4.1 Unauthorized migrants' previous migration experiences 215
11.4.2 Unauthorized migrants' social embeddedness 216
11.4.3 Unauthorized migrants' aspirations 219
11.5 Legal, moral and instrumental limits of the law 221
11.5.1 Towards a human-rights-based, empirically legitimate and differentiated approach 224

References 229

Abbreviations

AVIM	Afdeling Vreemdelingenpolitie, Identificatie en Mensenhandel (Police department regarding immigration affairs, identification and human trafficking)
AVR	Assisted Voluntary Return
AVRD	Assisted Voluntary Return from Detention
COA	Centraal Orgaan opvang Asielzoekers (Central Agency for the reception of asylum seekers)
DMB	Directie MigratieBeleid (migration policy directorate of the Ministry of Justice and Security)
DT&V	Dienst Terugkeer & Vertrek (Repatriation and Departure Service)
EU	European Union
Eurodac	European Dactyloscopy Database
EUROSUR	European Border Surveillance System
IND	Immigration and Naturalization Service
IOM	International Organization for Migration
Kmar	Koninklijke Nederlandse Marechaussee (Royal Netherlands Marechaussee)
LVV	Landelijke VreemdelingenVoorziening (National Shelter for Unauthorized Migrants in specific positions)
NGO	Non-Governmental Organization
SIS	Schengen Information System
VIS	Visa Information System

1 Understanding unauthorized migrants' legal consciousness

European nation-states aim to manage migration (Geiger and Pécoud, 2013). They want to limit the arrival *and* residence of migrants without the required legal status in order to protect their national sovereignty (Bosworth and Guild, 2008; Kaufman, 2015; Koulish and Van der Woude, 2020) as well as the security, labour markets, housing markets and social-security systems within their territory (Anderson, 2013; Burgers and Engbersen, 1999; Franko, 2020; Staring and Van Swaaningen, 2021). Additionally, they fear the presence of a large number of migrants on their territory without a legal status, given the notions of crime, fear, chaos and danger that surround them, especially in times of increased fear of terrorism (Anderson, 2013; Franko, 2020; Van der Leun and Van der Woude, 2011). Nation-states believe that this comes at the cost of the integration of migrants who are allowed to reside within its national territory (Bosworth and Guild, 2008). They are afraid that the presence of these migrants contributes to the idea of a loss of the nation-state's national identity (Weber and Bowling, 2008). For these and many other reasons, European nation-states have introduced entry restrictions which – in their view – are needed to manage the mobility of people (Franko, 2020; Koulish and Van der Woude, 2020). From the late 1980s onwards, they have become increasingly occupied with selecting who is (and who is not) allowed to enter the country and with preventing the arrival of unwanted others (*Ibid.*). Moreover, they have increasingly focused on ending the residence of so-called 'unwanted others' within their territory (Albrecht, 2002; Broeders and Engbersen, 2007) and have extended their opportunities for, *inter alia*, controlling, identifying and deporting unwanted others from their territory (Aas, 2011; Guiraudon and Joppke, 2001; Staring and Van Swaaningen, 2021).

As part of their migration management strategies, European nation-states turn to 'the law' (Anderson, 2013; Calavita, 2005; Dauvergne, 2008; Mainwaring and Walton-Roberts, 2018), the law referring to *all* legal norms in society and the institutions and practices associated with them (cf. Deflem, 2008). By using the law, the European Union (EU) strives for an 'unequivocal commitment to respect and protect the dignity, human rights and fundamental freedoms of all migrants as well as to ensure that migration takes place in a safe, orderly and well-managed way'.[1] By using the law, they ultimately define who is allowed to enter a nation-state's territory, under what conditions and for how long (Aarrass, 2021). It is also the law which prescribes what kind of measures a nation-state may take to

1 https://ec.europa.eu/commission/presscorner/detail/en/statement_19_6791, accessed 05/14/2023.

prevent the arrival of unwanted others, to control them and to deport them from the nation-state's territory (*Ibid.*). Furthermore, the law is the foundation of all collaborative, digital, military and other strategies that European nation-states use to prevent and control both the arrival and the residence of unwanted migrants as well as to deport those unwanted migrants from the nation-state concerned (Franko, 2020; Rijken, Staring and Van der Woude, 2022). It is also the law that sets whether and how migration may be governed through control (Bosworth and Guild, 2008; Rijken, Staring and Van der Woude, 2022), artificial intelligence (Bircan and Korkmaz, 2021), paperwork (Borrelli and Andreetta, 2019), death (Squire, 2017), partnerships (Kunz, 2013) or other means (Kreichrauf, 2023; Stel, 2021).

Yet, the functioning of the law in the migration domain may, I believe, be severely questioned given the turbulence that has accompanied both the arrival and presence of migrants in recent years. Questions have arisen as to whether migration actually does take place in the safe, orderly and well-managed way that the EU intends. In 2015, for instance, the world was confronted with the iconic picture of the Syrian toddler Alan Kurdi, whose body was found on a Turkish beach after he and his family fled the Syrian civil war in search of a safe haven and tried to reach Greece on a small inflatable boat (Smith, 2015). Alan is just one of the migrants who has died in the Mediterranean using the sea route into Europe (Cuttitta and Last, 2020). Likewise, migrants using land routes to enter Europe – or specific countries in Europe – are confronted with deadly and hazardous routes, a deterioration of human rights and a lack of required (health) care (Snel, Bilgili and Staring, 2021; Župarić-Iljić and Valenta, 2019). Additionally, on arrival, migrants may face a shortage of reception facilities, meaning that they have to sleep in tent camps or rough it without essential amenities and adequate services. This can be seen on the Greece, Italian and Spanish islands where migrants tend to arrive in Europe (Ambrosini, 2018; Kourachanis, 2018) as well as in so-called destination countries in Northern Europe such as the Netherlands and Belgium (De Backer et al., 2022; Larruina, 2023). While not all migrants take such a hazardous route, those who eventually end up residing without a legal status in a European nation-state's territory are confronted with harsh material and immaterial living conditions given the countries' exclusion and control policies (e.g. Eule et al., 2019; Staring, Boesveldt and Kox, 2022; Wyss, 2022). This applies – more or less – to the differentiated groups of migrants who decide to stay in the EU without the required residence rights, including asylum seekers, labour migrants, family migrants, visa overstayers and many others (Düvell, 2006). Some migrants protest against the law for being too restrictive and repressive, without taking their basic needs and potential to contribute to society into account (Ataç, Rygiel and Stierl, 2016; Hajer and Bröer, 2020). This occasionally results in (collective) hunger strikes or migrants committing suicide once they are no longer capable of coping with their situation (e.g. Barbero, 2012; Laban, 2017; Vanobberghen et al., 2020).

These de-personalized events are the outcome of people leaving their home country for a myriad of different reasons. Some decisively choose to migrate to and/or reside in European countries, despite their lack of travel and residence documents. Others just leave their home country and may, after months, years or decades, find themselves somewhere in Europe – in an asylum centre, an urban shelter or working somewhere in the informal economy. The law forbids these people to do so but they, nevertheless, decide to move to and reside in Europe without the required documents. This raises issues concerning how the law matters to these migrants as well as its implications for the functioning of the law in the migration domain.

1.1 Why migrants' perspectives on the law matter

These concerns have not yet been addressed, leaving the perspective of migrants without the required legal status stipulated by the law under-represented in the societal and academic debate (although see Abrego, 2011, 2015; Calavita, 2005; Ryo, 2011). Several scholars call for studies that include the voices of migrants without residence rights (Brouwer, 2020: 14–15; Côté-Boucher, Infantino and Salter, 2014; Pickering, Bosworth and Aas, 2015). Moreover, migrants who lack a legal status are themselves also looking for ways to be heard in this debate (Hajer and Bröer, 2020). Additionally, there are, I believe, moral, instrumental and academic reasons for drawing on the emic perspective of these migrants and giving them a voice in this debate on the functioning of the law in the migration domain.

First, there are moral reasons which call for a better understanding of how the law matters to migrants without residence rights along with concerns for the law. Even if the law is legally valid, its moral authority is not self-evident (Beetham, 1991). Tamanaha (2001: 241) therefore claims that 'every application of law or action in the name of law that increases human misery must be carefully scrutinized, regardless of whether it does or does not mirror society or enhance social order, and must stand up to a test of rightness'. This means that the law – including what nation-states do with the law – must be good and right to withstand this test. There are reasons to believe that the law in the migration domain cannot pass this test. Previous research, for instance, shows that specific immigration laws are racializing (Turnbull, Bhatia and Lousley, 2020), inflict harm (Bhatia, 2020) and have cumulative injurious and painful effects for migrants (Menjívar and Abrego, 2012). Some scholars (e.g. Menjívar and Abrego, 2012; Soliman, 2021) believe that states should be held responsible for the harmful and violent outcomes of the law. While courts have condemned some specific legal practices in the migration domain, they have not recognized the outcomes of these laws as large-scale human-rights abuses, which implies that the basic principles of the law in this context are considered legally valid.

However, these earlier studies do raise moral questions on the current use of the law in the migration domain. With this study, I aim to provide more insights into the functioning of the law for migrants without residence rights by using an insider's perspective. Through deep immersion in the research field, I hope to demonstrate what the law does to and for these migrants. According to Ryo (2017), such insights help to recognize the basic humanity and moral agency for these migrants as well as to appreciate the direct and indirect costs of the current use of the law in the migration domain.

Second, there are instrumental arguments for better understanding how the law matters to migrants without residence rights. European nation-states want to limit unauthorized migration but are currently confronted with several factors that negatively impact on their migration management strategies – which includes the migrants' unwillingness to leave their country of unauthorized residence (e.g. Maliepaard et al., 2022; Van Zwol Committee, 2019). Yet, people's understandings of and experiences with the law are supposed to influence their obedience to it (e.g. Hough, Jackson and Bradford, 2013; Jackson et al., 2015; Tyler, 2006). Social psychologist Tom Tyler (2006: 277), an authority in this research field, argues that all state authorities should govern based on the consent of those whom they govern in order to make people obey the law, consent that is developed from the experience of fairness when dealing with the authorities (see also Tyler and Darley, 2000). As it cannot be fully anticipated in advance how people will respond to the law, looking at the ways in which people interpret, understand and experience the law is needed to fully understand how it works in everyday practice (cf. Hasselberg, 2016). A grounded or constructivist approach that focuses on how the law matters to migrants without a legal status may contribute to a deeper knowledge of how the law is enacted, how migrants understand it and how they interact with it on an everyday basis (cf. Chua and Engel, 2019; Halliday, 2019; Ryo, 2017). Such understandings provide insights into the functioning of the law in the migration domain, insights which are valuable to law- and policy-makers and to practitioners working in this domain as they may help to understand the migrants' (non-)compliance with the law. They can be used to (better) develop equitable and effective immigration laws (Ryo, 2017; see also Leerkes, 2016).

Third, there are academic reasons for putting the migrants' perspective – in relation to the law – centre stage in this study as this perspective is still under-represented in the academic debate. There is a rich tradition of anthropological, ethnographic research on the subsistence strategies of migrants without the required residence rights which provides insights into their living conditions and social networks (e.g. Burgers and Engbersen, 1999; Chavez, 1998; Coutin, 2000; Massey et al., 1998; Staring, 2001; Van der Leun, 2003). Additionally, there are many socio-legal studies on how people give meaning to and interact with the law on an everyday basis – studies which help to better understand the functioning of specific laws (e.g. Ewick and Silbey, 1998; Merry, 1990; Nielsen, 2000; Sarat,

1990; Silbey, 2005). Furthermore, there is a vivid and flourishing border criminology scholarship – that is, the academic discipline which, *inter alia*, addresses topics such as (unauthorized) migration, globalization, bordering processes, migration controls and/or citizenship (Aas, 2007; Aas and Bosworth, 2013; Barker, 2012; Bowling, 2013; Brandariz, 2021; Brandariz and Fernández-Bessa, 2020; Pickering and Weber, 2006; Pickering et al., 2015; Van der Woude, 2022).[2] Yet the voices of the unauthorized migrants themselves on their relationships with the law are still under-represented in this discipline (cf. Aas and Bosworth, 2013; Brouwer, 2020: 14; Côté-Boucher et al., 2014; Ryo, 2017). Therefore, I combine elements from anthropology, socio-legal studies and border criminology studies in this study, as using such an interdisciplinary approach enables me to enrich the current academic debate on the powers of the law in the migration domain.

1.2 GUIDING RESEARCH QUESTIONS

These moral, instrumental and academic reasons made me decide to try to find answers to the intriguing puzzle of how the law matters to migrants lacking a legal status entitling them to reside on a nation-state's territory and what this means for the functioning of the law in this domain. I have translated this puzzle into the following central research question:

> How does the law matter to migrants lacking a legal status entitling them to reside on a nation-state's territory and what does this mean for the functioning of the law?

For feasibility reasons, I decided to explicitly focus on migrants who reside without the required legal status in the territory of a nation-state. These migrants constitute a heterogeneous group in terms of countries of origin, ethnicities, migration motives, incorporation strategies and aspirations (Vertovec, 2007; 2019). The group includes, *inter alia*, rejected asylum seekers, visa-overstayers, unauthorized labour migrants, family migrants and many others who lack a residence permit allowing them to reside on the nation-state's territory. Throughout this study, I use the term 'unauthorized migrants' to refer to this legal category of people who stay on the territory of a nation-state without formal permission to do so. This term has some limitations, as the adjective 'unauthorized'

2 This discipline is also known under the name of 'criminology of mobility' but is nowadays referred to as border criminology as the latter, according to Bosworth (2017), 'captures more clearly the way in which this is a field of study which is trying to understand both things that are happening at the border but also things that are happening in our criminal justice system' (https://www.socialsciencespace.com/2017/06/mary-bosworth-border-criminology/, accessed 05/14/2023).

wrongfully implies a state of being while it actually concerns a legal classification of the migrants' permission to reside on the nation-state's territory (see also Van Meeteren, 2014). Besides, such a legal classification is surrounded with ambiguity as it is constantly subject to change and the authorized–unauthorized nexus is not as clear-cut as the term implies (Kubal, 2013). Furthermore, this wording does not align the legal terminology that the Dutch authorities use for these migrants as they speak of foreign nationals without permission to stay in the Netherlands. However, there is no consensus (yet) on the most appropriate and accurate terminology for people lacking a legal status. In the current debate, they are called 'unauthorized migrants', 'irregular migrants', 'illegal migrants' 'undocumented migrants', 'semi-legal migrants', 'illegalized migrants', '*sans-papiers*' or 'clandestine migrants' (Baldwin-Edwards, 2008; Cvajner and Sciortino, 2010; De Genova, 2002; Donato and Armenta, 2011; Düvell, 2008; Espenshade, 1995; Guild, 2004; Kalir, 2019; Kubal, 2013; Portes, 1978; Triandafyllidou, 2010). All terms lack legal precision (Van Meeteren, 2014: 6–9), are criminalizing (Bauder, 2014) or present an unjustified dichotomy between those with and those without a legal status (Kubal, 2013). Yet, despite its limitations, I prefer to use the term 'unauthorized migrants' as it, in my view, clearly implies that unauthorized migrants are a socially and legally constructed group that is produced by – and subjected to alteration because of – nation-states' laws (cf. Donato and Armenta, 2011). Besides, this term fits in the terminology that is being used within border criminology (e.g. Bosworth, Franko and Pickering, 2018; Brouwer, 2020).

To better understand how the law matters to unauthorized migrants and what this means for the functioning of the law for this specific legal category, I have translated the central question into the following sub-questions:

1. How do unauthorized migrants understand the law on an everyday basis?
2. How does the law manifest itself in unauthorized migrants' everyday lives and how is it being experienced by these migrants?
3. How do unauthorized migrants give meaning to the law in terms of empirical legitimacy and how to understand these meaning-making processes?
4. How are the migrants' understandings of, experiences with and meaning-making processes translated into unauthorized migrants' interaction with the law and *vice versa*?

To find answers to these questions and do justice to unfolding the migrants' perspectives on their relationship with the law, I conducted multi-sited ethnographic fieldwork in different areas in the Netherlands as well as in Nigeria, Surinam and Guyana between early 2015 and mid-2018. I included more than 100 unauthorized migrants and parts of their social networks in this research. This bottom-up methodological journey, which unfolds in more detail in Chapter 3 of this book, enabled me to give a voice to migrants without a legal status, provide insights in the functioning of the law and contribute to the current debate on the powers of the law in the migration domain.

1.3 THE DUTCH LEGAL CONTEXT AS A CASE OF RESTRICTING UNAUTHORIZED RESIDENCE

This study is situated in the Netherlands, a North-Western European country which has external land borders with Germany to the east and Belgium to the south and is surrounded by sea to the west. It is one of the founding members of both the EU and the Schengen area, a group of nowadays 27 countries which – except for specific threats or under specific conditions – have abolished their internal land borders to enable its citizens to freely travel between them without passport or visa. The country counted just over 17.8 million citizens in early 2023,[3] excluding the unknown number of unauthorized migrants who reside in the Netherlands.[4]

The Netherlands used to be known for its tolerance and openness towards foreigners (Brouwer, 2020). Migrants – including unauthorized migrants – were initially welcomed and tolerated by the Dutch authorities[5] (Burgers and Engbersen, 1999; Van Eijl, 2012). Yet, due to – *inter alia* – an increased influx of migrants and refugees, a deteriorated labour market and an assumably changed societal position towards migrants, the Dutch authorities started to see the arrival and presence of these migrants as a social problem (Burgers and Engbersen, 1999; Van Eijl, 2012). Issues of migration and integration began to dominate political and public discussions (Van der Woude, Van der Leun and Nijland, 2014). In 1989, unauthorized migration was initially mentioned in the coalition agreement of the government (Obdeijn and Schrover, 2008). From then on, the liberal stance towards unauthorized migrants and the somewhat liberal aliens act were being replaced by more restrictive admissions policies, an increased exclusion of unauthorized migrants, intensified control collaborations, extended voluntary return programmes and a greater urgency for migration control policies (Engbersen, Van San and Leerkes, 2006; Van Eijl, 2012). These policies and practices have partly been the result of increased European collaboration in the migration domain that has been taken place since the end of the eighties. These have been translated in an extensive legal framework consisting of international and European legalisation, Dutch immigration and non-immigration laws and policies and other types of regulations. As such, the Dutch authorities try to restrict

3 https://www.cbs.nl/nl-nl/visualisaties/dashboard-bevolking/bevolkingsteller, accessed 06/07/2023.
4 Van der Heijden et al. (2020) have estimated that between 18,370 and 27,051 unauthorized migrants used to reside in the Netherlands between July 2017 and June 2018.
5 Throughout this study, I use the term 'authorities' to refer to the government *and* its executive services as unauthorized migrants themselves do not necessarily distinct between them.

the unauthorized entry of migrants, discourage unauthorized migrants from remaining in the country and prevent unwanted situations for these migrants. Leerkes and Van Houte (2020) characterize this Dutch legal context as a 'thick enforcement regime' given the Dutch state's strong enforcement interests and capacity. This regime is discussed in more detail in Chapter 2.

The Netherlands stands out in Europe given its strong enforcement interests and capacity (Leerkes and Van Houte, 2020). However, the value of this study moves beyond the country's specific geographical location as – like the Netherlands – other EU-states are also characterized by mobility (Barker, 2012; Bloch and Chimienti, 2012). They are all, to some extent, concerned with migration management strategies and all somehow turn to the law as part of this. While their strategies, interests and capacities may differ (Leerkes and Van Houte, 2020), there is increasing collaboration in the migration domain between these nation-states (Micinski, 2022). This could also be seen in their responses to the so-called 'refugee crisis' of 2015, the arrival of Ukrainians after Russia's invasion of the country and the current shortages on European labour markets. Just before summer 2023, the asylum and migration ministers of 27 EU-states reached an agreement on an asylum-procedure regulation and on the distribution of asylum seekers across EU countries.[6] Moreover, European nation-states – if they are members of the EU and Schengen – are bound by a similar legal framework of directives, guidelines etc. that set the boundaries within which they have to operate. This brings more uniformity to the EU's legal approach in the migration domain. While there are and will be legal and other differences between the EU states, the mechanisms behind the functioning of the law may be quite similar. Therefore, the answer to the question of how the law matters to unauthorized migrants and what this means for the functioning of the law is relevant to other EU states and countries outside the EU.

1.4 Drawing upon legal consciousness

This study takes the socio-legal concept of legal consciousness as its theoretical starting point. This concept has several definitions and has been applied in various ways (Chua and Engel, 2019; Horák, Lacko and Klocek, 2021; McCann and March, 1995; Silbey, 2005). Usually, it is understood as 'all the ideas about the nature, function, and operation of the law held by anyone in society at a given time' (Trubek, 1984: 592). The concept moves beyond the idea of legal awareness or knowledge of laws (Chua and Engel, 2019) but focuses on what (disadvantaged) people think and do with regards to the law and what

6 https://www.consilium.europa.eu/nl/policies/eu-migration-policy/migration-timeline/, accessed 06/09/2023.

this means for the law's powers (Silbey, 2005). The basis of the concept is the idea that the law is, in principle, similarly and equally applied but that people might give different meanings to it because of their different experiences with and knowledge of it (Merry, 1990). Therefore, legal consciousness scholars examine how people understand, experience, give meaning to and interact with the law in their everyday lives (Ewick and Silbey, 1992, 1998; Merry, 1990; Nielsen, 2000; Sarat, 1990; Silbey, 2005).

Over the years, different legal consciousness research schools have come about that differ from each other in terms of research purposes, conceptual operationalization and research methodology (see also Chua and Engel, 2019; Halliday, 2019; Hertogh, 2018). Chua and Engel (2019), for instance, distinguish the identity, hegemony and mobilization school. Halliday (2019) speaks of a critical approach, an interpretive approach, a comparative cultural approach and a law-in-action approach while Hertogh (2018) urges scholars to shift their focus from legal consciousness to legal alienation. These schools are not discussed in depth in this study as they should be considered Weberian ideal types that are more blurred in reality and may not find the approval of legal consciousness scholars who have been categorized in these schools themselves. Yet, I mention these schools to illustrate that there is no longer a monolithic approach in legal consciousness research. Instead, Halliday (2019: 872) contends, legal consciousness should be regarded an adaptable concept that may be 'applied widely across an eclectic range of subjects, drawing on diverse theoretical traditions, shedding light on many of the core interests of law and society scholars'. In this study, I make use of the adaptability of the concept. This means, more concretely, that I draw upon the aforementioned sub-questions in order to be able to understand how the law matters to unauthorized migrants as well as its consequences for the functioning of the law.

Firstly, I look for answers to the question of how unauthorized migrants understand the law on an everyday basis. Despite the central role of 'the law' in legal consciousness studies, its scholars do not unambiguously define the term (Halliday, 2019). It has long been a tradition in the legal consciousness research field to focus on positivistic law and determine the subject of the study in advance (Hertogh, 2004, 2012; see also Merry, 1990; Nielsen, 2000). Early legal consciousness scholars drew on the assumed gap between 'law in books' and 'law in action' (cf. Pound, 1910) and, consequently, looked at the law's effects to examine whether it worked as intended and what social results could be attributed to that particular law (Levine and Mellema, 2001: 172). However, Hertogh (2012) criticizes this approach as he believes that knowledge of prevailing law in society is small and the extent to which civilians recognize themselves in the law differs. He argues that legal consciousness not only refers to formal law but includes people's own ideas about laws, as the law is 'a notion that lives in people's heads and can be identified "on the basis of people's attitudes"'. This means that the question of what a specific research subject considers to be law should be included in the empirical research, which Engel (1998: 141) calls legal consciousness 'from below'. Following up on the call of Engel (1998) and Hertogh (2004, 2012) and previous studies that show that unauthorized migrants' understandings of specific laws may differ from those of the authorities (Alpes, 2011; Hiah and Staring, 2016), I move beyond a formal or positivist notion of the law in this study and use 'the law' to refer to the entirety of legal norms in society *and* the institutions and practices that unauthorized migrants associate with them (cf. Deflem, 2008). This means, more specifically, that I first explicitly address the issue of how unauthorized migrants understand 'the law'.

Secondly, I examine how the law manifests itself in unauthorized migrants' everyday lives and how they experience it. Many legal consciousness scholars use a law-first approach and prioritize law over other forces and institutions in their interpretation of a person's legal consciousness (e.g. Ewick and Silbey, 1998; Sarat, 1990). Yet, the salience of the law in a person's daily life cannot be taken for granted (Levine and Mellema, 2001; Sarat and Kearns, 1993: 55). The importance of the law should not be treated as a given or constant as focusing primarily on the law carries the risk of neglecting the imprints of other important structures that may affect people's ideas, impressions and consciousness (*Ibid.*). As the law might be secondary or tertiary to other structures in a person's meaning-making processes of it, Levine and Mellema (2001) argue that scholars should first examine the salience of the law in people's everyday lives. Questioning the salience of the law is supposed to generate information on non-legal and quasi-legal factors that develop or influence someone's legal consciousness, something that will be missed when focusing primarily on law or legal structures (Kennedy, 1980: 23). Although it has been argued that the unauthorized legal status of migrants that the law produces is 'a dominant social characteristic overshadowing all other personal characteristics' (Engbersen, 2001: 240), I do not take for granted the salience of the law in unauthorized migrants' everyday lives. Instead, I explicitly examine how the law manifests itself in unauthorized migrants' everyday lives and how they experience it.

Thirdly, I describe and explain how unauthorized migrants give meaning to the law. I explicitly focus on the migrants' meaning-making processes in terms of empirical legitimacy – that is, the migrants' thoughts on the justification of the authorities' right to hold power over them (Beetham, 1991). The latter includes people's perceptions of the authorities acting in ways that accord with prevailing notions of appropriate moral conduct and exercising their powers morally, justly and appropriately (Jackson et al., 2015). Taking empirical legitimacy as a theoretical starting point in order to understand how unauthorized migrants give meaning to the law enables me to gain greater insights into the law's moral authority, which is one of the aims of the study (e.g. Ryo, 2017; see also Leerkes, 2016). However, I do not draw upon the pre-set criteria that are often used in empirical legitimacy studies (see Chapters 7 and 8 for more details). Instead, I use an open angle that suits legal consciousness studies and helps to better understand how and why the migrants' meanings have come about. After all, Levine and Mellema (2001) argue that the focus in legal consciousness studies should be directed towards the structures that have a role in a person's meaning-making process concerning the law and how these impact on how one gives meaning to it. This includes structural factors at a macro level such as the power relations in society and the hegemony of the law that makes the 'haves come out ahead' (cf. Galanter, 1974) and impacts on a person's legal consciousness (Ewick and Silbey, 1998; Merry, 1990; Nielsen, 2000; Sarat, 1990). Additionally, it includes micro factors that may impact on one's meaning-making process and legal consciousness, which develops through individual experiences, socialization processes and other structures (cf. García-Villega, 2003; see also Sarat, 1990). This means that legal consciousness studies should include all such factors as may help to explain a person's thoughts on the law (cf. Cowan, 2004; Marshall and Barclay, 2003). Therefore, I describe and explain how unauthorized migrants give meaning to the law in terms of legitimacy and provide insights into how the migrants' meaning-making processes have come about.

Fourthly, I examine how the migrants' understandings of the law, their experiences with it and their meaning-making processes are translated into interactions with the law as well as how these interactions with the law, in turn, impact on the migrants' understandings of it. Legal consciousness refers not only to a person's ideas or understandings of the law. Consciousness, after all, denotes what unauthorized migrants both say and do, as it may be 'discursively deployed as reflexive consideration about day-to-day activities whereas it is also tacitly enacted as competent social action' (Ewick and Silbey, 1998: 46). This means that legal consciousness scholars also examine how people – intentional (deliberate) and unintentional (habitually) – act in relation to the law (Merry, 1990; Silbey, 2005). Such acts are often categorized based on Ewick and Silbey's (1998) renowned study on the commonplace of law in which they distinguish three predominant types of legal consciousness that express both what someone thinks about and does with the law (e.g. Gehring, 2013; Schwenken, 2013). The first type concerns people who are *before the law*, meaning that they accept and obey the law as they consider it to be fair. The second type refers to people who are *with the law*, meaning that they consider the law a game or commodity which can be played and used to gain advantage. The third group consists of people who are *against the law*. This usually concerns disenfranchized or marginalized groups who feel they are being caught with the law and may start to resist it if they are confronted with it. Fritsvold (2009) distinguishes a fourth category consisting of people who are *under the law*, meaning that they have an alternative conception of the law and believe that it cannot be used as a tool for social change. These people may turn themselves to civic obedience in search for justice (see also Halliday and Morgan, 2013). These predominant types are frequently used in legal consciousness studies but are also firmly criticized, since they are not new, not distinctive and not suited to marginalized groups (Levine and Mellema, 2001; Mezey, 2001). I take these predominant legal consciousness types into account although I also use an open angle to describe and explain how unauthorized migrants interact with the law in their everyday lives over time.

These four steps examining how unauthorized migrants understand, experience, give meaning to and interact with the law in their everyday lives are needed to illustrate the migrants' legal consciousness processes over time. The insights into these processes finally enable me to answer the question of how the law matters to unauthorized migrants and the consequences for the functioning of the law in the migration domain.

1.5 This book

This book builds on previous studies on unauthorized migrants' legal consciousness. These studies were initially mainly situated in North America (e.g. Abrego, 2008, 2011, 2018; Galli, 2019; Gleeson, 2010; Ryo, 2011, 2013), but there is an increasing number of studies on (unauthorized) migrants' legal consciousness in the European context (e.g. Alpes, 2011; De Hart and Besselsen, 2021; Gehring, 2013; Güdük and Desmet, 2022; Haddeland, 2021; Kubal, 2014; Kulk and de Hart, 2013; Miežanskienė, 2020; Schwenken, 2013). Such studies usually focus on a specific act in relation to the law, a specific group of unauthorized migrants, or a specific moment in time (e.g. Abrego, 2011, 2018, 2019; Haddeland, 2021; Kubal, 2014; Ryo, 2011; Schwenken, 2013). Moreover, some of these studies provide a rich description of unauthorized migrants' thoughts on or acts in relation to the law without comprehensively explaining the migrants' underlying motivations for their thoughts and acts (see also Young, 2014). By now, it is generally accepted that unauthorized migrants differently think about and interact with the law on an everyday basis, as is illustrated in more detail in Chapter 10. Yet, there is still little insight into how the migrants' (differentiated) thoughts and acts come about, making both Abrego (2011) and Güdük and Desmet (2022) call for studies that explain – the differences within – unauthorized migrants' legal consciousness. This study follows up on this call. Chapters 4 to 10 show how unauthorized migrants view, experience, give meaning to, and interact with the law, as well as how these views, experiences, meanings, and interactions have come about. Afterward, Chapter 11 presents three interrelated, interacting factors that mitigate unauthorized migrants' relationships with the law over time and help to explain – the differences within – unauthorized migrants' legal consciousness processes. In what follows, I further discuss the structure of this book.

The first three chapters of this book, including this underlying general introduction, establish the theoretical, legal, and methodological context for this study. **Chapter 1**, which serves as the introduction, has illustrated the rationale behind this study as well as its theoretical starting points. The next chapter, **Chapter 2**, sets the scene by providing an overview of current trends in the migration domain to illustrate the legal context in which unauthorized migrants' legal consciousness processes are situated. It also outlines some important legal developments that have taken place in the migration domain in the Netherlands since the late 1980s. As it is a book in itself to provide a historical overview of all laws, policies, and practices and how these are enacted in everyday practice in the Netherlands (see Van Eijl, 2012), I limit myself to those legal developments assumed to have the most impact on unauthorized migrants' everyday lives (e.g. Staring et al., 2022; Van der Leun, 2003; Van Meeteren, 2014).

Then, in **Chapter 3**, I discuss the methodological approach underlying this study. I elaborate on my methodological approach and address the different stages in the fieldwork and analysis. Furthermore, I reflect on my own role as a researcher and discuss how I dealt with ethical concerns in a period when ethical boards were still absent in the Netherlands. Finally, I address the limitations of the study.

Afterward, Chapters 4 to 10 provide answers to the sub-questions that have guided this study and present its main empirical and theoretical findings. The focus in these chapters is mostly on migration controls, as previous studies and my data analysis show that unauthorized migrants equate the law with their lack of legal status, given the legally embedded limitations, migration controls, and exclusion processes they may face because of their legal status. For example, North African Fazil[7] exclaimed, 'the law is papers' when we discussed his position towards the law. Such experiences directly impact unauthorized migrants' understandings of the law as well as the shaping of their legal consciousness, as will be illustrated throughout these chapters, either directly or more indirectly.

Chapters 4 and 5 provide answers to the first sub-question of this study on how unauthorized migrants understand the law on an everyday basis. Both chapters reveal that unauthorized migrants' understandings of the law are predominantly shaped by their lack of legal status and the limitations that come with it. **Chapter 4** illustrates that unauthorized migrants perceive the law as a system that initially produces their unauthorized residence and subsequently reduces them to their lack of a legal status. The migrants depict a comprehensive and multi-layered control system that includes laws and policies outside the migration domain, is executed by a myriad of state and non-state actors and extending across different geographical locations. This comprehensive nature leads them to refer to the law as a system. **Chapter 5** demonstrates that humanitarian organizations, established to support unauthorized migrants due to their disagreement with the state's exclusionary migration policies, have become part of this control system. This may be explained by the gradual and subtle responsibilization process by the Dutch authorities, during which specific measures were employed and monetary flows redirected to incorporate humanitarian organizations into broader migration control policies. This has resulted in a paradoxical merger of humanitarian care and securitization imperatives characterizing

7 Pseudonyms are used throughout this book to protect research participants.

these organizations' support today. Consequently, unauthorized migrants using this support have come to believe that humanitarian organizations have become part of the system. These chapters demonstrate that unauthorized migrants have a broad understanding of the law that extends beyond the law's formal, positivistic definition.

This also affects the migrants' experiences with the law, as illustrated in **Chapter 6**. This chapter addresses the second sub-question of this study on how the law manifests itself in unauthorized migrants' everyday lives and how it is experienced by these migrants. It illustrates that the law is omnipresent for unauthorized migrants, given the wide range of legally embedded limitations, control mechanisms, and exclusionary practices it imposes on these migrants, affecting their ability to generate an adequate income, arrange housing, and access healthcare or other rights, among other things. By referencing Sykes' (1958) renowned study on the pains of imprisonment, the chapter demonstrate that unauthorized migrants believe the law deprives them of, *inter alia*, healthy and secure living conditions, social and geographical mobility, and citizenship. These diverse forms of deprivation impact the migrants' self-esteem, health, and security. Although the impact, salience, and severity of these deprivations vary among migrants, they all share the sense of being punished for their unauthorized residence in the country, with no opportunity to either legalize their residence or escape their situation. Considering previous research with similar insights as well as Hayes' proximity model, the conclusion is drawn that Dutch authorities are aware of these collateral consequences of their control system and deliberately inflict these pains on unauthorized migrants. This implies that migration control is not only experienced as punishment by those subjected to it but is also intended to be punitive. This leads to what I have termed 'the pains of being unauthorized' in this chapter.

Afterward, Chapters 7 and 8 provide answers to the third sub-question of this study on how unauthorized migrants give meaning to the law in terms of empirical legitimacy and how these meaning-making processes can be understood. **Chapter 7** illustrates unauthorized migrants' differentiated thoughts on the law, specifically the Dutch immigration system. It reveals that these migrants may consider restrictive immigration systems to be empirically legitimate. However, they all believe that the Dutch system suffers from an extensive legitimacy deficit, as important substantive values are currently inadequately included in it. This comes at the cost of their consent with the system. While the system may be legally valid, unauthorized migrants question its morality, contributing to the delegitimation of the powers of the Dutch authorities in the migration domain. **Chapter 8** provides further insights into how the migrants' meaning-making processes should be understood, namely, in the context of substantive values included in human rights treaties. The chapter also addresses the substantive values which, according to my research participants, should underlie a justified immigration system. While other substantive values are important as well, this chapter specifically focuses on the importance of the Dutch authorities respecting their security, the best interest of the child, and their right to liberty. The chapter shows that these values are included in immigration laws and policies in the Netherlands. Yet, the migrants believe that these fall short in everyday immigration practice in the country. Given the perceived lack of respect for human rights that apply to them as well, they consider the current use of the law in the Netherlands to be empirically illegitimate.

Thereafter, Chapters 9 and 10 provide answers to the fourth and last sub-question of this study on how the migrants' understandings of, experiences with, and meaning-making processes towards the law are translated into interactions with the law. Both chapters connect unauthorized migrants' understandings of, experiences with, and thoughts on the law with their interactions with it. **Chapter 9** discusses how immigration detainees perceive the legitimacy of their detention and how this impacts their willingness to continue their unauthorized residence in the Netherlands. It shows that unauthorized migrants find detention quite painful, partly because of its perceived illegitimacy. Yet, respondents' interests in continuing their stay in the Netherlands typically outweighed their interests in ending the immigration detention experience, meaning that these respondents were reluctant to participate in their (forced) return process. It is only when unauthorized migrants attach some level of empirical legitimacy to their detention that the detention pressures them to leave the country, which demonstrates the importance of perceived legitimacy in bringing about law-abiding behaviour. A similar conclusion is drawn in **Chapter 10** on unauthorized migrants' legal consciousness over time. In this chapter, I distinguish two legal consciousness processes among unauthorized migrants that substantially differ from each other in terms of the migrants' proximity to and expectations of the law, their thoughts on the empirical legitimacy of the law, and their motivations (not) to interact with it. These different processes help us understand whether and why unauthorized migrants contest, obey, mobilize, resist, protest, or give up on the law. These also show that the impact of the law on unauthorized migrants' law-abiding behaviour is limited, as unauthorized migrants do not feel legally nor morally obliged to obey the law. Their perceived illegitimacy of the law in the Netherlands triggers defiance rather than compliance among these migrants. Even the last resort of immigration detention only puts limited pressure on unauthorized migrants to leave the Netherlands – and then only if these migrants attribute some level of empirical legitimacy to it. This exposes the powerlessness and powers of the law, raising severe questions about the current functioning of the law for unauthorized migrants.

Finally, in **Chapter 11**, I connect the insights from all chapters to answer the central research question of how the law matters to unauthorized migrants and what this means for the functioning of the law for this specific legal category in society. The chapter reveals that the law seriously matters to all these unauthorized migrants, albeit differently. They all have a rather similar understanding of the law, but they experience, give meaning to, and interact with the law differently. Building on the previous chapters, I use the final chapter of this book to present three interrelated, interacting factors that help understand the migrants' different relationships with the law and explain the powerful and powerless functioning of the law for unauthorized migrants. The chapter shows that the law may be considered very powerful given its constitutive effects; these are the law's indirect effects on the migrants' internal meaning-making processes and behaviour that come to the fore on an everyday, existential, social, legal, and well-being level. Yet, the law is also powerless if seen through an instrumental lens – i.e. when researchers examine whether the law inspires or deters unauthorized migrants to act in particular ways – as the law barely inspires unauthorized migrants to leave the country nor deters them from continuing their unauthorized residence in the Netherlands. The powerful and powerless functioning of the law exposes, I believe, the law's legal, moral, and instrumental limitations. I, therefore, use the last section of this study to advocate for a human-rights-driven, empirically legitimate, and differentiated legal approach towards unauthorized migrants that better suits the principles of law in society.

2 Setting the scene: Regulating migration

The lack of a legal status and the laws with which unauthorized migrants are consequently confronted are considered key factors in the shaping of unauthorized migrants' legal consciousness (Miežanskienė, 2020). This fits with previous research on unauthorized migrants' everyday lives which illustrates that immigration laws, policies and practices play a decisive role in the allocation of life changes to these migrants (Menjivar, 2006; Van Meeteren, 2014). The lack of a legal status is sometimes even considered 'a dominant social characteristic overshadowing all other personal characteristics' (Engbersen, 2001: 240). While I am aware that other legal arrangements or non-legal factors may be more important than immigration laws, policies and practices in the shaping of a person's legal consciousness over time (cf. Cowan, 2004; García-Villega, 2003; Levine and Mellema, 2001), this implies that insights into the latter are needed to understand the shaping of unauthorized migrants' legal consciousness. This chapter, therefore, provides an overview of recent immigration laws, policies and practices. As it would be a book in itself to provide an historical overview of all laws, policies and practices that are aimed at regulating migration (see van Eijl, 2012), I limit myself to those legal developments that are assumed to have the most impact on unauthorized migrants' everyday lives (e.g. Staring, Boesveldt and Kox, 2022; Van der Leun, 2003; Van Meeteren, 2014). Yet, during both the fieldwork and the analysis for this study, I keep an eye open to all other legal and non-legal factors that affect how the law matters to unauthorized migrants as well as its consequences for the functioning of the law. In what follows, I first provide an overview of what is done in the European context to regulate unauthorized migration. After this, I outline some important legal migration regulation developments in the Netherlands from the late 1980s onwards. This sheds light on the context in which the shaping of unauthorized migrants' legal consciousness should be understood.

2.1 Regulating migration in a European context

After timeframes of respectively recruiting, welcoming and tolerating migrants, European nation-states have started to believe that entry restrictions are needed to manage mobility flows and protect national security systems (Burgers and Engbersen, 1999; Franko, 2020; van der Woude, 2022). Since the late 1980s, they have become increasingly occupied with selecting who is and who is not allowed to enter the country (Burgers and Engbersen, 1999; Guiraudon and Joppke, 2001; Staring and Van Swaaningen, 2021). Their immigration *policies* to solicit international migration were gradually replaced by immigration – or migration – *controls* meant to protect the nation-state's territory from those who are not allowed to enter (Bosworth, 2008; Guiraudon and Joppke, 2001). European nation-states use such controls to manage the flow of people and protect the nation-state's territory as well as its social-security system (Guiraudon and Joppke, 2001: 2). They have introduced a wide range of control mechanisms to filter those who are allowed to enter and remain on the nation-state's territory (Franko, 2020). This includes, on the one hand, external migration controls which are directed at preventing unauthorized entry onto the nation-state's territory. These external controls may consist of 'metaphorical walls' (Finotelli and Sciortino, 2013) of – *inter alia* – joint visa requirements, pre-admission requirements, carrier sanctions, shared identification databases, common standards for border control, Frontex (the European Border and Coast Guard Agency), physical barriers, joint surveillance of the maritime borders and the use of state-of-the-art technology (Broeders, 2009; Carling, 2007; Dekkers, 2019; Scholten, 2014; Vavouli, 2022). On the other hand, it concerns internal migration controls aimed at the prevention of unauthorized residency and the deportation of unauthorized migrants. These enfold a wide range of exclusions, identification instruments and control mechanisms such as immigration detention, re-entry bans and deportation practices (Albrecht, 2002; Brandariz, 2021; Brochmann, 1999).

States adjust their internal and external migration controls in different directions under the influence of both geopolitical and national political developments (Guiraudon and Lahav, 2000; Lavenax, 2006; Leerkes and van Houte, 2020; Staring and Van Swaaningen, 2021; Van der Woude, 2022; Weber, 2006). Yet it is possible to distinguish seven coexisting, related trends that have substantially changed the nature, structure and reach of these controls in Europe since the early 1990s. Firstly, there has been a trend of strengthened migration controls in European nation-states (Aas, 2011; Aas and Bosworth, 2013; Vollmer, 2011; Wonders, 2017). European nation-states have introduced and/or tightened new laws, policies and practices in order to prevent unauthorized entry and residency (Aas, 2011; Albrecht, 2002; De Genova, 2002; Doomernik and Jandl, 2008). For instance, physical barriers, fences and walls are built – or planning to be built – to obstruct unauthorized migration and protect territorial borders. Examples of such physical blockades include the fences at the Spanish enclaves of Ceuta and Melilla, the increased border patrols at land and sea, and the walls that were built at European Union member-states' internal borders during and in the aftermath of the so-called 'refugee crisis' (Andersson, 2014; Staring and Van Swaaningen, 2021). Not only are European nation-states no longer preoccupied solely with their external borders, but they have also introduced and strengthened their internal migration policies and practices, which should make unauthorized migrants leave the territory (De Giorgi, 2010; Guild, 2009). Several European countries have criminalized unauthorized residency and/or support for unauthorized migrants (Guild, 2009). European countries have also introduced a wide range of controls such as the exclusion of unauthorized migrants from social services, detention and deportation practices and the introduction of re-entry bans that forbid deportees to return to the EU for a pre-set period (Albrecht, 2002; Baldacinni, 2009). While (announcing that) these measures also have a symbolic meaning (Aliverti, 2012; Fabini, 2017; Van der Woude and Van der Leun, 2017), these usually do impact on unauthorized migrants' opportunities to make a living in their destination country (Eule et al., 2019; Van Meeteren, 2014).

Secondly, migration control has shifted upwards from the national level to the international, intergovernmental and supranational levels by the increased (institutionalized) collaboration between European states (Guiraudon and Lahav, 2000; Lavenax, 2006). Such collaboration is assumed to strengthen and increase migration control capacity and effectiveness. For instance, the EU has agreed on the Schengen Borders Code which, in principle, abolishes checks at its internal borders and tightens the controls at its external ones. The latter includes a common visa regime, uniformed border controls, police cooperation and the use of electronic databases. As a consequence, participating countries have one system and border patrol agency for protecting the territorial borders of the EU, while all these countries are – within the EU legal framework – responsible for controlling unauthorized migrants within their territory.[8] The EU keeps on trying to expand its controlling capacity by looking for new forms of cooperation within the migration domain and discussing new EU migration and asylum policy that covers migration routes, asylum reforms, readmission agreements etc.[9] European states not only cooperate in order to prevent unauthorized admission but they also try to collaborate in order to realize both the forced and independent departure of unauthorized migrants. As forced return might be hampered by a lack of cooperation from the receiving country (Leerkes and Kox, 2016), both individual countries and state unions try to realize re-admission agreements with countries that are known for their unauthorized migration. These agreements ideally set out clear obligations and procedures for the authorities of the receiving country regarding when and how, in turn, to accept their unauthorized migrants for financial or other types of support (Billet, 2010; Cassarino, 2009).

Thirdly, migration control has shifted outwards due to European nation-states' externalization strategies, meaning that geographical borders are functionally or virtually moved outwards and detached from a state's territorial borders (Gammeltoft-Hansen and Sørensen, 2013; Weber, 2006). This has also been called 'remote control' (Zolberg, 1997 in FitzGerald, 2020). Based on unilateral, bilateral and/or multilateral state engagement, extraterritorial actions are undertaken to prevent immigrants' unauthorized entry and/or

8 https://ec.europa.eu/home-affairs/what-we-do/policies/borders-and-visas/schengen_en, accessed 09/26/2018.
9 https://www.consilium.europa.eu/en/policies/eu-migration-policy/, accessed 07/07/2023.

to effectuate unauthorized migrants' forced return (Frelick, Kysel and Podkul, 2016). For instance, already in 1968, admission into a country has to be obtained while in the country of origin by obtaining documents at the embassies or consulates there and meeting all kinds of requirements (Bonjour, 2010; Van Amersfoort, 1999). More recently, the EU and Turkey closed an EU–Turkey deal, which consists of Turkey enhancing its border controls towards Europe and preventing unauthorized migrants from crossing the EU external border. In response, the EU is supposed to accept up to 72,000 Syrian migrants from Turkey for each migrant who was deported from Greece to Turkey and to financially support Turkey with 6 billion euros to improve its border protection, physical infrastructure and state institutions (Heck and Hess, 2017).[10] This agreement functions as a blueprint for deals with other countries such as Tunisia, Egypt, Algeria and Morocco (Peeperkorn, 2023). Other examples of Europe's externalization strategies include the use of offshore detention camps in North African countries which disable migrants' onwards journeys into the EU (Bialasiewicz, 2012) as well as the so-called pushbacks that European nation-states are assumed to use to prevent the arrival of migrants on the move in European countries (Aulsebrook, Gruber and Pawson, 2021; Barnes, 2022). By using such strategies, European nation-states attempt to control migration from far outside their own territory and to extend their reach to control unauthorized migration.

Fourthly, controlling unauthorized migration has shifted downwards. Due to responsibilization processes (cf. Garland, 2001), the responsibility for migration control has partially moved from central state actors to private actors, agencies, organizations and individuals outside the direct realm of the state (Gammeltoft-Hansen and Sørensen, 2013; Gilboy, 1997; Lahav, 1998; Menz, 2009; Pham, 2007; Pratt, 2005; Walsh, 2020; Weber, 2013). Consequently, both state and non-state actors deal with questions of entry, stay and exit, including monitoring, reporting, identity verification, service denials, arrest, detention, return and the forced return of unwanted or unauthorized migrants (cf. Lahav, 1998; Walsh, 2020). This includes decentral and non-state actors such as universities, hospitals and, to a lesser degree, civic society which are all encouraged either by law or by a more-or-less-imposed sense of societal duty to identify and report unlawful immigrants to the authorities. Others point to the role of carriers (Lahav, 1998; Menz, 2009; Scholten, 2014), landlords (Sitkin, 2014), employers (Mitsilegas, 2013), private contractors who run immigration detention centres (Bosworth, 2014; Welch, 2012), and the public (Aliverti, 2015; Walsh, 2014) in controlling unauthorized migrants. If these private actors do not fulfil the migration control tasks that national states have outsourced to them, they might be sanctioned (Lahav, 1998). This means that a wide – and expanding – range of actors has started to police non-citizens in recent decades.

10 The EU-Turkey statement, European Council 2016.

Fifthly, scholars signal a trend of crimmigration – that is, the intertwinement of migration control and crime control at the levels of legislation, policy and enforcement practices (Aas and Bosworth, 2013; Stumpf, 2006, 2013; Van der Leun and Van der Woude, 2013). This is not only a legal or policy process but is also part of a broader social reality in which migration and crime have become more associated (Aliverti, 2012; Barker, 2012; Van der Woude, Van der Leun and Nijland, 2014). The use of criminal law to combat immigration offences is defended by the argument that these crimmigration measures are necessary to deter both immigration and criminal-law violations (Stumpf, 2013). Therefore, violations of administrative migration law – such as overstaying a visa, unauthorized entry into a country or ignoring return decisions or deportation[11] orders – are dealt with by criminal law instruments such as stop and searches, arrests and detention (Stumpf, 2006). Criminal offences may have consequences for a migrant's legal status as these may result in the withdrawal of a residence permit, the imposition of a re-entry ban or a prohibition on obtaining a state's citizenship. This trend entails an extension of the migration domain without unauthorized migrants being offered criminal safeguards (Chacón, 2009). Pakes and Holt (2017: 70) argue that states revert to non-criminal-justice modes as it is considered easier (see also Aliverti, 2012; Brouwer, 2020). Border officers may interchangeably and instrumentally use both legal frameworks in order to achieve the intended, desired results (Brouwer, 2020). This crimmigration trend has changed the nature of migration controls and extended the migration domain.

Sixthly, migration controls have become more digitalized, meaning that states use a digital infrastructure as a tool for the surveillance of unauthorized entry and residence (Broeders, 2007; Dekkers, 2019). States have equipped their migration controls with a number of computerized information systems that expand the reach of these controls from the moment migrants want to cross (digital) borders up to their deportation (Broeders, 2007; 2009). They have, for instance, introduced biometric identification documents to hamper unauthorized entry, something that has brought about biometric borders (Besters and Brom, 2010). They have also started to use different large-scale electronic surveillance systems such as the Schengen Information System (SIS and SISII), Visa Information System (VIS), a European Dactyloscopy database (Eurodac) and the European Border Surveillance system (EUROSUR) in order to control who enters and who leaves the territory of the EU or an individual state (Broeders, 2007; Dekkers, 2019; Vavouli, 2022). Furthermore, several countries use intelligence-led immigration checks in its border areas, meaning that border officers use digital information systems in their

11 Throughout this book, I use the term 'deportation' to refer to unauthorized migrants' forced return processes as this terminology is commonly used in the academic migration debate. This terminology contradicts the Dutch authorities' terminology who make use of the terms 'forced return' and 'repatriation' given the negative connotation of the term 'deportation'.

decisions on who to select and stop in border areas (Dekkers, 2019). Finally, states use digital instruments to identify, document and register unauthorized migrants. As such, they – in the words of Broeders (2009) – break down these migrants' anonymity in order to prevent them from entering the country, to exclude them from the social-security system and to deport them to their home country. Given the increased role of digital and technical surveillance techniques, information has become a key factor in controlling both unauthorized migration and unauthorized residency (Ericson and Haggerty, 2006; Koslowski, 2002; Lyon, 2007).

Finally, there is a trend for humanitarianism in the migration domain, which refers to the paradoxical merger of humanitarian care and securitization imperatives during Search and Rescue operations (Cuttitta, 2018; Pallister-Wilkins, 2017a), at external geographical borders (Walters, 2011) or upon reception (Feischmidt, Pries and Cantat, 2019; Social Inclusion, 2019; Vandervoordt and Verschraegen, 2019a, 2019b). Care has become confused with or has overtaken control imperatives (Garelli and Tazzioli, 2018; Pallister-Wilkins, 2015, 2017a, 2017b), meaning that migration control institutions have incorporated humanitarian discourses and practices and have become more concerned with compassion (Hadjimatheou and Lynch, 2018; Khosravi, 2009). At the same time, there is an increasing presence of humanitarian organizations at the border which – sometimes on behalf of the state – provide relief to and lessen the suffering of migrants (Fassin, 2011; Vandevoordt and Verschraegen, 2019a, 2019b). Although humanitarian organizations concerned with migrants' flight, arrival or reception focus on morality, have respect for human life and alleviate suffering, they have also become involved in securitization imperatives and reinforce existing architectures of control (Cuttitta, 2018; Fassin, 2011; Walters, 2011). This shows that humanitarianism and migration controls shape and consolidate each other (Pallister-Wilkins, 2017a), which partly tones down the negative effects of the EU's migration controls.

These seven trends show that European nation-states have started to use a more holistic approach to regulating migration which is said to have resulted in the so-called 'fortress Europe' (Albrecht, 2002; Koulish and Van der Woude, 2020). This fortress is supposed to hamper unauthorized entry and onward migration in the EU. While there are some counter processes that limit the effects of this holistic approach (see also Brandariz, 2021; Staring and Timmerman, 2021), this approach is not always executed as strictly as proclaimed (Aliverti, 2013; Van der Woude and Van der Leun, 2017), the European – and especially the Dutch – approach is generally considered to be a strict immigration enforcement regime (Franko, 2020; Koulish and Van der Woude, 2020; Leerkes and Van Houte, 2020). It is within this context that unauthorized migrants' legal consciousness is being shaped over time.

2.2 REGULATING MIGRATION IN THE NETHERLANDS

These migration regulation trends can also be seen in the Netherlands, the country in North-West Europe in which this study is situated. The Netherlands used to welcome and tolerate unauthorized migrants (Burgers and Engbersen, 1999; Van Eijl, 2012). However, due to an increased influx of migrants and refugees, a deteriorating labour market and an assumably changed societal position towards migrants, the Dutch authorities started to consider the arrival and presence of unauthorized migrants as a social problem and became more occupied with the regulation of (unauthorized) migration (Burgers and Engbersen, 1999; Van Eijl, 2012). In 1989, they first included unauthorized migration in the coalition agreement of the government (Burgers and Engbersen, 1999; Obdeijn and Schrover, 2008). From then on, the liberal stance towards unauthorized migrants and the rather liberal Dutch Aliens Act were gradually being replaced by more restrictive admission policies, the increased exclusion of unauthorized migrants, intensified control collaboration, extended voluntary-return programmes and an increased urgency for migration-control policies (Engbersen, Van San and Leerkes, 2006; Staring and Van Swaaningen, 2021; Van Eijl, 2012). These policies and practices have partly been the result of increased European collaboration in the migration domain that has been taken place since the end of the eighties. This is how the Dutch authorities tried to restrict the unauthorized entry of migrants, to discourage unauthorized migrants from remaining in the country as well as to prevent unwanted situations for these migrants (Van Eijl, 2012). The authorities first said that they were aiming for 'strict but fair' policies towards unauthorized migrants (e.g. Parliamentary documents 2010/11 19637 nos. 1435, 1566, 1630), which they later replaced with – what they called – a 'fair *and* effective' approach (coalition agreement 2021–2025, italics by author). In what follows, the most conspicuous legal developments aimed at the regulation of (unauthorized) migration and residence are addressed.

2.2.1 Protecting the Dutch external borders

The Dutch authorities collaborate with other European nation-states to protect their external borders. They are, for instance, one of the founders of the Schengen Area, a European zone in which systematic national border controls are abolished to facilitate the movement of goods and people across borders. In 1985, they agreed with four other European countries to replace their national border controls for a joint protection of the area's external sea, air and land borders and which consisted of, *inter alia*, pre-border checks, strict visa requirements, digital surveillance techniques and other barriers. These agreements have now been laid down in the Schengen Border Code which has been ratified by 27 European countries.[12] This means that Schengen members are mostly concerned with protecting the external borders of the Schengen Area, such as the coastline, seaports and airports in the Netherlands. The Dutch authorities make use, *inter alia*, of 100 percent identity checks, digital tools and dog guards to protect these external Schengen borders (Lucassen and Van Houtum, 2016). Yet members of the Schengen Area still have the opportunity to protect their own national borders under specific conditions – as could especially be seen during the so-called refugee crisis of 2015, perceived terrorism threats and the Covid-19 pandemic (Gülzau, 2021). The Dutch authorities also use so-called Schengen-proof, non-systematic, spot checks in the 20km zone around its land borders with Belgium and Germany in order to prove migrants' lawful entry into the Netherlands (Van der Woude and Brouwer, 2017; Van der Woude, Brouwer and Dekkers, 2016). This means, more concretely, that passengers in suspect vehicle and on international trains may be randomly controlled, obliged to identify themselves and checked for the lawfulness of their entry (Dekkers, 2019; Van der Woude and Brouwer, 2017; Van der Woude et al., 2016). The Dutch authorities aim to prevent unauthorized entry in the country by using these measures.

Furthermore, the Dutch authorities aim to limit the opportunities for migrants to legally enter the country as well as to obtain admission rights (Ellermann and Goenaga, 2019). In recent years, they have introduced, *inter alia*, a wide range of pre-admission requirements in order to stimulate migrants to apply for admission while still in their home country (Bonjour, 2010; Van Eijl, 2012). These are accompanied by more-restrictive admission terms, meaning that migrants have to meet extra requirements such as visa restrictions, study and work contracts, proof of relationships, income requirements, civic integration tests and financial fees in order to be allowed to enter the Netherlands and legally reside here. Additionally, they implemented the Marriage of Convenience Act to more strictly control whether someone should be granted a residence permit on the basis of their marriage (De Hart, 2003; Staring, 1998). At the moment of writing, the authorities are discussing (temporary) measures to limit the arrival of members who want to reunite with family in the Netherlands (Meijer and Righton, 2023). All these measures increase the threshold for admission into the Netherlands, which is already considered to be high compared with the admission criteria in other European countries (Ellermann and Goenaga, 2019). If migrants are not capable of meeting the applicable admission requirements and cannot make use of a tourist visa, they cannot legally enter the Netherlands. This means that they can only travel unauthorized to the Netherlands. As such, the authorities try to limit the number of migrants who legally enter the Netherlands and continue their stay after the expiry of their legal entitlements. This should contribute to the prevention of unauthorized residence.

12 https://www.consilium.europa.eu/en/policies/schengen-area/, accessed 07/09/2023.

2.2.2 *Using internal migration controls*

Yet despite the reinforced external migration controls and strengthened admission policies, it is complex – perhaps even impossible (Finotelli and Sciortino, 2013; Van Meeteren, 2014) – to fully prevent unauthorized entry into a country. Research shows that migrants still succeed in entering Europe unauthorized over land (Van Eijl, 2012: 174–175) or to remain there after their legal entitlements have ended (Black et al., 2004; Van Meeteren, 2014). Once in Europe, they may easily travel – again, unauthorized – to other EU countries due to the abolishment of systematic internal border controls in the Schengen Area. This means that it is hard to fully prevent the unauthorized entry and thus unauthorized residence in a country. While the Dutch authorities are themselves aware of this, they do want to try to end unauthorized residence given the problems it is supposed to cause on the labour and housing markets, to end the migrants' vulnerability and to prevent various forms of nuisance and crime (Parliamentary Documents 1990/91 22146 no. 1; 2007/08 19637 no. 1207; see also Kox, 2010; Van Eijl, 2012). Although it is not certain that the presence of unauthorized migrants actually causes such problems (Diepenhorst, 2012), the authorities have been using a two-tier approach whereby their return programmes are directly linked with the Netherlands' internal migration controls to make unauthorized migrants leave the country since the late 1980s (Kox, 2010; Mommers and Velthuis, 2010). They have, on the one hand, developed a wide range of return policies and programmes to convince and assist unauthorized migrants to – voluntarily – return to their home country (Staring and Kox, 2020). On the other, they have strengthened their internal borders in a bid to discourage and deter unauthorized migrants to reside without permission in the Netherlands (Broeders, 2009; Van Eijl, 2012).

2.2.2.1 (Forced) return policies

As part of this two-tier approach, the Dutch authorities have been further developing their (forced) return policies since the early 1990s. Their starting point is that unauthorized migrants who have received a return decision of the IND and who have exhausted all legal remedies independently leave the Netherlands, as such independent – or voluntary[13] – return is considered easier, cheaper and more sustainable than deportation (Van Eijl, 2012). Therefore, the Aliens Act 2000 made the unauthorized migrants themselves primarily responsible for their departure: those whose legalization claims are rejected as well as those migrants who received a return decision are automatically forced to leave the Netherlands (Kox, 2010). They are usually allowed 28 days to leave the country. During

13 The voluntariness – or – independency of these returns has repeatedly been questioned as these voluntary returns are partly enforced by discouragement policies leaving unauthorized migrants with little options (e.g. Webber, 2011).

this period, they may turn for return support to the authorities and different organizations. The latter include the International Organization for Migration (IOM), which has been provided with funding for Assisted Voluntary Return (AVR) projects for unauthorized migrants – and particularly asylum seekers – since 1992, as well as different non-governmental organizations (NGOs) which, at a later stage, were also given subsidies for AVR projects (Mommers and Velthuis, 2010; Staring and Kox, 2020). Unauthorized migrants in immigration detention may also use AVR since 2007 (Kox, 2011). AVR support usually includes practical help in organizing the migrants' flights and a (differentiated) reintegration budget and/or medical assistance which helps the migrants to reintegrate in their home countries (Mommers and Velthuis, 2010). The Dutch authorities hope that the AVR projects will convince unauthorized migrants to leave the Netherlands (e.g. Parliamentary Documents 1989/90 21132 no. 8; 1996/97 25386 no. 1; 1998/99 26646 no. 1; 2001/02 19637 and 26646 no. 648; 2003/04 29344 no. 1; 2007/08 19637 no. 1207; 2007/08 29344 no. 67; 2007/08 31018 no. 33; 2008/09 19637 no. 1263; 2009/10 30573 no. 54; 29344 no. 80, 85). What is more, they expect that these organizations – trusted by the migrants – are better capable of reaching out to unauthorized migrants and supporting their return processes (*Ibid.*; Mommers and Velthuis, 2010; Staring and Kox, 2020). Additionally, they expect that the financial support will enable unauthorized migrants to better reintegrate in their home country, which could encourage their return (*Ibid.*). Therefore – and with the incentive of funding from EU programmes, the opportunities for AVR and the funding for organizations that offer AVR have repeatedly been extended in recent decades, which fits with the aforementioned trend of responsibilization in the migration domain (see also Chapter 5).

Unauthorized migrants who do not independently leave the country run the risk of being subjected to a deportation process. In 2007, the Dutch authorities established the Repatriation and Departure Service (DT&V) to increase the efficiency of the Dutch return policies. This new organization – which consisted of employers of the immigration police, the Royal Netherlands Marechaussee (Kmar) and the Immigration and Naturalization Service (IND) – has become responsible for all tasks regarding unauthorized migrants' return and deportation. The DT&V first focuses on the migrants' independent return but may switch to forced return if the former fails. Using case-management strategies, they try to make unauthorized migrants at freedom-restricted (family) locations, in detention centres and at other locations leave the country.[14] Yet, unauthorized migrants' deportation is not that self-evident as the Dutch authorities are confronted with myriad limitations

14 At the moment of the fieldwork for this study, the DT&V introduced a new approach aimed at motivational treatment to stimulate unauthorized migrants' willingness to return (see also Breuls, 2022). Some case managers were already using this method, others were still learning how to use it or using their old strategies.

that hamper them to actually deport unauthorized migrants to their home country (Maliepaard et al., 2022). These limitations vary from the migrants' home countries reluctance to provide travel documents that are required for the migrants' deportation to the unauthorized migrants' unwillingness to arrange such documents; from the authorities' dependence of other actors for deportation to a lack of adequate collaboration and information in the state's deportation process; and from a lack of priority for the deportation in intranational negotiations to all kind of organizational matters (e.g. Advisory Council on Migration, 2021; DT&V, 2023; Leerkes and Kox, 2016; Maliepaard et al., 2022). The travel restrictions during the Covid-19 pandemic caused an extra barrier to deport unauthorized migrants at that time. For these reasons, the authorities – often in collaboration with other European countries – continue to look for new strategies such as readmission agreements, joint deportation flights and reintegration budgets that may help them to deport unauthorized migrants from the Netherlands (Maliepaard et al., 2022). To date, however, the authorities are not satisfied with the results and continue exploring new opportunities to increase their return and deportation rates (see also Verbaten, 2022).

2.2.2.2 Identification and exclusion policies

The Dutch authorities have increasingly coupled the country's return policies with its internal migration control policies in order to stimulate unauthorized migrants' willingness to leave the country. They use a wide range of internal migration controls to complicate unauthorized migrants' everyday lives in the hope of discouraging them from continuing their unauthorized residence (e.g. Parliamentary Documents 1990/91 22 146 no. 1; 1992/93 22 981 no. 1; 2003/04 29 537 no. 2; see also Broeders and Engbersen, 2007; Kox, 2010; van Meeteren, 2014). This includes different identification and exclusion policies, meaning that a person's identification is linked with his or her legal status and becomes more important for participating in Dutch society (Broeders, 2009; Van Meeteren, 2014).

By the early 1990s, for instance, unauthorized migrants were no longer eligible for a personal service number; these were linked with their legal status, meaning that newly arriving unauthorized migrants could no longer make use of social services or access the labour market (Benseddik and Bijl, 2004; Kox, 2010).[15] While these measures were resisted by a parliamentary commission (Commission Zeevalking, 1991) and local authorities (Van Eijl, 2012), the Dutch authorities decided to do so to prevent a semblance of legality and the potential abuse of social benefits (Parliamentary Documents 1990/91 22146 no. 1;

15 Asylum seekers do receive an ID document – a W document – during their asylum procedure which states that they are allowed to reside in the Netherlands while awaiting a decision in their procedure. Migrants may also receive an ID document – a W2 document – if they meet certain conditions that allow them to await a decision in their legalization procedure in the Netherlands. These documents, which include a migrant's name and nationality, are usually valid for one year. Migrants who are unauthorized in the Netherlands are not eligible for such W documents.

1992/93 22 981 no. 1; see also Kox, 2010; Van Eijl, 2012: 184). A couple of years later, in 1994, the Dutch authorities introduced the Compulsory Identification Act, which obliged everyone above twelve years old to identify themselves for employers, social security institutions, banks etc. This act was aimed at combatting fraud and crime but also limited the opportunities for unauthorized migrants to make a living. On the one hand, the act complicated the migrants' opportunities to (formally) access the labour market and participate in society. On the other, it made these migrants more prone to detection by the authorities as it created legal opportunities for the police and the Kmar to ask for identification on the grounds of a reasonable suspicion of unauthorized residence (see also Kox, 2010; Van der Woude et al., 2016). In 2005, this act was replaced by the Extended Compulsory Identification Act which did not change the rules for unauthorized migrants in terms of identification, but did enable special investigative officers and administrative institutions to ask someone to show their ID and to transfer unauthorized migrants to the immigration police. As such, this act entailed an extension of the actors involved in migration control, which increased the likelihood of unauthorized migrants again being controlled (Parliamentary Documents 2003/04 29218 no. 3; see also Kox, 2010).

These identification policies provided the Dutch authorities with opportunities to exclude unauthorized migrants from social services and formal markets and to prevent them from receiving benefits, entering the labour market and enabling their unauthorized residence (Parliamentary Documents 1994/95 24233 no. 3; see also Pluymen, 2008). The introduction of the Linking Act in 1998, which implied an adjustment of 25 other laws, enabled the systematic linking of information from the police on migrants' legal statuses with information from social services. This served to exclude those without a legal status from access to a wide range of public and semi-public provisions such as child benefits, insurance, social housing etc. (Parliamentary Documents 1994/95 24233 no. 3). Moreover, the act made officers working for a wide range of social institutions – such as schools, health professionals and the municipality – responsible for excluding unauthorized residence from these social provisions as they dealt with such applications, despite them not being willing to do so (Pluymen, 2008; Van der Leun, 2003; Van Eijl, 2012: 185). The introduction of the act substantially changed the position of unauthorized migrants in the Netherlands as they were now only entitled to necessary medical care, legal aid and – until the age of eighteen – education (Pluymen, 2008; Van der Leun, 2003). Some may also make use of shelter facilities if they meet certain eligibility criteria (see below).

In the same timeframe, the Dutch authorities limited unauthorized migrants' access to the formal *and* informal labour markets in order to eliminate the migrants' reason(s) for migrating and to complicate their unauthorized residence (Van Meeteren, 2014: 61). The authorities believed that the Foreign National Employment Act of 1994, the increased identification requirements and the introduction of the Linking Act would result in insufficient opportunities to do so (Van Eijl, 2012: 159), which is why they intensified control of the labour market by both the police and an Inspectorate (Parliamentary Documents 2003/04 29537 no. 2; De Lange, 2007; Van Eijl, 2012: 182). They also replaced the criminal fines for unauthorized labour with administrative fines as these were supposed to be less time-consuming and more effective, especially as they raised the fines to € 4,000 for private employers and € 8,000 for commercial employers for each unauthorized employee (Parliamentary Documents 2003/04 29537 no. 2). These amounts could be raised in cases of recidivism of the employer, after which criminal prosecution of the employer was also an option. While this does not automatically mean that more unauthorized migrants were caught on the labour market (Kox, 2010), these politics of identification and exclusion were – again – supposed to hamper unauthorized residence (Parliamentary Documents 2003/04 29537 no. 2; see also Broeders, 2009; Kox, 2010; Van Meeteren, 2014). The Dutch authorities believed that this act would be helpful in complicating unauthorized residence and counteracting unauthorized migration as well as in preventing a false sense of legality (Van Eijl, 2012: 184; see also Kox, 2010).

Finally, the Dutch authorities wanted to exclude unauthorized migrants from shelter and living allowances as well. In 1998, for instance, the Dutch authorities excluded Dublin claimants[16] and asylum seekers – who started another legalization procedure – from shelter and living allowances (Parliamentary Documents 1998/99 19637, no. 367). In 2001, after the implementation of the new Aliens Act 2000, asylum seekers and unauthorized migrants whose legalization claims were rejected also lost their entitlement to shelter and living allowances, meaning that they were forced to leave the asylum centre where they had been staying (Parliamentary Documents 1998/99 26732 no. 3). Only those who were believed to participate in their return process received shelter and living allowances in a sober, freedom-restricted location where they were imposed a daily reporting duty and obliged to participate in a return process in collaboration with a case manager (Koppes, 2017). This encouraged a wide range of humanitarian organizations to spring up to support migrants without a legal status in response to – and given their disagreement with – the state's policies. These were partly funded by municipalities which invoked their 'duty of care' as well as their responsibility for public order and safety and started such emergency shelters when they saw themselves confronted with a large number of asylum seekers ending up on the streets given the lack of adequate national-return policies (Staring and Kox, 2016). Over time, societal pressure as well as legal obligations forced the Dutch authorities to change their policies. In 2002, for instance, Dublin claimants were provided shelter again (Tussentijds Bericht Vreemdelingencirculaire TBV

16 The Dublin-regulation (EU-Regulation 604/2013) determines which EU-member state is responsible for examining an asylum application. This is usually the state where the asylum seeker first enters the EU, meaning that asylum seekers who apply for asylum or are stopped in another member state may be transferred to the state that is held responsible for the application. These asylum seekers are referred to as Dublin claimants.

2002/48). In 2012, a court ruling forced the Dutch authorities to end their policies to send minors back to the streets once their legalization claims were rejected and to offer shelter to families with minor children until the youngest child reached the age of eighteen. This resulted in freedom-restricted family locations (Parliamentary Documents 2010/11 29344 no.79; see also Brouwer, 2018). Likewise, in the aftermath of a complaint by the Conference of European Churches to the European Committee of Social Rights and Dutch court rulings, the Dutch authorities were forced to provide financial compensation to municipalities to arrange shelter for those unauthorized migrants who had been excluded from shelter and social services; this resulted in so-called 'Bed, Bath and Bread' arrangements from 2014 onwards (Parliamentary Documents II 2014/15 19637 no. 1944; see also Koppes, 2017; Pro Facto, 2018). At the end of 2018, after the fieldwork for this study had ended, this resulted in a national pilot scheme consisting of local support organizations providing shelter to and looking for perspectives for unauthorized migrants (the so-called '*landelijke vreemdelingenvoorzieningen*' – LVV, see Parliamentary Documents 2017/18 28345 no. 187). While a substantial number of unauthorized migrants are still eventually excluded from shelter and living allowances, this shows that the state's policies are not always as strictly executed as (initially) proclaimed (cf. Aliverti, 2013; Van der Woude and Van der Leun, 2017).

2.2.2.3 Detection, detention and deportation

Furthermore, the Dutch authorities increasingly focused on what Brouwer (2020) calls the detection, detention and deportation of unauthorized migrants. Over the years, the authorities created new legal opportunities to control unauthorized migrants and extended its capacity as well as the urgency for these controls (Parliamentary Documents 2003/04 29344 no. 1; 2003/04 29537 no. 2; see also Kox, 2010). The Dutch authorities have, for instance, increased the legal opportunities for the police, the Kmar and other actors to control a person's identity, nationality and legal status with the implementation of the Aliens Act 2000. These institutions used only to be allowed to control a person's documents if they had concrete indications that he or she was unauthorized in the country, but the new Aliens Act allowed them to also stop unauthorized migrants on the basis of a reasonable doubt about unauthorized residence. This lowered the threshold to stop someone and ask for their ID (art. 50 Aliens Act 2000; see also Kox, 2010). Additionally, these institutions obtained more opportunities to enter and search unauthorized migrants' assumed homes if they suspected that the migrants would be there (art. 53 Aliens Act 2000). These controlling institutions also made use of digital features such as fingerprints and databases that enabled them to link information to different internal and international databases (Broeders, 2009). The Dutch authorities had thus more opportunities to detect unauthorized migrants during their residence in the Netherlands. Yet, for pragmatic and rights-based reasons, the local police in Amsterdam, in collaboration with local support organizations and the central authorities, started a 'free in, free out' policy to enable unauthorized migrants to report the victimization of crimes without – at least on paper – running the risk of immigration enforcement (Timmerman et al., 2020). This shows that such local initiatives may limit the effects of the state's strict discouragement policies.

In the same timeframe, the Dutch authorities increased their control by extending the police capacity and making more institutions responsible for migration control. In 2003, for instance, the police reorganized and established a specialized department for immigration police – called Immigration Affairs, Identification and Human Trafficking (AVIM) – which contributed to an extended focus on and capacity for migration control (Boekhoorn and Speller, 2006). This same year, the then Minister of Immigration Affairs and Integration announced a further extension of the controlling capacity for the police and declared migration control as one of the police's priorities (Parliamentary Documents 2003/04 29344 no. 1; 2003/04 29537 no. 2; see also Boekhoorn and Speller, 2006; Kox, 2010). The minister declared that the police had to work with apprehension quota, meaning that they were forced to apprehend a minimum number of unauthorized migrants a year. In 2004, this was followed by new and increased migration control collaboration between different government institutions, such as the labour inspectorate, the tax service, municipalities etc., increased as part of the state's new, interdisciplinary intervention approach (Parliamentary Documents 2002/03 17050 no. 248). The identification, exclusion and detection of unauthorized migrants was now be done by other actors and at different levels, which shows the extended urgency for migration control (Broeders, 2009). Yet, despite the rise in capacity and urgency for migration controls in the early years after the turn of the century, there was no actual active focus on the detection of unauthorized migrants by the police at that time, as police officers in the four largest cities of the Netherlands decided not to prioritize migration controls as they did not want to go after unauthorized migrants who were not involved in crime (Van Eijl, 2012: 167; Van der Leun, 2003; Van der Woude and Van der Leun, 2017). They preferred to focus on crime and threats to public order in their everyday practice (*Ibid.*). Officers at street level, such as the police, do have a certain degree of discretion, meaning that they may stretch these rules and limit the impact of strict controlling policies (Van der Leun, 2003; Van der Woude, 2016). The translation of migration control in the books to migration control in action as well as the pressure on the police's capacity are some of the reasons why the central authorities were confronted with local limits in the execution of these policies.

Finally, the Dutch authorities have extended the opportunities to detain unauthorized migrants with the purpose of removal. Since the Aliens Act of 1965, it has been possible to use immigration detention for unauthorized migrants (Baudoin, Van de Burgt and Van Kalmthout, 2008; art. 59 Aliens Act 2000) but it has become easier to do so since the implementation of the Aliens Act 2000 (Baudoin et al., 2008). Nowadays, unauthorized migrants may be detained if this is considered necessary to protect public order or national security and if there are no less-intrusive alternatives available.[17] While there was initially no maximum duration for immigration detention, the EU Return Directive proscribed that immigration detention may last for six months, unless the detainee is considered uncooperative in revealing his/her identity or has been convicted of certain crimes. Then, the detention may be extended to eighteen months. The principle of this administrative measure is to deport unauthorized migrants from the Netherlands, something that succeeded in about 50 percent of the number of immigration detainees without Dublin-claim in 2020 and 90 percent of those with a Dublin claim that could be deported to another Schengen country in the period 2015–2019 (Advisory Council on Migration, 2021). If there is insufficient view to deportation or if the government has made insufficient progress toward deporting the individual, the detention has to be terminated. Released detainees are usually given a day train ticket and an order to leave the country. Despite the return order that is imposed on them, they may continue their unauthorized residence. However, they can be re-detained if they are caught again by the authorities (Timmerman, 2018).

2.2.2.4 Criminalization of unauthorized residence?

Finally, it should be noted that unauthorized residence – or support to unauthorized migrants – is not criminalized in the Netherlands. It is considered an administrative offence and is mainly dealt with by administrative and other non-criminalized laws, although it has been argued that the Dutch authorities have also included crime-control elements and actors in its migration policies (Staring and Timmerman, 2021; Van der Leun, 2010; Van der Woude et al., 2014). The Dutch authorities have repeatedly proposed to criminalize unauthorized residency as well as support for unauthorized migrants and launched a bill to do so in 2011 (Parliamentary Documents 2011/12 33512 no. 1–13; see also Terlouw, 2013; Van Eijl, 2012: 198). These plans received much criticism from the executive controlling institutions, NGOs for unauthorized migrants and others and was, after lengthy political and societal debates, withdrawn in 2014 (*Ibid.*). The topic comes up every now and then in political debate and there are still political parties in the Netherlands who aim to criminalize unauthorized residence. Thus far, unauthorized residence is included in administrative law, which means that unauthorized residence is not criminalized *and* that unauthorized migrants have fewer legal safeguards available than if unauthorized residence were dealt with in criminal law (cf. Chacón, 2009).

---

17 The Aliens Act further specifies when unauthorized migrants may be detained with the purpose of removal. Authorities have to motivate their decisions to detain an unauthorized migrant. This concerns a more extended motivation since the implementation of the EU Return Directive in the Netherlands in 2011.

2.3 To conclude

This chapter has set the scene in which unauthorized migrants' legal consciousness processes are situated. It has outlined the seven trends which have substantially changed the nature, structure and reach of the European migration regulation approach. Additionally, the chapter has shown that the Dutch authorities try to convince unauthorized migrants to – independently – return to their home country and fund AVR programmes to facilitate their return since the early 1990s. They combine this with politics of identification, exclusion, detection, detention and deportation in order to complicate unauthorized migrants' everyday lives and make them leave the country. Whereas it has been argued that the Dutch migration control approach is relatively strict in comparison with other European states (Leerkes and van Houte, 2020), the state's laws and policies are not always as strictly executed as proclaimed in everyday practices (Aliverti, 2013; Van der Woude and Van der Leun, 2017). Other processes may also take place which limit the effects of these strict controls on an everyday basis (Brandariz, 2021; Staring and Timmerman, 2021). While other legal and non-legal factors also shape the migrants' legal consciousness processes, it is within this legal context that unauthorized migrants' experiences with, thoughts on and interactions with the law come about.

3 METHODS: A MULTI-SITED ETHNOGRAPHY AMONG UNAUTHORIZED MIGRANTS

Ethnographic research is considered the most suitable to understanding how ordinary people think and act in relation to the law as well as the power of the law in their everyday reality (e.g. Ewick and Silbey, 1998; Merry, 1990; Nielsen, 2000; Sarat, 1990).[18] To date, there is no well-defined meaning of ethnographic research (Wincup, 2017). It usually includes being in the field, immersing oneself in a specific research study for a longer period and collecting and digesting all the data that enable the researcher to understand a group's social reality and cultural practices within its wider context (cf. Wincup, 2017; Zaitch, Mortelmans and Decorte, 2009). This is exactly what I have done in the context of this study.

Between early 2015 and mid-2018, I conducted ethnographic fieldwork among migrants who (used to) reside without a legal status in the Netherlands. I immersed myself in their everyday lives in order to be able to present 'thick descriptions' of these migrants' everyday social reality (cf. Geertz, 1973). I used a multi-sited approach, meaning that I met research participants at different localities and different moments in time in order to obtain more contextual information on their everyday lives and the role of the law in them (see also Siegel, 2008). Such a multi-sited method best fits migration research as the migration phenomenon has a significant trans-local nature (King, 2018) and migrants are not geographically bound or confined to a single place (cf. Hannerz, 2003). In order to be able to include (retrospective) perceptions of the law of unauthorized migrants who find themselves in different positions and different stages of their unauthorized residence as well as to observe changes in the migrants' perceptions on the law over time, I followed unauthorized migrants over time *and* space during the course of the fieldwork. This took me to many different areas in the Netherlands, Nigeria, Surinam and Guyana. It allowed me to better understand unauthorized migrants' emic perspectives of the law as well as the consequences for the functioning of the law. In this chapter, I further unfold my methodological approach and reflect on my positionality, ethics and the limitations of the research.

---

18 Legal consciousness scholars mostly turn to ethnographic research (e.g. Ewick and Silbey, 1998; Merry, 1990; Nielsen, 2000; Sarat, 1990), while Horak, Lacko and Klocek (2021) are in favour of a quantitative approach in legal consciousness studies. However, they claim that perceived legitimacy is equivalent to legal consciousness, which is – in my view – a too-limited definition of legal consciousness, as the latter includes what people consider to be the law and how they respond to it (see also Silbey, 2005).

3.1 Getting started: Accessing the research field

The first stage of the ethnographic research consisted of getting access to the research field in order to be able to unfold my research plans, which is a critical stage in qualitative research. Yet getting access is not self-evident when doing research among unauthorized migrants (Düvell, Triandafyllidou and Vollmer, 2010; Van Liempt and Bilger, 2018). Unauthorized migrants constitute a hidden group in society which is characterized by invisibility (Burgers and Engbersen, 1999; Van Meeteren, 2014). This complicates getting access to unauthorized migrants for research purposes and may cause anxiety and frustration among researchers (Maillet, Mountz and Williams, 2017). To prevent such anxiety and frustration, I consciously created different strategies that could help me to get in touch with a diverse group of unauthorized migrants. I am, of course, aware that ethnographic research is about flexibility and intuition and about grasping all opportunities in the field (cf. Ferrel, 2018; Poulton, 2014) and realize that such research may be messy and unruly and may often not turn out as expected (*Ibid.*). Yet I hoped that the use of different research strategies would help me to gain access to this research group and kickstart this study – especially as I aimed for diversity within the research group, given the heterogeneity that results in wide variety in the migrants' social positions, relations and opportunities in society (Burgers and Engbersen, 1999; Vertovec, 2007; 2019). In order to be able to capture this diversity in terms of, *inter alia*, the migrants' countries of origin, ethnicities and migration motives, I used different strategies to access the research field.

First, in spring 2015, I reached out to gatekeepers – persons who could put me in contact with unauthorized migrants, given their specific position in relation to the research group (cf. Zaitch et al., 2009). I found myself in a privileged position because, before I entered academia, I had been involved in a project to gain greater insight into the support that was offered by ethnic communities, humanitarian organizations and religious groups to unauthorized migrants. As part of this project, I had been reaching out to the contact persons of these organizations, which had brought me in touch with potential gatekeepers (Stichting LOS, 2011). Furthermore, I had already conducted research among unauthorized migrants in different settings such as immigration detention centres (Kox, 2007, 2011), among former rejected asylum seekers (Kox, 2010) and in a transnational prison (Kox et al., 2014) before I started this study. My contacts, previous experience and name recognition in the migration domain helped me to make contact with gatekeepers who could put me in touch with unauthorized migrants. From spring 2015 onwards, I contacted, *inter alia*, humanitarian organizations that mainly support rejected asylum seekers by providing them with shelter, legal assistance, medical aid or return assistance. I also reached out to grassroots organizations who could help me to get in touch with unauthorized labour migrants working in the informal economy (or trying to do so). I additionally approached key figures in migration communities who might be in touch with unauthorized migrants from all types of background. It was not self-evident that these gatekeepers were (again) willing to help me, as participating in research may be burdensome to unauthorized migrants while its effects are uncertain. Some gatekeepers were, indeed, reluctant to help me out, given the time constraints. Yet I was fortunate in that some of them were willing to help me out. They approached migrants for me, after which I could call or text those who were willing to participate in the study in order to set up a meeting.

Within the same timeframe, I also reached out to migrants of the We Are Here group, a protest group of rejected asylum seekers who came together to collectively step out of the shadows of society and reveal the – in their view – shortcomings of the law in the Netherlands (see also Hajer and Bröer, 2020). They wanted to inform the wider society on what they call the 'asylum gap', which refers to them not being granted asylum while they cannot or will not return – nor are deported to – their home country.[19] As the group was looking for ways to be heard in the migration debate, I believed that some of its members might be willing to participate in my research. This turned out to be right. When I contacted one of the spokespersons of the group by phone, the answer was: 'I always want to discuss our situation' (fieldnotes 03/25/2015). I was invited to the old, cold leaking parking garage they were squatting in at that time given their lack of housing or shelter, which were my first exciting steps in the field in the context of the study. We had a lengthy, interesting conversation on the group's situation and protests as well as on the aims of my research. The spokesperson was quite curious about my thoughts on the migration debate, which made me struggle not to open up too much on this matter to prevent any influencing. At the same time, I wanted to make sure that the spokesperson felt safe discussing everyday life without papers with me. After having spoken about other personal things and having moved the discussion away from my thoughts on the policies and more towards the interviewee's ones, the latter was willing to meet me more often. This probably had more to do with these migrants grasping all opportunities to get their voices heard in the migration debate than with me as a person. Like Bosworth (2014) showed for immigration detainees in the UK, this spokesperson hoped that an account of the group's experiences with the law in the Netherlands would change people's minds about the current immigration system. This was the start of more frequent contacts between the two of us and of me getting to know other members of the group.

Furthermore, I used site selection strategies at the start of the fieldwork, meaning that I included different research sites in the hope of meeting a diverse group of unauthorized migrants (see also FitzGerald, 2012). For this reason, I also applied for authorization for this study at the migration policy directorate of the Ministry of Justice and Security

19 See also http://wijzijnhier.org/who-we-are/, accessed 07/12/2023.

[Directie Migratiebeleid, DMB) in March 2015. Formally, I did not need any state authorization to conduct this research among unauthorized migrants. However, I hoped that authorization would convince organizations within the Dutch immigration system – such as the COA, immigration police, DT&V, immigration detention centres and the Kmar – to put me in touch with unauthorized migrants who found themselves in a different position to those living out of sight of the Dutch authorities.[20] In response to my application letter, I was invited for a meeting with two representatives of the DMB in August 2015 and – after some further correspondence – was granted permission for the research. While some organizations required a (extended) security check or a nondisclosure agreement in which I promised that I would let them check all publications for factual inaccuracies and would not disclose information that could harm persons who participated in the research, all organizations within the system were willing to help me. They enabled me to conduct participant observations at several locations and introduced me to unauthorized migrants. The immigration police in The Hague, for instance, informed me about the arrest of unauthorized migrants to enable me to meet and interview them at the police station. The COA helped me to get in touch with unauthorized migrants residing in the freedom-restricted (family) locations in Ter Apel, Emmen and Katwijk. The penitentiary institution for foreign-national offenders in Ter Apel allowed me to interview some unauthorized migrants and I was also able to interview those in immigration detention centres. This resulted in more research participants who found themselves in a different position to other participants – which provided me with more insights into the migrants' different relationships with the law.

The use of multiple strategies initially helped me to get in touch with a diverse group of unauthorized migrants. From here, I moved forward by using snowballing strategies. This means that I asked my participants whether they could put me in contact with other unauthorized migrants who might be willing to participate in my research (see also Mortelmans, 2009). This strategy is considered suitable for research among hidden populations such as unauthorized migrants and has been successfully used in other studies on the living conditions of these migrants (e.g. Burgers and Engbersen, 1999; Chavez, 1998; Staring, 2001; Van Meeteren, 2014). Yet, this method also has some downsides, as snowball sampling may result in the production of bias, thus needing the number of referrals per respondent to be kept to a minimum (Van Meeteren, 2014). Additionally, migrants may be reluctant to help establish contacts because they might not want others to know about their unauthorized status; in this way they can limit the risks of betrayal

20 Additionally, I wanted to observe the different organizations within the Dutch immigration system – such as the COA, the immigration police, DT&V, immigration detention centres and the Kmar – to better understand their work and unauthorized migrants' stories (see Section 3.2.3). In Section 3.5, I discuss some ethical considerations related to this approach.

(Staring, Boesveldt and Kox, 2022). Furthermore, migrants may only have small networks, meaning that they were not able to help me to establish other contacts (*Ibid.*), as I experienced myself while being in the field. Only a few migrants were able to put me in touch with other unauthorized migrants, while others were somewhat reluctant to do so. Yet, while being at different sites in the field, I encountered other unauthorized migrants who were able to help me to get access to the research group and to gain new leads.

3.2 Collecting data: Being in the field

From the moment I entered the field, I tried to immerse myself in the research group. As discussed below, I used different data-collection techniques to better understand how the law matters to unauthorized migrants and how this is of concern for the law. I (repeatedly) interviewed research participants in a wide range of settings and conducted participant observations both among them and within the immigration system. Finally, I made research visits to returned and deported migrants in Surinam, Guyana and Nigeria before I left the research field.

3.2.1 *Interviewing unauthorized migrants*

As part of my fieldwork, I conducted interviews with unauthorized migrants to obtain in-depth understandings of their legal consciousness processes. Gatekeepers and other unauthorized migrants usually provided me with the phone numbers of unauthorized migrants who were willing to participate in my research. Additionally, officers working at different state institutions in the immigration system put me in contact with migrants situated there. This enabled me to approach the migrants by phone or in person in order to ask them whether we could meet (again). In our first contact, I let the migrant choose a specific location for the interview to make sure that s/he would feel comfortable. Consequently, I held interviews in a wide range of settings – such as on a bench in a park, in fast-food restaurants, facilities for unauthorized migrants, a person's accommodation, in the consultation room in an immigration detention centre or a freedom-restricted (family) location, in prison or at the police station. At the start of each first meeting, I introduced myself, tried to comfort the respondent and discussed all ethical aspects of the study (see Section 3.5.2 on ethics). When I was sure that the migrant wanted to participate in the study and believed that s/he understood that participation could be withdrawn at any moment without explanation, I started the interview. The interviews usually lasted between 45 minutes and four hours and were sometimes spread over multiple occasions. After the first time, I tried to interview the migrant more often in order to be able to observe changes in the migrant's legal consciousness over time.

In the first interview, the unauthorized migrant's everyday life was central. As is common in legal consciousness studies (e.g. Ewick and Silbey, 1998; Levine and Mellema, 2001: 204; Nielsen, 2000), I started with open-ended, relatively unstructured interviews on unauthorized migrants' everyday lives that helped me to understand the salience of the law for them. Ideally, legal consciousness scholars do not address the law themselves in their study to prevent influencing the research subject. They usually wait to see whether, when and how the law or legal concepts and constructs of interpretations are brought to the fore (see also Levine and Mellema, 2001). Afterwards, it is the precarious task of the researcher to analyse the data in order to understand a person's legal consciousness and to distinguish legal structures from – and relate them to other – broader social structures (Cowan, 2004). I tried to use such an approach, meaning that I tried to 'organically' study the migrants' legal consciousness (cf. Nielsen, 2000: 106). Yet, it soon turned out that the migrants' accounts of their everyday lives were permeated with legal elements, given the salient role of the law – and particularly of migration controls – in their everyday lives. Consequently, the law took on a central role in the interviews, which made it more complex for me as a researcher to stay away from it myself. I did try, though, to leave the initiative to the migrants themselves to see whether, how and why they brought up the topic in the interviews.

The follow-up interviews, as well as those that were conducted at a later stage of the fieldwork, were more oriented towards the sub-research questions and the relevant theoretical concepts that were being brought to the fore (cf. Nielsen, 2000). While I still tried to wait and see what migrants' main focus would be, I asked more structured follow-up questions to better understand unauthorized migrants' understandings of, experiences with, thoughts on and interactions with the law over time. For instance, when it became clear that it was helpful to draw on the concept of empirical legitimacy to capture the migrants' thoughts on the law, I included elements of the operationalization of this concept in my conversations with them. This means that, *inter alia*, I asked questions about the perceived lawfulness and justification of the law in the Netherlands, as these elements are considered necessary to bring about empirical legitimacy (see Chapters 7 and 8). I used a similar approach in relation to other theoretical concepts that are used in this study. As such, I could combine my inductive approach with more deductively used theoretical concepts that appeared to be relevant in order to capture the migrants' legal consciousness.

Qualitative research with a vulnerable group is always characterized by getting your research participants to open up to you. This means seeking a balance between objectivity and participation, between compassion and a critical attitude, between sensitivity and diplomacy (Liebling, 2001). This is what I also tried to do in my interviews – I tried to carefully listen to the migrants and show compassion. Yet, as previous legal consciousness research has shown that individuals may evoke contradictory images of the law at different moments and even within the same sentence (Ewick and Silbey, 1998), I also critically – but in a friendly way – probed further if I encountered such contradictions, if the information otherwise did not feel right or if I felt that bringing in other perspectives could be helpful. I did this in either the same conversation or a follow-up conversation to gain a better understanding of the migrants' legal consciousness. Whilst I do not know what the research participants may have not told me and what I have not been able to observe, I can say that the interviews usually took place in a constructive atmosphere. Research participants could get very emotional and sometimes angry while discussing their experiences with the law, but they were usually pleased that they had someone carefully listening to them without interrogating, mistrusting or judging them. Some even said that participating in this research was quite therapeutic as it enabled them to share and rethink their life-stories. Others also disclosed potentially harmful information to me – such as their having lied to the immigration authorities or having used falsified documents. Being blessed with dark, wide eyes that somehow invite people to talk, I had very open conversations that helped me to understand the migrants' different relationships with the law.

3.2.2 *Participant observation with unauthorized migrants*

Participant observation with unauthorized migrants was another important data collection method of this study. This includes the immersion of the researcher in a particular social setting or group in order to gain insights into the natural settings of the research groups' everyday lives (Decorte and Zaitch, 2009). During the fieldwork, I immersed myself in unauthorized migrants' everyday worlds – for instance, I hung out at different research sites where unauthorized migrants used to spend time, including living rooms that were offered by humanitarian organizations to unauthorized migrants to hang out, do their laundry, enjoy a hot lunch, drink coffee and participate in a wide range of activities. I regularly went there myself to meet interviewees and to get to know other unauthorized migrants. I also joined unauthorized migrants during their everyday activities such as football tournaments, information meetings, protests and demonstrations. I usually accompanied migrants whom I had met before although I occasionally just went there myself to get to know people in the context of this study. Furthermore, I was invited to research participants' 'homes' for tea or a meal or just to hang out with them, which was usually at freedom-restricted (family) locations, small rooms or their shelters. I was then often introduced to family members, compatriots or friends. As is common in ethnographic research, it was important to go with the flow and see what this approach would bring me. The participants' observations provided insights into the natural settings of their everyday lives and helped me to understand what their lives were like and to shed light on the role of the law in the migrants' lives as well as the salience of it on an everyday basis. Besides, it allowed me to have informal conversations with these respondents based on my observations, which helped to create more depth to the conversations and interviews. This enabled me to create a better rapport with the migrants, gain additional insights and validate their narratives.

Furthermore, if possible and permitted by the research participants, I observed them in their interactions with the law. For instance, I attended some return meetings with the DT&V, I observed interrogations by police officers, I watched respondents interacting with the COA and I observed respondents during their return process in immigration detention. On these occasions, too, I had many informal conversations with my participants in a bid to better understand how they understood and experienced their interactions with the law as well as the consequences of it for their legal consciousness. Here, I use an example based on an observation of a research participant's return meeting with his case-manager from the DT&V during his stay in an immigration detention centre to illustrate how I could use my observations in some informal conversations.

> Samir tells me that he is tired. He had just got out of bed, hadn't had any coffee or a cigarette when his case manager called him to come downstairs for a meeting to discuss his return process. After the meeting finished, Samir first wanted to go upstairs to wake up a bit more, have a coffee, breakfast and a cigarette. Then he wanted to come downstairs again to have a talk with me. (...) When he comes back, Samir says: 'Well, it doesn't matter. The case manager is just doing his job, but I don't understand that he said that, already three months ago, he would contact the consulate. And now he says that I have to call the consulate myself as this will take less time. I don't get that. Why do I have to stay in detention this long then? The case manager could have done that three months ago, then it wouldn't take that long.' This is hard for Samir. He tells me that he will not call the consulate himself because it does not make sense for him to go there. In his view, is up to the DT&V to decide if they are going to hold him there (fieldnotes 04/26/2017).

My observations gave me a better understanding of migrants' interactions with the law and with the immigration system in particular. Besides, as I had observed in the return meeting between Samir and his case manager, I could directly ask follow-up questions on what has happened there and how he gave meaning to it. With Samir, I could go deeper into the discussion on the call to the consulate; this was invaluable to me as I more often heard negative stories about the DT&V and their approach in return meetings without having a full understanding of what happened during these meetings. Having observed the meeting created more depth to my data.

3.2.3 *Participant observation within the immigration system*

The emic perspectives of unauthorized migrants are central in this study. Yet I also pragmatically observed sites, actions and state actors within the Dutch immigration system. For instance, I twice joined the immigration police in The Hague when they went to check three different houses for the presence of unauthorized migrants. I joined their team – consisting of multiple police officers in three cars and a van – who entered these houses. I observed the police officers communicating with the migrants concerned, searching their rooms and – afterwards at the police station – interrogating the apprehended migrants. I have also observed several case managers from the DT&V during return meetings with unauthorized migrants in immigration detention centres, at freedom-restricted (family) centres and at an asylum seekers' centre to see how they tried to encourage these migrants' willingness to return and to realize their departure from the Netherlands. Furthermore, I joined COA employees on several occasions during their work in the freedom-restricted (family) locations in Emmen, Katwijk and Ter Apel. There, I also observed the migrants during their reporting duties, meetings with case managers, social activities and at other occasions to gain an impression of what life in such a location was like. Furthermore, I joined the Kmar during their mobile border controls along a highway as well as on international trains. I observed how they approached people, who they selected for controls and how they communicated during these controls. There was one asylum seeker who came to them to claim asylum during one of the shifts that I observed. In addition, I joined the immigration police in Rotterdam while they were controlling the work and residence permits of sex workers who worked from home. I also visited the location where newly arriving refugees were being taken for their identity checks and controls as this could not be done in the regular reception centre in the aftermath of the so-called refugee crisis. Furthermore, I participated in a course run by the Kmar in which they teach employees who escort unauthorized migrants, upon deportation, to their country of origin. Finally, I observed two deportations from the Netherlands. I was present at the airport when these unauthorized migrants entered the airport, could observe the deportation process on the plane and left when the flight was about to take off.

During the participant observation, I observed how the law was enacted in everyday practice. I also had ample opportunity for informal conversations with the state officers from – among others – the COA, Kmar, DT&V and the police. They informed me about (the motivations for) their actions, the legal regulations and their own thoughts on them. They also dug up memories from the past to provide me with more insights into their work and what goes with it. As such, these participant observations in the immigration system provided me with contextual knowledge that is rarely available from previous studies. This helped me to better probe during the interactions with my research participants. I again provide an example from Nestor, an African man who had been detained in immigration detention during the course of this study, to show the added value of this approach. Nestor told me that he was almost deported from detention to his home country and explained the first steps of his deportation process to me, as my fieldnotes reveal:

> Nestor tells me that the Kmar used a van to take him to the airport. There, a man in uniform took him into a room, searched him and checked his luggage. Then, he was taken into a (smoking) room. Nestor explains that there was a formally dressed man – no uniform though – who came to sit down next to him. There was another man who came to sit on his other side and another who positioned himself opposite him. One of these men started talking to Nestor and told him that it was up to Nestor how things – the deportation – would work out that day. If Nestor participated in the process, everything would be fine. Otherwise, the Kmar would be forced to use other means to deport Nestor. Nestor explained to me that he told the man right away that he did not want to cause any problems and that he would cooperate on the process as he did not want any fuss. After this conversation, Nestor stayed in the smoking room. Two officers stayed with him and kept on talking about what was going to happen (fieldnotes 11/03/2017).

As I had observed all the rooms through which unauthorized migrants must pass before being escorted to the plane, I was aware of the different steps that are taken at the start of the deportation process. I was informed about the (de-escalation communication) techniques that escorts make use of in the deportation process. This contextual information made me appreciate Nestor's experiences, which helped me to better question him in our conversation. I could probe deeper into the different rooms as well as the escorts' de-escalation techniques. Nestor himself also noticed that I knew what I was talking about, meaning that he would recall in greater detail his memories, which improved the validity of the research approach.

This approach did carry the risk that I would come across some of my research participants while joining officers on duty in the immigration system. To limit this risk and prevent any harm being done to research participants, I informed the latter directly at the start of the research that I would also observe actors in the Dutch immigration system. If I were to come across them, then at least they would have been forewarned and would – hopefully – understand my role as a researcher. I tried to limit the likelihood of being confronted with research participants by focusing my participant observation within the immigration system on different localities. I mainly observed in The Hague and Rotterdam while my fieldwork with unauthorized migrants mainly focused on other localities such as Amsterdam, Utrecht, Ter Apel, Emmen and Katwijk. This seemed successful as I did not come across any respondents during this fieldwork. While I did observe some of them in their encounters with controlling institutions, this was only with their permission and they knew in advance that I would be present (see the previous section).

3.2.4 *Fieldwork with returned and deported migrants*

Almost at the end of the fieldwork, I was awarded a Talent Fund by the Erasmus School of Law, which enabled me to visit deported and returned unauthorized migrants and to gain the migrants' retrospective reflections on their positions towards the law in the Netherlands. In the initial research design, I only aimed to stay in touch with deported and returned migrants by WhatsApp, Skype and other digital means. This award, together with funding from the Erasmus Trust Fund, offered me the opportunity to go to Nigeria (Lagos and Benin City), Surinam (Paramaribo) and Guyana (Georgetown) to add an extra layer to my multi-sited approach. While I had already included interviewees who were participating in AVR projects as well as those who had returned to other countries in the research, these visits allowed me to also include the retrospective experiences of deported migrants in the research which may differ from the experiences of unauthorized migrants in the Netherlands. Besides, visiting both returned and deported migrants enabled me to observe their living conditions myself, to have in-depth conversations with them and to gain a better understanding of their everyday life after their (forced) departure from the Netherlands. This helped me to create more depth in this part of the research than staying in touch by phone and other digital means would have allowed me to do. This helped me to obtain extra – and perhaps different – insights into how the law (retrospectively) matters to unauthorized migrants as well as its consequences for the functioning of the law, which contributed to reaching data saturation.

For these reasons, I spend eight valuable days in Nigeria in February 2018; I mainly stayed in Lagos but also made a two-day trip to Benin City. In May 2018, I spend nine days in Paramaribo in Surinam and made a daytrip to Georgetown, Guyana, to where a research participant had recently returned.[21] These countries were chosen because of my involvement in the evaluation of the AVR programme Vice Versa 4.0 of Stichting ROS at that time (see Staring and Kox, 2020). A relatively high number of their clients – including two of my research participants – returned to these countries. Additionally, these countries differ from each other as Nigeria is mainly known for its labour migration while Surinam

21 Marko de Haan, a research assistant who participated in the evaluation of the return project of Stichting ROS and wrote his Master's dissertation on this topic (De Haan, 2018), was doing fieldwork in Surinam at the same time. We did some of the interviews together and divided other respondents between the two of us. Lotte Servaas conducted similar fieldwork in Indonesia (Servaas, 2019). These data are only used in Chapter 5 of this book, which focuses on the role of humanitarian organizations.

is a former colony of the Netherlands and known for its chain migration to the country. There were relatively few language barriers with inhabitants from these countries.

As part of my preparations for my fieldwork abroad, I approached a wide range of organizations and key figures that could have contact with returned or deported migrants in the regions that I planned to visit. Besides, Stichting ROS tried to put me in contact with their returned clients in these countries as part of the aforementioned evaluation of their return project (see also Staring and Kox, 2020). The International Organization for Migration (IOM) also arranged some conversations with their former clients situated in these countries. Further, I had also set up some appointments with key figures who were in contact with returnees or deportees or could tell me more about their situation. Given the limited time I could spend in these countries, I wanted to have made as many appointments as possible in order to make the best use of my time. However, as is common in ethnographic research, things did not always work out as planned, as some potential research participants were out of town, forgot the appointments or could no longer be reached by phone. At the same time, the snowballing method and reaching out on different occasions helped me to get in touch with other returnees and deportees who were willing to participate in my study. This is evidenced in the following note from my fieldwork at a funeral in Paramaribo that I visited together with research assistant Marko de Haan at the invitation of a stakeholder:

> Our contact person starts to talk with an older, somewhat shabby man who tells him that he has been living in the Netherlands as well and that he has been back in Surinam for some time. We join the conversation and have a little chat about the funeral and funeral customs in Surinam, while our contact person is talking with 'his' visitors from the Netherlands. When our contact person walks away from us to order some drinks, he asks us to go with him. Marko joins him while I wait a bit to have another chat with the shabby man. I explain to him why we are in Paramaribo and that we are looking for people who returned or were deported because of their lack of a legal status in the Netherlands. He then tells me that his entire family is still legally in the Netherlands. He himself did not have a legal status back then and spent several years unauthorized in the Netherlands. He was eventually deported to Surinam but would love to go to the Netherlands again (fieldnotes 05/11/2018).

We talk a bit more, after which I ask him whether we could make an appointment to further discuss his experiences in the Netherlands. He invites me to his house where we could hold the interview. Throughout all my research visits, I used a similar approach. I just tried to go with the flow and see whether I could get in touch with people who could help me to better understand unauthorized migrants' relationships with the law.

These were exciting and challenging research trips. In advance, my lack of experience with fieldwork abroad as well as time constraints, made me doubt whether the research visits would not end in complete failure. Given my limited time over there, I feared that I would not be able to find people who fit the research criteria and were willing to talk to me. Yet, my concerns turned out to be unfounded. People did not want to set a date in advance, as is common in the Dutch agenda culture. However, when contacting them once I was there, research participants were willing to meet me the next day, which resulted in a packed research schedule. I hung out with them, was guided to important places and interviewed them on their return experiences as well as their retrospective experiences with the law. Returned and deported migrants even felt honoured that someone from the Netherlands was visiting them so they could pretend to still have close friends there. However, there was one respondent in Nigeria who was rather angry with me, as she believed that I should not have spent money on a flight to visit her but should have given it to her as she needed it more. As her whole family was present, I first talked to them and she later opened up a bit. These very dense and intense research stays provided me with some additional insights into the law as well as into how unauthorized migrants relate to it, as can be read throughout the following chapters. As such, my fieldwork provides an extra layer to this study.

3.2.5 Leaving the research field

After having been in the field on and off for about three years and having gathered thousands of pages of data on the migrants' relationships with the law, I decided to end the fieldwork in the Netherlands at the end of 2017 and finish the fieldwork abroad in May 2018. In this period, I followed 45 research participants, meaning that I had been talking to and hanging out with them anything from three to more than twenty times between March 2015 and June 2018. Additionally, I included 60 unauthorized migrants whose participation was limited to a single meeting as it was too burdensome to participate on a more extensive basis.[22] It is not possible to make statements about the representativeness of the research group, as it is always problematic when researching a hidden population (Van Meeteren, 2014). Moreover, it is not the aim of qualitative research (cf. Zaitch et al., 2009). Yet, the heterogeneity within the research group limits the risk of sample bias. Additionally, the differences and similarities in the stories of unauthorized migrants made me believe that I had been able to capture the variation in the migrants' legal consciousness processes and to provide insights into how the law matters to them as well as the

22 This only includes those migrants who came to the fore in my fieldnotes and interviews, meaning that I also encountered other unauthorized migrants about whom I do not have sufficient data to include in my study.

consequences for the functioning of the law. The extensive period of fieldwork had allowed me to achieve theoretical saturation of unauthorized migrants' legal consciousness processes, meaning that I reached the point that (it seemed that) no additional issues or insights emerged from the data anymore and all elements of unauthorized migrants' legal consciousness processes were identified (cf. Strauss and Corbin, 1998: 143). While I would have loved to collect more data and continue immersing myself in unauthorized migrants' everyday reality, this made me decide to leave the research field.

Leaving the research field is a precarious task as it puts an end to or changes relationships with the migrants concerned (cf. Zaitch et al., 2009). I had built a good relationship with some of my respondents, who really appreciated seeing me every now and then to talk about their personal situation. That is why I tried to warn respondents that the end of the period of fieldwork was fast approaching and that I would not be around much more. I tried to manage their expectations and, when possible, we stayed in touch on WhatsApp, even after they returned to their country of origin. At the moment of writing, I am still in touch with a few research participants on WhatsApp.

3.3 The research group

The fieldwork was conducted with a very diverse research group of 65 unauthorized male migrants and 40 unauthorized female ones who varied in age from eight up to 70 years old. Their length of (unauthorized) stay in the Netherlands varied from almost a year to 38 years. They had many different motives for their migration which varied from claiming asylum to reuniting with family members and from searching for medical health care to aspiring a better life in terms of income, work or study. These migrants come from different continents and countries of origin. Some had had a residence permit which was withdrawn or not renewed, while others had never applied for a legal status or their applications had been rejected. The migrants were residing in different locations, including renting a room or staying at a support organisation, in immigration detention centres, at freedom-restricted (family) centres, in criminal detention or with family or friends, etc. By the end of the data-collection period, some migrants had obtained a (temporary) legal status or were undergoing (again) a legalisation procedure, while others had returned/were deported or still remained unauthorized in the Netherlands.[23]

Although it is common in ethnographic research among unauthorized migrants to provide a more extended description of the research group (e.g. Burgers and Engbersen, 1999; Van Meeteren, 2014), I have decided not to do so. The reason is that I was put in

23 There were no respondents residing (un)authorized in a third country, which would have been another option.

touch with some of the research participants by officers working in the immigration system. I am afraid that revealing more individual information on them might compromise their anonymity and mean that individual persons might be traceable. As discussed in more detail in Section 3.5, I fear that providing more information on the research participants might endanger them, especially as some of them disclosed potentially harmful information. That is why I limit myself to the brief description above and only add additional information in the chapters concerned.

3.4 THE ANALYSIS

For the analysis of the data, I recorded and literally transcribed the interviews.[24] I wrote down all my observations and conversations as well as methodological reflections and theoretical deliberations in extensive fieldnotes as soon as possible after returning from the field. All transcripts, fieldnotes and other documents are imported in the qualitative data analysis software Atlas.ti, which facilitates the analysis process. Nonetheless, it still the precarious task of the researcher to make sense of the data (Evers, 2015). It is up to the researcher to unravel a respondent's legal consciousness and to determine how and in which legal and broader social structures it is being shaped (Cowan, 2004). Legal consciousness scholars therefore usually use an interdisciplinary approach which integrates psychological, sociological, legal and other perspectives in their analyses in order to make sense of the data (Horak et al., 2021), as I also did.

At first, I planned to conduct my analysis on the principles of grounded theory that Glaser and Strauss (1967[2006]) introduced. This inductive approach consists of 'systematic, yet flexible guidelines for collecting and analysing qualitative date to construct theories "grounded" in the data themselves' (Charmaz, 2006: 2). Researchers who adopt a grounded theory approach do not draw upon and formulate research questions based on existing theories. Instead, they inductively code the data. Afterwards, based on constant comparison, grounded theorists look for patterns and categories in the data and come up with relevant ideas and theoretical concepts. They try to build typologies on the basis of axial and focused codes and by using memos. This theory is not solely aimed at describing the social reality of a specific group or setting – as tends to be done in pure ethnography – but focuses on the construction of theories that emerge from the data (Glaser and Strauss, 1967[2006]). The latter construction has been criticized as it is not possible to approach the research field as a '*tabula rasa*' without pre-conceived theoretical ideas. Charmaz (2006), for instance, argues that it is better to draw upon so-called sensitizing concepts while being in the field. This is what I also planned to do. I wanted to centralize

24 I am really grateful to Laura Heijnen, who transcribed some of the interviews.

legal consciousness in my study and, over time, draw upon different theoretical concepts emerging from my data in order to give meaning to the various elements of a person's understandings of, experiences with, thoughts on and interactions with the law and to produce some new theoretical notions.

Yet I felt somewhat overwhelmed by the sheer quantity of data I had collected and the numerous pages I needed to code as part of the analysis process. I had already started the analysis while in the field, but it soon began to seem like an impossible task to code all the documents according to the principles of grounded theory. As Bosworth (2014) did in her study on the experiences with immigration detainees in the UK, I quickly abandoned my primary ideas on my analysis strategies. While I always teach my students following qualitative research methods courses to code all that seems relevant and not to assume too quickly that something is irrelevant, I simply lacked the time to do this myself given the – to use Bosworth's words (2014: 81) – 'mountain of material' I had collected throughout the fieldwork. This is why I eventually used a more pragmatic, less-finely meshed coding strategy to analyse the data. I somewhat pragmatically applied open and thematic coding strategies for discovering the data, as well as pattern analysis to find meaningful linkages across the full dataset (Saldaña, 2016: 235). First, I labelled all research participants, laws, actors, encounters with the law, control mechanisms and other relevant topics to make sure that I could seek and find whatever I needed in my dataset, which is also an important aspect of coding (Evers, 2015). I then inductively explored which topics were in the data and used open codes to label these fragments. I also deductively coded the data on the basis of theoretical concepts that appeared to be important and that are central in Chapters 4 to 10 of this book.[25] This required reading and rereading the data over and over again, making notes and memos and creating networks that helped me to make further sense of the data. While there might still have been more in the data, I did not include it in this (already rather extended) book. It would have been both infeasible and unnecessary to describe and explain unauthorized migrants' legal consciousness processes over time as well as to contribute to several theoretical debates.

In the analysis as well as the upcoming chapters, the unauthorized migrants' perspective has been central. I examined how these migrants understand, experience, give meaning to and interact with the law during the analysis process. However, Ewick and Silbey (2020) argue that the perspective of the research group should not be the central focus of legal consciousness studies. Instead, these studies should centralize the law in the analytic

25 Chapter 9 of this book is based on other data that have not been collected as part of this study. I have decided to include this chapter in this book as it helps me to answer the fourth sub-question of study on how the migrants' understandings of, experiences with and meaning-making processes towards the law are translated into interactions with the law. The chapter focuses particularly on the experiences of unauthorized migrants in immigration detention as well as their interactions with the law in terms of their participation in their (forced) return process. This will further be explained in chapter 9 itself.

process to see what the law does and to understand the (hegemonic) powers of the law in society. Yet, as said in the introduction, I made use of the adaptability of the concept by focusing initially on the migrants themselves. However, at the end of my study, I switched perspective. I no longer solely focus on the migrants' perspective but – following up on Ewick and Silbey's (2020) approach – I include what the law does as well as the consequences for the functioning of the law for this specific group in society in order to better understand the law's powers.

3.5 Some reflections on my positionality, ethics and limitations

Both my fieldwork and my analysis show the impact of my positionality as a researcher on the research process, which fits with the idea that the research process is intertwined with the person of the researcher (see also Hiah, 2019). While researchers often strive for neutrality in qualitative research, this is simply impossible as personal, communal and political sympathies inform our choices both before entering the field, while being in the field and during the analyses process (cf. Becker, 1967; Liebling, 2001). The researcher and the research subject jointly constitute the social reality (cf. Hammersley, 2013). The choices which researchers make impact on the outcomes of their research processes. This is why careful consideration by the researcher on his or her own role, the ethical concerns that arise during the study as well as the study's limitations are all needed to better understand the researcher's impact on the study (see also Lumsden and Winter, 2014). This requires reflexivity as well as transparency by a researcher to provide insights into the situatedness of knowledge production (Rose, 1997; see also Hiah, 2019)).

3.5.1 *Positionality*

Positionality refers to the researcher's recognition and declaration of his or her position within a research process and its effects on the outcome of the research, which is why it is important to reflect on my own positionality and how this affected the research process. Rose (1997) shows that this requires looking 'inward' to the identity of the researcher as well as looking 'outward' to the researcher's relation to the research topic in its wider social context.

Therefore, I first look inward and discuss how I impacted on the research process. I am part of the majority population in the Netherlands, meaning that I may be considered not to be a member of the research group of unauthorized migrants (cf. Carling et al., 2014). Yet, this is not immediately obvious from the outside as, phenotypically, I am a somewhat tanned, brown-eyed and dark-haired woman. This made my research participants – like many others – assume that I was an immigrant in the Netherlands myself. Many of them asked me where I came from and seemed somewhat disappointed if I said that I was Dutch and that neither myself nor my (grand)parents were immigrants. While I was not initially aware of the effect my appearance might have had, this might have positively affected the migrants' openness towards me, as they perhaps assumed that, as an immigrant myself, I would understand them. Me not being an immigrant usually came arose after the first contact/interview with the migrant when there was already some level of rapport between us and my origins seemed to matter less. Yet, it did make my participants aware of my privileged position. The latter could also be seen in my family situation – I was visibly pregnant during the initial phase of the fieldwork. This directly stimulated all kinds of conversations on the research participants' (wishes for) families. While this topic would probably also have come up later in my conversations with research participants, it emphasized the deprivation of a family life which migrants experienced and which contrasted my own situation. Furthermore, my gender might have had a positive impact while being in the field. Being a woman facilitated my contact with women and did not seem to negatively affect my interactions with male migrants. On the contrary, it made some male respondents – who were not aware of me having just given birth – even more willing to talk to me as they were interested in my marital status; this is not uncommon in research with unauthorized migrants who are occupied with legalizing their residence in the country (see also Van Meeteren, 2014). My not being interested in a relationship did not seem to affect their willingness to talk to me. I am not sure whether there was any relation to my physical appearance – as migrants never explicitly expressed it as such and we did not discuss it during the research process – but its impact is certainly there.

Looking outward involves discussing my own relation to the research topic and, more particularly, explaining whose side I was on during the project. Becker (1967) argues that it is impossible to be neutral in qualitative research and that it is important to acknowledge this. Yet, as Liebling (2001) shows, it is not necessary to sympathize with one side only in a project as a researcher may also sympathize with subordinates and powerholders. I agree with her. Being inspired by my experiences before I entered academia, I had deep sympathy for unauthorized migrants, given the position they were in due to their not having a legal status and their subjection to the powerholders. This does not mean that I could no longer sympathize with others. The multiple informal meetings with officers working in the immigration system, for instance, contributed to my understanding of the officers' motivations for their work and why they did it. I felt consideration for them as well, especially for those officers who deliberately thought about the work they did and the powers it involved. I believe that this sympathy for both sides is necessary to collect data and understand what is really out there (see also Liebling, 2001). After all, ethnographic research is about 'genuine humility, acknowledged ignorance, eagerness to learn, and willingness to engage that which you study on its own terms' (Ferrell, 2018: 148).

Later, during the analysis of the data, I tried to forget about this sympathy. I tried to create greater distance from both perspectives without forgetting the people – both migrants and officers – about whom I was writing. I tried to move from an insider to an outsider perspective again and to appreciate the merit of having different perspectives included in the research as it gave greater context to the migrants' stories. Migrants, for instance, considered it disproportional that they were escorted by numerous officers when being deported,[26] while officers informally explained that they needed to have that many people present on the flight given the duration of the deportation process and Dutch labour laws. Despite the perspective of unauthorized migrants being central throughout this study, such information helped to give weight and recognition to the powerholders too and to limit the potential for bias in the research (cf. Liebling, 2001). As such, I tried to illustrate what was out there in the research field – as done throughout this study – in its wider social context while giving recognition to its possible moral, political and academic implications. Because, as Becker (1967: 246) argues, researchers need to meet the standards of good academic research, regardless of the points of view we hold as researchers. Otherwise, the research results would not be valid and may harm those who participated in the research.

Finally, looking outwards also includes a discussion on how a research project is situated in its wider social and political context. My study fits with the long tradition of legal consciousness studies which find their basis in studies on power and inequality and, more particularly, the lack of equality for marginalized and disadvantaged groups (Ryo, 2011; Silbey, 2005). In line with critical criminology, this project aims to understand how unauthorized migrants' meaning-making processes in relation to the law fit within the broader structures in the complex societal context. After all, the phenomenon of unauthorized residence is 'a thing itself and on its own terms' (Ferrel, 2018: 148) and it is the job of ethnographers to better understand the phenomenon in its wider context. This context, which is discussed in Chapter 2, consists of the increased use of borders which are currently no longer solely situated at states' territorial lines but have become invisible and are located everywhere and nowhere (Balibar, 2002). These borders produce migrants with unauthorized residence; there would not be a category of unauthorized migrants if there were no borders in the world (De Genova, 2013). These borders are based on (post) colonial thinking and produced on the basis of race, ethnicity etc. (Bosworth, Parmar and Vázquez, 2018). These produce illegality that has become an existential condition which shapes large groups within society (Franko, 2020). It is within this wider context that unauthorized migrants' legal consciousness processes come about. I take this wider

26 If unauthorized migrants' behavior gives reason to do so, they may be escorted upon deportation by officers from the Kmar.

context into account in order to be able to explain unauthorized migrants' understandings of, experiences with, thoughts on and interactions with the law over time.

3.5.2 *Ethical considerations*

The fieldwork was conducted at a time when ethical committees for the social sciences were still absent in the Netherlands. Yet, evidently, I did think about ethics before, during and after the research, especially given the vulnerability of unauthorized migrants and specifically of minors. I wanted to protect my research participants, that is, the migrants themselves, members of their social networks, gatekeepers, and officers from the immigration system. I sought to make sure that participating in this research would not harm them in any way. Informed consent was therefore extremely important, although this can be ambiguous during ethnographic research at different research sites with a wide range of people. Yet, to be clear about my role as a researcher, I used an overt and obtrusive approach (Noaks and Wincup, 2004), meaning that research participants were aware of my role as a researcher and that I subtly reminded them of my role every now and then (see also Van Meeteren, 2014). On making contact with a potential research participant, I first used some small talk to create a rapport. After this, I verbally informed him/her of my research objectives. I also provided them with a letter which offered more information on my research. As I was aware that unauthorized migrants could be rather suspicious about signing papers given their previous negative experience with the authorities and as I did not want to write their real names down given the risks which this might entail for them, I did not ask them to sign the letter. I signed the letter myself, though. The letter mainly functioned to inform them and make sure that they knowingly consented to participate in the research. When I felt confident that my participants realized that it was up to them what information they chose to share with me, that they could end their participation in the research at any moment without further explanation and that the information would only be anonymously reported, I started to include them in the research. Only from then onwards did I try to collect all relevant data by observing, participating, talking and collecting stories, images and other relevant information in the field (cf. Zaitch et al., 2009).

If my participants agreed to take part in my study, I tried to protect them, as I was aware that partaking in research may be quite burdensome for them. Yet most migrants were happy to participate in this rather demanding study as they considered it important to be heard by the Dutch and European authorities as well as civil society and believed that this study provided them with just such an opportunity. They felt that little was really known about their situation and believed that people deserve information on this matter (see also Hajer and Bröer, 2020). They wanted to make the invisible *in* society visible *to* society by telling their stories. The unauthorized often feel as if they are not treated as human beings, therefore my study could show that they are flesh-and-blood people with real stories, which contributes to their humanization in society (see also Brotherton, 2019). They often have little power themselves to do so but participating in research can contribute to the migrants' empowerment (see also Maillet et al., 2017). Brotherton and Barrios (2011), for instance, have shown with their research on Dominican deportees that ethnographic research has the capacity to give the highly marginalized a voice in the debate, which may turn out to be powerful, unsettling narratives that make a difference in individual legal cases as well as in the immigration system itself. Migrants who participated in my study sought to have such power as well and were usually grateful to be given a voice. Yet, it should be said that this does not apply to all the unauthorized migrants I met during my fieldwork. Some did not want to participate in the study unless they were financially rewarded. 'Time is money' said a man whom I repeatedly met in a living room and who wanted me to pay him for his participation. As I lacked the funding to give financial rewards and as there are some disadvantages that come with payments for research participants, I could not do so. Others considered it important to tell their stories but were emotionally not capable of doing so as it would be too demanding. I did try, though, to give those who were open to it a voice in the migration debate in the hope that it would humanize and empower them.

Unauthorized migrants' vulnerable position as well as their risk of being deported represent a great level of responsibility for the researcher, which I was fully aware of at all times. This dates from a past discussion in the Netherlands on whether it is ethical to conduct research among unauthorized migrants. There has been quite extensive research with unauthorized migrants in the Netherlands (e.g. Burgers and Engbersen, 1999; Staring, 2001; Van der Leun, 2003; Van Meeteren, 2014). Yet there have also been some concerns about whether these studies do actually harm unauthorized migrants by disclosing too much information on their subsistence strategies (e.g. Westerink, 2000). Some representatives of Dutch NGOs believed that this information prevented unauthorized migrants from living unauthorized in the Netherlands and provided the authorities with the opportunity to further complicate unauthorized residence. Research among unauthorized migrants may, as such, actually support current migration-control practices in the Netherlands. This also applies to my study, which uncovers a wide range of information on unauthorized migrants' everyday lives. Researchers have to be constantly mindful of the risks. As Casas-Cortes et al. (2015: 63) argue: 'Migration scholarship cannot [...] only be seen as a scientific endeavour, but must rather critically engage with its own place in the politics of mobility'. That is what I have also tried to do – I have taken on the responsibility to protect my research participants, meaning that I did not disclose any information on the strategies that unauthorized migrants use during their unauthorized residency unless these strategies were already known by the authorities and did not further harm the group. I made deliberate choices as to what – and what not – to report to prevent any harm being done to the migrants. As the research focuses on their understandings of and experiences with the law and what this means for their relationship with it, this was not problematic in terms of answering the research questions. Furthermore, as Maillet et al. (2017) illustrate, it is important to include the voices of the migrants themselves in the debate.

In line with this, I took precautions to try to ensure the research participants' confidentiality and anonymity. As some officers working in the immigration system were already aware of a few migrants' participation in this study – as they helped me to recruit them – I provide very little information on the individual participants, as discussed in Section 3.3. The immigration police, for instance, knew who I was talking to during my fieldwork, as they called me as soon as an unauthorized migrant was on his or her way to the police station. The same applies to the authorities of the immigration detention centres and in freedom-restricted (family) locations, as I had to register to enter the premises or make use of their consultation rooms. Officers from other organizations in the immigration system were also aware of the participation of some unauthorized migrants. For this reason, I have left out any information that could immediately be traced back to these migrants to better ensure their anonymity. This may concern a migrant's nationality or age; it may also concern specific occurrences in the immigration system, meaning that I decided to exclude these quotes or stories. I also decided to use different aliases for the same person in different chapters. While the use of different pseudonyms for one migrant comes at the cost of the reader's opportunity to visualize the respondents and of the transparency of my approach, I considered this necessary to protect the respondents' anonymity and prevent harm being done to them.

During the fieldwork, I was constantly occupied with not causing any emotional harm to my research participants, as previous research has shown that sharing their stories may be quite upsetting for unauthorized migrants. In this study, too, participants regularly started to cry during our conversations; they were really upset by their experiences in the Netherlands and afraid of being detained or deported. Some were consumed with anger due to their experiences, which caused them to lose sleep. While I comforted these migrants and transferred them to a caregiver if I thought this might be necessary, this made me wonder whether participation in this research project was not too emotionally burdensome and whether or not I should continue like this. At the same time, these respondents told me that they were very grateful to have someone listening to their full story and paying attention to them, which made me realize that this was also an important task for me as a researcher – not only to give them a voice but also to continue listening to them, as they found this reassuring. Their emotions might have influenced the migrants' narratives: they might have blocked or forgotten particular facts or information in a bid to protect themselves, they might have a certain interest in not sharing everything or they might have certain emotions that make them emphasize one particular topic in their story. Due to my observations with the migrants themselves and within the immigration system, I had ample tools with which to bring such topics to the fore. Luckily, it was not that burdensome for all respondents – some really enjoyed hanging out together and showing me the different aspects of their lives. They invited me to join them in a wide range of activities and smiled when they met me and my children in the city. For them, it was nice to have another contact in their everyday lives.

The aforementioned ethical concerns particularly apply to the minor unauthorized migrants who participated in this research. After all, minors are considered to be exceptionally vulnerable due to their young age, legal status, and unstable living conditions (cf. Vervliet et al., 2015). Furthermore, they may be grappling with different backgrounds, experiences, and expectations during their residence in their country of arrival (cf. Castillo Goncalves, 2020), especially given their deportability. Additionally, it is uncertain to what extent minors are intellectually and emotionally capable of understanding the risks of participating in qualitative research and able to provide fully informed consent for the research (Vervliet et al., 2015). These aspects may exacerbate the already uneven power balance between a researcher and research participants (cf. Castillo Goncalves, 2020). For these reasons, I initially did not intend to include minors in the research group. Yet, while spending time at locations where unauthorized migrants gather and during the interviews, I also encountered minor unauthorized migrants who initiated conversations with me. I did not want to formally interview them as I was concerned that it might be too burdensome and could trigger unwanted memories and fears. However, I did engage in small, informal conversations with them about their everyday lives, including their housing, schooling, friends, etc. During these conversations, the minors spontaneously shared other aspects with me. For instance, while in Nigeria, a young girl whispered in my ear whether I could bring her back to the Netherlands. Others spoke about attending Chinese language classes despite feeling Dutch and not realizing they were deportable. Finally, an eight-year-old boy illustrating how his pregnant mother faced confrontation and mistreatment by the police prior to the family's deportation. I listened to the minors, but I did not pose sensitive questions to them and refrained from probing deeply during these conversations; instead, I allowed the minors to talk whenever they wanted to. With the permission of the minors and their parent(s), these informal conversations, as well as my own observations of them, were included in this research to enhance the understanding of the shaping of unauthorized migrants' legal consciousness processes.

To conclude, the fieldwork has been an emotional journey for me, too. I encountered upset and sometimes desperate research participants, observed a failed deportation that was accompanied by physical resistance, saw children being apprehended and heard much personal misery during my fieldwork, both in the Netherlands and abroad. These emotions are an accepted part of research in the migration domain (Bhatia, 2014; Maillet et al.,

2017) but it made me sometimes uncertain as to whether it was the right thing to do to ask migrants to go over their stories again. At the same time, silence is not an option as it is important to share these stories and provide insights into what happens (*Ibid.*). Migrants felt relieved to talk to me and be part of the research. Additionally, my fieldwork created lots of laughter, joy and fun. It enriched me in multiple ways, both as a researcher and as a person. Hopefully, its outcomes positively add to the current migration debate.

3.5.3 *Limitations of the study*

Finally, I want to say some words on the limitations of this study as well as the consequences this might have had for its outcomes. A first limitation has to do with the composition of the research group. I was, for instance, only able to conduct interviews myself in English or Dutch (with sometimes a mixture of Spanish, French or German) or with the assistance of a translator.[27] Few migrants were interviewed in their mother tongue, which prevented some from adequately expressing themselves or sharing all the required information. While most unauthorized migrants with a lengthy residence in the Netherlands had mastered either Dutch or English, my inability to speak the migrants' own language negatively affected communication during the fieldwork and impacted on who could participate in my research. Furthermore, I went to Nigeria, Surinam and Guyana in order to understand how returned and deported migrants retrospectively reflect on their relationship with the Dutch law. However, these countries are known for their labour, family and chain migration and not for their asylum migration. This means that I might have missed the experiences of rejected asylum seekers who had either decided to return to their home country or were deported by the authorities. While I did include rejected asylum seekers who participated in voluntary-return projects and who might have had a different understanding of the law, I may have missed some of their stories. Yet, as argued above, much qualitative research is not about representativeness (Van Meeteren, 2014; Zaitch et al., 2009).

Furthermore, negotiating trust is an indispensable element of qualitative research in general and research with unauthorized migrants in particular. At the same time, it is questionable whether it is possible to be trusted by unauthorized migrants in the context of research activities. After all, these migrants are prone to detection, detention and deportation due to their unauthorized presence in the Netherlands, which makes opening up to a researcher a risky endeavour (see also Van Meeteren, 2014). This means that qualitative research is perhaps more about creating a more-or-less symmetrical and equal relationship between the researcher and the researched, which provides the latter with the

27 I have translated all quotes and fieldnotes into English to widen the readability of this study.

opportunity to share those things that are of importance to them (Staring and Kroese, 1991). It involves creating a level of closeness with participants that encourages them to open up during the interview (cf. Bhatia, 2014). It is about ensuring migrants that the results will not be taken out of context for research purposes (cf. Fitz-Gibbon, 2014) and involves convincing migrants that the research will give them a voice and make them visible in the debate, which may contribute to their empowerment (see also Brotherton and Barrios, 2011). At the same time, the unauthorized migrants themselves have certain interests. Some explicitly asked me what was in it for them if they participate in the research (see also Bosworth, 2014). They will – sometimes deliberately – choose what to say and what not to say during the study in a bid to accomplish certain things through their participation. This means that the researcher constantly needs to renegotiate trust, create openness, show his or her own integrity and reconvince research participants to open up (see also Staring and Kroese, 1991) – as I tried to do, especially in cases where I encountered contradictions in the migrants' stories or the interviews and observations. While this resulted in participants disclosing harmful information and very intimate stories with me, it will also have resulted in them not revealing all of their story, which is common in qualitative research. While this is a limitation of this study, I luckily had a quite extensive research group, meaning that I was able to collect a wide range of in-depth stories on unauthorized migrants' legal consciousness processes.

3.6 To conclude

This chapter has further unfolded the methods on which this study is based– that is, a multi-sited ethnographic approach involving 105 unauthorized migrants who were situated at different locations in the Netherlands, Nigeria, Surinam and Guyana. I interviewed migrants, conducted participated observation with migrants as well as in the immigration system and visited returned and deported migrants who used to reside in the Netherlands. All the data were analysed in Atlas.ti. In the following chapters, I present my theoretical and empirical findings which – all together – help me to understand how the law matters to unauthorized migrants in the Netherlands and what this means for the functioning of the law.

4 'I call it a system.' Unauthorized migrants' understandings of the long reach of Dutch internal migration controls*

Abstract

Drawing upon the concept of deportability, this chapter addresses the first sub-question of this study on how unauthorized migrants understand the law on an everyday basis. It demonstrates that unauthorized migrants possess a broad understanding of the law that extends beyond its positivistic notion and centres around their unauthorized status. The migrants associate the law with their lack of a legal status due to legally embedded limitations, migration controls and exclusion processes they face as a result. This leads them to perceive the law as a system that initially produces their unauthorized residence and subsequently reduces them to their lack of a legal status. The migrants identify three important, interlinked layers within this system, considering that the system is 1) executed by a myriad of state and non-state actors, 2) encompasses laws and policies outside the migration domain, and 3) extends across over different geographical locations. This results in a comprehensive, multi-layered control system that unauthorized migrants perceive as 'the law'. This understanding of the law forms the foundation of unauthorized migrants' legal consciousness processes.

4.1 Introduction

> 'Yeah. I run from Ivory Coast because of the war and because of my opinion on the ones in power in that time. Now, plenty of things have changed. [...] I have run for more than 10 years, 12 years from my country and I think that it is now time to go home. Because now, I feel that I am wasting my time here in the Netherlands. I don't have my legal status here. I still continue to be in a freedom-restricted location. And you want to know something about this?

* This chapter has been published as Kox M and Staring R (2021) 'I call it a system' Unauthorized migrants' of the Long Reach of Dutch internal Migration Controls. *International Journal for Crime, Justice and Social Democracy* 10(3): 87–100.

> This looks like another prison for me. [...] The problem I face for more than four years now is the embassy. They tell me that they have a rule: "Ibo, you are intelligent. You used to work in some company where you do wood. You used to plant wood." [...] And sometimes they send this wood to a foreign country. [...] Can you send wood to another country, if they don't give you all the papers that are required to send it? [...] It is the same thing. "We recognize you. You are from the Ivory Coast. We call around in the country, but we don't see papers of you. We cannot sign some paper for you. It is difficult. If we do like that, it will destroy our work as administrators. It is not possible." Thus, because of the law in the Ivory Coast, they cannot sign the papers. And because of the Dutch law, the Netherlands cannot give me my papers. I am between two laws, that is my big problem now. [...] I call it a system. It is a system.'

This quote is by Ibo from the Ivory Coast, who arrived in the early 2000s in the Netherlands to seek asylum. His request was rejected, after which he saw himself confronted with – what he calls – 'some difficult situations'. During his interviews, he reflects on a wide range of what Albrecht (2002) and Doomernik and Jandl (2008) have labelled 'internal migration-control mechanisms' and that other scholars situate in the context of bordering practices (Aliverti, Milivojevic and Weber, 2019; Newman, 2006). These internal migration-control mechanisms are defined as those policies and practices that are enacted within the controlling nation-state and aimed at the discouragement of unauthorized residency *and* the return or deportation of unauthorized migrants (Albrecht, 2002). These internal controls are posited next to external migration controls that specifically deal with the intensified closing, fortifying and policing of the territorial lines of nation-states or supranational entities such as the European Union to prevent unauthorized entry. Both forms of control may consist of assemblages of technologies, laws, institutions, representations, discourses, or practices that are used in and beyond border areas (Genç, Heck and Hess, 2018).

Our broader ethnographic research amongst migrants living without a legal status in the Netherlands shows that the experiences and meanings that Ibo presents us are not restricted to a single, isolated unauthorized migrant. Many other unauthorized migrants agreed on this tangle of internal migration controls which, according to them, was not only hard to permeate but also impacted on multiple domains in their everyday lives from the moment they started considering migration to the Netherlands until long after their return or deportation. These migrants' lived experiences are directly related to Western nation-states' intentions to govern through migration controls, meaning that they strictly select who is allowed to reside on the state's territory and exclude or ban the unwanted others (Bosworth and Guild, 2008). In recent decades, states have strengthened their internal control mechanisms (Aas, 2011; Aas and Bosworth, 2013) and moved their borders in different directions (Guiraudon and Lahav, 2000; Lavenax, 2006; Staring and Van Swaaningen, 2021; Weber, 2006) to increase capacity and effectiveness. These developments have brought about a multi-layered structure in the Dutch internal control system, often referred to as a multi-layered border regime (cf. Van der Woude and Staring, 2021).

This chapter draws on the concept of 'deportability' as the omnipresent awareness of the possibility of being deported from the 'space of the nation-state' (De Genova, 2002: 439) to unpack these layers of the internal border regime from the perspective of unauthorized migrants (who used to be) in the Netherlands. After an elaboration of the theoretical concepts and the method, we illustrate how these internal migration controls interact with the daily lives of unauthorized migrants and shape their experiences while living in the Netherlands *and* after return/deportation. Untangling internal migration controls not only illustrates how unauthorized migrants experience these different interlinked layers of the Dutch internal control system but also reveals that the migrants themselves experience even more layers of control than often assumed in the theoretical debate on (governing through) migration controls. This can be seen particularly after the migrants' return or deportation to their home countries where they are still being confronted with the legal, social *and* existential consequences of internal migration controls practiced thousands of miles away. We argue that the internal migration management of an individual nation-state like the Netherlands, due to its multi-layered character, is directly linked and has similar consequences to external migration-control management. This not only implies that individual nation-states, through their internal control mechanisms, also contribute to the externalization of migration control at a supranational level but also shows that the state's approach brings about immobility in home, transit and destination countries, something that raises severe questions over the current controlling approach.

4.2 Internal Migration Controls, Deportability and the Netherlands

The multi-layered bordering regime is the result of different, related developments that have brought about a proliferation of border sites, meaning that borders are no longer solely situated at states' territorial lines but have become invisible and are located everywhere and nowhere (Balibar, 2002). On the one hand, this refers to the externalization of borders or 'remote controls' (Zolberg, 1997 in FitzGerald, 2020), meaning that geographical borders are functionally or virtually moved outwards and detached from a state's territorial border (Weber, 2006). Based on unilateral, bilateral or multilateral agreements, states undertake extraterritorial actions to prevent immigrants' unauthorized entry, effectuate unauthorized migrants' deportation policies, and strengthen external borders (Frelick, Kysel and Podkul, 2016). Using externalization strategies such as strict visa requirements, offshore detention camps, and outsourcing border controls, migrants are being stopped and held in their home countries and (former) transit countries (Staring and Van Swaaningen, 2021).

On the other, internal control mechanisms have been substantially changed, which extends their reach. For instance, policing unauthorized migration and residency has shifted from the national level upwards to the international, intergovernmental, and supranational level as states increasingly use (institutionalized) collaboration (Guiraudon and Lahav, 2000; Lavenax, 2006). Another example refers to processes of responsibilization that have taken place both in crime control and with respect to migration control (Staring and Van Swaaningen, 2021). In this process of responsibilization, migration control has partially moved from central, public state actors to private agencies, organizations and individuals at the local level and/or outside the direct realm of the state (Kox and Staring, 2020; Lahav, 1998; Weber, 2013). Further, there is an increased intertwinement between the criminal and migration domains: 'crimmigration'. While this trend also evokes counter processes that change the effects of crimmigration (Staring and Timmerman, 2021), it expands states' bordering strategies as administrative migration-law violations may also be sanctioned with criminal law(like) instruments (Stumpf, 2006), and criminal offences may have migratory consequences (Chacón, 2009). Finally, states increasingly use technical surveillance infrastructures and digitalize their borders to facilitate deportation processes. Therefore, information has become a key factor in controlling unauthorized migrants; this has also relocated migration control away from a state's territorial borders to inside its territory (Broeders, 2009). This brief overview shows the layered structure of internal control regimes in terms of localities, actors, policy domains, and tools and how these mechanisms, through the notion of deportability, dominate migrants' daily lives.

The effect of internal control mechanisms on unauthorized migrants' everyday lives has been discussed in the context of deportability – that is, the unauthorized migrants' vulnerability caused by the ever-present risk of being deported and the (possible) accompanying encounters with everyday forms of exclusion, surveillance and repression (De Genova, 2002). Coutin (2000: 40) argues that the lack of a legal status may be irrelevant for most unauthorized migrants' everyday activities but that their 'legal reality is superimposed on daily life' (see also De Genova, 2002). It produces a 'deeply interiorised mode of being' (De Genova and Peutz, 2010: 14) caused by internal migration controls. This is represented by their exclusion from the formal labour and housing market, complicated access to healthcare, difficult social relations, and lack of perspective for the future (Coutin, 2000; De Genova, 2002). Kox, Boone and Staring (2020) show that the lack of a legal status may bring about all kind of 'pains of being unauthorized'. This may result in so-called 'migrant struggles', which refers to the process whereby migrants 'openly challenge defeat, escape or trouble the dominant politics of mobility' as well as their 'daily strategies, refusals and resistances through which migrants enact their (contested) presence' (Casa-Cortes et al., 2015: 80). Some migrants are non-deportable as the receiving state is not able to actually arrange the necessary documents (cf. Leerkes and Kox, 2016). They may use the extra opportunities to circumvent internal controls (Fabini, 2019), but this non-deportability does not provide them with any extra rights during their unauthorized stay.

These different internal migration-control mechanisms and the accompanying deportability are, to a greater or lesser extent, applicable to many Western countries that are uncomfortable with irregular migration flows (cf. Leerkes and Van Houte, 2020). This also applies to the Netherlands, where this study is situated. Here, the Dutch label of a relatively open and tolerant country has made way for a much harsher social reality characterized by restrictive admission policies, the increased exclusion of unauthorized migrants, and the extended capacity of and urgent need for migration controls (Engbersen, Van San and Leerkes, 2006). For instance, the Dutch authorities have extended their policies of identification by implementing the Extended Identification Act [*Wet op de Uitgebreide Identificatieplicht*] which requires all persons over fourteen to show valid proof of identification upon request by the police or other designated officers. This extension also concerns the increased use of biometrical features – iris scans, fingerprints or digital facial images – to facilitate the surveillance, identification and deportation of unauthorized migrants from the Netherlands (Broeders, 2009). Further, the Dutch authorities introduced the so-called Linking Act [*Koppelingswet*] in 1998, which ensures that only migrants with valid residence permits can access the formal labour and housing markets, social security benefits and public services (Van der Leun, 2003). Due to the linking of residence status with these public and semi-public services, unauthorized migrants are only eligible for essential healthcare, legal aid and – until the age of eighteen, – education (Hintjens, Siegmann and Staring, 2020). This Linking Act is added to other measures that strengthen unauthorized migrants' exclusion from society, such as the introduction of administrative fines for employers of unauthorized migrants and the lack of subsidy for local authorities for providing shelter to homeless unauthorized migrants (Van Meeteren, 2014). Finally, the Dutch authorities implemented a new Aliens Act in 2001. Unauthorized residency is not criminalized in this act, but it does provide more opportunities to stop, detain and deport unauthorized migrants on the basis of a reasonable suspicion of unauthorized residence. Although the implementation of the Return Directive in 2011 includes safeguards for immigration detention of unauthorized migrants and increased the threshold to detain unauthorized migrants (Klaassen and Rodrigues, 2021), the increased detention opportunities have also been criticized for the lack of proper individual assessment before detention (Busser, Oosterhuis and Strik, 2019). While the effects of this exclusion and control are determined by the everyday interactions between border officers and unauthorized migrants (Van der Woude and Van der Leun, 2017) and the embeddedness of unauthorized migrants in supportive social networks, studies on unauthorized migrants in the Netherlands show that it has become increasingly difficult and painful to survive in the Netherlands without a residence permit (Kox, Boone and Staring, 2020).

4.3 METHODOLOGY

This chapter shows how unauthorized migrants experience and give meaning to the wide range of internal border-control practices in their everyday lives in the Netherlands or their home country following deportation or return. It focuses on internal border controls, whose outcomes are still felt after return and deportation. This chapter is grounded in multi-sited ethnographic fieldwork with 105 unauthorized migrants that was conducted between March 2015 and May 2018, observing them in their everyday lives and during their interaction with controlling institutions. I followed 45 unauthoirzed migrants over time; I repeatedly interviewed or informally talked to these migrants and had frequent contact by phone or WhatsApp. The number of contacts varied from three to over 20 times. I also interviewed, informally spoke to, or observed another 60 unauthorized migrants who wanted to be involved in the research but only at one moment in time. The respondents were mainly based in the Netherlands but also included migrants who were deported or returned from the Netherlands to Surinam (10), Nigeria (6) and Guyana (1). I also pragmatically observed sites, actions and state actors within the Dutch border regime such as the police (arrests and interrogations), the Repatriation and Departure Service (DT&V, return counselling meetings), and deportations to better understand and question the respondents' experiences.

Given the assumed differences between unauthorized migrants (Burgers and Engbersen, 1999), I tried to create a diverse group in terms of age, gender, country of origin, length of stay in the Netherlands, migration motive and family situation. I recruited unauthorized migrants with different backgrounds at different locations and stages of their unauthorized residency, including those who were living out of sight of the authorities, just being arrested by the police, living at freedom-restricted (family) locations aimed at removal or staying in immigration detention centres. I made contact with these migrants through support organizations, migration institutions, and the snowballing method. This resulted in a heterogenous research group that may, to some extent, be considered exceptional, as many migrants never reach their European destination country. Simultaneously, there are also migrants who never aspired to cross the European borders but ended up – for different reasons – in Europe (Snel, Bilgili and Staring, 2020).

In all interactions during the fieldwork, unauthorized migrants could recall their situation in the country of origin and their migration journey but also discussed their everyday lives, experiences with migration controls and visions of their future. Given the vulnerability of the research group, they were provided an information sheet and repeatedly reassured that they could stop their participation in the research whenever they wanted without further clarification. While some respondents decided to limit their participation to a single meeting as they considered it too emotional to discuss their experiences and existential uncertainties, most were very grateful to be given a voice. For some, it seemed even quite therapeutic to have someone listen to their life stories in the context of their unauthorized residency. Returned and deported migrants even felt honoured that someone from the Netherlands was visiting them so they could show their current social environment to still have close friends there. This approach and the open attitude of these migrants enabled me to follow them and observe the consequences of current control practices over time. Field notes were kept of all observations and informal conversations, while interviews were recorded and literally transcribed. The data were all analysed in qualitative data analysis software, ATLAS.ti, using thematic and open-coding techniques for discovering the data and pattern analysis to find meaningful linkages across the full dataset (Saldaña, 2016: 235).

4.4 Deportability in the Netherlands: Confrontations with a multi-layered system

Dealing with the presence of internal migration controls is an everyday reality for unauthorized migrants given its impact on all domains of their daily lives (cf. Pickering and Weber, 2006) and the state of deportability it brings (cf. De Genova, 2002).[28] These control mechanisms deprive them of healthy and secure living conditions, limit their social and geographical mobility and affect their feelings of belonging (see chapter 6). These controls also have emotional effects (cf. Paasi, 2011), as in the story of Joseph, an African asylum seeker whose claim has repeatedly been rejected and who believes that the Dutch authorities are playing a psychological game by excluding unauthorized migrants from comprehensive support and subjecting them to internal controls:

> 'From there, they [immigration authorities] just starting and asking… They asked me a lot of questions, really, they asked me a lot of questions about my

28 The effects of these Dutch internal controls on the migrants' working, housing, and health conditions have repeatedly been discussed (e.g., Burgers and Engbersen, 1999; Hintjens, Siegmann, and Staring, 2020; Staring and Aarts, 2010), so they are not discussed here.

> asylum. I am staying in Amsterdam, I just am here. I just explained because I was used to sleeping in the park, you know. I was sleeping in the park, begging on the street you know. It was a hard time. Then from there, they didn't tell me anything. Then I go, go to [immigration] detention. (…) And eh every month, the first of every month, you have to go to meet the people they call DT&V [Repatriation and Departure Service]. And those people are kind of eh… I don't know how I can explain this, it is a kind of psychological thing so… It is… When they are coming to you, the only things they ask you is that you leave the country. No comments, just that. (…) For me, honestly, I grew up in a war country. I grew up in war. I have seen war in my lifetime, so for me… (…) I can say: it is better to be in the war than to let somebody play with you psychologically. Because, in the war, the things I've experienced – if some can shoot you, can kill you and then it is finished. But their psychology is … is a kind of … it is more dangerous because they don't kill you.'

After six months, the man was released from detention as he could not be deported. Like other respondents who were ambiguous or explicitly negative toward return, he suffered from severe pains that are inherently linked to his subjection to migration controls and the – in his view – psychological game the Dutch authorities play. For some, this resulted in trauma, something that is more often found among unauthorized migrants, and asylum seekers in particular (Bäärnhielm et al., 2017).

Another profound emotion is the constant fear of deportation, something that is part of – or the intention behind – the current system, according to several respondents. Amado, a Filipino domestic worker who lived with his wife and son in an apartment and who had a relatively vibrant social life within his ethnic community, explains how he is hampered by this fear:

> 'Every time you get out of your house, you are aware. You just always think you know: "Maybe it is my time now". So, you know, you are a bit worried all the time. Especially because I wasn't ready and did not yet have the money to go back to the Philippines. That is… the fear is there every time I go out of the house.'

Respondents said they were afraid that the police – or other officers – would stop them and discover that they do not have a valid legal status to remain in the country. Then, in line with the Aliens Act, they may be detained in an immigration detention centre and eventually deported to their home country. Most respondents fear this deportation for different reasons. Some – mainly rejected asylum seekers – are mainly concerned with security in their home country while others point to their strong social ties or greater opportunities to make a living in the Netherlands compared to their home country. Others fear that the legal consequences of the return directives after deportation would prevent them from returning to the Netherlands or another EU country. Amado, for instance, wants to earn a specific amount of money to enable him to build a life in his home country, something that has become more complicated due to the exclusion of the labour market and the administrative fines for employers. This shows how internal controls can contribute to migrants' reluctance to return to their home country despite the wide range of control mechanisms they are confronted with.

Finally, these migrants' deportability is being fed by the layered structure of the Dutch internal control system in terms of the different actors and institutions involved, the increased use of non-migration policy domains and the different localities in which the effects of these controls are experienced. As illustrated below, these three layers are interlinked with and strengthen each other, which contributes to migrants' experiences of subjection to an encompassing control system.

4.4.1 *The first layer: Different controlling actors*

First, respondents experience the different state and non-state actors in the control system. They refer to state actors, such as the Immigration and Naturalisation Service, which decides upon legalization; the (immigration) police who controls them; the Repatriation and Departure Service, which holds return meetings with unauthorized migrants; and the Royal Netherlands Marechaussee (KMar), which might escort unauthorized migrants during their deportation. In line with the aforementioned trend of responsibilization, respondents highlight the controlling role of non-state actors. For instance, respondents searching for work recount that employers ask for their ID upon recruitment, something that has limited their opportunities for work and pushed them into the informal economy. Others point to the role of relatives, acquaintances or unknown others who have betrayed them to the police. Furthermore, as Chapter 5 discusses in more detail, rejected asylum seekers sometimes doubt whether they can still trust those organizations that provide support to unauthorized migrants given their focus on selection, exclusion and increased return. Some respondents explicitly state that they consider these non-state actors as part of the migration control system; this also applies to lawyers, the IOM, the Refugee Council and airlines. The latter – implicitly – is evident during the observation of the deportation of Selahattin, a Turkish man who tried to use the Dutch authorities' dependency on the airline to hinder his deportation. Airlines not only have to control passengers' documents upon departure but are also used to deport unauthorized migrants (cf. Walters, 2018).[29] During these flights, the captain is responsible for the passengers on board, including the deportee. Selahattin seemed aware of this. He was quiet during the entire deportation process until the moment when he – restrained in a body cuff and escorted by the KMar – entered the Turkish Airlines plane. Once on board, he tried to shout, bite, escape the grip of his escorts and draw attention to his situation. Extra escorts entered the plane to oppose this firm resistance. When passengers noticed this struggle, they asked the escorts what was happening and were told that it was better for the migrant to return home. I then had to leave the plane as I was not flying to Turkey myself. By then, Selahattin was exhausted and could no longer resist. However, the Belgian flight captain decided to cancel the deportation as he feared unrest during the flight. After another stay in immigration detention, Selahattin was released in the Netherlands. This shows that the inclusion of controlling, non-state actors hampers unauthorized residency and, at the same time, also offers unauthorized migrants' opportunities to fight the system. These interactions with state and non-state actors can also result in upsetting and traumatic experiences, as described above, in migrants' desperate attempts to prevent being deported 'back home'.

Further, respondents – mainly rejected asylum seekers – mentioned the Dutch authorities' use of digitalized actors to expand the reach of their control, especially in their use of fingerprinting. Upon arrival in the EU or once unauthorized migrants are apprehended within the EU, they were forced to provide fingerprints which are registered on several databases to see whether they had been in another Schengen member-state before or whether they were registered criminals. Respondents say that these fingerprints hamper their geographical mobility as they will be deported to the Netherlands if they are detected in another European country on the basis of the Dublin Convention (cf. Picozza, 2017). A rejected asylum seeker explained, 'Since they took my fingerprints, I cannot go anywhere'. He tried to apply for asylum in other European countries following his rejection in the Netherlands but was deported back there. He is afraid to return home given the ongoing political unrest in his origin country but realizes that it will be difficult to return to the Netherlands again due to his registered fingerprints taken when entering Europe for the first time. Therefore, he, like other respondents, opted for 'safety first' and decided to continue his unauthorized residency. In doing so, these migrants challenge the Aliens Act that is focusing on increasingly fast and austere asylum procedures. However, these migrants decided not to take the risk of a 'definite return' and continued their unauthorized stay. It turns out that immobility or prolonged stay is one important and unintended outcome of these measures.

29 The authorities also use EU charter flights (https://frontex.europa.eu/media-centre/multimedia/videos/return-operationsBbo2NH, accessed 07/01/2020).

4.4.2 *The second layer: Policies and laws within and above migration management*

The layering of the Dutch internal control system comes to the fore in the authorities' use of different policy domains to increase their legal opportunities to stop, detain and deport migrants with no legal status. While some respondents believe that the police will find a reason if they want to stop them, others point to the inclusion of criminal laws in the migration domain, something that aligns with the aforementioned trend of crimmigration. Yaro, from Ethiopia, explains:

> 'You know *khat*? The green leaf? The Somalian, the Ethiopian and the Kenyan, we eat it as a normal thing... It is just a matter of enjoyment. I went to buy it in Amsterdam. When I came out of the shop, three or four people stepped in the light. They said: "Mister. Mister, stop!" (...) They ask: "Can I see your ID? Your ID. And can you open your jacket?" Then they said: "What is this?" I said: "This is *khat*". "You don't know that *khat* is not allowed?" I said: "I didn't know." (...) So, they seized it, blablabla and took me to the foreign police. There, they dropped the charge, got me a lawyer and said: "Now you are free from the *khat* but now you are facing being illegal in the country." It is an eh... two-stager: they had to criminalize me for buying *khat*, but then that charge was dropped and I faced the crime of illegality.'

Staring (2014) argues that, with the criminalization of *khat* in 2013, the Dutch government created a legitimate opportunity for the police to apprehend *khat* users – who happen to be a selective group of migrants originating from the Horn of Africa, Eritrea, Ethiopia and Somalia. This implies that some criminal laws intentionally or unintentionally target specific nationalities and, consequently, can be used for controlling migration. Yaro's story illustrates this as he was not prosecuted for the possession of *khat* but did end up in immigration detention.

Respondents not only provided examples of the inclusion of criminal law in the migration domain but also referred to the use of development-aid policies to facilitate deportation (cf. Cassarino, 2009). The inclusion of these different policy domains within the control system has extended the latter's reach and expanded the number of actors. For instance, respondents argued that the Dutch authorities increasingly collaborate with other nation-states to both prevent unauthorized entry *and* facilitate deportation. Some referred to the migration partnerships introduced since 2005 between the EU and migration source countries (cf. Billet, 2010; Cassarino, 2009), partnerships which entail migration source countries receiving development aid, visa facilitation, or other incentives *if* they accept and provide the required travel documents for those nationals whom the

Dutch authorities want to deport. These collaborations are, thus, an extension of the Dutch authorities' deportation policies and actors. Several respondents were aware of these partnerships, which increased the feeling of being subjected to a system. This also applies to Taner, a Burundi man who left his home country due to the civil war. He believes that the Burundi President uses the partnership money to supply his soldiers with weapons instead of strengthening the justice system in the country. Taner explained:

> 'We are refugees, we come to Europe for help. But those people, the rebels, the Burundi president was a rebel, they kill people. And then they get money from the Netherlands for us. The Dutch authorities say: "We have illegal migrants, so we will help you financially". The Burundi president signs and the Dutch pay. That's corruption! (…) In Guinea as well, and in eh… in Iraq, I don't know exactly which countries, but I heard about the Congo too. Yes, they are being paid, huge, very huge amounts. And the president… what do you think? He gets, like, a million but do you think he cares about me? No! They don't care about me. The money, that's important.'

Some respondents said they felt powerless due to the increased collaboration of the Dutch authorities with others included in the control system, against whom the migrants cannot compete due to the merger of different laws and policies within the migration control domain. Simultaneously, the Dutch authorities – and the EU – face complications in ending such partnerships, given the reluctance of migration source countries to accept their own nationals. This provides respondents with the opportunity to ask the representatives of their home country to refuse the provision of a travel document.

Finally, respondents point to the inclusion of other policies and laws in the control system. For instance, as we illustrate later in more detail, they found that current civic integration policies select who deserves admission and who should be held in the home country (cf. Bonjour, 2010). Further, they refer to the inclusion of social policies in the domain of labour, housing, and family affairs (cf. Bowling and Westenra, 2020; Hiah and Staring, 2016). The extension of the migration control domain with these other legal domains complicates living without a legal status in the Netherlands and causes immobility in the migrants' home countries. A substantial number of respondents question whether such an encompassing, criminalizing system is needed, as they are not criminals but simply lack the legal documents entitling them to remain in or migrate to the Netherlands.

4.4.3 *The third layer: Dutch internal control mechanisms contributing to the EU's externalized control*

Finally, the effects of internal control mechanisms are not only felt by respondents living in the Netherlands. These internal controls also influence these migrants' daily lives in their home countries after deportation or voluntary return. The different localities where these mechanisms perpetuate add to the image of an interlinked, layered structure of Dutch internal migration control, which the migrants perceive as a system.

Respondents were confronted with the stigma of being deported, meaning that, they are – as in their destination country – not considered full citizens and are to some extent excluded from fully participating in society. This may result in feelings of loss (cf. Peutz, 2010). This can be seen in the narrative of Jeffrey, a deported Surinamese man. In the early 1990s, he left his job at Paramaribo airport after a traumatizing plane crash and migrated to the Netherlands where he worked unauthorized for several years before he was arrested, detained for 2.5 months and deported given his lack of a legal status. After his deportation, Jeffrey arrived at the airport with two plastic bags. He, like other Surinamese deportees, pretended to be on holiday, as he felt ashamed of his former unauthorized residency. He was aware of the powerful stigma that rests on deportees who are considered failures or criminals. However, he explained:

> 'They are bullying me. I could get into a fight with someone because it is so annoying. 'They have posted him. The Netherlands have posted him', that's what they say. That it just annoying someone, right? I no longer go out in the evenings to avoid meeting anyone. Now, it has become quiet (…). It really hurts me; I am still really sad that I had to leave my country [the Netherlands].'

Jeffrey continues to describe how he eschews certain places or people, thereby showing how he had already internalized his label as an outcast (cf. McDowell and Wonders, 2010). After deportation, he continued feeling miserable and developed an alcohol addiction, something he denies later in the interview. His legal and social exclusion in the Netherlands was socially perpetuated during his stay back home in Surinam, as his former neighbours and friends believed that deportees do not rightfully belong in their country either – Jeffrey also struggled with this. He preferred to be in the Netherlands, given the opportunities to work and the presence there of legally residing families, especially as he could not live up to his wife's expectations in Surinam. This illustrates how bordering practices and the accompanying deportability not only have enormous long-term legal and social consequences for deportees but also seriously influence their mental and physical health even long after deportation. Dingeman-Cerda and Coutin (2012) believe that such unwanted deportations bring about not only individual suffering but also what they call 'social suffering', which affects society as a whole, at least in the Salvadorian context (see also Schulz, 2021).

Respondents also account for the immobility they face in their home country as the outcome of Dutch internal control mechanisms. Many deportees and returnees considered a return to the Netherlands as a solution for their ongoing economic or social problems in their home country. A lack of opportunities on the labour market, social exclusion and feelings of not belonging in their home country all lead to cyclical migration, where these migrants attempt to travel back and forth within their transnational network. As they have obtained migration experience and built transnational ties, migration has become a more real and closer solution to them (cf. Schuster and Majidi, 2013). However, their previous subjection to internal migration controls contributed to their immobility post-return. For instance, respondents in both Nigeria and Surinam were, again, considering migration to the Netherlands as this felt more like their home country than did their actual country of origin given their social and cultural ties there, the length of their residency or other forms of connection. However, migration to the Netherlands or another European country after deportation has become more complicated due to the entry bans and the pronouncement of undesirability that the EU/Netherlands have introduced and that are registered in digital databases.[30] This prevents further migration to the entire EU – considered a double punishment. Priya, a Surinamese woman who has been back in Surinam for three years, is a case in point. She is still involved in many legal procedures in the Netherlands to reduce her three-year prison sentence in cassation, as this would allow her to undo the imposition of the entry ban. She has relatively few opportunities to fight this decision, though, as she is already far away, which complicates communication with her lawyer. During these years, the cruel situation means that Priya is not able to see her son, who lives in the Netherlands, as she is not allowed to enter the country:

> 'Your child doesn't forget that, like, "Ow, three years my mother wasn't here. Three birthdays that my mum didn't attend. Three mothers' days." Can you give that back to me? Can you give that back to my child? No! you cannot give that back.'

Entry bans seriously limit people's opportunities to travel legally to both the Netherlands *and* other EU countries, which is why migrants consider cyclical migration within their transnational network to be a solution to the life events or issues they are confronted with.

30 An entry ban is an administrative measure that prohibits migrants, for a pre-set time, from returning to EU countries. The pronouncement of undesirability also aims to ban unauthorized migrants but is mainly used after a criminal conviction. See also https://ind.nl/en/Pages/entry-ban-return-decision-and-pronouncement-of-undesirability.aspx, accessed 07/31/2020.

Internal migration control mechanisms, such as the entry ban or the pronouncement of undesirability, have actually become part of and further added to the external migration-control mechanisms as they prevent migration to Europe and create immobility in the home countries.

Further, some returned and deported respondents are confronted with civic integration requirements that hamper their return to the Netherlands. In 2005, the Dutch authorities introduced pre-admission integration requirements as part of its policies to ensure that only sufficiently motivated migrants who will probably successfully integrate into Dutch society are admitted. Some of these requirements include a sufficient income level and a test of Dutch language fluency and societal knowledge. This relatively strict selection measure makes entry rights conditional on participation in or successful completion of the programmes (Bonjour, 2010). This shows that the Dutch authorities use a broad range of policies – within and beyond migration *and* integration policies – to govern unwanted migration. By such means, they strictly select who is welcome in the Netherlands and try to close the net for unwelcome others. The fieldwork in Surinam and Nigeria illustrated that the merger of these policy domains once again hindered respondents' (re)migration to the Netherlands. Chioke, a Nigerian who was deported four years earlier and whose wife and son were still legally residing in the Netherlands, is one such case. During each phone conversation, Chioke's son asked him when he would return to the Netherlands, which his father would love to do; however, this was still impossible given his wife's lack of sufficient income. He worked the entire time during his (unauthorized) stay in the Netherlands and was able to support his family, but now he is stuck in Nigeria until he is able to meet these preadmission requirements. Chioke continues to look for a way to circumvent these requirements. He believes that it is hard that the Dutch authorities tear families apart with these measures. Other respondents and their family members were looking for partners, jobs, and other resources to facilitate their legal migration to either the Netherlands or another European country, as they preferred legal migration over clandestine routes and living unauthorized in the Netherlands (again).

4.5 To conclude

This chapter started with sketching the context of a globalizing world in which opposing processes – increased restrictive and selective bordering practices and the increased mobility of *bona fide* travellers and crimmigrants within transnational networks – go side by side. It is in this context of increased mobility, cyclical migration, transnational networks and increased migration control that this chapter focused on the interaction between unauthorized migrants and Dutch internal migration-control mechanisms as well as how these interactions shaped the daily lives of unauthorized migrants in the

Netherlands and their mobility during their unauthorized stay, post-return or deportation. The chapter shows that the so-called internal migration-control mechanisms seriously contribute to the 'deportability' of unauthorized migrants, defined as their omnipresent awareness of the possibility of being deported from the 'space of the nation-state'. This deportability has a serious legal, social and existential impact on these migrants which are felt long after their return or deportation, even for those respondents who returned to their home country using financial return assistance (see also Chapter 5).

This chapter shows how the multi-layered structure of the different Dutch control mechanisms is being perceived by those subjected to it – that is, as 'one system of control'. The analysis of the migrants' stories gives meaning to three important, interlinked layers within the system: the different actors, a broad range of laws and policies not restricted to migration policies, and different localities. First, the migrants discern a whole range of public and private actors who are involved within this system of internal migration control, including (immigration) police, immigration officers, officers from the Immigration and Naturalisation Service, departure supervisors from the DT&V, border officers, employers, acquaintances, citizens, lawyers, flight captains, landlords and IOM employees. A second input to the layered structure of the internal migration control is presented by the different laws and policies that all try to control the mobility of the unauthorized migrants in the Netherlands and which, as such, also add to the encompassing control system: criminal laws, development aid, civic integration requirements, labour laws, housing laws and social rights. The chapter shows how these layers are interlinked, as the merger of these policy domains with the migration domain also implies an extension of the controlling actors with whom unauthorized migrants are confronted from the moment they choose to migrate until their post-return or deportation. Third, this chapter illustrates that specific internal migration-control mechanisms dealing with entry bans and deportations have severe consequences that go far beyond internal migration controls, with their national policy goals of withstanding unauthorized stay. As a consequence, migrants returned or deported to their home country often experience immobility, economic or social exclusion, as well as traumas related to their separated families. As shown, the individual nation-state, through its internal migration management, adds directly to the externalization of migration control at a supranational level. These insights, based on the migrants' experiences, reveal that multi-layered bordering regimes have an even wider reach than is usually assumed in the theoretical debate on this topic and that the interlinkage of these layers strengthens its effects.

Nation-states attempt to govern through migration controls (Bosworth and Guild, 2008) and create a comprehensive multi-layered system to do so. However, this chapter shows that unauthorized migrants also try to deal with the nation-state's intended policy goals. They prolong their stay in the Netherlands based on ideas of safety first, instead of answering their marginalized and criminalized position by returning home. The migrants' narratives simultaneously illustrate the self-evident character of mobility in their lives. Once people have migrated, this generates movement in different directions, even after return or deportation (cf. Glick Schiller and Salazar, 2013). The effects of internal migration-control mechanisms here and there raise serious external barriers to this self-evident nature of international cyclical migration. It challenges the creativity of migrants' agency in resisting these bordering practices, as it also fuels criminal networks facilitating irregular border crossings (Snel, Bilgili and Staring, 2020). Finally, Ibo, who was quoted at the beginning of this chapter, is quoted again.

> '...I call it a system. It is a system. Sometimes I laugh when I see these young people who come here and who see the system. The legalization opportunities give them hope that there are some good things ahead of them but these are not there. It is empty, empty hope.'

Ibo, who could be labelled as a hands-on expert in migration control due to his long-lasting experience of living unauthorized in the Netherlands, is far from optimistic about the direction that migration management takes. He realizes the comprehensive and devastating impact of migration control on his daily life long after returning home.

5 'If you don't have documents or a legal procedure, you are out!' Making humanitarian organizations partner in migration control*

Abstract

This chapter contributes to answering the first sub-question of this study regarding how unauthorized migrants understand the law. It reveals that unauthorized migrants hold the belief that humanitarian organizations – initially established to support migrants without legal status in response to, and in disagreement with, the state's exclusionary migration policies – have become entangled in migration control due to the gradual and subtle responsibilization process by Dutch authorities. As part of this process, authorities have implemented specific measures and redirected financial resources to integrate these organizations into their broader migration control policies. Consequently, there has been a decline in the number of support organizations for unauthorized migrants, a reduction in their independence and autonomy, and an increased emphasis on selection and return. The merging of humanitarian care and securitization imperatives by these organizations, as a consequence of the Dutch authorities' responsibilization process, contributes to unauthorized migrants' experiences of exclusion, selection, and enforcement by these organizations. These experiences lead unauthorized migrants to perceive humanitarian organizations as integral parts of the aforementioned control system that they consider as the law. This perception comes at the cost of the migrants' trust in these organizations.

5.1 Introduction

The unaccompanied minor Magomed arrives early 2013 in the Netherlands and claims asylum. His asylum application is rejected and he has to return to his home country, but he stays unauthorized in the Netherlands. As he is struggling with the pains of being unauthorized, he goes in and out of immigration detention and is anxious about his future.

* This chapter has been published: Kox M and Staring R (2020). 'If you don't have documents or a legal procedure, you are out!' Making humanitarian organizations partner in migration control. *European Journal of Criminology* 19(5): 974–993.

He has one safe haven, which is a non-governmental organization (NGO) that provides him with housing and legal assistance. Magomed considers one of its employees as his 'father'. Recently, though, Magomed has started relating his disappointment with this substitute father because he had warned him that he had to leave the NGO's housing within a couple of months if he did not cooperate with his 'voluntary' return. Magomed feels indignant and betrayed by his 'father', who knows that it is impossible for him to return. He does not understand the NGO's changed mood other than the fact that the NGO is dependent on governmental money linked to unauthorized migrants' return. While discussing his future situation with us, Magomed expresses strong feelings of insecurity and stress about where to go because his time in the shelter is running out.

Magomed's story is not an isolated case. Ethnographic fieldwork amongst migrants without a legal status in the Netherlands – which is presented in this chapter – shows that these migrants also experience exclusion, selection and enforcement by humanitarian organizations that sprang up to support these migrants (see also Van Meeteren, 2014; Staring and Aarts, 2010). These migrants' experiences seem directly related to the Dutch authorities' responsibilization strategies, meaning that they seek to act upon migration 'not in a direct fashion through state agencies (police, courts, prisons, social workers) but instead by acting indirectly, seeking to activate action on the part of non-state agencies and organizations' (Garland, 1996: 452). Garland (1996, 2001) developed this theory to explain modern crime control strategies, but this process is also observed within the migration domain as agencies, organizations and individuals outside the direct power of the state have been made responsible for controlling migration (see Lahav, 1998; Weber, 2013). This includes, amongst others, carriers (Scholten, 2014), employers (Mitsilegas, 2013), universities and hospitals (Weber, 2013), and citizens (Aliverti, 2015). This chapter argues that humanitarian organizations too have become actors in controlling migration and shows how migrants lacking a legal status experience these developments.

It draws on the concept of humanitarianism, referring to humanitarian organizations that provide relief to and lessen the suffering of migrants while they simultaneously reproduce the causes of the migrants' suffering and legitimize restrictive migration policies (Fassin, 2011; Vandevoordt and Verschraegen, 2019b). Migration scholars have illustrated this paradoxical merger of humanitarian care and securitization imperatives during Search and Rescue operations (Cuttitta, 2018; Pallister-Wilkins, 2017), at the geographical border (Walters, 2011) or upon reception (Feischmidt et al., 2019; Social Inclusion, 2019). However, borders are no longer solely situated at states' territorial boundaries because states have also developed comprehensive policies and practices aimed at the prevention of unauthorized residence and the deportation of migrants without a legal status (Albrecht, 2002; see also Chapter 4). These internal border controls made some migrants without a legal status (temporarily) dependent on the material and non-material support of humanitarian organizations (Staring and Kox, 2016; Van der Leun and Bouter, 2015). As illustrated in this chapter, Dutch authorities have incorporated parts of these organizations into its broader system of migration control. This means that these organizations have manoeuvred themselves into the ambiguous position of simultaneously advocating the interests of migrants and serving the government by acting as a loyal player within the immigration system. This has brought an extension of what Walters (2011: 145) calls 'the humanitarian border', that is, the 'uneasy alliance [of] a politics of alienation with a politics of care, and a tactic of abjection and one of reception'.

This chapter continues with some reflections on humanitarianism and the methodology. Then, based on secondary sources, it distinguishes different types of humanitarian organizations supporting migrants without a legal status living in the Netherlands. Next, it shows how the Dutch government incorporated humanitarian organizations within their system of migration enforcement and discusses how these organizations deal with their new position. Drawing on the aforementioned ethnographic fieldwork, it illustrates migrants' experiences with the responsibilization of these humanitarian organizations and the consequences of these processes. It concludes with a discussion on the implications of these broader developments of welfare states increasingly denying non-citizens access to their services and compelling migrants without a legal status to turn to humanitarian organizations, while, at the same time, using various strategies to disarm such organizations.

5.2 The ambiguous roles of humanitarian organizations

Humanitarianism and securitization are part of the same dynamic continuum (Župarić-Iljić and Valenta, 2019). Although humanitarian organizations concerned with migrants' flight, arrival or reception focus on morality and have respect for human life and alleviate suffering, they have also become involved in securitization imperatives (Fassin, 2011; Walters, 2011). Both state and non-state actors use the organizations' higher moral purposes to normalize or legitimize current border practices, even if these have inhumane effects (Fassin, 2011; Pallister-Wilkins, 2018). This mutes the counter-narratives of those who are confronted with border practices and masks the effects of migration policies (Pallister-Wilkins, 2017; Župarić-Iljić and Valenta, 2019). As such, it both contrasts with and reinforces these policies (Cuttitta, 2018; Pallister-Wilkins, 2017; Walters, 2011). Although state border officers may also be concerned with compassion (Hadjimatheou and Lynch, 2018; Khosravi, 2009), humanitarian organizations are often more supportive than state actors. However, their support may be 'compromised by the nature of their relationship with the government and the securitization strategy of diluting access to legal, economic and social protections', something that prevents these organizations from promoting their clients' best interests (Gerard and Weber, 2019: 277). Securitization and humanitarianism can therefore result in similar outcomes for people on the move (Pallister-Wilkins, 2017).

There are comparable tensions between humanitarianism and securitization for humanitarian organizations that support unauthorized migrants, that is, migrants without a valid form of authorization, such as – amongst others – failed asylum seekers, visa overstayers and migrants whose residence permit has been withdrawn. These organizations are not directly aimed at saving unauthorized migrants' lives, but may be characterized as humanitarian because they try to achieve humane living conditions and alleviate the migrants' suffering by providing material or non-material assistance in terms of shelter, living allowances, legal/medical assistance, empowerment initiatives and advocacy (see Vandevoordt and Verschraegen, 2019b). National immigration policies and opportunities for humanitarian organizations to support migrants may differ between countries, but in most countries, there is humanitarian support available for unauthorized migrants (Garkisch et al., 2017).

However, European states are trying to co-opt, influence or take over such humanitarian organizations for unauthorized migrants (Feischmidt et al., 2019; Vandevoordt and Verschraegen, 2019a). Although these organizations do not passively fill institutional gaps and take over the state's responsibilities (Sinatti, 2019; Garland, 2001), these organizations – or their employees/volunteers – may face consequences if they do not meet the state's expectations or they may not be able to continue their support otherwise (Gerard and Weber, 2019; Lahav, 1998). This includes humanitarian support for unauthorized migrants. Vandevoordt and Verschraegen (2019b) point, for instance, to the exclusion of unauthorized migrants from a Belgian humanitarian organization after the state co-opted this organization. Fleischmann (2019) illustrates how German authorities are trying to (re)gain control and power over organizations that assist migrants by institutionalizing citizen commitment in its municipal policies. Cullen (2009: 102) argues that the Irish NGO sector 'is harnessed to the state through service provision and a reliance on state and foundation funding', a development that limits their impact. Similar processes can be seen in France (Nicholls, 2013), Germany (Castaneda, 2007; Ellermann, 2006) and the UK (Statham and Geddes, 2006). Finally, because of the availability of funding, humanitarian organizations have become involved in Assisted Voluntary Return programmes, something that has been defined as 'soft deportation' because these programmes function only in addition to – or as a replacement for – state deportations and the voluntariness of such returns has been questioned (Leerkes et al., 2017; Webber, 2011; see also Vandevoordt, 2017).

Because these developments have mainly been described from a theoretical perspective or from the NGOs' point of view (Feischmidt et al., 2019; Social Inclusion, 2019), the question arises of how these developments are experienced by unauthorized migrants who are subjected to these processes and what the consequences are for unauthorized migrants in need of humanitarian support.

5.3 Methodology[31]

This question will be answered on the basis of this research on unauthorized migrants' legal consciousness for which I followed 45 unauthorized migrants between March 2015 and May 2018. I observed these migrants in their everyday lives and during their interaction with regulatory institutions; interviewed and informally talked to them several times; or had frequent contact by phone or WhatsApp. The number of contacts with this group of migrants varied from three to over 20 times. In addition, I interviewed, extensively informally spoke to and observed another 60 unauthorized migrants who wanted to be involved in the research but on a limited basis. In all interactions during the fieldwork, unauthorized migrants could talk about their situation in the country of origin and their migration journey as well as discuss their everyday lives, their experiences with migration control and their visions of their future. All observations and informal conversations were written down in field notes and interviews were recorded and transcribed verbatim. The data were then analysed using Atlas.ti (qualitative data analysis software).

I aimed to create a heterogeneous group of unauthorized migrants in terms of age, gender, country of origin, length of stay in the Netherlands, motive for migration, family situation, and current situation given the previously assumed differences between these migrants (see Burgers and Engbersen, 1999). I therefore focused on unauthorized migrants at different locations and at different stages of their unauthorized residence, including unauthorized migrants living out of sight of the authorities, those who had just been arrested by the police, those living at freedom-restricted (family) locations or those staying in immigration detention centres. To prevent an overrepresentation of respondents who remain unauthorized in the Netherlands and have different thoughts on current migration controls, I also involved unauthorized migrants who were participating in return programmes or who had already returned or been deported to Surinam (16), Indonesia (11), Nigeria (6) and Guyana (1). I gained contact with these migrants through support organizations, immigration institutions and these migrants' social contacts. This approach – which includes seventeen interviews by research assistants[32] – resulted in a research

31 The Methodology section is based on the methods section in the previous chapter.

32 The research assistants Lotte Servaas and Marko de Haan conducted fieldwork in Indonesia and Surinam as part of their master's theses (De Haan, 2019; Servaas, 2019) and a study of an Assisted Voluntary Return project in which both Kox and Staring are involved (Staring and Kox, 2020). Their fieldwork is only included in this chapter of this book.

group of 122 unauthorized men and women who vary in age from eight to 70.[33] They cover a variety of countries from all continents. Their length of (unauthorized) stay in the Netherlands varies from almost one year to 38 years. Some of them had a residence permit that had either been withdrawn or not extended; others had never applied for a legal status or had been rejected.

The analysis revealed that unauthorized migrants consider the aforementioned humanitarian organizations to be part of the Dutch migration control system. This is why a policy analysis to understand how these organizations have become involved in selecting, excluding and enforcing unauthorized migrants was included as well. This analysis included parliamentary documents between 2000, which was when local governments started financial support of NGOs for unauthorized migrants, up to December 2018 as the political debate and the discussion between national and local levels were reflected in these documents. The analysis also involved secondary sources to gain insights into these organizations' perspective on these processes and the impact on their modus operandi.[34]

5.4 Local humanitarian organizations in the Netherlands

The Netherlands used to be internationally known for its tolerance towards migrants, but it is currently better characterized by its restrictive admission policies, increased exclusion of unauthorized migrants, and greater pressure for migration control (Engbersen et al., 2006; Van der Woude et al., 2014). Unauthorized migrants are excluded from all formal markets and welfare arrangements and are allowed only essential healthcare, legal aid and – until the age of eighteen – education. Besides, they may be eligible for shelter if they meet certain eligibility criteria, which often include willingness to return (see Chapter 2). Although the effects of this exclusion and control are often determined by the everyday interactions between border officers and unauthorized migrants (Van der Woude and Van der Leun, 2017), studies on unauthorized migrants in the Netherlands show that it has become increasingly difficult to survive in the Netherlands without a residence permit (Burgers and Engbersen, 1999; Engbersen et al., 2002; Kox, 2010; Staring, 2001; Staring and Aarts, 2010). Some groups of migrants are – temporarily – entitled to state shelter in freedom-restricted institutions, others are not.[35] They are faced with harsh living conditions and constantly run the risk of being stopped, detained or deported (see Chapter 4).

33 Minors were spoken to only informally in the presence of or with permission of their parents.

34 These studies provide important qualitative insights into the perspective of the humanitarian organizations but offer little quantitative data on these organizations.

35 This concerns migrants who have minor children, are vulnerable/ill or willing to return to their home country. Besides, migrants receive twelve weeks of shelter in a freedom-restricted centre after their legalization claim has been rejected. In recent years, Bed, Bath and Bread arrangements have been established as will be discussed later onwards in this chapter.

Consequently, the support of family members, friends and compatriots is becoming ever more important. If unauthorized migrants do not have such an (ethnic) network to fall back on, they are dependent on local humanitarian organizations (Engbersen et al., 2002; Staring and Aarts, 2010).

The first local humanitarian organizations emerged in the late 1970s and 1980s and originated within Dutch church organizations or protest/squatter movements that were dissatisfied with asylum decisions taken by the Immigration and Naturalization Service and with unauthorized migrants sleeping rough (LOS Foundation, 2014). At that time, these local organizations consisted of a small number of volunteers who offered shelter, living allowances and other types of material and non-material support. In addition, they organized protests and demonstrations against Dutch migration policies. These early organizations operated autonomously and independently of governments and their eligibility criteria. There were around 30 such organizations in 2000 (Bouter, 2013: 15).[36]

However, these emergency structures proved to be insufficient owing to the introduction of the Linking Act (1998), the revised Aliens Act 2000 (2001) and some policy changes that excluded specific groups of asylum seekers from state shelter. Consequently, local municipalities were faced with a large number of asylum seekers ending up on the streets when there were no adequate national return policies. Many municipalities invoked their 'duty of care' as well as their responsibility for public order and safety. They decided to financially support these organizations for assisting unauthorized migrants who were expected to legalize their residence in the Netherlands or resettle in their home country and those who found themselves in extreme and pressing difficult circumstances within their municipality.[37] Whereas some of the early organizations refused support from the government as a matter of principle, others accepted financial compensation from local authorities in exchange for services aimed at the unauthorized migrants. From then on, these organizations worked hand in hand with their municipality, something that limited their capacity to resist central migration policies (Kalir and Wissink, 2016).

Municipalities not only subsidizes existing organizations for unauthorized migrants, they also subsidized new organizations offering emergency assistance to unauthorized migrants. Even though the central authorities have always been against this form of support for unauthorized migrants, local municipalities supplied funds to be spent in consultation with the municipality or as a lump sum for each supported unauthorized migrant. These new locally institutionalized organizations often consist of one paid

36 In 1979, several organizations merged into VluchtelingenWerk Nederland (https://www.vluchtelingenwerk.nl/over-ons/onze-geschiedenis, accessed 05/29/2020).

37 These criteria differ per organization; see LOS Foundation (http://www.stichtinglos.nl/noodopvang, accessed 05/29/2020).

employee helped by volunteers. They are completely dependent financially on municipalities and can generally assist only those migrants who met pre-set eligibility criteria, that is, migrants looking either for legal residency or to return and migrants who need assistance on humanitarian grounds. These support organizations that are entirely funded by municipalities have become known as 'emergency relief' (Koppes, 2017; LOS Foundation, 2014). In contrast to the existing organizations, these emergency relief organizations are forced to exclude unauthorized migrants who do not meet these criteria from support because local municipalities do not subsidize these migrants' support and there is a lack of other funding. In 2002, there were around 170 of such local emergency relief organizations in the Netherlands that offered assistance to unauthorized migrants in exchange for financial governmental support (Parliamentary Documents 2002/03 19637 no. 695).

5.5 Incorporating support organizations for unauthorized migrants

The document analysis shows that the Dutch central authorities have tried to incorporate these organizations into their broader policies of migration control. They believe that providing support to unauthorized migrants undermines the central immigration policies aimed at discouraging unauthorized residence. Besides, they assume that providing shelter attracts more unauthorized migrants and hampers their departure (Advisory Council on Migration, 2018: 3). Whereas local authorities and humanitarian organizations consider support for unauthorized migrants necessary to prevent inhumane situations, the state has repeatedly tried to force municipalities to end their financial contributions to these humanitarian organizations. Therefore, it also used administrative coercion and threatened to cut the municipalities' budgets (LOS Foundation, 2014; Parliamentary Documents 2002/03 19637 no. 695, 2004/05 19637 no. 892). These threats by the state – combined with volunteers' exhaustion and a decline in unauthorized migrants owing to a regularization scheme – led to a reduction in the number of organizations from 170 in 2002 to 50 in 2013 (Koppes, 2017; LOS Foundation, 2014; Van der Welle and Odé, 2009). The central government's constant threats to end emergency assistance not only reduced the number of support organizations but also led to conditional support, given the stricter selection of unauthorized migrants by the emergency relief organizations on the one hand and the reduced number of other organizations on the other (Van der Leun and Bouter, 2015).

Moreover, the state's threats restructured the organizations. Following a complaint by the Conference of European Churches to the European Committee of Social Rights and Dutch court rulings that state that Dutch authorities are required to offer unauthorized migrants so-called 'Bed, Bath and Bread' arrangements, the government decided to provide financial compensation to municipalities to arrange shelter for those unauthorized migrants who had been excluded from shelter and social services until there was greater clarity about the consequences of these court rulings (Parliamentary Documents 2014/15 19637 no. 1944; see also Koppes, 2017; Pro Facto, 2018). Although this resulted in some new organizations, their support was financially compensated only if migrants registered with the state's Repatriation and Departure Service (DT&V). This meant that the unauthorized migrants' use of support organizations would make them visible to Dutch authorities, even if they were to abandon their 'voluntary' return without obtaining legal residency.[38] After several legal proceedings and negotiations between the government and local municipalities, the state's financial compensation for municipalities providing support to unauthorized migrants stopped and the new requirements persisted, with profound consequences for unauthorized migrants (Parliamentary Documents 2016/17 19637 no. 2267). This 'inclusionary control' (Tomczak and Thompson, 2019: 9) introduced barriers for unauthorized migrants to make use of the available support.

Recently, the Dutch central government has gone one step further and started a pilot that includes local support organizations in national state shelters for unauthorized migrants (so-called 'landelijke vreemdelingenvoorzieningen' – LVV). These shelters are managed under the supervision of the municipality in cooperation with the DT&V and humanitarian organizations (Mack et al., 2022).[39] The latter must either encourage migrants' 'voluntary' return or find another permanent solution because they are expected to accomplish better results than the state given the migrants' trust in these organizations (Pro Facto, 2018). Unauthorized migrants may stay in these shelters for two weeks without any conditions, after which they need to cooperate in either legalization or return. If not, the migrant might be disqualified from shelter (Parliamentary Documents 2016/17 19637 no. 2375).[40] This latest development completes the restructuring of these humanitarian organizations as they are incorporated into the state's broader system of migration control and decide – together with the state – on the migrants' selection or exclusion. Previous research shows that several Dutch organizations use comparable excluding rationales as

38 See the Association of Netherlands Municipalities' 'Factsheet Bed-bad-broodregeling' (https://vng.nl/onderwerpenindex/asiel/asielbeleid-en-integratie/publicaties/factsheet-bed-bad-broodregeling, accessed 05/29/2020).

39 See Government of the Netherlands, Regeerakkoord 2017: 'Vertrouwen in de toekomst' (https://www.rijksoverheid.nl/documenten/publicaties/2017/10/10/regeerakkoord-2017-vertrouwen-in-de-toekomst, accessed 10/17/2018).

40 See also Association of Netherlands Municipalities (https://vng.nl/files/vng/brieven/2018/attachments/20181130_getekende-samenwerkingsafspraak-lvv.pdf and https://www.rijksoverheid.nl/binaries/rijksoverheid/documenten/kamerstukken/2018/11/29/tk-stand-van-zaken-locaties-vreemdelingen-voorzieningen-lvv/tk-stand-van-zaken-locaties-vreemdelingen-voorzieningen-lvv.pdf, accessed 05/20/2020).

the DT&V because of these responsibilization processes (Cleton and Chauvin, 2020; Kalir and Wissink, 2016).

In this same timeframe, humanitarian organizations have also become more involved in the 'voluntary' return of unauthorized migrants. There are several probable reasons for this. Since the 1990s, for instance, the failing repatriation policies have prompted pleas to engage support organizations to help organize the unauthorized migrants' return (Rusinovic et al., 2002: 81). In the last decade, advocacy groups that appeal for a reduction in immigration detention have argued that assistance from support agencies is less damaging and more effective than detention when it comes to return. They have therefore suggested the use of alternatives to detention and more frequent use of return projects set up by support organizations (for example, Advisory Council on Migration, 2013a; Amnesty International, 2011). Consequently, additional funding has been made available for – (partly) sub-contracted – organizations that promote the return of unauthorized migrants (Parliamentary Documents 2012/13 19637 no. 1721). Further increased funding, combined with an aversion to immigration detention, has persuaded several agencies to branch out into this type of project, including those organizations that sprang up to support unauthorized migrants. These organizations require the approval of the DT&V to assist potential returnees, which also means that those migrants who ultimately do not return are registered with the Dutch authorities.

In addition, the support organizations' increased focus on return – in combination with their dependence on or wish for return subsidies – results in a more specific approach in terms of selecting migrants who are eligible for assistance (see Staring and Kox, 2020). The Dutch authorities fund return assistance for unauthorized migrants – and sometimes only rejected asylum seekers – from designated countries. This means that migrants from non-designated countries will not receive support from an organization because their assistance would not be funded (Staring and Kox, 2020). Given the level of discretion of these support organizations, combined with the financial benefits for assisting migrants who return, organizations direct their assistance much more towards migrants from these specific countries at the expense of others, especially as organizations have pre-set targets for the number of returnees. This even results in competition amongst organizations as they all try to recruit those migrants whose return is easy to achieve (Staring and Kox, 2020). This means that the organizations' generic approach is replaced by a specific approach favouring particular countries of origin that are deemed more problematic by the Dutch authorities. This underlines the 'mixing of exclusionary and inclusionary forces' (Tomczak and Thompson, 2019: 7) because these organizations are aimed at including unauthorized migrants but now feel forced to exclude those migrants who do not meet the imposed criteria (see Van der Leun and Bouter, 2015).

The incorporation of humanitarian organizations in the state's migration control policies was the result of a gradual process characterized by both opposition from and cooperation by humanitarian organizations (see also Cantat and Feischmidt, 2019). During the fieldwork we learned that some organizations refused state funding because they feared a negative impact – and limitation – on their support. Other organizations are balancing between their goal to support unauthorized migrants and their obligations towards the municipalities (see Županić-Iljić and Valenta, 2019). They are facing different dilemmas but look for loopholes that enable them to act upon the migrants' wishes, such as postponing the migrants' registration at the DT&V or withdrawing passports that facilitate deportation (Staring and Kox, 2020). In addition, they use their position to lobby for policy changes that create a better situation for unauthorized migrants (Staring and Kox, 2020), although the question arises whether or not their changed position limits their transformative powers (see Gerard and Weber, 2019). Finally, some organizations have adapted the state's rationale, language and approach in their everyday practices (Cleton and Chauvin, 2020; Kalir and Wissink, 2016). This limits the organizations' negotiating space for alternative initiatives and has made them a part of the restrictive Dutch migration systems (Kalir and Wissink, 2016; Van der Leun and Bouter, 2015). Kalir and Wissink (2016: 35) argue therefore that the Dutch authorities and these humanitarian organizations constitute a 'continuum that is underlined by a dominant logic, common categories, shared political subjectivities and pre-agreed lines of political actions'.

5.6 Selection, exclusion, return and enforcement by humanitarian organizations

The fieldwork shows that these developments have consequences for unauthorized migrants' experiences with and perceptions of these organizations. Some of the respondents have been dependent – more or less – on humanitarian organizations. They, in general, appreciate these organizations, which provide them with material support in the form of shelter, meals and/or living allowances when they have nowhere else to go. In addition, these organizations assist them to get access to medical and legal aid, report victimization to the authorities, and help them resist abuse as a consequence of their vulnerable position. Respondents believe that the support organizations are safe havens. They feel like human beings again in this supportive environment where they are empowered. They emphasize the need for such organizations, given the lack of other available supporting networks; otherwise they would have nowhere to go because they do not consider return a realistic option (see Staring and Kox, 2016). This, again, shows that these organizations provide inclusionary mechanisms despite being situated in an exclusionary context (see Tomczak and Thompson, 2019).

However, academics as well as research participants are also critical of the newly adopted modus operandi of these organizations (Bouter, 2013; Cleton and Chauvin, 2020;

Kalir and Wissink, 2016; Koppes, 2017; Rusinovic et al., 2002; Van der Leun and Bouter, 2015). Although the organizations' selection of unauthorized migrants has been based on pre-set admission criteria since municipalities started to subsidize these organizations, these criteria were flexibly and arbitrarily imposed in practice on the basis of situation, needs, identity, attitude and reciprocity (Van der Leun and Bouter, 2015; Pro Facto, 2018). However, the migrants' opportunities in terms of legalization and especially return have become more prominent in these selection processes (see Van der Leun and Bouter, 2015). This means that those migrants whose residency cannot be legalized and who are not willing to return are more likely to be excluded from (comprehensive) support. In addition, some respondents bring to the fore that support organizations, in their view, strictly select whether unauthorized migrants are eligible for (comprehensive) assistance. This means that even migrants who fulfil the basic requirements for the organizations' support may be excluded from shelter or other forms of support. These different arguments come to the fore in the story of a 26-year-old East African migrant, Abdi, whose asylum application was rejected and who arrived late in the evening of the same day at an NGO in Amsterdam. He recalls the woman at the NGO stating: 'I don't have place to help you because you were rejected [as an asylum seeker]…. You have to find your own way'. After this 'secondary victimization experience', Abdi continues describing how he slept in a park in the centre of Amsterdam for weeks, feeling a nobody and not knowing what to do. Although he did find assistance elsewhere and received help for another asylum application, he still felt frustrated, misunderstood and hurt because of selection methods that prioritize others over him. This man, like other migrants, doubts whether those organizations are still willing to help them while, at the same time, they do not have anywhere else to go. Although there has always been a certain level of selection by these support organizations, given their limited resources (see Rusinovic et al., 2002), the organizations' exclusionary control seems to have increased as the number of organizations has decreased and the organizations' dependence on municipality funding on the basis of pre-set criteria has increased (LOS Foundation, 2014; Van der Welle and Odé, 2009).

The respondents' stories reveal that exclusion by support organizations takes place not only in the selection process when it is being decided whether or not a migrant will receive (comprehensive) assistance, but also once a migrant is already receiving comprehensive support. Several migrants highlight the fact that they were warned that their shelter would not be continued if they no longer met the eligibility criteria, meaning that respondents needed to participate in a 'voluntarily' return process if there was no prospect of legalization anymore. If not, they could be put onto the streets, as is shown in the story of Adrien, an African migrant who explained how he had not had his asylum permit renewed after it expired and his country of origin was considered to be secure again. He had been residing alternately lawfully and unlawfully in the Netherlands and wondered whether or not to return given his complicated situation in the Netherlands versus the insecure conditions in his country of origin. He continued:

> '[An NGO] helped me to arrange shelter, for a room and sleeping and so on. That is why I am here. But now, the support organization says: 'If you don't have a legal procedure, we can also …' [makes throwaway gesture] … And the support organization says … Because I am sleeping there, she says: "If you don't have documents or a procedure, you are out!"'

Ultimately, Adrien was arrested because of his unlawful residency and ended up in immigration detention. Given the instability in his country of origin, his residency was legalized again – partly owing to the advocacy efforts of this 'excluding' NGO – after which he received state shelter. This illustrates that the position of this NGO is characterized by ambiguity because they cannot support all unauthorized migrants and cannot unconditionally offer shelter given their lack of resources (see Van der Leun and Bouter, 2015). The chance to receive funding for returnees offers an incentive to these organizations to focus on those migrants who might return (Kalir and Wissink, 2016).

The tendency amongst support organizations to focus increasingly on the return of unauthorized migrants – at the expense of other kinds of support – created feelings of loneliness and uncertainty amongst some respondents. Although reviewing migrants' possibilities for return has long been part of many support organizations' approach (Staring and Kox, 2020), the current stronger emphasis on return makes some research participants point out that they no longer feel supported in their attempt to build a life in the Netherlands and that they are increasingly made to feel that they should return – or express a willingness to return – because otherwise they will be excluded from support. This is in line with Cleton and Chauvin (2020), who argue that such organizations present return as the only route to be taken. Nana, a West African unauthorized migrant who is under psychiatric treatment, partly caused by being unauthorized for over 20 years, recalls:

> 'I saw she dropped appointment and then I went there [NGO]. And then she raised the same topic: if I said I want to go to my country, then I can stay here. If I am not ready to go to my country, then I have to leave.'

Nana was actually put out onto the streets because the organization believed that he was not actively trying to achieve his return, whereas he states that he was not able to obtain the documents required for return. His lawyer has been able to find other temporary shelter at the Salvation Army. Other respondents also feel anxious about the support organization they once experienced as a safe haven and some have actually lost – or were about to lose – support if they did not explicitly express a willingness to cooperate with their 'voluntary' return. The perceived risk of being made homeless, regardless of whether that would actually happen, threatens unauthorized migrants' safe havens.

5.7 The changed character of humanitarian organizations

Whereas the majority of our respondents are in principle still positive about the support they receive from these organizations, some emphasize that a support organization convinced or forced them to do things in order to be eligible for assistance. Otherwise, the organization threatened to stop their support. This not only involves cooperation in the return process as illustrated above, but – according to the respondents' narratives – also includes demonstrating, volunteering and working in tough conditions (see Staring and Aarts, 2010). Jacob, an African respondent reveals, for example, that he and other unauthorized migrants move from squat to squat. They used to be grateful for the organization's chairperson, who is responsible for their finances and who has done a lot for their cause. However, this chairperson now requires them to do things they do not want to do while threatening that they will not receive money for their groceries otherwise. He explains:

> 'The chairperson says: "No, you guys, you have to do like actions. You have to be on the streets. You have to do that, like demonstrations." We have to go to the mayor and show them… tell them and speak with the mayor. We have to go to the city hall. But yeah… So the chair can go and ask for money. But even the people here are fed up with all that kind of stuff, demonstrations for four years, etcetera. Because demonstrations are no solution… It is what this person says. The demonstrations are only for getting donations, for getting the money, but that is not… It is not what people really want. People just want to be seen and just want to have their cases looked at and… to know if they can find some solution.'

Despite the chairperson's good intentions and efforts to achieve a better situation for the migrants, this example illustrates the organizations' powers over unauthorized migrants and the ever-present risk of the use of these powers, which resulted in negative experiences for some respondents (cf. Staring and Aarts, 2010).

Furthermore, the research visits to the unauthorized migrants who had returned to Guyana, Indonesia, Nigeria and Surinam reveal that some migrants feel disappointed with the support organizations after their return. Despite – or perhaps because of – positive experiences in the Netherlands during preparations for their return, these migrants feel that the organizations are rather indifferent to what happens to them after their return.

According to some respondents, these organizations pay little attention to what to do straight after arrival in the country of origin and how to tackle factors that might hamper a sustainable return. For instance, during our stay in Surinam, a migrant sent us a WhatsApp message asking whether we could find him a place to live as he had no idea where to go after his arrival in Surinam the next day. Although he had told the organization who offered him Assisted Voluntary Return that everything would be settled, nothing was settled after his arrival in Surinam, meaning that he – like other returning respondents – was mainly concerned with basic provisions before actually being capable of considering or achieving their business plans. As a consequence, these migrants have often spent part of the money that was meant for a business on food, housing and relatives, and in doing so diminish the chances of a sustainable return (see Staring et al., 2012; Staring and Kox, 2020). Other academics raise questions about the sustainability of the return of those who made use of Assisted Voluntary Return programmes (Lietaert et al., 2013; Van Houte et al., 2014).

The unauthorized migrants' narratives provide insight into the support organizations' changed character (see Staring and Kox, 2016). Given their increased focus on selection, return and enforcement, combined with a lack of commitment, these support organizations reflect the state's approach and rationale. Although not all humanitarian organizations are involved in such processes and organizations do question whether this is the right approach or how to legitimize their work (see Cleton and Chauvin, 2020), in practice it makes respondents question the intentions of these organizations. They doubt whether these humanitarian organizations are concerned with their well-being and whether or not to make use of their support. These organizations' changed approach has created a new group of marginalized unauthorized migrants that have nowhere else to go. On the one hand, there are the non-deportable migrants who cannot return for reasons outside of their sphere of influence and have nowhere to go, such as the accompanied minor Magomed reported at the beginning of this chapter. On the other hand, there are the migrants who are not willing (yet) to return to their home country. However, the current exclusionary and deterrent approach is a modest incentive to return (Leerkes and Kox, 2017) and, meanwhile, it does contribute to 'the pains of being unauthorized' (Kox et al., 2020).

5.8 To conclude

This chapter illustrates the expansion of 'the humanitarian border' (Walters, 2011: 145). The paradoxical merger of humanitarian care and securitization imperatives can be seen not only at external and externalized borders but also at internal borders. The Dutch authorities have used a responsibilization strategy to make humanitarian organizations part of – and sometimes partially responsible for – migration management (see Fassin, 2011; Gerard and Weber, 2019). Although, given their disagreement with the state's exclusionary migration policies (LOS Foundation, 2014), these organizations originally developed to support unauthorized migrants, the Dutch authorities have incorporated these organizations into their broader migration control policies by using specific measures and by redirecting monetary flows. During this gradual process, the number of support organizations for unauthorized migrants has decreased (Koppes, 2017; Van der Welle and Odé, 2009). Moreover, many humanitarian organizations have lost full autonomy by accepting funding from local authorities, meaning that they are bound by pre-set criteria and have less flexibility in deciding who to support (see Van der Leun and Bouter, 2015). This dependence on municipality funding has resulted in exclusionary support. Furthermore, organizations have become more concerned with unauthorized migrants' return and have been obliged to register their clients with state institutions in order to receive funding. Consequently, these organizations bring these migrants to the attention of the authorities and may pressure them – (un)consciously – to return. Finally, some organizations are currently being completely incorporated into state institutions and as such enhance the state's migration control practices.

Whereas some organizations refuse state funding for principled reasons or struggle with this new role and the associated dilemmas (Staring and Kox, 2020), others have adopted the changed role in their everyday practices (Cleton and Chauvin, 2020; Kalir and Wissink, 2016). They have manoeuvred themselves into an ambiguous position where they serve the government by acting as a loyal participant within the immigration system while simultaneously supporting the interests of the unauthorized migrants. These organizations' Janus face is not without consequences because it compromises their support (see Gerard and Weber, 2019). In particular, the most vulnerable and marginalized unauthorized migrants who depend most on humanitarian support are experiencing further exclusion, selection and enforcement by both the state and humanitarian organizations. They question whether the organizations they used to trust are still capable of and willing to promote their best interests and whether they will not be urged to return against their will. Given their previous experiences of rejection and exclusion at the state level, they experience the rejection and exclusion at the level of humanitarian organizations as particularly painful. This results in feelings of uncertainty, frustration and misunderstanding amongst migrants, especially if decisions are not adequately explained by these humanitarian organizations (see Staring and Kox, 2016). It makes them question whether or not to make use of such organizations. Not only does this threatens these unauthorized migrants' safe havens, it may also result in further withdrawal and increased vulnerability of these migrants.

Humanitarian borders are context specific (Walters, 2011: 146) but these developments are not limited to the Netherlands. Other European states also try to 'disarm' humanitarian organizations for unauthorized migrants by using two – sometimes combined – strategies. On the one hand, states make use of responsibilization strategies – like the Netherlands – by incorporating humanitarian organizations into their broader systems of migration control. This enables the state to police unauthorized migrants from a distance and limits the organizations' negotiating space for alternative initiatives. As such, it makes these organizations a part of current restrictive migration systems (Ambrosini and Van der Leun, 2015; Castaneda, 2007; Kalir and Wissink, 2016; Van der Leun and Bouter, 2015; Vandevoordt, 2017). These processes can be seen in Belgium (Vandevoordt, 2017), France (Nicholls, 2013), Germany (Castaneda, 2007; Ellermann, 2006; Fleischmann, 2019), Ireland (Cullen, 2009) and the UK (Statham and Geddes, 2006). On the other hand, some states criminalize humanitarian organizations that support unauthorized migrants. Carrera et al. (2016) show that these humanitarian organizations experience harassment and intimidation in their work and fear administrative sanctions, even though humanitarian assistance may not be formally criminalized. We do not observe this trend in the Netherlands,[41] but others report the criminalization of humanitarian organizations in Spain (López-Sala and Barbero, 2019), in Belgium, France and the UK (Fekete, 2009), and in Italy and Greece (Carrera et al., 2018). This criminalizing approach affects all kinds of support, including shelter, medical aid and advocacy/protests. This sometimes deters volunteers, activists and humanitarian organizations from getting involved in providing humanitarian assistance (Sigona, 2018) and may result in civil actors being forced to limit or end their humanitarian assistance (see Carrera et al., 2016; López-Sala and Barbero, 2019). Making support organizations a full partner in migration control and/or criminalizing such organizations threatens the unauthorized migrants' safe havens in an increasing hostile environment (see Sigona, 2018).

Humanitarian organizations for unauthorized migrants can – despite being compromised by these developments – function in the current exclusionary migration domain (see Tomczak and Thompson, 2019). However, the humanitarian approach has a downside – like support in other contexts. For instance, it masks the effects of current controlling policies in terms of homelessness, marginalization and vulnerability. In addition, it facilitates governments' neglect of their clear responsibilities towards unauthorized migrants in terms of offering 'Bed, Bath and Bread' arrangements, something the authorities are obliged to do according to a court ruling (see Vandevoordt and Verschraegen, 2019a). Furthermore, it normalizes and legitimizes the state's exclusionary migration control policies aimed at the migrants' departure, something these humanitarian organizations currently contribute to (Kalir and Wissink, 2016; Leerkes et al., 2017). Nevertheless, we do support offering humanitarian organizations the opportunity to

41 A draft bill – later withdrawn – proposed criminalizing unauthorized residency but excluded humanitarian assistance from this criminalization (Parliamentary Documents 2014/14 33512 no. 3; 13).

provide – uncompromised – support to unauthorized migrants. Such support reduces the pains of being unauthorized and the negative – inhumane – effects of current migration policies (Engbersen et al., 2006; see Chapter 6). Incorporating humanitarian organizations runs the risk that unauthorized migrants will withdraw from this type of assistance altogether when there are no alternatives available as long as they consider return not to be a realistic option. This may increase the risks of further marginalization, health concerns and vulnerability in terms of victimization, exploitation and betrayal. Although the merger of control and care by such humanitarian organizations may be opportune from the state's perspective (Hadjimatheou and Lynch, 2018), it would make sense from a humanitarian perspective to break the current security–humanitarianism continuum and allow humanitarian organizations to continue unconditional and uncompromised support of unauthorized migrants. Such an approach seems more appropriate from a pragmatic perspective too, because the causal relationship between exclusion and return is still unclear (Leerkes and Kox, 2017). Moreover, migration systems based on legitimacy and diplomacy seem to be more effective (Leerkes and Kox, 2017; Van Houte and Leerkes, 2019). Another – more humane – option would be to adapt current migration policies in such a way that they no longer cause inhumane and painful effects for both unauthorized migrants and society and therefore make humanitarian assistance to unauthorized migrants redundant.

6 The pains of being unauthorized in the Netherlands*

Abstract

This chapter addresses the second sub-question of this study, exploring how the law manifests itself in the everyday lives of unauthorized migrants and how it is perceived by the migrants. The chapter illustrates that the law is omnipresent in various moments, places, and contexts in the lives of unauthorized migrants. This ubiquity arises from a wide array of legally embedded limitations, control mechanisms, and exclusionary practices imposed by the law on unauthorized migrants. By referencing Sykes' (1958) renowned study on the pains of imprisonment, I demonstrate that unauthorized migrants believe the law deprives them of, *inter alia*, healthy and secure living conditions, social and geographical mobility, and citizenship. These diverse forms of deprivation impact the migrants' self-esteem, health, and security. Although the impact, salience, and severity of these deprivations vary among migrants, they all share the sense of being punished for their unauthorized residence in the country, with no opportunity to either legalize their residence or escape their situation. Considering previous research with similar insights as well as Hayes' proximity model, the conclusion is drawn that Dutch authorities are aware of these collateral consequences of their control system and deliberately inflict these pains on unauthorized migrants. This implies that migration control is not only experienced as punishment by those subjected to it but is also intended to be punitive. Consequently, being unauthorized in the Netherlands becomes an exceptionally painful experience for migrants.

6.1 Introduction

> 'Why? If they give a permit after seven years, after eight years, why do you [Dutch authorities] make me all these years illegal? Why do you [Dutch authorities] treat me badly here? That is the complaint! It is allowed by the law to arrest you. You get punishment just to get… They detain you! You just do not get benefit from the socials! You are completely out of the society! You

* This chapter has been published: Kox M, Boone M and Staring R (2020) The pains of being unauthorized in the Netherlands. *Punishment & Society* 22(4): 534–552.

> cannot do anything! And later on, they say: 'Congratulations.' Does it make sense?'

This is a quote from Danel, an East African man who fled to the Netherlands in 2011 to seek asylum. His asylum application got rejected, but he stayed in the country despite the lack of a legal status. During his unauthorized residency, Danel got excluded from social services, apprehended for the lack of a legal status and detained in immigration detention. The Dutch authorities could not deport him, so he got released within the Netherlands. He continued his unauthorized residency until he obtained a temporary residence permit on medical grounds. Danel is severely upset by these occurrences and feels punished by the Dutch authorities.

This man's story is not an isolated case. Ethnographic fieldwork amongst 105 migrants without a legal status in the Netherlands reveals that these unauthorized migrants feel punished and hurt by their subjection to migration controls. Their experiences show parallels with the pains of those deprived of their freedom, captured by Sykes (1958) in the pains of imprisonment. This pains-concept contributes to understanding (the subjective experiences of) punishment, minimalizing the suffering it causes and evaluating the realization of its aims (cf. Hayes, 2015; Sykes, 1958: 130–134). Nonetheless, there was some doubt whether to use this concept for unauthorized migrants as it is usually applied within criminal settings and we want to prevent fortifying the criminalization of unauthorized migrants by using penal vocabulary (cf. Düvell et al., 2010). However, there are three arguments in favour of using the pains-framework to analyse unauthorized migrants' experiences with migration control, especially as Sykes (1958: 66–67) drew a parallel between prisoners and people without legal citizenship himself.

First, Sykes was not solely interested in imprisonment, but wanted to study a system of total power and focused on a maximum security prison as it represented 'a social system in which an attempt is made to create and maintain total or almost total social control' (Sykes, 1958: xiv). Also Goffman (1961) and Mathiesen (2006) show that social control mechanisms that are revealed in penal studies may have implications for other (total) institutions. This indicates that 'penal' concepts are not limited to prisons. Besides, there are similarities between the subjection to migration control and penal institutions. Engbersen (2001: 242), for instance, believes that the irregularization of migration constitutes a panopticon as migration control functions – and is being experienced – as an open prison. This panopticon is not aimed at disciplining or correcting unauthorized migrants, but at excluding and detecting these migrants in order to guard public institutions and labour markets. Aas (2014) calls this a 'banopticon' as the state's priority is on banishment and territorial exclusion. This argumentation's value has increased given the recent irregularization of migration and the asymmetrically incorporation of criminal laws and instruments in the migration domain (Aas and Bosworth, 2013; Legomsky, 2007).

Second, the pains-framework offers an opportunity to describe the unauthorized migrants' experiences with migration control and to study its consequences for those subjected to these controls, like Sykes (1958) did for prisoners. Sykes (1958) introduced his study at a moment that prison sentences were no longer intended to be painful and severe bodily suffering had been abandoned. He showed that imprisonment brought unintended consequences that constituted a profound and unprecedented attack on prisoners' personality, self-esteem and feelings of security. This made imprisonment as painful as the physical maltreatment it replaced, according to Sykes (1958). He believed that these unintended – partly acceptable or unavoidable – deprivations and their consequences had to be explored and should play a substantial role in the discussions on the functioning of prisons. As several studies show that current migration policies negatively affect several domains of unauthorized migrants' everyday lives (Bloch, 2014; Martinez et al., 2013), it is important to include the possible pains of being unauthorized and its consequences in the discussion on the functioning of migration control.

Third, examining the pains of being unauthorized may contribute to the current discussion on the boundaries of punishment. Several scholars argue that these boundaries have shifted under the influence of globalization processes while the 'punishment and society' scholarship tends to overlook the immigration domain (Bosworth, 2019; Bosworth et al., 2018a; Hannah-Moffat and Lynch, 2012). Punishment is supposed to consist of five elements: (a) it must involve pains, (b) in response to a violation of legal rules, (c) be directed towards the one who has breached the legal rules, (d) imposed intentionally by state authorities that are (e) acting under the authority of the breached law (Bosworth, 2019: 85–86; Hayes, 2018: 236). States usually consider the subjection to migration control no punishment as it concerns administrative laws that are not aimed at causing pains. However, the question is whether this statement is justified. Bosworth (2019), for instance, argues that it is not useful to dissociate administrative and criminal penalties given its convergence. Aas (2014), too, believes that the current focus on the absence of formal membership has changed the nature of penal interventions as these prioritize territorial exclusion over reintegration, something she calls 'bordered penality'. This is supposed to impact the system's effects and rationales and reshape the nature of penal power. Applying the pains-framework to the lived experiences of those subjected to migration controls may as such contribute to this current discussion on the boundaries, roles and purposes of punishment (Hannah-Maffat and Lynch, 2012).

These three arguments make us believe that the pains-framework is a well-suited tool to analyse unauthorized migrants' experiences with migration control. Therefore, these are central in this chapter. After notes on the pains and the methodology, the unauthorized migrants' experienced deprivation of 1) healthy and secure living conditions, 2) social and geographical mobility and 3) citizenship is illustrated. Then, the differences in experienced pains is explained. The conclusion, finally, addresses the absolute character of migration control, its (unintended) consequences and the implications for the understanding of punishment.

6.2 THE PAINS OF IMPRISONMENT

The perceptions of those being subjected to punishment are usually framed as 'pains' (Ugelvik and Damsa, 2018). Sykes (1958) introduced these pains to illustrate that prisoners were – despite the abandoning of physical pains – still suffering but now from the deprivation of liberty, goods and services, heterosexual relationships, autonomy and security. Over the years and with changing penal systems, Sykes' list of pains has been revised (Crewe, 2011) and adjusted to specific prison populations such as juveniles (Cox, 2011), fathers (Ugelvik, 2014) and lifers (Crewe, 2011). Besides, the concept has been used to understand the experiences of those subjected to other penal phenomena or situated elsewhere in the punishment continuum including community penalties (Hayes, 2015), open prisons (Shammas, 2014) and probation (Durnescu, 2011). These studies have resulted in a long list of pains over time.

Warr (2016) and Ugelvik and Damsa (2018) reveal specific pains of foreign-national offenders who are imprisoned in 'crimmigration prisons' in the UK respectively Norway, i.e. prisons where immigration purposes are added to – or replacing – traditional aims of prisons such as punishment, deterrence and rehabilitation (Ugelvik and Damsa, 2018). This concerns the pains of certitude, hope, legitimacy, discrimination, long-distance relationships and deportability of unauthorized migrants. Both studies reveal the indeterminacy that foreign-national offenders are experiencing as they do not know if and when they will be released, transferred to immigration detention or deported. They are dependent of the immigration apparatus for decisions in these matters, but communication with this apparatus is complicated given language barriers and officials being located elsewhere (cf. Kaufman, 2015). Foreign-national offenders feel treated differently in comparison with regular prisoners. This decreases the experienced legitimacy of being imprisoned and hampers them envisaging their future, something that is also complicated by the lack of proper rehabilitation opportunities (cf. Boone and Kox, 2012) and little opportunity to maintain long-distance relationships. These findings are in line with other studies on the experiences of foreign-national offenders and seem to be caused by the lack of a legal status and confinement in non-inclusionary prisons (Kaufman, 2015; Kox et al., 2014; Turnbull and Hasselberg, 2017). While these findings cover the experiences of criminally imprisoned unauthorized migrants, the question arises whether and what kind of pains unauthorized migrants experience due to their subjection to administrative migration controls.

6.3 METHODOLOGY[42]

The argument in this chapter is based on ethnographic fieldwork on unauthorized migrants' legal consciousness. Between March 2015 and May 2018, I followed 45 unauthorized migrants, meaning that I observed these migrants in their everyday lives and during their interaction with controlling institutions; repeatedly interviewed and informally talked to these migrants; and had frequent contact by phone or WhatsApp. Besides, I interviewed, extendedly informally spoke or observed another 60 unauthorized migrants who wanted to be involved in the research though on a limited basis. In all interactions during the fieldwork, unauthorized migrants could recall their situation in the country of origin and their migration journey, but also discuss their everyday lives, experiences with migration control and visions on their future. All observations and informal conversations are written down in field notes while interviews are recorded and literally transcribed. When the data were saturated, I ended the fieldwork.

I tried to create a heterogenic group of unauthorized migrants in terms of age, gender, country of origin, length of stay, migration motive and family situation given the at forehand assumed differences in their thoughts on migration control (cf. Burgers and Engbersen, 1999), Therefore, I focused on unauthorized migrants at different locations and in different stages of their unauthorized residency, including unauthorized migrants who were living out of sight of the authorities, were just apprehended by the police, living at freedom-restricted (family) locations aimed at removal and staying in immigration detention centres. I obtained contact with these migrants through support organizations, controlling institutions, and via via. The respondents were mainly based in the Netherlands, but it also includes migrants who I visited after their (forced) return from the Netherlands to Surinam (10), Nigeria (6) and Guyana (1). This approach has resulted in a research group of 105 unauthorized men and women who vary in age from eight to 70. They cover a variety of countries from all continents. Their length of (unauthorized) stay in the Netherlands varies from almost a year to 38 years. They have all different kind of migration motives including seeking asylum, reuniting with family, looking for better opportunities or a combination of these motives. Part of them has had a residence permit which was withdrawn or not prolonged, others never applied for a legal status or got rejected.

The data are analysed using Atlas.ti (qualitative data-analysis software). During the analyses, I noticed that – despite myriad studies on pains of punishment – academics are

42 The Methodology section is based on the methods section in the previous chapters.

not very specific about what constitutes a pain: some scholars consider all hardship that only one respondent brought to the fore as pain, while others only speak of pain when it is more profound in the data. Hayes (2018: 239) defines pains as 'a personal experience of physical, mental, or emotional suffering by a penal subject, arising from their punishment by agents of a criminal justice system'. He notes that pains include both 'intentionally inflicted forms of suffering and unintended consequences for the offender' (Hayes, 2015: 86). This is in line with Sykes (1958: 63–64) who used an inductive approach and mainly illustrates extreme forms of frustrations and deprivations that hurt prisoners in a maximum-security prison and are a serious attack on one's personality or self-esteem. This approach is followed in this chapter, meaning that if focuses on personal experiences of physical, mental, or emotional suffering that arose from the subjection to migration controls and were profound in the data.

This study is situated in the Netherlands. This country used to be known for its tolerance towards migrants, but its open attitude has made place for an excluding and repressive society characterized by restrictive admission policies, increased exclusion of unauthorized migrants, and extended capacity and urgency for migration control (Engbersen et al., 2006). Unauthorized migrants are excluded from formal markets and social services and only entitled to necessary healthcare, legal aid and – until the age of eighteen – education. While all unauthorized migrants are legally similar and equally treated, those who have minor children, are vulnerable or willing to return are – temporarily – entitled to state shelter in freedom-restricted institutions. Others are not. They make either use of all kind of informal networks to make a living or they turn themselves to charity initiatives for their basic needs.[43] During their unauthorized residence, these migrants may be subjected to all kind of migration controls including identity controls, police stops, return meetings and immigration detention and deportation. They are living in a constant state of deportability as they are forced to leave the Dutch territory while they are for varying reasons not actually deported nor leaving the country independently (cf. De Genova, 2002; Hasselberg, 2016; Leerkes and Kox, 2016, 2017).

6.4 The pains of being unauthorized in the Netherlands

The unauthorized migrants' narratives revealed all kind of pains that were caused by their subjection to migration controls. Three forms of deprivations were most profound.

43 Despite the lack of legal differences between unauthorized migrants, such charity initiatives are mainly open for rejected asylum seekers.

6.4.1 *Deprived of healthy and secure living conditions*

First, it concerned their deprivation of healthy and secure living conditions. This is mainly caused by these migrants' exclusion from the formal labour market and social services, the administrative fines for employers who hire unauthorized migrants and controlling practices that harden the migrants' living conditions and thrive them underground. This negatively impacts both unauthorized migrants' health and security.

For instance, the fear of being subjected to migration controls is very salient in most respondents' everyday lives, although some respondents report that controlling policies are not as strictly executed as is being argued (cf. Aliverti, 2013). This fear is being fortified by them observing others to be arrested, hearing stories about deportations and previous experiences with migration control. Although there are no legal differences between different groups of migrants, this especially applies to two groups of respondents. The first concerns black African respondents who feel discriminated on the basis of their skin colour (cf. Van der Leun and Van der Woude, 2011: 445).[44] The second group consists of rejected asylum seekers who are not living in a war zone and not directly subjected to violence anymore, but who fear deportation to the (assumed) unsafe situation they fled. Its impact is shown in a field note of a conversation with Hamza and Simin, an Iraqi couple who live with their three children in a freedom-restricted family location:

> 'That's scary for the kids. When they go to school, they see police to arrest families who are brought to a detention centre for deportation. This damages the kids.' (…) The family tells that they are temporarily safe given the current deportation moratorium, but afterwards, they could be arrested and perhaps deported like other families. The oldest daughter of sixteen has seen this before. She tells that she would open the window and jump if the police come to arrest them. Her mother tells her not to do that because she will die, but the daughter says she will jump anyhow. The mother hasn't forgotten her remark as it really hurts her.

Hamza, the father tells that their daughter has to cry a lot and is not sleeping properly because of the constant fear they are confronted with. It makes respondents – including non-asylum migrants – feel insecure. While this fear constitutes an enduring process (cf. Hasselberg, 2016), a few respondents has become numb though as they have repeatedly

44 Moroccans and other North Africans are – amongst others – prone to ethnic profiling (cf. Van der Leun and Van der Woude, 2011) and migration controls are supposed to have a racialized character (Bosworth et al., 2018b).

been stopped and detained in immigration detention while the authorities cannot deport them (yet). This mitigates their anxiety.

Nevertheless, almost all respondents prefer to stay under the radar. This withholds them reporting victimization to the authorities, despite initiatives of the Dutch police to provide such opportunities. A Moroccan woman is a case in point. She arrived at the age of fifteen in the Netherlands, after which she was hold inside and abused by the man who helped her to flee her abusing father. After several years, she escaped and slept some nights in the streets as she had no one around to support her. She was found by some Moroccan women who forced her to prostitute herself. She was afraid to escape and report her victimization to the police though as she thought – and was being told – that the police would arrest and deport her, something she feared given her previous experiences of violence in Morocco. More respondents said not to have reported victimization of criminal offences, labour exploitation or traffic accidents as they were afraid of possible consequences or found themselves in complex dependent relations. This shows that current controlling practices (indirectly) increase the migrants' vulnerability for victimization, exploitation and betrayal and deprive them of security (cf. Timmerman et al., 2019).

Many respondents say that these hard material and immaterial living conditions and the uncertainty that accompanies living without a legal status bring severe distress and negatively impact their health. They mention several health problems that not rarely started during their unauthorized stay or specifically in immigration detention. A mother who lives with two children in a freedom-restricting family location repeatedly narrates on the problems her daughter is – according to her – facing as a consequence of being unauthorized. Her – then potty-trained daughter – moved to this location at the age of two. Five years later, she is very angry, sleeps late and wets her pants again. She tells her mother that she is 'constantly very busy' in her head and cannot sleep because of that. The daughter is currently receiving treatment, but her doctor believes that the problems are caused by the lack of a legal status. This complicates recovery. Mainly rejected asylum seekers and respondents who are struggling to survive without a legal status report health issues that are – according to them – related to their unauthorized status or migration history. Also, research shows that living without a legal status – and the uncertainty and stress that come with it – negatively affects these migrants' health and may harm children's' physical, emotional or social development (Martinez et al., 2013; Scherder et al., 2018).

Unauthorized migrants are entitled to necessary health care, but respondents experience several difficulties in claiming these rights. They are not only afraid to go and see a doctor given their aforementioned fear for authorities, but they also face language and cultural barriers and may be rejected by doctors who are unfamiliar with arrangements for patients who cannot financially afford care (cf. Hintjens et al., 2018). Respondents in immigration detention feel humiliated if they are referred to a specialist outside the detention centre as their hands used to be cuffed and feet tight to a stick. This was for a few respondents reason not to visit specialists anymore as they felt not seen or treated as humans. This severely hurts them. As such, current migration policies deprive unauthorized migrants – or at least makes them feel deprived – of healthy living conditions.

6.4.2 *Deprived of social and geographical mobility*

The fieldwork further shows that unauthorized migrants feel deprived of their social and geographical mobility. Respondents tell not to know what the next day will bring given the everyday risks of being controlled, let alone where they will be in five years. This uncertainty that accompanies the migrants' state of deportability hampers them visualising their future as is illustrated by the story of Ramin, an Afghan rejected asylum seeker:

> 'The future is dark to me. Like. ... Like in a room in the night when there is no light, that's it like for me. I don't know. If you think... if it's light, then you can see there is a computer, here is a phone, here is a window, there is a plant of a tree, there is a painting. Yes, but if the lamp is turned off, then you don't know what exactly is where. (...) I just don't know. The future, I just don't know'.

Some respondents were not foreseeing a bright future in their country of origin either given the lack of perspective or security over there. However, they believe that their current perspectiveless situation is caused by restrictive migration policies. This makes them not only feel that their lives are on hold, it also withholds them from planning their future: especially rejected asylum seekers have lost faith that better times will come and feel blocked in their mobility given the little opportunities to develop themselves. Besides, some Black Africans say to feel disadvantaged and discriminated in comparison with other migrants who – according to them – do get a status, social services and so on.

The lack of perspective can be seen in the professional domain as unauthorized migrants have little opportunities to study after the age of eighteen and are excluded from the formal labour market. A 27-year-old woman who returned to Surinam after 22 years of unauthorized residency tells for instance that she really wanted to go to university after her graduation from gymnasium. However, she ended up being stuck at home, crying on the couch, and struggling with how to feel towards her parents. She gets very emotional when she remembers that there were no opportunities to obtain a residence permit and that she could neither study nor have a formal job. She started to isolate herself to prevent having to answer painful questions about her live. Respondents who were unauthorized in the Netherlands at the age of eighteen report similar stories and regret they have not been able to develop themselves. They are still struggling with its consequences, also after their return to their country of origin (cf. Khosravi, 2018). Something similar can be seen amongst adult respondents whose professional careers are blocked by the lack of a legal status and the exclusion from the formal labour market. These migrants are usually designated to low-skilled informal jobs such as babysitting, housekeeping, or working in the catering or construction industry. For some this is not problematic as they are less educated and only concerned with sending remittances and saving for their return, others are frustrated as this exclusion deprives them of a professional career.

The subjection to migration control also affects unauthorized migrants' relationships because 'it's always about the documents' (Ilyas): if a potential partner finds out the respondent does not have documents, the (chance for a) relationship is over. Some of the respondents – especially labour migrants – did start a relationship after their arrival in the Netherlands though, not rarely with someone in a similar position. While respondents were open to or even longing to be in a (scam) relation given the possibilities to obtain a residence permit, this applies less to starting a family. Many respondents without a family, often young men, said that they would love to have children but only once legalized. They felt that the opportunity to become a father was taken away from them by not granting them a legal status, something they regret. For a very few interviewed men, the wish to start a family – in combination with getting older – was reason to leave or consider leaving the Netherlands. While the majority of the respondents feel limited in their social mobility, this does not apply to all respondents: mainly female or labour migrants gave birth or were expecting during their unauthorized residency. On the one hand, it concerns planned births as not everyone felt hampered by the lack of a legal status, on the other these pregnancies were the result of the lack of contraceptives.

Unauthorized migrants have – in principle – the opportunity to end the pains of being unauthorized by legalizing their residency or leaving the country. However, this is more complicated in practice given current restrictive admission policies. Besides, their geographical mobility is limited as they cannot or will not return. For instance, an African migrant whose asylum was rejected wants to leave as he feels imprisoned and is wasting his time. Despite his efforts with the Repatriation and Departure Service and an NGO that offers voluntary return assistance, he has not been able to obtain a travel document that enables him to return. Consequently, this man is literally stuck in place. Although the Netherlands formally provides unauthorized migrant who cannot obtain a residence permit, it is in practice difficult to proof that one cannot return and is entitled to such a permit (Advisory Council on Migration, 2013b). The majority of the research group does not want to return though as they prefer staying unauthorized in the Netherlands over returning given their expectation to be subjected to even more pain in their country of origin.

Finally, the Dublin regulation hampers some respondents leaving the Netherlands and move (unauthorized) to another European country. They know that they will be deported to the Netherlands if they get caught or report themselves to the authorities. The fear of being detained and possible deported after travelling to another country makes them stay in the Netherlands. This fear is realistic given the experiences of a woman who went together with her partner and son to Austria, hoping to legalize her residency there. However, they got detained and deported to the Netherlands as they were registered here first. While some migrants do not consider leaving the Netherlands given their embeddedness in Dutch society, these rules limit the geographical mobility of part of the respondents. These respondents feel stuck in both time and place: they cannot physically move elsewhere given the abovementioned regulations and limitations while their lives are on hold. This constitutes a waste of time.

6.4.3 *Deprived of citizenship*

Finally, some respondents believed they deserved formal citizenship or at least a legal status in the Netherlands given their lengthy stay and socialization and did not understand that their legal status was denied/withdrawn. They considered it painful not to get what they thought they deserved. This is illustrated in the story of Guy, a 27-year-old Congolese man who came as a teenager to the Netherlands to reunite with his family. He has spent four years lawfully in the Netherlands and socialized in the country before his residence permit was not prolonged. Guy tells:

> 'I went to school, I was doing some … I was playing football in a team, a real football team. I was in [name team], I was playing there you know. And after the four years, you have to go back? It was a surprise for me, I didn't know about going back. I didn't know about detention, about deportation, I didn't know about all that. I didn't hear about that. I was not even like … my mind was even surprised, like: 'Boom, you have to go.' Ah! That was really, really, really, really the hardest moment for me'.

These migrants feel that they have become 'too Dutch' to be deported to a country they do not know or familiarize with (anymore). Their feelings of being a Dutch citizen resulted in a mismatch with their new everyday reality of being controlled, excluded and possibly detained and deported.

The fieldwork reveals three partially overlapping groups of respondents that experience this specific pain. This concerns youngsters who were born or grew up in the Netherlands, respondents with lengthy (unauthorized) residency in the country, and respondents who had (temporary) legal residency and – mandatorily – integrated here. These groups have in common that they are embedded in Dutch society. They speak Dutch, sometimes better than the language of their country of origin. Youngsters have been/are going to school in the Netherlands while adults have been/are working and sometimes paying taxes, volunteering or contributing to society in other ways. These migrants are embedded in Dutch society, but their residence permits were not prolonged or withdrawn as – amongst others – they became eighteen, their country of origin was considered safe again or they were convicted for a criminal offense. The end of their regular residency was difficult to accept for these migrants. These respondents felt frustrated by the Dutch authorities that – according to them – pretended that they had no right to be here while they felt a Dutch citizen. For instance, Safouan, a northern African man who came to the Netherlands as a child was after almost 40 years of legal residency being told that his residence permit would be withdrawn due to several convictions for – addiction related – petty offenses. He had plenty of opportunity to obtain a Dutch passport, but repeatedly postponed the application. When he was arrested and brought to the immigration police, Safouan was very angry when the police called him 'illegal' as he did not see himself like that. Eventually the decision to withdraw his residence permit was cancelled in court, but these experiences severely hurt him and felt like an attack on his personality. This story also shows the prolonged conditionality of legal residency statuses, something that increases these migrants' vulnerability and generates different levels of membership (cf. Bosniak, 2006).

6.4.4 *Differences in experiences explained*

The above shows that some respondents are frustrated in the extreme by being unauthorized and subjected to migration controls, where other migrants seem less affected by it. Although it is – barring exceptions (e.g. Crewe, 2011; Hayes, 2018) – not common to explain differences in experienced pains, this chapter offers three explanations for these differences. The first concerns the respondents' social embeddedness in society that helps them to negotiate the experienced deprivations of proper living conditions and mobility. Although all respondents are legally equal, their social incorporation varies (cf. Burgers and Engbersen, 1999; Staring, 2001). Respondents with a relatively strong incorporation and a tight supportive network were less confronted with pains as their networks helped to arrange housing and work, obtain health care, report victimization, etc. Consequently, these respondents found themselves both materially and immaterially in an advantaged position in comparison with respondents without such a network. The latter concerns on the one hand rejected asylum seekers who usually do not have a settled community to fall back on or whose community has less opportunities to support their unauthorized compatriots in a comprehensive and structural way (Dourleijn and Dagevos, 2011). On the other, it includes some respondents from settled communities as current controlling practices have increased the migrants' dependency of their networks while these network members simultaneously are not able or willing to provide this anymore. These migrants depend – if not entitled to state shelter – on caritas and NGO's. Consequently, they are confronted with harder living conditions which makes them less capable of negotiating the pains of being unauthorized.

The second explanation is related to the respondents' personal aspirations. Van Meeteren (2014) distinguishes three types of aspirations. This concerns 'investment aspirations', i.e. migrants who want to make money during their temporary stay abroad with which to return to the country of origin. The second group consists of migrants with 'settlement aspirations' who – regardless their legal status – aspire personal gain in their destination country. The third group concerns migrants with 'legalization aspirations' who aspire legalization of their residency. Migrants with investment and settlement aspirations seem less deprived as they do not consider legalization a basic requirement to live their lives, meaning that they do not put their lives on hold like migrants with legalization aspirations tend to do. Contrary to migrants with legalization aspirations, these respondents do start relationships or families, they do work and often under better conditions then they used to, and they are involved in social networks. This does not mean that these respondents do not experience pains at all. However, these pains seem less intrusive as these complicate but not completely obstruct achieving their aspirations. Those migrants with investment and settlement aspirations who do consider it impossible to realize their aspirations either left the Netherlands or altered their aspirations into legalizing their residency. Migrants with legalization aspirations report relatively much pains as they want to settle their legalization before they continue to shape their lives. This means that they usually put their lives on hold and wait with relationships and children and that they do not work, something that negatively impacts their social mobility. Besides, they fear that leaving the Netherlands will negatively influence their legalization procedures, something that affects their geographical mobility. This negatively impacts their health, while they are relatively afraid of putting themselves on the radar of the authorities by looking for health care. As part of these migrants with legalization aspirations believes that they deserve a residence permit given what they have been through, they feel not only frustrated that current migration policies hamper them realizing their aspirations, but are also hurt that they have to live under hard and uncertain conditions while wasting substantial years of their lives. This makes the subjection to migration control more intrusive for these respondents with legalization aspirations.

Finally, the respondents' perceived legitimacy of their subjection to migration control offers an explanation for the differentiation in the experienced pains. The legitimacy of current migration controls has repeatedly been questioned (Aas and Bosworth, 2013; Webber, 2012), but this study reveals a more differentiated picture than comes to the fore in the literature. Next to those respondents who emphasize the illegitimacy of (the execution of) migration controls, part of the research group does consider immigration policies, its enactment or their subjection to these controls legitimate. These differences in the perceived legitimacy are directly related to the experienced pains as the higher the perceived legitimacy, the less experienced pains. A contrary, pains are more salient if respondents perceive their subjection to migration controls less legitimate, something that Leerkes and Kox (2017: 923) call 'the pain of perceived illegitimacy'. Those respondents who aspire legalization in the Netherlands usually consider the Dutch system of migration control – or the way it is being executed – less legitimate in comparison with respondents with investment and settlement aspirations. Also, because migrants with legalization aspirations often believe that they deserve citizenship in the Netherlands, which results in more pains as this right is denied. They start to fight these decisions and continuously try to legalize their stay, something that severely occupies their thoughts and affects their health. Some have lost the power to fight these decisions and have withdrawn from both society and their personal networks. This makes that these migrants are frustrated in the extreme. This applies less to respondents with investment and settlement aspirations who are – already before their migration – aware of the (calculated) risks of being subjected to migration controls. They understand these migration controls and, consequently, experience less pains.

6.5 To conclude

This chapter shows that unauthorized migrants are experiencing several pains due to current migration controls of which the deprivation of healthy and secure living conditions, social and geographical mobility and citizenship are the most profound. The pains of being unauthorized resemble the pains of punishment and especially those of national-foreign offenders who have similar experiences with uncertainty, deportability and illegitimacy (Ugelvik and Damsa, 2018; Warr, 2016), especially if they did not commit a criminal offense. They live in a painful enduring state of deportability, feel blocked and have little opportunities to either legalize their residency or evade their situation. The Dutch authorities seem to attempt to create and maintain (almost) total social control over unauthorized migrants in this banopticon in the hope that these migrants will leave the territory (cf. Aas, 2014). This approach shows parallels with the expurgatory function that Mathiesen (2006: 141) reveals for the prison context and that refers to the state's use of institutions to maintain, control and conveniently forget about unproductive or non-accepted groups in society. The current migration control system seems to have a similar expurgatory function as it deprives unwanted migrants of full membership and places them out of society, something that results in further deprivations and pains for these migrants. The impact, salience and severity of the subjection to migration controls differ though, something that is explained on the basis of the migrants' embeddedness, aspirations, and legitimacy perceptions. These elements influence to what extent respondents are able to negotiate the pains and determine as such the dominancy of the lack of a legal status.

These constant and far-going efforts to control unauthorized migration bring several negative consequences for unauthorized migrants. First, the illustrated pains hurt and frustrate many respondents in the extreme and form a severe attack on their personality, self-esteem and security (cf. Sykes, 1958). Second, studies show that the lack of a legal status negatively influences these migrants' health while they experience difficulties with claiming the health care they are entitled to (Hintjens et al., 2018; Martinez et al., 2013; Scherder et al., 2018). Third, the unauthorized migrants' fear for authorities drives some underground, something that withholds them from reporting victimization or exploitation to the authorities. It puts them in a vulnerable position and limits the authorities' opportunities to prosecute offenders (cf. Timmerman et al., 2019). Fourth, the far-going exclusion may drive unauthorized migrants into the clandestine circuit (Engbersen et al., 2006). Finally, several scholars raise normative concerns on current control systems (Aas and Bosworth, 2013).

The question arises whether these consequences and the imposed pains are intended by the authorities as there must be some pains to speak – legally – of punishment (Bosworth, 2019; Hayes, 2018). Hayes (2018) presents a model of penal severity that is based upon the proximity of the experienced pains to the state's actions. This model can be used to discuss the rationale behind Dutch migration controls. Hayes (2018) distinguishes four pains, i.e. direct pains that are straightforwardly intended by the state, oblique pains that are assumed to be indirectly intended by the state, contextual pains which are unintended but causally related to the severity of the penal intervention, and entirely unrelated pains that coincidentally come to the fore. According to Hayes (2018), policy makers have – except for specific oblique pains – the opportunity to inform themselves on these pains. If his reasoning is applied to the pains of being unauthorized, it is seen that the Dutch authorities could and should be informed on these pains given previous studies that reveal the impact of living without a legal status and the pains and feelings of punishment it causes (Burgers and Engbersen, 1999; Di Molfetta and Brouwer, 2019; Martinez et al., 2013). Indeed, the negative consequences of current migration controls are only partly new, other experiences are just reframed as pains. While the Dutch authorities do provide – the legally required – provisions for unauthorized migrants in terms of necessary health care, education until the age of eighteen, legal aid, state shelter for vulnerable migrants, and reporting victimization, they seem to ignore these academic insights on the consequences of their migration policies (cf. Engbersen et al., 2006). This indicates that the authorities accept the collateral consequences of (possibly) being subjected to migration controls, including the pains it causes for unauthorized migrants who are subjected to these controls.

I believe therefore that migration controls are intended as punishment (cf. Bosworth, 2019; Bosworth et al., 2018a) as also other elements that are required to speak of punishment are assumed to be salient (Aas, 2014; Di Molfetta and Brouwer, 2019; Ibid.). Nation-states like the Netherlands may claim that these controls are for preventive or regulative purposes and not meant as punishment, but 'to re-label measures as non-punitive is often nothing less than a cynical subversion of the criminal process and its human rights protections' (Zedner, 2016: 4; see also Bosworth, 2019: 81). Besides, such a claim would deny the lived reality of unauthorized migrants who are subjected to these controls and feel punished (cf. Bosworth, 2019). The current system of migration control has as such expanded the reach of penal power and altered its justification as it is not about one's culpability anymore, but about one's identity (cf. Bosworth, 2019) and it is not only about punishment, deterrence and rehabilitation, but also about deportation (cf. Aas, 2014). This finding implies that the current 'punishment and society' scholarship is too narrow as it focuses mainly on macro-sociological or legally structured forms of punishment and tends to overlook what happens on the ground (cf. Hannah-Moffat and Lynch, 2012: 119). Penal phenomena outside the criminal domain – including the migration domain but also other (preventive) practices in the penal continuum – are largely neglected (Bosworth et al., 2018a; Hannah-Moffat and Lynch, 2012; Hannah-Moffat and Maurutto, 2012). However, states' expanding penal strategies calls for a grounded sociological understanding of punishment that includes – and questions – the rationales behind, purposes of and experiences with the subjection to all different forms of state power. In order to understand contemporary punishment, 'punishment and society' scholarship should look beyond the borders of both nation-states and criminal laws.

7 'Where is the justice?' Unauthorized migrants' perceptions of the legitimacy of Dutch immigration system*

Abstract

This chapter addresses the third sub-question of this study, focusing on how unauthorized migrants give meaning to the law in terms of empirical legitimacy. The chapter outlines unauthorized migrants' varied perspectives on the legitimacy of the Dutch restrictive immigration system, considering their association of the law with this system. Drawing upon Beetham's conceptualization of legitimacy (Beetham, 1991), the chapter delves into the migrants' considerations regarding the perceived lawfulness of the law, the justification of its execution, and their level of consent to it. The chapter reveals that unauthorized migrants may view restrictive immigration systems as legitimate. However, they unanimously assert that the current Dutch system suffers from a significant legitimacy deficit, lacking the inclusion of crucial substantive values. This deficiency comes at the expense of their consent to the system and contributes to the delegitimization of immigration authorities' powers. While immigration authorities strive to legitimize the use of restrictive immigration systems, a pertinent question arises regarding the justifiability of such systems. These systems may be legally valid but appear not to withstand the test of rightness.

7.1 Introduction

> 'This immigration system is no humanity! If you put unauthorized migrants on the street without shelter, without benefits, without medical services. … It's like sending them to their grave, to go and die. And this is what happened to us for the past few years!'

This quote belongs to Jacob, a 39-year-old West-African man who arrived in the Netherlands in the late 1990s. Ever since, he has tried to legalize his residence by repeatedly claiming asylum and using other legalization trajectories. The immigration authorities

---

* This single authored chapter is revised and resubmitted to the *British Journal of Criminology*.

rejected all Jacob's legalization applications, meaning that he was unauthorized in the country and – among others – subjected to frequent police stops, numerous return meetings, immigration detention ten times, a deportation attempt and a re-entry ban. Despite these efforts to make Jacob leave the country, the Dutch immigration authorities have not been able to deport him. Jacob tells me that he is suffering from severe psychiatric complaints which, he believes, are being caused by twenty years of unauthorized residence. He considers it inhumane that his residence is not legalized while he cannot be deported either, especially as the Dutch immigration authorities continue subjecting Jacob to the Dutch immigration system. The latter refers to a wide range of immigration laws, policies and practices aimed at preventing, controlling and ending unauthorized residency (Franko, 2020; Guiraudon and Joppke, 2001). Jacob, as well as other unauthorized migrants, consider these laws, policies and practices a comprehensive, multi-layered immigration system with serious legal, social and existential effects on them (see Chapter 4).

Several scholars question whether elements of restrictive immigration systems such as border enforcement strategies (Ryo, 2015), immigration detention practices (Bosworth, 2013; Breuls, 2022; Van Houte et al., 2021) and deportation policies (Cleton, 2022; De Genova and Peutz, 2010) can be considered legitimate by unauthorized migrants subjected to them. Some believe not, because the rationale behind these systems is generally driven by the interests of receiving states and does not automatically reflect the beliefs of hyper-diverse groups of unauthorized migrants (e.g. Bosworth, 2013; Van Houte et al., 2021). Besides, these systems – or specific elements of them – may be racializing (Turnbull et al., 2020), inflict harm (Bhatia, 2020) and have cumulative injurious and painful effects on unauthorized migrants (Kox et al., 2020; Menjívar and Abrego, 2012). Some scholars (e.g. Menjívar and Abrego, 2012; Soliman, 2021) therefore believe that states should be held responsible for the harmful and violent outcomes of such immigration systems. Courts have not recognized these systems as large-scale human rights abuses (yet) but there is an increasing number of studies that illustrate that unauthorized migrants perceive specific (control) instruments within the immigration system to be illegitimate (e.g. Bosworth, 2014; Breuls, 2022; De Genova and Peutz, 2010).

This raises the question of whether restrictive immigration systems at all can be considered legitimate by the unauthorized migrants subjected to them and why (not). This question has not been answered yet, but its answer may bring deeper knowledge of how immigration systems are enacted and understood by those subjected to it. Côté-Boucher et al. (2014), for instance, argue that insights into how different actors involved in the immigration system perceive their roles contribute to a better understanding of the everyday practices within the immigration system. While these authors mainly refer to actors who enact bordering practices, the effects of the immigration system are determined by their everyday interactions with (unauthorized) migrants (Van der Woude and Van der

Leun, 2017). This implies that insights into unauthorized migrants' legitimacy perceptions of the immigration system are necessary as well. Moreover, such insights may contribute to the understanding of the normative legitimacy of such systems (Tankebe, 2013; see also Chapter 8) – that is, whether these controls are in accordance with the rule of law (Jackson and Bradford, 2019). Furthermore, these insights help to understand – and perhaps critique – the use of power by the authorities (Bottoms and Tankebe, 2012), thus contributing to the development of more ethical, equitable and effective immigration systems (Ryo, 2015, 2017). This chapter, therefore, draws on the experiences of 105 unauthorized migrants in the Dutch immigration system to illustrate whether restrictive immigration systems can be considered legitimate by those migrants subjected to them and, if yes, what minimal requirements are needed to bring about legitimacy in the eyes of those subjected to a restrictive immigration system.

The study is situated in the Netherlands, a country that used to have an open attitude towards migrants. Since the late 1980s, however, the country has started to problematize the arrival and residence of unauthorized migrants (Van Eijl, 2012). Its lenient attitude towards unauthorized migrants has been gradually replaced by restrictive admission policies, a greater exclusion of unauthorized migrants and an extended capacity and urgency for migration control (Engbersen et al., 2006; Leerkes and Van Houte, 2020; Van Meeteren, 2014). While the Dutch authorities have not criminalized unauthorized residence itself, they have excluded unauthorized migrants from all formal markets and welfare arrangements and only allowed them access to essential healthcare, legal aid and – until the age of eighteen – education. Over time, some groups of migrants have (temporarily) become entitled to state shelter in different types of freedom-restricted institutions. Those who are (no longer) eligible for such shelters either survive in the informal economy and/or have become dependent on their social networks' support or on local humanitarian organizations (Staring et al., 2022). They may be subjected to several instruments of the immigration system such as police stops, return meetings, reporting duties, freedom restriction, immigration detention, deportation and others (Kox and Staring, 2021). While the effects of these instruments are not always as severe as proclaimed (Van der Woude and Van der Leun, 2017), previous research shows that it has become increasingly painful to survive without a residence permit in the Netherlands (Staring et al., 2022; see also Chapter 6). It is in this context that the migrants' legitimacy perceptions are being shaped.

In what follows, I first discuss the current understanding of legitimacy and the methods. Then, I illustrate unauthorized migrants' thoughts on the legitimacy of the immigration system in the Netherlands. I show that unauthorized migrants may consider immigration systems – and even restrictive immigration systems – to be legitimate if these are lawfully enacted and do justice to important substantive values. However, this is currently inadequately done in the Netherlands, which comes at the costs of the migrants' consent with the Dutch immigration system and contributes to the delegitimation of the immigration authorities' powers. Immigration authorities try to legitimize the use of such an immigration system. However, as I show in the conclusion, the question arises as to whether such systems can be justified as such restrictive immigration systems may be legally valid but do not seem to stand up to the test of rightness.

7.2 The current understanding of legitimacy

The term 'legitimacy' arises from the Latin word *legitimus*, which means 'lawful', 'appropriate' or 'just' (Tankebe and Liebling, 2013: 1). There is no consensus on exactly how to understand and operationalize the concept, since it has myriad definitions and operationalizations which are used within and across different academic disciplines (Noyon et al., 2023; Roberts and Plesničar, 2015). In criminology, legitimacy is assumed to have a normative component which objectively addresses whether powers, policies and practices are legally permissible, given the substantive criteria that specify how institutions ought to rule (Hinsch, 2010). This means that the authorities meet 'certain substantive requirements – say standards of justice and rationality expressed in a normative conception of legitimacy – irrespective of whether people believe that they are met or not' (Hinsch, 2010: 40). Besides, there is a subjective component of legitimacy which refers to the approval of authorities and laws by those who have to abide by it (Hinsch, 2010; Jackson and Bradford, 2019). The subjective component, usually referred to as empirical legitimacy, addresses people's thoughts on the justification of the authorities' right to hold power over them (Beetham, 1991). This includes people's perceptions as to whether the authorities act in ways that accord with prevailing notions of appropriate moral conduct and whether they exercise their powers morally, justly and appropriately (Jackson et al., 2015). It is this empirical notion of legitimacy that is central in this chapter.

Beetham (1991) – a leading social scientist in the legitimacy debate (e.g Bottoms and Tankebe, 2012) – conceptualizes empirical legitimacy based on three complementary and cumulative conditions. These imply that 1) the execution of power is in accordance with established rules, 2) that these rules can be justified by reference to powerholders' and subordinates' shared beliefs and 3) that subordinates express their consent to defer to the powerholders. The first condition – conformity with established rules or lawfulness – means that powerholders both acquire and exercise their power in accordance with established (unwritten and formal) rules (Beetham, 1991; Tankebe, 2013). The second condition – justification based on shared beliefs – prescribes the need for a certain level of moral alignment between powerholders and subordinates because, in the words of Beetham (1991: 69), 'without a common framework of belief (…) the powerful can enjoy no moral authority for the exercise of their power, whatever its legal validity'. This requires agreement between powerholders and subordinates on what authorities should and should not do (Beetham, 1991, 1993; Jackson et al., 2012). Finally, the third condition – consent – refers to the 'demonstrable expression of consent on the part of the subordinate to the particular power relation in which they are involved' (Beetham, 1991: 18). This may be both in words as well as in acts according to Beetham (1993), although it has been argued that assuming consent based on acts is too simplistic given the authorities' power to (unconsciously) enforce or incite people to consent without people actually accepting its use of powers (Harkin, 2015).

Beetham's conceptualization of legitimacy has been widely used in legitimacy studies (e.g. Hough et al., 2013; Jackson et al., 2015; Sunshine and Tyler, 2003a; Tankebe, 2013). These studies are usually characterized by a quantitative approach and mainly focus on procedural justice aspects – that is, whether people believe that legal authorities fairly and respectfully exercise their powers (Jackson et al., 2015; Tyler, 2006). Some scholars also include lawfulness, equal outcomes (distributive justice) and effectiveness (Sun et al., 2018; Tankebe, 2009) or focus on trust or moral alignment facets in their research design (Jackson et al., 2012). However, such operationalizations of empirical legitimacy are assumed to be too narrow, as they impose the preconditions of legitimacy on their research subjects (cf. Harkin, 2015; Jackson and Bradford, 2019; Tyler and Jackson, 2013). Besides, such a narrow operationalization of empirical legitimacy only limitedly reflects the concept's theoretical framing (Jackson and Bradford, 2019; Tyler and Jackson, 2013). For instance, it barely includes subordinates' beliefs in the research design while shared beliefs are considered important to bring about empirical legitimacy and may especially differ between groups and cultures (Boone and Kox, 2023; Jackson et al., 2012). Several scholars, therefore, advocate for qualitative studies that do more justice to (the operationalization of) the legitimacy concept (Harkin, 2015; Radburn and Stott, 2019). This chapter follows up on this call.[45]

7.3 Methods[46]

This chapter is based on ethnographic fieldwork with 105 migrants who (used to) reside between a few months and up to 38 years, unauthorized, in the Netherlands. Between March 2015 and May 2018, I followed 45 of these migrants over time, meaning that I hung out with them in their everyday lives, observed their interactions with controlling

45 These scholars also argue that a qualitative approach is better suited to developing and extending the current conceptualization of empirical legitimacy and call for a reconceptualization of it. I have addressed this part of the call elsewhere (see Chapter 8) in order to be able to fully focus on the unauthorized migrants' perceptions of the legitimacy of the Dutch immigration system in this chapter.

46 This methods section is based on the methods sections in previous chapters.

institutions, (repeatedly) interviewed them and had frequent informal talks, phone calls and WhatsApp conversations with them. The number of contacts with these migrants – and sometimes members of their social networks as well – varied between three and 20+. I also had one-off contacts with another 60 unauthorized migrants whom I interviewed or with whom I extensively and informally talked during participant observations. The migrants in the research group were between eight and 70 years old and originated from different countries and continents. They were situated at different locations and at various stages of their unauthorized residency during the first contact in the context of this study. While most respondents were based in the Netherlands, I included some who participated in assisted voluntary return programmes or who had left or were deported from the Netherlands to Surinam (10), Nigeria (6) and Guyana (1). The inclusion of these migrants was supposed to prevent any over-representation of respondents who consider the current system illegitimate and are – according to legitimacy theories (e.g. Tyler, 2006; Van den Bos, 2018) – less willing to comply with their return orders. Hence, this approach should provide insights into the differentiation within unauthorized migrants' perceptions of empirical legitimacy.

The fieldwork was conducted as part of a broader research project on unauthorized migrants' legal consciousness. The latter refers to 'the ways in which people experience, understand, and act in relation to law' (Chua and Engel, 2019: 336). This angle enabled respondents to discuss a wide range of topics during our interactions, including their experiences with the Dutch immigration system, their thoughts on the legitimacy of (specific elements within) the system and their ideas on whether restrictive immigration systems such as the Dutch one can be legitimate. The interviews were literally transcribed and all observations and informal conversations were laid down in extensive fieldnotes. Data were analysed by using thematic and open coding strategies in the qualitative data-analysis software Atlas.ti (cf. Saldaña, 2016: 235). For the analysis of this chapter, I drew upon Beetham's tripartite conceptualization of legitimacy. I first analysed unauthorized migrants' thoughts on the Dutch immigration system in terms of lawfulness, justification and consent. Following up on the aforementioned calls of Harkin (2015) and Radburn and Stott (2019), I moved beyond a procedural focus and examined how unauthorized migrants give meaning to these three aspects; I also openly explored migrants' other ideas on the legitimacy of immigration systems. This approach enabled me to answer the question of whether restrictive immigration systems can be considered legitimate by those unauthorized migrants who are subjected to them and, if yes, what minimal requirements are needed to bring about legitimacy in the eyes of those subjected to it.

7.4 Unauthorized migrants' legitimacy perceptions

My analysis showed that respondents have differentiated thoughts on the lawfulness, justification and acceptability of the Dutch immigration system. Yet, as illustrated below, they all believe that the current immigration system – or specific elements within it – suffer from extensive legitimacy deficits. This is not to say that immigration systems cannot at all be considered legitimate by those unauthorized migrants subjected to them. However, in the latter's view, substantive values are currently inadequately included in the Dutch system. This comes at the cost of the migrants' consent to the current system and contributes to the delegitimation of the powers of the immigration authorities.

7.4.1 Lawfulness

Unauthorized migrants attach considerable importance to the lawfulness of the (enactment of the) immigration system as comes to the fore in the words of the northern African Nasim: 'They [immigration authorities] have to respect the laws, that is important!' Beetham (1991) also believes that lawfulness is a first condition to bring about legitimacy. This involves, in his view, authorities both acquiring and exercising their powers in accordance with established unwritten and formal rules (Beetham, 1991; see also Tankebe, 2013). A breach of rules may result in an illegitimate use of power, which a substantial number of my respondents had experienced in their home and transit countries, where dictators, war, violence and money directly impacted on their rights. While referring to their previous experiences, respondents emphasized the value of the democracy in the Netherlands. Nasim, for instance, said he did not trust the authorities in his home country as they 'just do whatever they want' without considering people's human rights. He is more positive on how the Dutch immigration authorities acquire and organize their powers: 'The Netherlands are a democratic country; they have a constitution'. This makes Nasim, as well as other respondents, believe that the Dutch authorities have fairly acquired their powers. 'The law in the Netherlands? It is according to the rules', states Arnaud, a West-African migrant who is about to return to his country of origin. While scholars still debate whether the power to coercively enforce borders can be legitimately acquired (Abizadeh, 2010; James, 2021), my respondents recognize the Dutch authorities' right to rule over them by using a restrictive immigration system.

Respondents have differentiated thoughts on the lawfulness of the Dutch immigration authorities' use of their powers, although it should be said that their ideas on what the law entails do not necessarily coincide with how the law is actually laid down in the books. Some respondents believe that the Dutch authorities act in accordance with international and national immigration laws and standards. As Ali, an older African man, explained to me: 'The law tells them what to do: "Do this, do that". They cannot act differently to the law'. This point of view is mainly found among respondents who temporarily migrated to the Netherlands to enter the labour market. In contrast with other respondents, these unauthorized labour migrants do not expect a residence permit, as they mainly migrated to improve their living conditions. They initially had no experience with legalization procedures and little interaction with the immigration authorities, meaning that their previous encounters with the latter do not impact on subsequent perceptions of or experiences with the immigration system. These respondents are usually confident that Dutch immigration officers – to use the words of the North-African Abdou – 'just follow the rules that are created by the government', i.e. that these officers exercise these rules and use their powers in accordance with the law. Nevertheless, some do question the laws and standards themselves as these are, in their view, not always justified, as will be shown later. However, 'these are the rules of the government', as the South-East Asian, Mark, argues. While these respondents' views may change over time after disempowering experiences with the immigration authorities (see chapter 10), they initially do not doubt the lawful enactment of the Dutch immigration system. They say that they trust the authorities.

This view contrasts with the thoughts of other respondents, in particular rejected asylum seekers as well as others who believed they were entitled to a residence permit in the Netherlands. These respondents – who have plenty of experience of Dutch legalization procedures – claim that the Dutch authorities do not exercise their powers in accordance with established rules. While referring to international treaties and human rights standards, they argue that – in their view – it is unlawful for their admission and (continued) legalization to be rejected by the Dutch authorities. Dejan, for instance, believes that he is entitled to a residence permit given the lack of accessible healthcare for his severely disabled daughter in his home country in the Balkans. He claims that the Immigration and Naturalisation Service (IND) does not act in accordance with (international) laws by denying their admission: 'The IND doesn't use laws, they make their own rules. They do whatever they want. I cannot believe them, I cannot trust them'. These respondents consider the (enactment of the) system to be arbitrary and believe that they do not have sufficient opportunities to support their legalization claims or find justice in court – thoughts which echo the recent findings of Amnesty International (2020). IND officers themselves are struggling as well to come to decisions in which human values are adequately respected given the politically inspired legal framework they are bounded by (IND, 2022). The perceived unlawful use of powers by the Dutch immigration authorities negatively impacts on the respondents' thoughts on the trustworthiness of the authorities, while the latter are needed for the acceptance of and obedience to laws (Tyler and Huo, 2002).

Consequently, the latter group of respondents also considers all (repetitive) chain reactions that follow the rejection of their legalization applications to be unlawfully imposed on them, which confirms that previous experiences with the authorities influence one's thoughts on what comes next (cf. Van den Bos et al., 1997). Respondents refer to a wide range of measures such as the exclusion from social services, return decisions, immigration detention and entry bans. Amr, a North-African man who used to have Dutch citizenship but who was, he believes, wrongly advised to give it up, is a case in point. He was convicted for a criminal offence and held in a separate prison for national-foreign offenders, where identification and deportation are added to – or replace – the traditional aims of imprisonment (Ugelvik and Damsa, 2018). Amr was positive about his treatment in this prison but felt doubly punished as he resides in a more sober prison that offers fewer rehabilitation opportunities. What is more, he may face a longer sentence given his transfer to immigration detention if deportation from prison fails (Brouwer, 2020). He considers unlawful the imposition of a longer prison sentence because of the withdrawal of his citizenship:

> 'I think it is strange that someone who has always been lawful in the country and who has served his sentence is detained for another six months in immigration detention. Then, he is released in the Netherlands because he cannot be deported. That is not fair, not in accordance with the law. I have been in the Netherlands for 27 years, working and paying taxes. I was Dutch myself but, because of misinformation, I have a worse sentence! As I cannot stay in the Netherlands, I have to stay longer in prison…'

Such first- or second-hand experiences make respondents believe that immigration officers act unlawfully. Yani, a rejected asylum seeker from Iraq, believes that these officers 'play with the law', given the perceived inconsistency in the authorities' use of power. While the controlling actors may have proceeded in accordance with immigration laws in my respondents' case files and their use of power does not entail a breach of the rules, this is not perceived as such by the respondents concerned. They refer to an illegitimate use of powers by the immigration authorities.

7.4.2 *Justification based on shared beliefs*

Regardless of whether respondents believe that the Dutch immigration authorities lawfully exercise their powers, they (eventually) almost all believe that there is currently no adequate justification for the immigration system *or* specific elements within it. The rejected asylum seeker Adam, for instance, starts to shout when we discuss the justification of Dutch immigration laws, policies and practices: 'That is injustice, you know! It is injustice!' The experienced lack of justification for (elements within) the current immigration system is mainly due to the powerholders' and subordinates' lack of shared beliefs that underly the system, which is the second element that is assumed to be necessary in order to bring about perceived legitimacy (Beetham, 1991). This means that laws – or the laws, policies and practices of the immigration system in this case – are an expression of values that are recognized and accepted by both those in power *and* those subjected to it (Coicaud, 2002). After all, 'rules cannot justify themselves simply by being rules but require justification by reference to considerations which lie beyond them' (Beetham, 1991: 69). Without such a justification, rules suffer from a legitimacy deficit (Beetham, 1991). While respondents who came to work in the informal economy were (initially) less outspoken on the legitimacy deficit of the Dutch immigration system, their thoughts changed after (repeated) interactions with the immigration authorities (see also chapter 10).[47] Like other respondents, they eventually brought (multiple) substantive values to the fore that are, in their view, currently inadequately included in the Dutch system while being necessary for a justified immigration system.

Recognition of migrants' membership is one of the values that is brought to the fore by respondents who consider themselves to be members of Dutch society. These respondents argue that the system should only be used for 'real unauthorized migrants', which – as Dean from Surinam believes – is currently inadequately done in the Netherlands. While the immigration authorities considered all respondents to be unauthorized in the country, several respondents see themselves as members of Dutch society who should not be subjected to the immigration system. This also applies to the North-African Salim who, with his parents, arrived in the Netherlands in the 1970s and whose residence permit was withdrawn after more than 32 years of authorized residence, given his multiple drug-addiction-related convictions. We first meet at the police station shortly after his apprehension for his unauthorized residence. While referring to his lengthy residence and socialization in the Netherlands, he cries: 'They call me illegal, but I'm not!' The respondents' ideas on their membership fit the notion of 'denationalised citizenship', which means that (partial) membership is not restricted to formal, acknowledged citizens of a national society but may also be obtained on other grounds (Joppke, 1999; see also Van Houte et al., 2021). Such denationalized citizenship can also be seen in the story of Quincy, a Surinamese man who used to hold Dutch citizenship until Surinam gained independence from its Dutch colonizer in 1975. As he was on Surinamese territory at that time, he lost his Dutch citizenship. He argues that he was 'born under the Dutch flag' which – in his view – implies that the Dutch authorities have a debt to fulfil towards him

47 My strategies to recruit unauthorized migrants were initially solely directed towards those who had somehow interacted with the immigration authorities, meaning that almost all respondents somehow interacted with them. This impacted on their thoughts on the immigration system as discussed in Chapter 3 in more detail.

and other Surinamese citizens.[48] Quincy's as well as other respondents' thoughts align with Fraser's (1999: 28) idea that recognition of (full) membership is needed to bring about justice in the current globalized world. While states such as the Netherlands increasingly use different forms of probationary membership which may be withdrawn under specific conditions (Stronks, 2014; Stumpf, 2006), respondents point to the importance of the recognition of their socialization in the country, their cultural and social ties with the Netherlands and their contribution to Dutch society. They believe that these factors – over time – result in membership which should be recognized by the Dutch immigration authorities in order to bring about a justified immigration system.

Respect for peoples' security is another substantive value which – especially in rejected asylum seekers' views – is needed to bring about a justified immigration system. The Dutch authorities *have* ratified and implemented several treaties, directives and human right standards for the protection of refugees (Aarrass, 2021), which shows some level of congruence between the authorities and unauthorized migrants on values that should underly a justified immigration system. However, respondents argue that the Dutch authorities' view on security – or on those whose security is in danger – is too limited in everyday practice, which points to a lack of agreement between the authorities and unauthorized migrants on how to give substance to this value (see also Chapter 8). While the Dutch ministers responsible for the immigration system believe that their immigration system is strict but fair, respondents disagree. Like lawyers and migration scholars (Geertsema et al., 2021; Terlouw and Groenendijk, 2009; SVMA and VAJN, 2021), they point to the many barriers and the distrust experienced in legalization and court procedures that hamper them in obtaining asylum and force them to return to unstable and perceived insecure countries. They believe that this negatively impacts on their security, which comes at the cost of the justification of the current system. As Adam explains, for instance: 'Justice? What should it be like? Justice should be like, erm … Yeah. Once people really, really have problems, you for sure should look on the situations in the countries of the, erm, people and, erm … help these people'. He believes that this is currently not common practice in Dutch legalization and return practices. Adam points to the consequences: 'People are dying from that. People are dying there every day, every day. And then you want to send someone there. So, what will happen? That is what the Netherlands do not realize'. This is one of the reasons why Adam as well as some other respondents call the current system a 'crime against humanity'. This exposes the conflict between the migrants' internalized norms on who deserves admission for security reasons and the current implementation of the Dutch immigration system in everyday immigration practice.

48 There is currently societal and political debate on a regularisation scheme for Surinamese unauthorized migrants (see also Groenendijk and Den Heijer, 2022).

A similar conflict can be seen in the research participants' and Dutch immigration authorities' approach to safeguard the best interests of the child in everyday immigration practice. The Dutch authorities have – among others – ratified the United Nations Convention on the Right of the Child, which proscribes that 'the best interests of the child shall be a primary consideration' (see also Klaassen et al., 2020). However, respondents believe that, in practice, children's interest are subordinate to immigration laws, policies and practices, which – again – shows the immigration authorities' and respondents' differing thoughts on how to give substance to substantive values in everyday immigration practice. This particularly applies to respondents with children. The Surinamese Patricia, for instance, believes that immigration authorities 'have to look at the children'. While referring to the situation of her children, who are severely struggling with and psychologically damaged by their legal position, she cries that the Dutch immigration authorities fail to do so: 'If the child is central, it won't be like this!' Patricia and other respondents report both first- and second-hand experiences of children being subjected to unstable and insecure living conditions, separated from one of their parents, withheld legalization, retained in immigration detention centres and deported to unstable countries. These are – in their view – directly related to the immigration authorities' restrictive admission policies and repressive return and deportation practices. Like several scholars (Cleton, 2022; Kromhout et al., 2015; Liefaard, 2020; Rap, 2020), they question whether the immigration authorities do respect the best interest of the child in practice. Liefaard (2020), too, claims that 'the focus of migration control often lies heavily on safety and security, often at the cost of adequate human rights protection and the best interests of the child'. This comes – in the respondents' view – at the expense of the justification of the current immigration system.

Furthermore, respondents argue that a justified immigration system requires the inclusion of respect for unauthorized migrants' human dignity. This is also laid down in the EU Return Directive, which prescribes speedy and efficient return procedures for unauthorized migrants while fully ensuring respect for migrants' fundamental human rights and human dignity. This Directive has been implemented in the Netherlands. However, once respondents have (uselessly) interacted with the Dutch immigration authorities, they experience a lack of respect for their human dignity in everyday immigration practice. They feel that they are treated as 'criminals' while unauthorized residence is, in itself, not a criminal offence. Mandisa, an African woman who, together with her four children, was deported and dropped at the cargo bay of the airport in her home country, is a case in point. She said that the officers escorting her deportation were very friendly but questions the authorities' criminalizing approach towards unauthorized migrants: 'I mean, we are not criminals, my children are not criminals. (…) Why do they… I mean, why are we being treated this way?' This criminalizing approach comes – *inter alia* – to the fore when respondents are being apprehended and arrested by a myriad of immigration police officers, held in prison-like immigration detention centres, mistrusted in legalization and return procedures and have re-entry bans imposed for many years. The use of a criminalizing approach towards unauthorized migrants fits with the crimmigration trend – that is, the intertwining of crime control and migration control practices (Van der Woude et al., 2014). Yet, respondents consider this systemic criminalization of unauthorized migrants to be disrespectful, as the African Hakim explains: 'That is not fair at all! It would be fair if… if they would think about them as human beings'. The respondents' experiences transcend the notion of procedural justice, as they do not solely refer to their treatment by the immigration authorities, as the procedural justice concept implies (Tyler, 2006). Instead, they argue that an immigration system cannot be justified if its laws and policies themselves are criminalizing and disrespect people's human dignity. This aligns with findings from an earlier study on perceived procedural fairness in immigration detention in the Netherlands, in which an immigration detainee exclaimed: 'Moral? I'm in jail, there is nothing moral about that. I don't care about this procedure' (De Gier et al., 2020). This shows that the system itself should entail respect for migrants' human dignity in order to be justified in unauthorized migrants' eyes.

Finally, respondents argue that immigration systems need to be proportional and effective in order to be justified. Almost all respondents claim to have experienced a disproportional and ineffective use of immigration control mechanisms. They refer – *inter alia* – to their (far-reaching) exclusion from social services, the (repeated) imposition of immigration detention under prison-like conditions and the use of (lengthy) re-entry bans. Unauthorized labour migrants initially understand the authorities' use of such instruments, as becomes evident in the story of the Indonesian Henry: 'I understand that the Dutch authorities choose who may and who may not come to the Netherlands. I get it that they detain those who are not allowed to come'. However, they do not understand why such instruments are disproportionally and ineffectively used, as they have experienced in the Netherlands, especially as subjection to the immigration system is considered to be painful (see also Chapter 6). They argue that their residence is not legalized nor are they being deported while they are (repeatedly) subjected to painful immigration control mechanisms (cf. Staring et al., 2022). While their own attitude may impact on the authorities' efforts to deport them, there are often other factors that hamper the deportation process (Leerkes and Kox, 2016). Respondents therefore believe that they should not be continuously subjected to immigration control mechanisms. Jacob explains:

> 'There are three options, there are only three options for immigration laws: either you grant the person a residence permit, or you deport the person, or you set the person free. You have to set his life free. If you cannot help the person and if you cannot deport the person, then you have to set his life free.

> But if you are not granting the person a permit and if you cannot deport the person and if you are not setting the person's life free, then what is it? Where is the justice?'

The effectiveness of immigration detention in the Netherlands has somewhat increased over the years but almost half of the immigration detainees were – without authorization – released in the Netherlands and ordered to independently leave the country (Advisory Council on Migration, 2021). This makes respondents believe that the Dutch immigration authorities – in the words of Beetham (1991: 137) – cannot 'satisfy the ends which justify its enormous concentration of powers'. The unauthorized migrants believe, therefore, that the current Dutch immigration system suffers from a serious legitimacy deficit.

7.4.3 *Consent*

The experienced lack of justification for the Dutch immigration system comes at the cost of the respondents' consent with this system while the subordinate's demonstrable expression of consent is considered to be the third and final element needed to bring about legitimacy (Beetham, 1991). This does not mean, though, that unauthorized migrants can in no way consent to immigration systems which consist of restrictive admission procedures and strict control mechanisms. Respondents tell me that they do understand the use of immigration systems to protect nation-states. Arnaud, for instance, explains: 'The authorities need to protect the country, if we want it or not. My experience in the Netherlands is that it is a rich country. So, if the Netherlands opens the country for everybody, they will all come'. This applies not only to entry and admission rules but also to more repressive control mechanisms aimed at ending unauthorized residence. Elshan, an eighteen-year-old who has been socialized in the Netherlands and who believes that he deserves to be there, explains:

> 'It [the current immigration system] does make some sense because … if I were from the DT&V [Repatriation and Departure Service] and wanted to deport someone, I wouldn't be nice either. Not: 'Hi, would you please return?' No, I wouldn't do that either. Actually, I do understand them [Dutch authorities].'

Like others, he understands that the Dutch immigration authorities make use of immigration detention and other strict control mechanisms to counteract unauthorized residence, which is 'actually normal' according to the Indonesian Farel. One might question whether these respondents have internalized the dominant ideas and values of current immigration systems (cf. Anderson, 2013) but we can see that unauthorized migrants do not automatically reject restrictive immigration systems. They could consent with immigration systems and may even be in favour of more restrictive ones, which shows that immigration systems may be considered legitimate by those unauthorized migrants subjected to them.

However, most respondents do not consent with the *current* Dutch immigration system as, in their view, it lacks adequate justification and is unlawfully enacted by the immigration authorities. This makes them believe that the current system is unacceptable. This came to the fore in an interview with Joseph, an African asylum seeker whose temporary asylum permit was not prolonged. He was about to be deported but, while he was walking to the plane, his deportation was aborted given the unsecure situation in his home country. He was released from immigration detention but was not granted a residence permit in the Netherlands. He is upset that the Dutch authorities leave him in limbo without providing him any security guarantees:

> 'I am not a criminal. I only want a safe space to sleep, sit, eat and that's it. If it is better in my home country, I will call them: 'Okay, I want to return.' But the DT&V shouldn't push me all the time. Don't push me, push me. You know, it is a psychological game, they keep on pushing you, pushing, pushing. (…) They can't keep on pushing people as they might die. No! I will never accept that! It is a big problem.'

While some respondents – especially labour migrants – initially consented to the system, their disempowering experiences, as well as the realisation that important substantive values are lacking within the system, come at the cost of their consent with it (see also Chapter 8). A system of power that is chronically unable to meet the interests of the subordinate is subject to power erosion (Beetham, 1991: 209). This obviously has consequences for the attitudes and behaviour of the subordinate groups and may impact on the state's ability to secure cooperation from them (Beetham, 1991; Bottoms and Tankebe, 2012). This could also be seen in this study. Respondents not only expressed their lack of consent to the current immigration system during the interviews but also showed this in their behaviour. They started to circumvent the immigration authorities, mobilize the law, participate in protests and demonstrations, resist the immigration authorities and create loopholes to continue their residence in the Netherlands (see also Breuls, 2022). The withdrawal of consent may eventually result in the delegitimation of the power-holder according to Beetham (1991), meaning that the powers of the immigration authorities become subject to erosion and a large-scale state of turbulence may arise. While the experienced legitimacy deficit of immigration systems has not resulted in the collapse of society as Bosworth (2013) would have expected on the basis of legitimacy theories, this does indicate the risks of such an approach.

7.5 To conclude

This chapter started with the question as to whether restrictive immigration systems can be considered legitimate by unauthorized migrants subjected to them and, if yes, what minimal requirements are needed to bring about legitimacy in the eyes of those subjected to them. After having analysed 105 unauthorized migrants' thoughts on the empirical legitimacy of the Dutch immigration system in terms of lawfulness, justification and consent, I can affirmatively answer this question. Respondents do understand the authorities' experienced need to make use of restrictive immigration systems. They may consider these systems legitimate. However, they can only consent to an immigration system if it is lawfully enacted *and* justified based on shared substantive values. In the respondents' view, this is currently not the situation in the Netherlands. They disagree on whether the Dutch immigration system is lawfully exercised by the immigration authorities, but they all believe that the current system – or specific elements within it – lacks an adequate justification. The justification of the use of power is usually inadequately operationalized in legitimacy studies that focus on procedural justice (Boone and Kox, 2023; Harkin, 2015), while the lack of shared beliefs of immigration authorities and unauthorized migrants is taken for granted in migration studies (Bosworth, 2013). This study, however, has shown the importance of including *and* expressing such values as it provides insights into unauthorized migrants' motivations to consider (elements of) the current system to be illegitimate. It shows the importance of substantive values such as the recognition of unauthorized migrants' membership, respect for their security, the best interests of the child, their human dignity and a proportional as well as effective treatment. Respondents believe that such values should underly immigration laws, policies and practices in order to make them justified. As the Dutch immigration authorities have not adequately included these in their immigration system, respondents cannot consent to it.

The Dutch immigration authorities do justify the current immigration system (e.g. Breuls, 2022; Cleton, 2022). They have intentionally developed the system and strengthened their immigration laws, policies and practices in order to restrict unauthorized migration (Engbersen et al., 2006; Van Eijl, 2012). They created a thick immigration enforcement regime which combines strong enforcement interests with extensive enforcement capacities (Leerkes and Van Houte, 2020). Such systems are considered painful by the unauthorized migrants themselves and have harmful effects on migrants and society (Bhatia, 2020; Kox et al., 2020; Menjívar and Abrego, 2012) but the immigration authorities aim to end unauthorized residency by using this system. As such, they want to serve other audiences in the immigration debate – i.e. other people who are addressed by these policies (cf. Bottoms and Tankebe, 2012). The current Dutch approach may, for instance, serve the sectors of Dutch society that is assumed to be in favour of a (more) restrictive immigration system given their ideas that unauthorized migrants pose a risk for society (Van der Leun and Van der Woude, 2011). Besides, immigration officers themselves may be in favour of such an approach and legitimize current immigration laws, policies and practices (e.g. Breuls, 2022; Cleton, 2022; Cleton and Chauvin, 2020; Kalir, 2019). While some immigration officers see themselves confronted with situations in which it is difficult to come to human decisions given the political legal framework they are bound by (IND, 2022; Vreemdelingenvisie, 2022), the picture arises of immigration officers themselves generally legitimising the current Dutch immigration system (e.g. Breuls, 2022; Cleton, 2022; Cleton and Chauvin, 2020; Kalir, 2019).

However, the question arises as to whether the use of the current immigration system can be legitimized. Beetham (1991: 69) argues that 'without a common framework of belief … the powerful can enjoy no moral authority for the exercise of their power, whatever its legal validity'. This chapter shows that the common framework of belief is lacking in everyday immigration practice. The authorities' aim to restrict unauthorized migration has become dominant over unauthorized migrants' personal experiences and feelings, which has resulted in a painful and harmful system that is considered unjustified by those subjected to it (see also Chapter 6). This fits Hannah Arendt's (1976) idea of 'thoughtlessness' – i.e. the absence of thinking – that she observed in modern democracies, meaning that authorities or individual officers distance themselves from the standpoint of others and do not (want to) accept their policies' consequences. Subsequently, people's needs and suffering go unnoticed or are ignored. The latter seems applicable to the Dutch authorities as the unseen injustice as a result of the Dutch immigration system is outlined by Geertsema et al. (2021; see also Chapter 6). This raises the question of whether the immigration authorities can still any enjoy moral authority in this domain, even if the system is legally valid. Tamanaha (2001: 241) claims that 'every application of law or action in the name of law that increases human misery must be carefully scrutinized, regardless of whether it does or does not mirror society or enhance social order, and must stand up to a test of rightness'. By this he means that what is being done must be good and right. Given the unseen – or neglected – injustice and pains that are being caused by this system as well as the system's harmful effects, the use of this immigration system does not seem to pass this test.

Kuschminder and Dubow (2022) argue that: 'dehumanisation is neither necessary nor sufficient for an effective returns policy'. As unauthorized migrants may consider an immigration system to be legitimate if these are lawfully enacted and justified on the basis of shared beliefs, immigration authorities do have the opportunity to create an immigration system that is considered justified by unauthorized migrants. This would require a different approach though, which prioritizes the well-being of unauthorized migrants over the current one-sided restrictive approach. This goes against the current trend in the migration domain but seems the only morally right thing to do. Let me close with the words of Hakim:

> 'Laws are created by human beings. These human beings are responsible for the creation of illegals. But what are illegals anyway? People cannot be illegal. Everyone is born as a human being and they do not have documents when they are born. It is human beings who decide that everyone needs documents. (...) Where is the justice? It is not about documents but about humanity, right?'

8 Reconceptualizing empirical legitimacy of situations of severely conflicting social interests*

Abstract

This chapter contributes to addressing the third sub-question of this study, exploring how unauthorized migrants assign meaning to the law in terms of empirical legitimacy and how these meaning-making processes can be understood. It illustrates that the migrants' meaning-making processes should be understood in the context of substantive values, which, according to unauthorized migrants, should underlie a justified immigration system. The migrants argue that authorities should, among other things, uphold significant substantive values in the immigration system, such as their security, the best interests of the child, and their right to liberty. They support their argument by referencing human rights that are applicable to them, implying that these rights should be respected by Dutch authorities. While these values and rights are enshrined in immigration laws and policies in the Netherlands, they currently fall short in everyday immigration practices in the country. The perceived lack of respect for these substantive values leads unauthorized migrants to believe that the current application of the law in the Netherlands is empirically illegitimate. This underscores that unauthorized migrants' meaning-making processes in terms of empirical legitimacy should be understood within the framework of substantive values rooted in human rights treaties.

8.1 Introduction

Legitimacy literally means 'lawful', 'appropriate' or 'just' (Tankebe and Liebling, 2013). It is considered a core concept in the legal domain since a legitimate approach helps to assess the 'quality' of the execution of power by powerholders. In addition, it may foster public acceptance and consequently contribute to the viability of institutions (Beetham, 1991). Furthermore, the concept is assumed to predict subordinates' willingness to cooperate with powerholders (Tyler, 1990). Despite the importance of legitimacy, there is no

---

* This chapter has been published as Boone MM and Kox MH (2023). Reconceptualizing empirical legitimacy for situations of severely conflicted interests. *Utrecht Law Review* 19(2): 13–25.

consensus on the meaning of the concept. There are myriad definitions and operationalizations of the concept that are being used within and across different academic research disciplines (Roberts and Plesničar, 2014). The focus in this chapter is on empirical legitimacy which refers to the approval of authorities and laws by those who have to abide to it (Jackson and Bradford, 2019). This concept *subjectively* addresses people's thoughts on the authorities' right to hold power over them (Beetham, 1991) as well as people's perceptions that those authorities act in ways that accord with prevailing notions of appropriate moral conduct (Jackson et al., 2015). Empirical legitimacy is considered the opposite of normative legitimacy, which objectively addresses whether powers, policies and practices are legally permissible given the substantive criteria that specify how institutions ought to rule (Hinsch, 2010). This means that authorities meet 'certain substantive requirements – say standards of justice and rationality expressed in a normative conception of legitimacy – irrespective of whether people believe that they are met or not' (Hinsch, 2010).

Although empirical legitimacy and normative legitimacy are conceptually distinguished in current debates on legitimacy, it is generally acknowledged that both conceptualizations are equally important when evaluating the legitimacy of the execution of power (Hinsch, 2010). Both concepts can be brought back to Beetham's work who, in response to Weber's view that the acceptance of power is a sufficient condition for the legitimacy of it (Weber, 2017), designed a conceptual framework for the analysis of legitimacy (Beetham, 1991). Beetham's conceptualization is based on three conditions, that 1) subordinates offer their willing consent to defer to authority and that this consent is 2) grounded in the authority's conformity to standards of lawfulness and 3) a degree of moral alignment between powerholders and subordinates that is reflected in shared moral values (Beetham, 1991). This scheme has become common sense for every legitimacy thinker, including empirical legitimacy scholars (Tankebe, 2013). However, this chapter raises questions on the operationalization of Beetham's third condition in current empirical legitimacy studies as we believe that this operationalization falls short in cases of severely conflicting societal interests where moral alignment between authorities and subordinates cannot be taken for granted.

This shortcoming is attributed to two dominant characteristics of the conceptualization of empirical legitimacy in current research. The first characteristic concerns the overwhelming procedural conceptualization of Beetham's third condition – moral alignment of subordinates and powerholders – of the empirical legitimacy concept. While Beetham (1991: 17) writes that moral alignment refers to shared values of powerholders and subordinates and what 'expectations people have about what government should and should not do', the operationalization of the empirical legitimacy concept is currently dominated by the procedural justice school. Procedural justice scholars believe that subordinates will feel aligned with the moral values of powerholders in the case of adequately demonstrated fair procedures, which belief primarily follows from the work of Tom Tyler (see Tyler, 1988). Such fair procedures contain two main aspects, that is *quality of decision-making* and *quality of interpersonal treatment* (Sunshine and Tyler, 2003b). *Quality of decision-making* entails the extent to which subordinates are able to take part in the decision-making (voice), the perceived consistency of the decision-making and the absence of subjective preferences in the decision-making (neutrality). *Quality of interpersonal treatment* means that powerholders approach subordinates with dignity, courtesy and respect. Even though Beetham (1991) argued that socially expected standards in the exercise of power vary across time and space, the procedural justice findings are supposed to equally apply to men and women, regardless of their age, ethnicity or social class (Rothe, 2010). The procedural justice perspective has become very appealing to policy makers and politicians since it is accompanied by the conclusion that enhanced procedural justice may bring about greater compliance with the law and – in the context of criminal law – reduced rates of recidivism. Consequently, procedural justice has been extensively tested in legal decision-making contexts (see Ansems, 2021; Beijersbergen and Dirkzwager, 2015; Hinds and Murphy, 2007).

Secondly, it is argued in this chapter that the current dominance of deductive, quantitative survey research in empirical legitimacy studies is unsuited to map legitimacy perspectives in situations of severely conflicting interests, which comes at the cost of the explanatory power of the concept. Empirical legitimacy has repeatedly been tested in quantitative survey studies (Hough et al., 2013). These studies constantly confirm the relevance of the previously mentioned procedural justice elements. However, these studies lack the – in our view necessary – inductive approach to detect additional elements that could play a role in the construction of these empirical legitimacy perceptions. As Beetham (2013) himself argues: 'the empirical study of legitimacy involves a discursive investigation of the grounds or criteria on which a claim to legitimacy is based'. This is also acknowledged by procedural justice researchers of the first hour who argue that it is time to broaden the concept as the importance of legitimacy perceptions to shape behaviour has been sufficiently proven (Jackson and Bradford, 2019). Tyler and Jackson (2013), for instance, argue that 'the operationalization of legitimacy has been narrow, reflecting the limited manner in which legitimacy has been theoretically framed'. Although they notice the difficulty that can arise in a multicultural society when moral values between powerholders and subordinates differ, they do not really elaborate on how these conflicting values should affect the empirical legitimacy construct. Jackson and Bradford (2019) also stress that the current subscales of the empirical legitimacy concept should be approached as possible sources of legitimacy and not as constituent components of it. They argue that researchers should not impose the preconditions of empirical legitimacy if they want to be sensitive to cultures that might have different values. Several scholars argue therefore for a more inductive approach in empirical legitimacy studies (Harkin, 2015).

This chapter draws upon ethnographic research among unauthorized migrants in the Netherlands to illustrate the shortcomings of current operationalization of empirical legitimacy. It focuses on the migration domain, but the argument is also valid in other situations of severely conflicting societal interests such as the debates on climate change and the COVID 19 pandemic. Previous research has shown conflicting and constantly changing opinions in the migration debate (Meuleman et al., 2016), which implies that there are multiple audiences in this debate who hold different opinions and (are believed to) have different interests (Bottoms and Tankebe, 2013). This makes it a suitable case study to substantiate the abovementioned argument. After a note on the methods, the argumentation is presented in more detail. It is shown that – even though there is differentiation in the legitimacy perceptions of unauthorized migrants (see Chapter 7) – most unauthorized migrants who participated in the study feel illegitimately treated because, in their view, fundamental values are insufficiently taken into account when immigration authorities use their powers, even in situations of perceived fair procedures and outcomes. Based on Beetham (1991) himself and Wilson (1993, elaborated on in the discussion), these fundamental values are equated with the moral values that require alignment between powerholders and subordinates to bring about legitimacy according to Beetham's conceptualization. These values are currently not adequately included in quantitative empirical legitimacy studies with a strong focus on procedural justice. While such studies do include questions regarding whether authorities 'have the same sense of right and wrong' as research participants, these mainly focus on procedural aspects (Hough et al., 2013). This means that the outcome of these studies might be that unauthorized migrants feel fairly treated, despite them considering the use of powers by the immigration authorities to be empirically illegitimate. As illustrated in the discussion, this also has consequences for the normative legitimacy of the use of powers in the migration domain.

8.2 METHODS

This chapter draws on a bottom-up approach to understand how unauthorized migrants perceive the legitimacy of the use of power by immigration authorities which make decisions concerning them. It is based on multi-sited ethnographic fieldwork with 105 unauthorized migrants on their legal consciousness. The study included unauthorized migrants' thoughts on the legitimacy of the use of power by immigration authorities such as the Immigration and Naturalization Service (IND), the immigration police, the Repatriation and Departure Service, immigration detention officers and the Royal Netherlands Marechaussee. In order to get an in-depth understanding of the unauthorized migrants' legal consciousness, I followed 45 unauthorized migrants over time and additionally interviewed, extendedly informally spoke to and observed another 60 unauthorized migrants between March 2015 and May 2018. In all interactions in the field, unauthorized migrants could (among other things) discuss their thoughts on the (legitimacy of the) use of power by Dutch immigration authorities. They were explicitly asked what was needed for a legitimate use of power in the migration domain and why this was needed. As this was a rather complex question for some of the research participants, they were also invited to discuss their ideas on the execution of powers by immigration authorities if they were the Prime Minister of the Netherlands and what should be taken into account in order to bring about empirical legitimacy in this domain. The interviews with the unauthorized migrants were literally transcribed and all informal conversations and observations were reported in extensive field notes.

The data were analysed using Atlas.ti (qualitative data-analysis software). In contrast with the dominant approach in empirical legitimacy studies (see Jackson and Bradford, 2019), this study was characterized by an exploratory, inductive approach. The preconditions of empirical legitimacy were used as a sensitizing concept, meaning that the conditions that are known from empirical legitimacy studies functioned as a starting point for data collection and analysis (Blumer, 1969). In addition, possible other criteria that shaped unauthorized migrants' empirical legitimacy perceptions were inductively explored. This means that all information that research participants brought to the fore when they discussed the perceived legitimacy of the use of power by Dutch immigration authorities, as well as their ideas on what was needed to bring about justice in the migration domain, was inductively coded. It was observed that unauthorized migrants believed that several elements were currently lacking in the migration domain which came at the cost of its empirical legitimacy. As such, the study moved beyond the narrow operationalization of empirical legitimacy in order to be able to contribute to the current understanding and operationalization of empirical legitimacy. This has resulted in an overview of substantive needs that should be included in the execution of powers in the migration domain to bring about empirical legitimacy, as well as more insight into the importance of procedures in cases of severely conflicting interests.

8.3 Unauthorized migrants' substantive needs

Unauthorized migrants have rather differing thoughts on the empirical legitimacy of the use of powers in the migration domain. While some of the research participants believe that the current use of powers by the immigration authorities is or can be legitimate, the majority points at its illegitimacy. The perceived illegitimacy is not the direct result of a procedural unjust treatment as assumed in many studies in which procedural justice is considered to be the strongest predictor of empirical legitimacy (Hough et al., 2013). On the contrary, research participants argue that important fundamental values are inadequately incorporated in existing immigration policies and practices which, in their view, comes at the cost of its empirical legitimacy. They bring several substantive criteria to the fore that are needed to bring about empirical legitimacy. These needs can be directly derived from the moral or fundamental values that are distinguished in the introduction as one of the three conditions of Beetham's conceptualization of legitimacy. While research participants point at many values as can be seen in Chapter 7, this chapter is based on three values that help to illustrate that migrants' needs are currently not covered in the dominant quantitative procedural approach in empirical legitimacy studies, even though these do have an important influence on people's perceptions of the legitimacy of powerholders' actions.

8.3.1 Security guarantees

Security guarantees is one of these substantive justice criteria that unauthorized migrants bring to the fore. Research participants consider it important that Dutch immigration authorities respect their security when they use their powers over migrants. The Dutch authorities have ratified the United Nations Refugee Convention 1951 as well as the European Convention on Human Rights. This means that it is part of Dutch immigration laws and policies to grant asylum and offer protection to those who have real reasons to fear persecution, death, torture or other inhuman treatment, and victimization of random violence due to an armed conflict in their home country. Additionally, Dutch immigration laws and policies offer the possibility of granting a residence permit to migrants if admission is required by (other) international obligations, is beneficial to Dutch society or required for pressing humanitarian reasons.[49] Given the principle of non-refoulement that is laid down in the Convention against Torture and Other Cruel, Inhuman or Degrading Treatment or Punishment (CAT) and the International Convention for the Protection of All Persons from Enforced Disappearance (ICPPED), Dutch immigration authorities are not allowed to deport unauthorized migrants to countries where they would face torture, cruel, inhuman or degrading treatment or punishment and other irreparable harm. This implies that security guarantees are incorporated in Dutch immigration laws and should be respected by the immigration authorities (see also Aarrass, 2021).

However, research participants argue that the Dutch authorities' view on security – or who is in danger – is too limited and does no justice to those who need protection, which echoes recent findings of Amnesty International that asylum seekers are too often given 'the disadvantage of the doubt' when the IND assesses the credibility of the asylum seekers'

---

49 Par. 13 Aliens Act 2000.

claims (Amnesty International, 2020). The IND itself argues that officers see themselves sometimes confronted with complex, painful casefiles in which they are struggling to come to decisions in which human values are adequately respected given the politically inspired legal framework they are bounded by (IND, 2022). They do not always experience that justice and a human approach are important on an everyday basis (IND, 2022). Research participants, especially rejected asylum seekers, believe that the current Dutch system provides too few opportunities for those in need of protection to obtain a residence permit – in contrast to the Dutch authorities' view that their migration policies are strict though fair. The migrants refer to their own position as well as that of other people. While discussing the fairness of the Dutch admission policies and what is needed for a fair use of powers by the immigration authorities, Hiba, a Turkish woman who is about to return to her home country, explains: 'I want the Dutch authorities to give them asylum. If you have real security problems, you don't get asylum'. Bah, an African man whose asylum claims have all been rejected, argues that the Dutch authorities currently 'forget the human beings' by using a too limited definition of security: 'Justice is ehm… I don't know much about justice, but justice is you try to find out where the truth is. And when you find out where the truth is, then you have to go on with the truth, not to deny it'. However, currently, the Dutch authorities do not help people in need according to some of these research participants. As security is considered a pillar of international refugee protection, these participants – and especially rejected asylum seekers – believe that universal human rights are inadequately reflected in the current use of power by the Dutch immigration authorities. This negatively impacts on unauthorized migrants' thoughts on the empirical legitimate execution of powers by the IND and other immigration authorities.

A substantial number of research participants argue that security guarantees – or at least respect for their security – is needed to bring about a fair or just use of powers by the immigration authorities. This also comes to the fore in the story of Christian, an African youngster whose asylum claim was being rejected while he believes that his life is at risk upon return to his home country:

> 'Justice? What it should be like? Justice should be like ehm… Yeah. Once people are really, really in problems, you for sure should look on the situations in the countries of the eh people and eh… (…) People are dying from that. People are dying there every day, every day. And then you want to send someone there. So, what will happen? That is what the Netherlands doesn't realize.'

Christian considers Dutch immigration practices a 'crime against humanity'. In line with other research participants, he believes that the Dutch IND should include security guarantees in their admission and return decisions which, in his view, is not currently adequately achieved in the Netherlands. These research participants use a broader definition of security that includes the general situation in the asylum seekers' home country as well as individual elements that may threaten their lives. 'It's illogical law or breaking the law' not to include such elements according to Daniel who, after several rejections of his asylum claims, received a residence permit after all. We believe that this comes at the cost of the moral alignment between Dutch immigration authorities and unauthorized migrants, while the execution of power can only be legitimate to the extent that the rules may, in the words of Beetham (1991), be 'justified in terms of beliefs shared by dominant and subordinate'.

8.3.2 *The best interests of the child*

Research participants also argue that the interests of the child are not adequately included in the migration domain, which undermines the perceived legitimacy of the execution of powers by immigration authorities. The Dutch authorities have ratified the United Nations Convention on the Rights of the Child. This Convention applies to all children within the jurisdiction of the state, including unauthorized children. Article 3(1) of this Convention provides that 'in all actions concerning children, whether undertaken by public or private social welfare institutions, courts of law, administrative authorities or legislative bodies, the best interests of the child shall be a primary consideration'. In line with this Convention, unauthorized migrants who participated in our research believe that the exercise of power by immigration authorities should consider the best interests of the child. However, as with the case of the perceived lack of security guarantees by immigration authorities, research participants argue that the best interests of the child are not or not adequately incorporated in practice when immigration authorities exercise their powers despite it being laid down in immigration laws and policies.

Research participants bring several examples to the fore in which immigration laws prevail over the best interests of the child. Among other examples, they share stories that are related to Dutch admission policies which allow children to be taken away from one of their parents. Migrants who were deported to Nigeria and Surinam, for instance, discussed that they were separated from their children and not allowed to return to the Netherlands as they did not meet Dutch admission criteria. This also applies to a Nigerian, Azibo, who was deported while his son was still in the Netherlands. He facetimes with his son on a weekly basis. Every time, his son asks him when his father will come to the Netherlands again. While the father would like nothing more than to be reunited with his son, he is not allowed to return to the Netherlands as his wife does not meet the income requirements for family reunification.[50] Consequently, his son has to grow up without his father being around. Regina, a Surinamese woman who has been deported and is not allowed to visit her daughter in the Netherlands, believes that her daughter 'will never forget that'. Furthermore, research participants point at the living conditions for unauthorized children in the Netherlands. Dutch authorities are no longer allowed to send children to live on the streets given a legal ruling of 2011. Consequently, Dutch authorities have arranged freedom-restricted family locations, aimed at removal, for children and their parents who are not authorized to be in the Netherlands. The living conditions at these locations have repeatedly been criticized for not being in the best interests of the child and for causing anxiety among children (Kromhout et al., 2015). This also applies to the conditions in immigration detention centres for minors which also cause anxiety and stress among children there (see also Chapter 6). This, among other things, makes Kromhout, Kloppenburg and Van Doorn (2015) believe that Dutch immigration authorities are not fulfilling their legal obligations towards unauthorized minors (see also Advisory Council on Migration, 2023; Klaassen et al., 2020).

Research participants say that the best interests of the child should be considered first and foremost when immigration authorities exercise their powers, otherwise there cannot be justice. They do not understand why children are treated in this unfair way in the Netherlands, especially as the best interests of the child are laid down in Dutch immigration laws and policies. Several research participants believe that the lack of respect for the best interests of the child harms the empirical legitimacy of the use of powers by Dutch immigration authorities. Rachel, a Surinamese woman whose children hold Dutch citizenship while she is not authorized to be in the Netherlands, is a case in point. She explains that her Dutch children are staying with her in a freedom-restricted family location aimed at her removal from the Netherlands, only because she is not allowed to remain in the Netherlands. Rachel believes that this hampers the opportunities of her children in terms of schooling, social life and safety which is not in their best interests:

> 'I cannot understand that this happens in the Netherlands. I believe, whatever I think of the Netherlands, I believe that a child should be central. But that's not the case. If a child is central... Do you know how many Dutch children... How many Dutch children and their parents are victims [of Dutch immigration laws] here? You know? They really should look at it, because a child cannot be central in their policies if they are acting like this. The Netherlands should

50 The Dutch authorities have introduced a wide range of pre-admission requirements in order to stimulate migrants to apply for admission while still being in their home country. Due to these new admission rules, migrants have to meet extra requirements in terms of visa restrictions, study and work contracts, proof of relationships, income requirements, civic integration tests and financial fees in order to be allowed to travel to the Netherlands and legally reside here (cf. Bonjour, 2010; Van Eijl, 2012).

> first… (…) Look, my child is here, because of me. Because I don't have a residence permit, because I don't have a personal service number. Because of that, my child doesn't receive child benefits, she cannot enjoy the Netherlands, I don't get that…'

Research participants experience that the best interests of the child are subordinate to immigration laws. Liefaard (2020), too, believes that 'the focus of migration control often lies heavily on safety and security, often at the cost of adequate human rights protection and the best interests of the child serving as a primary consideration for governments, policy makers and judiciaries.' While he refers to normative legitimacy, our study shows that the dominance of immigration laws over the best interests of the child comes at the cost of its empirical legitimacy as well. Research participants consider that the use of powers by Dutch immigration authorities is unfair and unjustified because the best interests of children are not put first and foremost when these authorities use their powers.

8.3.3 *The right to liberty*

A third value that research participants urgently bring to the fore is their right to liberty as they may only be deprived of their liberty on the basis of international legal standards. Unauthorized migrants refer here to the authorities' use of immigration detention, that is an administrative measure to ensure that migrants cannot abscond while preparations for deportation are being made (Cornelisse, 2010). Although most research participants acknowledge the legitimacy of immigration detention as such, they argue that it is now used by the Dutch authorities in an inhuman, inappropriate and ineffective way which does not align with international legal standards. Article 5 of the European Convention for the Protection of Human Rights and Fundamental Freedoms, for instance, states that everyone has the right to liberty and security and that this right may only be withdrawn in accordance with a procedure prescribed by law if it is, among other things, needed to prevent unauthorized entry into a country or if action is being taken with a view to deportation. Additionally, international human rights standards such as the EU Returns Directive,[51] European soft law measures as well as court rulings of the European Court for Human Rights state that immigration detention is a last resort. It means that immigration detention may only be used with the utmost reluctance if needed to achieve the unauthorized migrants' deportation and it should be used for a limited amount of time. In addition, unauthorized migrants may not be held under prison-like conditions. The

51 Directive 2008/115/EC of 16 December 2008 of the European Parliament and of the Council on common standards and procedures in Member States for returning illegally staying third-country nationals OJ L348/24.

detention conditions should fit the purpose of detention and entail a minimum of restrictions. Additionally, the UN Working Group on Arbitrary Detention (2008) has stated in its position document based on international law, as well as its own jurisprudence, that:

> 'The irregular entry and stay in a country by migrants should not be treated as a criminal offence, and the criminalization of irregular migration will therefore always exceed the legitimate interests of States in protecting their territories and regulating irregular migration flows. Migrants must not be qualified or treated as criminals or viewed only from the perspective of national or public security and/or health.'

The Dutch authorities have ratified these instruments and implemented them in their national immigration laws.

However, research participants argue that Dutch immigration authorities do not respect their right to liberty given the current use of immigration detention. They provide several examples to illustrate that, in their view, the organization of immigration detention in the Netherlands does not align with the human right standards discussed above. Their point of view is supported by a wide range of academics, NGOs and advisory committees, all of whom have criticized Dutch immigration detention policies in recent years (see for example Amnesty International, 2018a, 2018b; Cornelisse, 2010; De Nationale Ombudsman, 2020; Leerkes and Kox, 2017). First, they point at the frequent use of immigration detention in the Netherlands. While the number of immigration detainees decreased during the period of the fieldwork (Klaassen and Rodrigues, 2021), research participants believe – in line with NGOs and academics – that Dutch immigration authorities too often and too easily make use of immigration detention where alternatives are available. This is considered inhuman and inappropriate as the unauthorized migrants have not committed a crime and detention does have an injurious character. Second, unauthorized migrants believe that the detention conditions are not suitable for unauthorized migrants and are not in accordance with what is required on the basis of international human rights standards. This also comes to the fore in an interview with Christian. He has been detained in immigration detention many times. While discussing the fairness of the Dutch immigration system, he declared:

> 'It is like a prison, it is the same as a prison because doors are closed and only temporarily open. It is the same like in a prison, because it is closed and open. You cannot go outside, you cannot even... (...) There is no difference with jail there, it is jail only, you know? (...) It is a crime against human, against humanity. It is a violation, that's it. But some people here, they don't know.'

Several research participants argue that if the immigration authorities want to make use of immigration detention, they should carry out the measure in such a way that it suits the reason for the unauthorized migrants' deprivation of liberty. Third, research participants consider the use of immigration detention useless or ineffective, and coming at the cost of fairness. While the effectiveness of immigration detention in the Netherlands has increased over the years, almost half of the immigration detainees were released in the Netherlands without being granted residency rights (AZCV, 2022).[52] They are provided with a train ticket to the place of their apprehension and ordered to leave the country within 24 hours, something that is not realistic for most of them. This means that they are offered no solution but that they continue their unauthorized residence in the Netherlands.

The lack of a solution in the authorities' use of power is considered a form of injustice by the research participants, especially as they are excluded from most social services, possibly subjected to migration controls and confronted with several forms of deprivation that are hard to cope with (Kox et al., 2020; Kox and Staring, 2021). They feel stuck in the Netherlands where they are not allowed to reside, while they believe they cannot return to their home country or another country (see also Chapter 6). This applies in particular to elderly unauthorized migrants with lengthy unauthorized residence (Staring et al., 2022). They believe that the Dutch authorities should offer a solution and should not leave them in limbo as this causes injustice. Research participants believe that Dutch immigration authorities should protect and respect their right to liberty, otherwise the use of powers by these authorities is not fair. This aligns with the ideas of Rodrigues (2016) who argues that the authorities are responsible for all unauthorized migrants whom they cannot actually deport to their home country. Research participants explain that the protection of and respect for their liberty entails that they are treated as human beings and provided with some solutions. A labour migrant from the Philippines is a case in point. While he understands that the Netherlands sets rules to regulate migration and that not everyone is allowed to reside in the Netherlands, he considers the current Dutch approach to be unjustified: 'I think it is injustice you know to catch them [unauthorized migrants] and then they do just like they are criminal. I think that is not human, you know. Because they also have human rights to live'. The respondents' ideas are reinforced when Dutch immigration authorities apply their powers in vain, as such application does not result in legalization or deportation in their particular situation. This aligns with the ideas of Beetham who argues that authorities should be able to 'satisfy the ends which justify its enormous concentration of powers' (see also Tankebe, 2013). According to a substantial number of research participants, this is currently not the situation in the Netherlands,

52 This number refers to immigration detainees without a 'Dublin claim', meaning that they are not deported to another European country which is responsible for their legalization trajectory (Advisory Council on Migration, 2021).

given the ongoing infringement in their everyday lives by the immigration authorities which do not offer them a solution.

8.4 To conclude

This chapter started with a reference to Beetham's influential work in which he distinguished three conditions for a legitimate use of power by powerholders, that is consent, legality and moral alignment between powerholders and subordinates. It raised the question whether the third element – moral alignment between powerholders and subordinates – has been sufficiently incorporated in current empirical legitimacy studies given the strong focus on procedural elements. While these studies do include questions on whether authorities 'have the same sense of right and wrong' (Tankebe, 2013) as their research subjects, it seems that researchers in this field take the fulfilment of this element as a given, without feeling the need to explicitly operationalize or test it. Tankebe, for example, refers to Wilson's rise of universalism to state that all modern democratic societies are characterized by a universalistic ideology of human equality and takes this idea for granted in the subscales of the empirical legitimacy construction (Wilson, 1993). Although he sees that the universalist ideal is sometimes poorly fulfilled for certain groups in society, this does not fundamentally affect this common legitimacy framework. Tyler and Jackson (2013) do point at the difficulties that can arise when powerholders and subordinates do not share the same moral values but, in line with Tankebe, do not really elaborate on this possible conflict and hardly include it in their quantitative approach. This chapter shows that this poor operationalization of moral alignment comes at the cost of the explanatory power of current empirical legitimacy study.

This claim is substantiated on the basis of ethnographic fieldwork among unauthorized migrants. The data show that it is precisely this lack of moral alignment between powerholders and subordinates that can prevent feelings of a legitimate use of power by Dutch immigration authorities towards many of the unauthorized migrants who participated in this study. While the chapter shows there is congruence between powerholders and unauthorized migrants on the importance of certain values, these values are – in the view of our research participants – very poorly or inadequately implemented in immigration laws, policies and practices. This hampers a legitimate use of powers by the immigration authorities in the eyes of unauthorized migrants. This bottom-up approach shows that powerholders and subordinates have different views on how these values should be interpreted and what moral obligations follow from them. While Dutch immigration authorities have implemented security guarantees, the best interests of the child and the unauthorized migrants' right to liberty in national immigration laws and policies, research participants argue that these are not adequately implemented in practice. According to the migrants, immigration authorities do not take these values into account when they use their powers towards unauthorized migrants, meaning that these migrants feel adversely affected in their sense of justice. Procedural politeness cannot compensate for the perceived negligence of fundamental values in the authorities' use of powers.

One can seriously wonder whether these findings add something new to the already existing approaches in legitimacy research. While procedural elements are most commonly used to operationalize moral alignment in empirical legitimacy studies, there are also studies which include other elements in their operationalization of empirical legitimacy, that is perceived lawfulness, fair outcomes and effectiveness of the use of powers (Hough et al., 2013). It may be wondered whether these elements would help us to understand the unauthorized migrants' experiences. For instance, the different valuation of the extent to which security guarantees are included in decision-making about admission and return, may also be explained by a different interpretation of the international and national immigration laws and therefore by perceived lawfulness as a subscale of empirical legitimacy. It could also be concluded from these findings that unauthorized migrants simply prioritize outcome justice over procedural justice, because the (desired) result of giving more weight to their need for security will usually be that they receive permission to stay in the Netherlands. Contrary to the general idea that procedural justice dominates empirical legitimacy judgements, Tankebe (2009) found effectiveness to be more important in shaping cooperative behaviour than procedural justice which he explained through the history of violence and abuse by the police in colonial and post-colonial periods. Despite these already existing additions and nuances in the empirical justice debate, the added value of the insights presented in this chapter are threefold.

First, it has repeatedly been questioned whether the concept of empirical legitimacy – and its strong focus on procedural justice – fits the current globalized and polarized world. Tankebe and Liebling (2013), for instance, state that, despite the great insights which the procedural justice literature has brought with regard to people's normative expectations about power, there is a need to develop a broader theorization. Empirical legitimacy criteria – and the importance of these criteria – could differ between and within societies and depend on the way in which power is organized (Bottoms and Tankebe, 2012). This aligns with the ideas of Fraser (2005) who points at the importance of redistribution, recognition and representation moving beyond the territorial borders of the state to bring about justice in society. This chapter contributes to this broader theorization, by bringing to the fore unauthorized migrants' substantive expectations on the execution of power of a group of subordinates that normally stays under the surface but can be regarded as the weaker party in the social and political conflictual domain that is migration. While unauthorized migrants are directly confronted by immigration laws, policies and practices, their voices are hardly ever included in the debate on its legitimacy.

Second, while it is often assumed that empirical legitimacy and procedural justice findings seem to hold for minorities as well (see the Introduction of this chapter), it may be questioned whether quantitative surveys adequately access hidden groups in society which might hold different ideas and perceptions on empirical legitimacy. While quantitative scholars test for and correct missing groups in their data sets, we wonder whether the group central in this chapter is sufficiently represented in these surveys, or whether a group of sufficient size could be encouraged to participate in this type of research if one wanted to conduct a separate survey on their perceptions. After all, they are a hidden group in society and may not speak the destination country's language, which complicates reaching out to such a group to fill out a survey. Since the expertise of both authors is not in quantitative research, we seriously wonder whether it is possible to include such hidden groups as unauthorized migrants and others in a quantitative research design.

Third, these findings should also have consequences for the normative legitimacy claims that are made by powerholders in the migration domain. This chapter shows that moral alignments between powerholders and subordinates with regard to important fundamental values such as security guarantees, the best interests of the child and the right of liberty, are not or not adequately respected in the eyes of the subordinates. Although the Universalist ideal, as expressed by Wilson (1993), should protect nationals and non-nationals equally against infringements of rights that follow from these moral values, it is not experienced as such by the research participants. Despite this, decisions made against them with regard to topics discussed in the empirical part of this chapter are supported by the highest political institutions and courts. For Bosworth (2013), this is reason enough to step out of the existing legitimacy discourse in an attempt to understand the functioning of immigration detention centres. She argues that the concept of legitimacy 'with its intellectual roots in liberal communitarian societies' is simply not useful as a tool to either understand or critique the legitimacy of immigration detention centres. Following Beetham (1991), she reasons that these legitimacy judgements need 'congruence between a given system of power and the beliefs, values, and expectations of the subordinates' and in her eyes this congruence is missing in mobile, unbounded institutions such as immigration detention centres (Bosworth, 2013). Although she admits that a simple rejection of these institutions from a legitimate perspective would be a more obvious response to her observations of the daily routine in these institutions, she would not know 'what legitimacy claims she should make given the transitional and no man's land character of these institutions of which the residents don't seem to be fellows of a single political community'. Although we can go along with the inability that Bosworth feels when she compares the situation of unauthorized migrants to the existing frameworks of legitimacy, as academics we do not settle for that. Qualitative and quantitative researchers should jointly try to further refine these frameworks, so that the minority views of hidden groups in society about conflicting social interests can be better brought to light. In time this will hopefully also lead to a different interpretation of the normative frameworks of legitimacy, which still breathes a promise of universalism but for the time being mainly seems to protect the interests of the dominant majority.

9 Pressured into a preference to leave? A study on the 'specific' deterrent effects and perceived legitimacy of immigration detention*

Abstract

This chapter contributes to addressing the fourth and final sub-question on how unauthorized migrants' understandings of, experiences with, and meaning-making processes toward the law are translated into interactions with the law. The chapter relies on a different dataset, as will be discussed in the methods section of this chapter, but it is included in this book as its insights help me to find answers to the intriguing puzzle of how the law matters to unauthorized migrants. The chapter reveals that unauthorized migrants generally view immigration detention as a painful and distressing experience, partly due to its perceived illegitimacy. However, most migrants do not develop a preference to return to their country of citizenship in the hope of ending their (repeated) exposure to detention. On the contrary, the perceived illegitimacy of immigration detention triggers defiance rather than compliance with the law. Even as a last resort, immigration detention exerts limited pressure on unauthorized migrants to leave the Netherlands, and only if these migrants attribute some level of empirical legitimacy to it. This underscores that empirically legitimate laws are not only necessary for establishing morally acceptable laws, as demonstrated in previous chapters. Empirically legitimate laws are also crucial for instrumental reasons.

9.1 Introduction

Immigration detention is an administrative measure to ensure that migrants cannot abscond while preparations for deportation are being made (Cornelisse, 2010; Wilsher, 2012). Two main types exist: 1) preadmission detention at the border, involving foreigners not admitted to the state's territory, and 2) pre-expulsion detention of foreigners whose

* This chapter has been published as Leerkes AS and Kox MH (2017) Pressured into a preference to leave? A study on the 'specific' deterrent effects and perceived legitimacy of immigration detention. *Law and Society Review* 51(4): 895–929.

stay in the territory is, has, or is likely to become unauthorized. Although formally not a punishment, governments do use immigration detention to deter unwanted immigrants from the territory (Campesi, 2015; DeBono, 2013; Hasselberg, 2014; Kalhan, 2010; Leerkes and Broeders, 2010; Mainwaring, 2012; Martin, 2012; Pickering and Weber, 2014). That claim rests on three main observations: 1) barring exceptions, detention occurs under regimes resembling criminal imprisonment; 2) immigration detainees tend to experience the detention as a kind of punishment, and 3) various policy makers have publicly stated that immigration detention is meant to pressure detainees into leaving. For example, in the Netherlands, the country on which the present analysis focuses, a former Minister of Immigration and Asylum argued that the purpose of immigration detention is to 'incite to departure' ('prikkelen tot vertrek') (Parliamentary Documents 2010/11 19637 no. 1396).

It is illegal under international law to use immigration detention to deter future asylum seekers or to dissuade those who have commenced their claims from pursuing them (United Nations High Commissioner for Refugees, 1999; see also Mainwaring, 2012). It is less clear whether states can use it as a means to coerce rejected asylum seekers and other deportable migrants into a willingness to leave. Various nongovernmental organizations believe not and have criticized the lengthy maximum duration of immigration detention as well as the prison-like conditions under which immigration detention is carried out (see for example Amnesty International, 2009; Jesuit Refugee Service-Europe, 2010). Social scientists, too, have pointed at the harmful effects of immigration law more generally for the well-being and social incorporation of those with weaker legal statuses (see Menjíıvar and Abrego, 2012). Immigration detention should, in accordance with international and national laws, only be used as a last resort in order to prevent the risk of absconding and should be carried out under conditions adjusted to the administrative nature of the detention.

In addition to the legal-normative question of what uses of immigration detention are permissible and acceptable, there is also the empirical-theoretical question of whether and how immigration detention affects migration preferences, and, if so, whether its influences are a result of deterrence, or whether other mechanisms, such as the perceived (il)legitimacy of the detention, (also) play a role. The central question of this chapter is: How, and to what extent, does immigration detention – under conditions found in the Netherlands in 2011 – affect the willingness of detainees to leave the territory of the detaining state, and are eventual changes in detainees' migration preferences produced by deterrence? The analysis is based on unique data that was initially gathered in as part of a research project that I conducted for the International Organization of Migration (IOM) (Kox, 2011). Semi-structured face-to-face interviews were conducted with 81 immigrants who were being held in pre-expulsion detention in 2011, and information was obtained about the administrative outcome of their detention. In this chapter, detainees' attitudes as they were expressed *during detention* are analysed, the relationship between detainee attitudes and detention outcomes is discussed elsewhere (Leerkes and Kox, 2016). Post-deportation attitudinal changes lie outside the scope of the study. The data were fully reanalysed after the cooperation with IOM had ended.

It is conceivable that immigration detention indeed causes forms of deterrence that, in some ways, resemble what would be called 'specific deterrence' in the context of criminal imprisonment.[53] Here, the wish to prevent additional detention – either continued or repeated detention – possibly produces 'law-abiding behaviour' among those who have actually been detained. Three varieties of such deterrence potentially exist. First, detainees may be pressured into cooperating with the deportation procedure by giving up their claims to legal status or by disclosing their nationality or identity. The detaining state has an interest in identifying and documenting (undocumented) detainees, as no country of origin accepts undocumented returnees (Broeders, 2007; Ellermann, 2008). Second, those who are released because of a failed deportation procedure may try to leave the country on their own so as to prevent repeated detention. Third, deportees may refrain from re-immigrating in order to prevent repeated detention. This study focuses on the first and second variety of specific deterrence, so understood.

There is only fragmentary and contradictory evidence about whether and how immigration detention impacts detainees' migration preferences and behaviour. The present study seems unique in addressing these questions on the basis of a substantial number of interviews conducted in detention centres. Hasselberg (2014: 481) conducted ethnographic research among eighteen foreign-national offenders who were facing deportation from the United Kingdom but had been granted bail from immigration detention. Most respondents indeed perceived the detention as being designed to pressure them into leaving, and some of them – especially those who had been detained repeatedly – felt that the detention break[s] one down' to the point of agreeing to deportation.' Kalhan (2010), too, mentions in passing that for the United States, there is a deterrent effect in the sense that detainees may give up their claims to legal status and comply with deportation in order to end the detention. Mainwaring (2012), however, argues that economic hardship and political persecution give African migrants little choice but to continue their migration project regardless of the risk of being detained in Malta for eighteen months. Unfortunately, her analysis potentially suffers from selection regarding the dependent variable, as only unauthorized migrants were interviewed outside of detention, thereby possibly excluding individuals from the sample who were deterred by detention and no longer stayed on Malta. Van Kalmthout and colleagues (2004) conducted extensive fieldwork in two Dutch

53 Immigration detention may also produce what would be called 'general deterrence' in case of criminal imprisonment. Here, the fear of detention possibly controls the behaviour of migrants who have not actually experienced the detention centre, but who risk being detained. For example, rejected asylum seekers may decide to leave the state's territory 'voluntarily' because they wish to evade pre-expulsion detention.

detention centres but did not specifically investigate the eventual impact of detention on migration preferences. They do report that most respondents did not want to go to their country of citizenship in the short term, and that their preferences did not seem to change much.

The analysis focuses on deterrence, but ample attention is paid to how migrants perceive the legitimacy of immigration detention. There are different conceptualizations of legitimacy (see Fallon, 2005). As a legal concept, legitimacy refers to lawfulness and internal consistency of the law, such as a law being in accordance with the constitution. As a philosophical concept, legitimacy means that a law or institution is believed to be right and justifiable in the light of some philosophical principle, such as the principle of sovereignty. In this chapter, a *sociological* conceptualization of legal legitimacy is followed, which pertains to the normative acceptance of the law in society, especially among those who are targeted by the law. A practice can be in accordance with the law, while not being perceived as legitimate by the ruled. Criminal justice research has shown that perceived legitimacy of the law is crucial for compliance. Usually, normative models of compliance are even found to have more explanatory power than economic (rational choice) models of compliance such as found in deterrence theory (see for example Tyler, 2003; Tyler et al., 2010), and this also seems to hold for migration decisions that are reached outside of detention (Ryo, 2013). There also is the possibility that deterrence and perceived (il)legitimacy interact in complex ways. Defiance theory, for example, argues that deterrent effects require that the targets of a sanction perceive the sanction as legitimate (Sherman, 1993). This claim appears to be too strong, but it seems probable that deterrent effects become more likely when the detainee attributes some measure of legitimacy to the detention. Paying attention to perceived (il)legitimacy also is a way to do justice to, and provide more information about, the contested nature of immigration detention, or what Bosworth (2011, 2014) calls its 'legitimacy deficit', thereby strengthening the detainee perspective in this debate. In what follows, it is shown that immigration detention, though generally perceived as rather painful and distressing, produced limited specific deterrent effects at the attitudinal level, which were concentrated among respondents classified as labour migrants and, relatedly, among respondents who attributed some measure of legitimacy to their detention. It is argued that most migrants had interests that outweighed their interest in the detention being ended, and that the detention also triggered mechanisms – including resistance on normative grounds – that actually reinforced detainees' preferences to stay in the country of the detaining state.

The next section provides some contextual information on the Dutch case. Subsequently, the theoretical framework is discussed, the methods are unfolded, and the results are reported. The concluding section discusses the broader scientific implications of this chapter for the study of international migration and the study of legal compliance.

9.2 THE DUTCH IMMIGRATION DETENTION REGIME

As there are international differences in how immigration detention is organized (see Wilsher, 2012), it is useful to provide some contextual information on the Dutch case in 2011. According to the EU Return Directive, immigration detention may last for six months, unless the detainee is considered uncooperative in revealing his/her identity and/ or has been convicted of certain crimes, in which case the detention may be extended to eighteen months. Within this limit, there is considerable international variation in Europe. The Netherlands is in a cluster of countries also including Germany, Denmark and Italy, where the maximum detention duration is eighteen months. These countries in particular seem to use the detention for deterrence purposes given the long maximum detention duration, at least at the time of this research. In that respect, they resemble the United States, Australia, and the United Kingdom (which opted out of the EU Return Directive), which do not have a pre-set maximum detention duration and sometimes use it for years in a row. Other EU countries, such as France (45 days) and Belgium (five months), have considerably shorter maximum detention durations, or use the detention for relatively short periods (in 2008, the average detention duration in Sweden was 20.8 days).[54] In the Netherlands, about half of those detained in 2011 spent more than three months in detention, while a quarter were detained for six months or more. On average, pre-expulsion detention lasted 74 days (Van Schijndel and Van Gemmert, 2012). In 2011, the total inflow in Dutch immigration detention amounted to 6,104 persons, and 5,844 persons entered pre-expulsion detention (Van Schijndel and Van Gemmert, 2012).

Noncitizens can be detained under Dutch law if various conditions are met. These include the foreigner lacking a right to stay in the country (or being likely to lose that right) and there being a realistic probability of deportation. If there is insufficient view to deportation, or if the government has made insufficient progress toward deporting the individual, the detention has to be terminated. Released detainees are usually given a day train ticket and an order to leave the country. Those who stay can be re-detained, provided that there is a 'new fact' that supposedly increases the probability of deportation, such as new information about the individual's identity, or when at least a year has passed since the previous detention period. Immigration judges may decide that a detention is unlawful, and immigration attorneys have significant influence over such decisions (see Ryo, 2016), but such institutional safeguards have not prevented significant levels of repeated immigration detention. In 2010, 45 percent of the detainees were released because of a failed expulsion procedure, and 27 percent had been in Dutch immigration detention

54 Figures on detention duration were taken from http://www.globaldetentionproject. org (country profiles), accessed 06/01/2015.

previously (Kox, 2011). In the case of repeated detention, the cumulative detention duration may exceed eighteen months.

At the time of writing, a governmental proposal to develop a specific detention regime for immigration detainees is being discussed in parliament (Parliamentary Documents 2015/16 34 309 no. 1–9), but in 2011, the pre-expulsion detention regime was modelled after the regime for crime suspects who are detained before their trials. Detainees were to stay in their cells – mostly designed to hold two people – between 5 pm and 8 am, and between 12 noon and 1 pm. When out of their cells, they were to spend time in a common recreation room with cooking facilities, television, table tennis, and board games. A program of eighteen hours a week was on offer, including airing (one hour per day), sports (45 minutes twice a week), recreational activities (six hours a week), library visits (one hour per week), religious ceremonies (one hour per week), and visits (two hours per week). There were no 're-integration facilities' such as labour, educational programs or training courses. In the Netherlands, some detainees are given the option of leaving the country via 'Assisted Voluntary Return from Detention' (AVRD), instead of being deported. In case of AVRD, detainees are released at the airport where they meet an IOM employee in the departure hall. This happens under a number of conditions, which includes the 'removal' not being delayed.

An additional specificity of the European context is that released detainees have the option of (illegal) onward migration: migrating to other European countries is illegal, but not too difficult, since land borders are normally rarely policed within the Schengen Area, an area comprising 26 European states that have abolished all passport controls at their mutual borders. The Area includes the Netherlands and the two countries where it has land borders with (Germany and Belgium).[55] In the past, rejected asylum seekers and (other) unauthorized migrants could obtain *legal* stay in a different European country, if only temporarily – i.e. during the asylum procedure – by submitting an asylum request there. However, under the Dublin III Regulation (EC 604/2013), a successor of the Dublin Convention that became in force in 1997, those reapplying for asylum in a different European country, or who apply for asylum while they could have done so sooner in a different European country, may be rejected without further consideration and be returned to the 'responsible state' for examining the asylum claim, usually the state through which the migrant first entered the EU (see Thielemann and Armstrong, 2013).

Compared to the United States, where an estimated 52 percent of all unauthorized immigrants in 2014 were Mexicans (Passel and Cohn, 2016), the unauthorized population

55 It is allowed for Member States to conduct migration policing in border zones, away from the actual geographical border. Police may, under conditions, stop vehicles or check international trains for unauthorized migrants when there is a 'reasonable presumption of illegal residence'. After 2014, the border controls were – temporarily – increased in response to the elevated influx of asylum seekers in the EU.

in the Netherlands is quite heterogeneous in terms of national origin. In 2011, more than 60 percent of the detainees were from countries that, on their own, represented less than five percent of the detainees (Van Schijndel and Van Gemmert, 2012). The most prevalent nationality was Iraqi with 9.6 percent. It has been estimated that women represented almost one third (29 percent) of the unauthorized population in 2012 (Van der Heijden et al., 2015). Since women run significantly lower risks of apprehension than men (Leerkes et al., 2012), they only represented thirteen percent of all immigration detainees in 2011 (Van Schijndel and Van Gemmert, 2012).

9.3 Conditional deterrence?

Immigration detention in the Netherlands has three main direct 'migration outcomes': 1) deportation or AVRD to a country where the detainee's admission is guaranteed, usually the detainee's country of citizenship, 2) a continued unauthorized stay in territory of the detaining state, and 3) illegal onward migration to another European country.[56] Before being detained, each detainee will generally prefer continued stay in the territory of the detaining state, although this does not hold for all detainees.[57] 'Specific deterrence' at the attitudinal level can be said to have occurred when a preference for continued stay has changed into 1) a preference to return to the country of citizenship or 2) onward migration to a different European country – *and* that the change is due to the detention being experienced as frightening or discouraging.

Potentially, two aspects of the immigration detention experience could produce such attitudinal deterrent effects. The first involves the *perceived severity* of the immigration detention experience. Much like criminal prisoners, immigration detainees are subjected to various forms of deprivation, or what Sykes (1958) famously called the 'pains of imprisonment'. A reduction of autonomy and a loss of liberty are inherent in detention and most detainees experience a reduced access to social relationships as visitors face travel costs and visiting hours, internet access and opportunities to make phone calls are limited, and potential visitors who are unauthorized themselves are unlikely to visit the centres. Additionally, detainees experience material deprivation, especially those who were ordinarily employed. Detainees typically share a cell with a stranger and cannot work but receive some pocket money to buy some goods in the detention shop. Deprivation of security may also be relevant, as, in Sykes's words, each immigration detainee is 'thrown into prolonged intimacy' with other detainees. This can provoke anxiety, especially when

56 Other outcomes include legalization or a temporary deportation ban.

57 For example, some individuals are apprehended en route to a different country or while in the process of preparing their return or onward migration. Others prefer to return to their country of citizenship before being apprehended but lack the papers to do so.

other detainees have a criminal background or are mentally instable. Crewe (2011) recently argued that Sykes's pains of imprisonment, though still relevant today, represent only a part of the painfulness of imprisonment as detainees may also be subjected to what he calls the 'pains of uncertainty and indeterminacy'. This certainly also holds for immigration detainees as they do not know in advance how long they will be detained (within the maximally allowed detention duration), while it is often unclear whether they will be deported (see Becket and Evans, 2015).

The second aspect involves the *perceived risk* of repeated immigration detention. Being detained implies that one has been 'caught', and that one's unauthorized status is known to the authorities. People who have experienced a sanction tend to perceive the probability of similar sanctions in the future as higher than before the sanction was imposed (Matsueda et al., 2006; Piquero and Pogarsky, 2002), and this may also hold for the sanction of immigration detention. Perceived probability of a sanction, in turn, tends to increase rule compliance (see, for example, Tyler, 2003). In other words, detainees may be reasoning that it is in their interest to leave the territory of the detaining state because – having been apprehended and detained – they believe that repeated detention is likely should the deportation procedure fail.

For two reasons, detention may be perceived as painful and repeated detention as probable, without continued stay becoming the least preferred detention outcome. First – taking the rational choice perspective that is implied in deterrence theory – there may be a kind of threshold effect before actual deterrence occurs (see Tyler, 2003). After all, the 'utility' of staying in the country of the detaining state, though lowered by the 'costs' of the detention experience, may still be higher than the 'utility' of being sent to one's country of citizenship or, should the deportation procedure fail, of going to a third country. Similarly, it is conceivable that detainees experience the detention as painful, while they do not see it as a major deterioration of their situation, such as when the person concerned normally leads a strongly marginalized existence in the territory of the detaining state when out of detention.

Second, the deterrent effects may be offset by resistance should the detention be perceived as illegitimate. Normative models of rule compliance maintain that rules are followed because people believe that doing so is right or, as the neo-institutionalists emphasize (Scott, 2008), as 'normal', that is, 'as the way we do these things'. A distinction is usually made between the normative evaluation of outcomes and procedures (Tyler, 2003). Outcome legitimacy means that the law's content is considered fair; procedural legitimacy means that rules are enforced in ways that are perceived as just, by actors who are trusted. The first type of legitimacy encompasses a judgement about the acceptability of the official objective of (pre-expulsion) immigration detention, namely that the detainee leaves the territory over which the detaining state claims territorial sovereignty, usually by 'returning' to his or her country of citizenship. The second type of legitimacy encompasses a normative judgement about the acceptability of *how* and by whom that outcome is realized. This both entails a judgement about the use of immigration detention in cases like the detainee's, and a judgement about how the detention is organized in terms of detention duration, the possibility of repeated detention, available programs, interactional styles of the guards, and so forth. Migrants who perceive their deportation or their deportation procedure as illegitimate can be expected to try to obstruct the deportation procedure. Defiance theory has aimed to synthesize deterrence theory with legitimacy theories (Sherman, 1993). It argues that the deterrent effects of a sanction require that those subjected to the sanction perceive it as legitimate. While this claim seems too strong – we can conceive deterrent effects in the absence of perceived legitimacy – it does suggest the possibility of a kind of 'interaction effect' in the sense that people may be most likely to comply when the product of perceived severity, perceived certainty and perceived legitimacy reaches a kind of optimum. In this view, increases in perceived severity are likely to eventually undermine compliance by reducing perceived (process) legitimacy.

9.4 Data and method

The data were initially collected as part of a research project for IOM Netherlands that was directed by me. The IOM wanted to learn more about how detainees experienced the detention, and how they assessed IOM's presence in the centres in the context of AVRD. As part of this project, semi-structured interviews with 81 immigration detainees were conducted in May, June, and July 2011 in the three main detention centres that were operational in the Netherlands at the time (Rotterdam, Zaandam, and Zeist). All respondents were randomly selected from the resident lists. IOM employees working in the detention centres tried to approach 232 detainees; of these, 144 persons could not be interviewed: 1) 62 persons were not in the centres because of departure, release, or appointments at courts or embassies, 2) 51 persons were unwilling to be interviewed, or anticipated that it would be too emotionally demanding, and 3) 30 candidates faced communication issues. Apart from the 81 interviews, seven interviews were terminated prematurely due to unexpected language barriers or because these interviewees found the interview too emotionally demanding; these were excluded from the analysis. The interviews took place in the detention centres' consulting rooms and lasted between 45 minutes and three hours. The interviews were conducted by both authors of this chapter, by IOM employees who specialize in client contacts in the clients' mother tongue, and by a university research assistant.[58] All interviewers received interview training. While

58 We conducted 24 interviews. Seven IOM employees (who work as 'native counsellors') and the university research assistant conducted the remaining interviews. Native counsellors normally inform migrants about return, and originate from – and speak the language native to – relevant source countries.

some respondents criticized the IOM, most did not feel that IOM put pressure on them to leave the Netherlands, and we had the impression that respondents felt comfortable telling their stories, also given the detailed information they provided, including during the interviews with the IOM employees. The interviewers recorded the interview or took notes, depending on the possibilities for recording and the preferences of interviewee and interviewer. All interviews were held in the respondent's first or second language, with ten different languages being used in total. A telephonic interpreter assisted with five interviews. The respondents' case files held by IOM, the Dutch Immigration and Naturalization Service (IND) and the Repatriation and Departure Service (DT&V) were also studied in order to gather procedural information, including the respondents' juridical position and history, possible previous detainments, and the administrative outcome of the detention in terms of deportation, AVRD or release in the Netherlands. Respondents were guaranteed anonymity, but the Custodial Institutions Agency knew who participated, as respondents could only be interviewed by appointment in a detention setting.

Respondents were interviewed about their situation in their country of citizenship and the Netherlands, their stay in immigration detention, their thoughts on the future and their attitude with regard to staying in or leaving the Netherlands, and the possible consequences of their stay(s) in immigration detention for their migration preferences. Respondents might have perceived an interest in creating an impression that they were 'cooperating' with the removal procedure as detainees who are seen as uncooperative by immigration judges risk an extension of the detention period. In order to minimize that risk, relatively long and open interviews were designed, during which the interviewers attempted to create 'rapport'. For example, before sensitive questions regarding 'return' were asked, respondents were given the opportunity to explain in their own words why and when they had migrated, what their situation in the Netherlands had looked like, and what they thought of immigration detention. Additionally, respondents were not explicitly asked whether they were 'cooperating' with the Dutch authorities, but – using open questions – were interviewed about eventual changes in their migration preferences. For example, it was asked 'Have your return intentions changed during your stay in immigration detention? How? Why/why not?' Two questions measured the perceived legitimacy of the detention: 1) 'Do you think the Dutch government has a right to detain you? (Why/Why not?)' and 2) 'Do you think the detention conditions are appropriate given the reason for your detention? (Why/Why not?)'. Both questions incited statements about perceived process legitimacy. The first question in particular also provided information about perceived outcome legitimacy.

After the project for IOM had ended, all interviews were reanalysed. Both authors of this chapter independently coded the respondents' statements, including their migration preferences at the time of the interview and their (retrospectively reported) preferences before the detention period. For repeatedly detained respondents, the stated migration preference before the first detention period was also coded. There was insufficient information to systemically classify the respondents on perceived outcome and process legitimacy separately, but their statements did allow us to tentatively divide the respondent into a 'low' and a 'higher' perceived legitimacy group. The first group believed that the Dutch government had no right to detain and deport them whatsoever and also believed that the detention conditions were inappropriate in their case. Most respondents in the second group were also quite critical about at least some aspects of the detention, but either indicated that the government had some kind of right to detain people in cases such like theirs (be it for a shorter period, not repeatedly, and so forth) or found the detention conditions appropriate. If transcripts initially resulted in different codings, the final coding was decided on after discussion among the authors.[59]

While analysing the interviews, we inductively found indications that the effects of detention, and the reasons that respondents had to try to resist deportation, depended on respondents' migration projects. In order to examine such differences in a more systematic way, the respondents were classified into *family migrants*, *asylum migrants*, and *labour migrants*. This was done using the information that respondents provided during the interviews regarding their reasons for leaving their respective countries of origin. *Family migrants* were defined as respondents who mentioned that a desire to reunify with family or a partner in The Netherlands had been among the reasons for leaving their country of origin. *Asylum migrants* indicated that a desire to apply for asylum had been among the reasons for emigrating. Respondents who had come to Europe without reunifying with immediate family members, and without the intention to apply for asylum, were classified as *labour migrants*. Most of them had migrated to Europe and (eventually) the Netherlands to work; a few had come in hopes of being able to study in Europe or had left their country of origin without a clear plan for the future. This can be seen as a hierarchical classification. First, it was determined whether the respondent left his or her country or origin in order to reunify with family (yes: 'family migrant'; no: 'asylum or labour migrant'); as a second step, it was determined for each 'asylum or labour migrant' whether he or she had left the country or origin to apply for asylum (yes: 'asylum migrant', no: 'labour migrant').

The classification of respondents into these three groups – it may be better to speak of partially overlapping 'clusters of respondents' – served as a heuristic tool that helped us to understand and describe the implications of what are meaningful differences in respondents' migration projects. It should be emphasized that this categorization is not meant to essentialize immigrant categories. Evidently, people may migrate for more than one reason in complex 'configurations of motives', which may also change during the

59 Conflicting interpretations could mostly be resolved by fine-tuning definitions of the codings. In a few cases, the coding of the author who conducted the interview was followed.

migration project. Some respondents classified as asylum and labour migrants eventually obtained a partner in the Netherlands. A few respondents classified as labour migrants applied for asylum at a later stage. Various respondents classified as family or asylum migrants also mentioned economic reasons for leaving their country of origin. While all asylum migrants in our sample had migrated without reunifying with direct family members, some had remote relatives in the Netherlands.

We repeatedly discussed ethical aspects among each other, including the question of whether it is ethical to conduct research on the (in)effectiveness of immigration detention given the possibility that the results may be used in society to legitimize immigration detention, including the – ethically and legally dubious – use of lengthy immigration detention under prison-like conditions. Unfortunately, there is little scientific debate on such normative aspects (see Düvell et al., 2009), and we found that scientific codes of ethics provide limited, perhaps insufficient, guidance.[60] We eventually concluded that it is justified and important to conduct social scientific research on this topic. We consider the research not a priori harmful in democratic societies, where different publics may or may not use research findings for different purposes, including purposes that researchers do not personally advocate. We hope that our findings contribute to a richer scientific and public debate on the functions, human rights performance, and (il)legitimacy of immigration detention.

9.5 Results: Pressured to depart?

9.5.1 *Quantitative overview*

The analysis focuses on how the respondents experienced the detention. However, given the relatively large sample size and the use of probability sampling, it was decided to also present some quantitative findings to make optimal use of the data (see Namey et al., 2008 on the possibilities and limitations of quantifying qualitative data). Before describing how the respondents experienced the detention, a description of the main characteristics of the research group is being given which is followed by a quantitative overview of the reported migration preferences of the respondents.

60 The code of ethics of the International Sociological Association mentions that researchers should be aware that results may be used for various non-scientific purposes, and that they are entitled to intervene to correct possible misinterpretations, but is silent on whether certain research questions should perhaps not be asked or whether certain results should perhaps not be reported in the light of concerns about certain extra-scientific uses.

9.5.1.1 Research group

The respondents, 73 men and eight women, were from 36 different countries, mainly located in North and West Africa, South/Southwest Asia, the Middle East, and Latin America (mostly Surinam). Ages varied from eighteen to 67 and averaged around 34. The detention frequency varied from one to no fewer than eight times, and 33 respondents had been detained previously. The average duration of the most recent detention at the time of the interview was 4.4 months, varying from a few days up to fifteen months. Some respondents had only been apprehended because of illegal stay in the country, others also had police contacts due to suspicions regarding felonies and/or minor misdemeanours. All but five respondents were illegally residing in the Netherlands at the time of the interview: four had a precarious form of legal stay as part of a procedure to obtain a residence permit, and one risked losing his residence permit because he had been sentenced for a crime. Information by the Custodial Institutions Agency indicated that the sample was quite representative with regard to sex, age, and migration motive, with former asylum seekers making up about half of the detainee population. Detainees with longer detention durations were somewhat overrepresented, however, and some nationalities – including Somalian, Georgian, Algerian, Ghanaian, and Eritrean – were underrepresented.

As was mentioned in the previous section, respondents were classified into family migrants, asylum migrants, and labour migrants based on their initial migration motive. The three groups indeed differed on a number of characteristics that can be expected to be correlated with migration motive, including country of origin, number of former residence permit holders, and duration of stay in the Netherlands. The groups were quite similar in other respects, including age and sex composition, and there were no notable differences with respect to their detention duration.

The respondents classified as *family migrants* (N=13) mostly originated from countries that have been source countries of immigration to the Netherlands for some time, like the former colony Surinam, and the former 'guest worker' country Morocco, but others were from Tunisia, Pakistan, Egypt, and Syria. Family ties do not preclude an unauthorized status as the requirements for legal family migration include income and age requirements, while certain family relations, such as those between siblings or between parents and adult children, do not normally give a right to a residence permit (Leerkes and Kulu-Glasgow, 2011). Most family migrants had immigrated without state permission, but four used to have a residence permit, which had been ended because of criminal offending. The duration of stay of the family migrants varied from a number of months up to 32 years, with an average of fourteen years, making this the most 'established' group with the longest average duration of stay. The longer duration of stay was also reflected in a somewhat larger share of respondents who had been detained in immigration detention before.

The asylum migrants (N=39) originated from 25 different countries, mostly located in North or West Africa and Asia (including the Middle East), and, less so, Eastern Europe. A substantial number were from countries that were experiencing military conflicts at the time, or that had oppressive regimes, including Afghanistan, Iran, Iraq, Sudan, Ethiopia, Russia, and China. They had been in the country between some months and 27 years, with an average of six years. Some seemed to have weak asylum claims; others had possibly encountered difficulties in proving a well-founded fear of persecution or fled unsafe conditions that are not recognized as grounds for asylum. States may also end protection when conditions in countries of origin have improved only to some extent (see Black and Gent, 2006). Seven asylum migrants were former residence permit holders. Contrary to the family migrants, their permits had not been ended because of crimes, but because they were no longer deemed in need of protection.

The labour migrants (N=29) originated from thirteen different countries, mostly located in Africa and Asia, including Morocco, Nigeria, Egypt, China, India, and Turkey. Three were from South America, and one from Eastern Europe. In this group, the duration of stay in the Netherlands varied from some days up to 32 years, with an average of nine years. European countries have a rather strict admission policy for labour migrants, especially when it concerns 'unskilled' labour. Residence permits are only granted when the employer can prove that the work cannot be done by a native worker or (other) EU citizen. Indeed, only two respondents in this group had ever obtained a residence permit.

9.5.1.2 Migration preferences

Figure 1 provides an overview of respondents' migration preferences at the time of the interview and – retrospectively reported – just before the detention period during which the respondents were interviewed. The figure pertains to all respondents (N=81), regardless of whether they had been detained in immigration detention before.

Figure 1 Migration preferences before and during detention (all respondents)

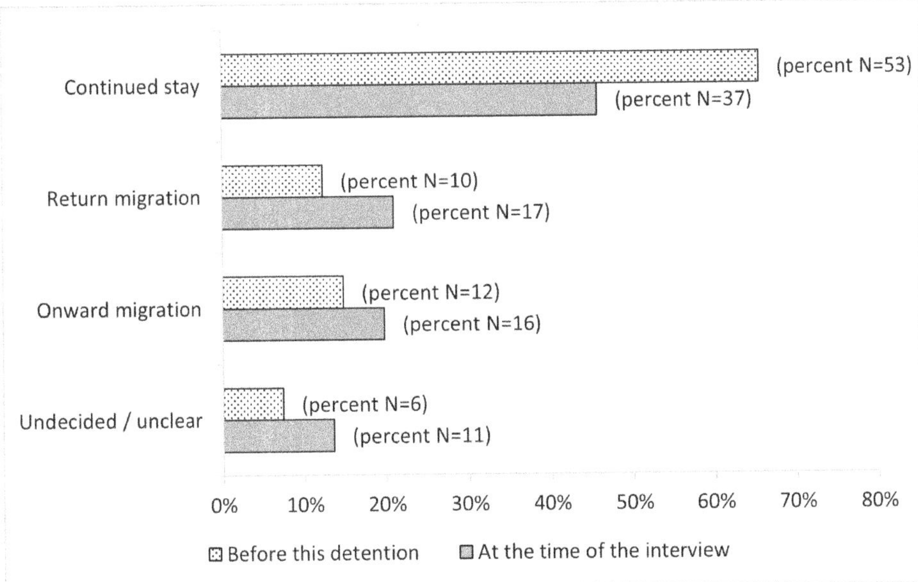

Figure 2 specifically pertains to the 33 respondents who had been detained in immigration detention repeatedly. It should be stressed that these figures are *indicative*, as they are based on our interpretation of the respondents' statements in a semi-structured interview.

Just before the detention, ten of 81 respondents preferred to go to their country of citizenship; against seventeen respondents (not necessarily the same individuals) at the time of the interview. The number of respondents expressing a preference for onward migration similarly increased somewhat from twelve to sixteen. Eleven respondents were still undecided or were unable to make their preferences clear. All in all, the number of respondents with a preference for continued stay decreased from 53 to 37 (19 percent of 81 respondents) during the detention. Among the 33 repeatedly detained respondents, migration preferences just before the detention had sometimes been produced by previous detention periods (see Figure 2). When these previous detentions are also taken into account, the number of respondents preferring return migration had increased by sixteen ([17–10]+[9–0]=16) during the detention, while the number of respondents preferring onward migration had increased by seven ([16–12]+[5–2]=7). These results suggest that immigration detention pressures a *notable minority* into a preference to leave the country.

Figure 2 Migration Preferences Before and During Detention (Repeatedly Detained Respondents)

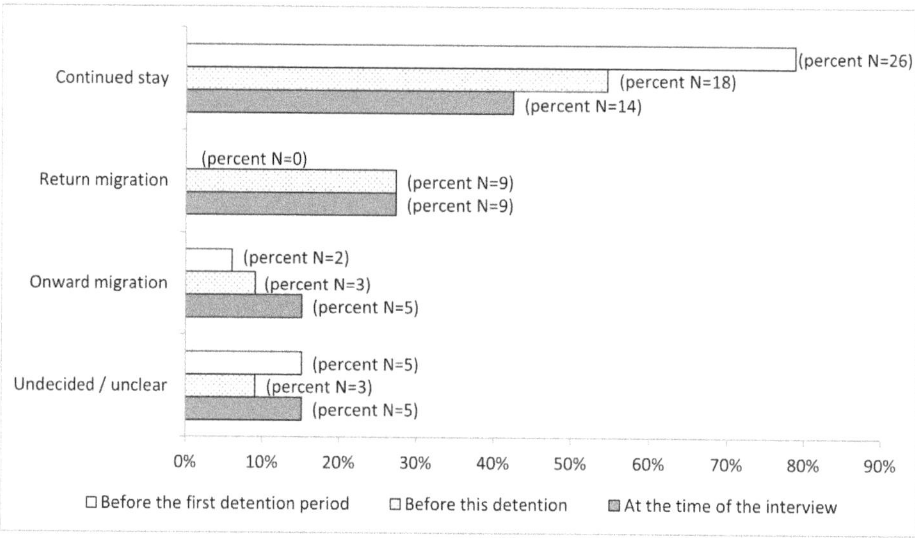

All changes in migration preferences were reported to be detention-related, but repeatedly detained respondents in particular also attributed eventual changes to factors other than detention or indicated that they were a more indirect result of detention. For instance, some of them had changed their mind because of difficulties they had encountered after previous detentions, for example because they had lost their jobs because of the detention. Labour migrants seemed to be more likely than family and asylum migrants to have changed their mind. Those classified as labour migrants represented 35 percent of the sample, but 63 percent of the additional respondents who eventually preferred 'return' (10 of 16), and 57 percent of the additional respondents who preferred onward migration at the time of the interview (4 of 7). As expected, respondents in the higher legitimacy group were relatively likely to report a preference to 'return': while only 38 of the 81 respondents (44 percent) attributed at least some measure of legitimacy to their detention, this percentage was 82 percent (14 of 17) among those who, at the time of the interview, preferred to go to their country of citizenship. This was not the case for those expressing a preference for onward migration; only 25 percent (4 of 16) of them were in the higher legitimacy group.

Part of the overrepresentation of labour migrants among those reporting a preference to go to their country of citizenship seemed to be related to an association between perceived legitimacy and type of migration. Nineteen of 29 labour migrants (66 percent) were in the higher legitimacy group, against thirteen of 39 asylum migrants (33 percent) and six of thirteen family migrants (46 percent). These differences echo culturally dominant beliefs and established regulations with regards to immigration rights – while labour migration is generally not considered a right, most countries do recognize a conditional right to asylum and family migration (see Walzer, 1983).

The gender composition of the research group reflected the underrepresentation of women among immigration detainees. Accordingly, the number of female respondents (N=8) was too small to make assertions about eventual gender differences. When comparing men and women, more or less similar patterns were observed, suggesting that immigration detention produces limited specific deterrent effects among men and women alike, which are concentrated among labour migrants and those attributing some measure of legitimacy to the detention, irrespective of gender. Three female respondents – all part of the labour migrant and higher legitimacy group – developed a return preference during the detention, five persisted in a preference to stay. After the project for IOM had been completed, we asked the Dutch government to provide us with information about the administrative outcome of the respondents' detention. We learned that more than two-thirds of them (59 of 81, 69 percent) had eventually been released in the Netherlands, including ten of the seventeen respondents (59 percent) who had expressed a preference to go to their country of citizenship.

The next section discusses how family migrants, asylum migrants and labour migrants experienced the detention and why immigration detention did or did not alter their migration preferences. The interview fragments also show that there was a notable degree of 'blurring' between the three types of migrants, and that migration motives sometimes changed during an individual's migration project.

9.5.2 *The voice of the detainee*

9.5.2.1 Family migrants

Most family migrants had a strong socio-cultural attachment to the territory of the detaining state due to their family ties *and* the length of their stay in the Netherlands. As a consequence, they generally tried to resist deportation and were reluctant to migrate to a different European country. They certainly did not consider detention a trivial matter, however. A Surinamese man, who had been reunified with his elderly mother as an adult and had lived in the country without state permission for thirteen years, was a case in point. Having been detained twice before – the last time had been for nine months – he found the detention quite stressful, yet he insisted on staying in the Netherlands.

> 'This is no life. I mean for illegal Dutchmen in general. It's not good for honest people. If you keep somebody here for nine months, you've stolen a year of his life … Last time I slept with four people in a cell [for nine months]. … My

> health is still fine, but I am a bit stressed about what's going to happen. I talk in my sleep and I've been to a psychologist.'

Like most respondents, the man primarily complained about the loss of freedom, the perceived unfairness of the detention, the uncertainly about the detention outcome, and his lack of perspective more generally. Additionally, he seemed to suffer from a loss of status that comes with cell-sharing. Several other respondents similarly experienced status deprivation, but focused more on material aspects, or at least articulated their concerns in these terms. A Moroccan man, for instance, lamented the quality of the food:

> 'It's distasteful. We only get bread and milk, one litre of milk for four days, half a loaf of bread for two days, 100 grams of sugar for four days. I try to make my own food, but the [detention] shop asks one euro per tomato! Outside that buys you a kilo!'

Despite experiencing deprivation, family migrants were generally reluctant to comply with arrangements for departure. Their local family ties, and the associated ambition to settle in the Netherlands permanently, was not easily offset by the 'pains of immigration detention', not even repeated and prolonged detention. Additionally, family migrants were quite critical about both the outcome and process legitimacy of the detention. A different Surinamese man, who had spent 3.5 months in his second detention, was another case in point. Beginning in the late 1960s, his whole family had gradually migrated to the Netherlands: first his eldest sister, then all of his remaining siblings and mother. When his marriage ended in 2001, he was the last family member to emigrate, after which he remarried and became a father:

> 'My wife and child are here. I want my child to make that decision when she's old enough, to decide herself where to live and be. My home is here because I've been living here for so long. The Netherlands is not the land of milk and honey, and it isn't easy [being unauthorized], but I'm in my fifties and I don't want to give up my life here. (...) You may protect your borders and you don't have to allow everybody, but the sanction needs to make sense and they need to listen to each story and pick the rotten apples. I have a permanent address with my wife and child, but I cannot officially register there [being unauthorized]. And now they say that I am at risk of absconding. I will not let myself be deported!'

Many family migrants also saw no viable alternatives but to stay in the Netherlands since they did not have any relatives, friends, or economic opportunities in their country of origin or third countries. The aforementioned Moroccan, for example, had lost one of his hands while working illegally for a butcher, without being entitled to disability insurance as an unauthorized immigrant. With the exception of his elderly mother, all of his family members lived in Europe, and even though he no longer had close contact with his family – which he attributed to his accident – he argued that he could not return to Morocco as a beggar: 'Here, I at least get some support from friends and a Moroccan foundation.'

As expected under deterrence theory, eventual changes in migration preferences sometimes also seemed to be related to increases in the perceived certainty of (repeated) immigration detention. A young man wanted to return to Surinam, since his sisters reasoned that he was likely to be re-caught – and perhaps become a burden to them – now that he had been apprehended for unauthorized residence:

> 'Well, look. When the detention wasn't there, it went well. But not anymore. Once they have you, they will catch you again just like that. And I've made some money and stuff, and now I want to return. I can work with my brother-in-law [until I have arranged my papers for the Netherlands]. So, my sisters told me to go back to Surinam.'

In some instances, detention actually seemed to reinforce preferences to stay in the territory of the detaining state. Group-wise detention sometimes seemed to enable migrants to exchange techniques to resist deportation:

> 'We talk a lot about how they can't really force us to return. And we advise each other regarding how it will be held against you in court if you do not sufficiently [give the impression that you] cooperate.'

Additionally, information on opportunities to deal with the challenges of being unauthorized is sometimes also shared: 'I can't work [being an unauthorized immigrant in the Netherlands], I can only deal drugs. A guy offered me to make some money [when I am outside] by receiving packages of drugs every other week. But I'm not into that kind of thing.'[61]

9.5.2.2 Asylum migrants

Most asylum migrants similarly considered the detention quite severe and were aware of the possibility of repeated detention even though this group was to a lesser extent

61 The respondent's claim that he can 'only deal drugs' is an overstatement, but it is true that unauthorized migrants in the Netherlands have increasingly become dependent on the informal and illegal economy (Leerkes et al., 2012).

repeatedly detained in comparison with the other two groups. Even more so than family migrants, most of them nonetheless tried to resist deportation. In their case, this was not primarily because of a strong socio-cultural attachment to the Netherlands, but rather because they 'feared return'. An Iranian woman, who claimed to have fled an abusive husband, explained why being deprived of liberty had not changed her mind:

> 'I am enclosed by four walls and it feels like I'm in prison. Outside you're free, you can call, go shopping. I've been here for four months.... The people here do their best but it's very difficult... Perhaps when you look at it from a higher level, that you can understand the system. But I don't see it for myself. I came for safety, received these rejections, and now I am locked up. It's not fair when somebody comes for safety.... I have children, and I want nothing more than to be with them. But I cannot return home due to the problems with my husband... I face a death threat when I return...'

Additionally, asylum migrants were even more critical about the legitimacy of the detention than family migrants. This is, for example, what a rejected Afghan asylum seeker said when an interviewer inquired how he perceived the legitimacy of the detention:

> 'What do you think yourself? I feel just like you if you would sit here. Everyday hundreds of people die in Afghanistan. There is injustice. Troops go there, but it only makes things worse. That's why I was forced to come here, and then I get locked up. If someone here [a European] dies because of the war in Afghanistan they organize a march and mourn for ten days; there, hundreds of people die each day, and nothing is done. There are no humane people here.'

Some respondents indicated, perhaps paradoxically, that a residence permit would make it easier to leave, as it would enable them to re-migrate should conditions be or become as unsafe as they feared. A Liberian respondent complained about the boredom of detention, the difficulty of communicating with the outside world, and his stress and associated medical problems including migraines, stomach aches, and depression. Yet this is what he said after almost a year of detention:

> 'I can't go back. This is only possible if I have a residence permit so I can come back if there are problems there. It's not safe right now because of the political situation and crime. I know that from the internet, friends, and CNN.'

Asylum migrants tended to emphasize asylum-related obstacles to returning, and to some extent this may have been a way for them to justify and articulate their right to stay in

Europe. Apart from safety issues, however, some of them also faced socioeconomic obstacles. Most of them had migrated to settle in Europe permanently, or for an indefinite period of time, and seemed to have left little to 'return' to. One of our interviewers reported the following about a West African man, aged 30, who had been in Europe for twelve years:

> He said his parents died in atrocious conditions, that he was imprisoned, and saved by accident. ... It's his second detention. He says that all days are the same, that there's nothing to do but to 'sit, sit, sit', and that he's only 'half a man'. His health has worsened, he eats badly. He doesn't consider return, because he feels that he's entitled to a residence permit, and because his parents have died and his house was destroyed. He also says he is not a criminal and doesn't understand why he can't stay at a regular address.

All detainees found immigration detention a painful experience, but a few valued at least some aspects of it. For example, one respondent, who had initially come to Europe to seek asylum, had been in the country for 27 years and was detained for the sixth time. 'I cannot return. I don't want to. My life's here. I'm detained, but it doesn't matter to me. Look, you're not free, but it's not bad.' This relatively positive evaluation of detention was probably related to the respondent's frame of reference. He had become addicted to drugs, had been living on the streets, and was regularly ill. Other strongly marginalized detainees were similarly negative about the loss of liberty and autonomy, but also valued certain aspects of the detention to some extent, such as the medical care facilities (also see Leerkes, 2016).

Compared to family migrants, asylum migrants were more likely to consider onward migration to another EU country or, in some cases, to Canada or the United States. Thus, despite the aforementioned Dublin Regulation, substituting a different European country for the Netherlands still turned out to be a way to continue migration projects, albeit irregularly. In fact, some respondents had actually lived elsewhere in Europe after their asylum claim had been rejected, or after previous deportation procedures had failed. Others still intended to go elsewhere in Europe should they be released. An Iraqi, for example, had gone to Belgium in hopes of obtaining a residence permit there. His statements show how a perceived severity of the detention without at least some measure of perceived legitimacy of the detention may pressure migrants into (illegal) onward migration rather than 'return'.

> 'It's not good. I have to go to Belgium again. There it's better. Here they keep you seven, eight, ten, eighteen months... In Belgium it's two, three, four, and you're free. And I can get a residence permit there [this is actually unlikely].'
> Interviewer: 'What specifically is so bad about this detention?'

> Respondent: 'Well, you're imprisoned. You don't know when you'll get out, you don't sleep or eat well, with others in a cell, showering together, just dirty. I don't get it! I don't come for money or something, I come for safety. I never had any problems with the police, and in Europe they lock me up.'

Those among our respondents who had actually been 'displaced' to a different European country had all been apprehended there and had been transferred to the Dutch authorities to be re-detained. After having experienced that the Dublin regulation ties asylum seekers to the (first) detaining state, some asylum migrants no longer preferred onward migration. A few asylum migrants wanted to go to their country of citizenship. This mostly occurred after several detentions in combination with other difficulties of being unauthorized. Such respondents also seemed to have weaker asylum claims – at least they expressed milder fears concerning return. Some of them were in the lower legitimacy group, suggesting that a perceived legitimacy of immigration detention is not, as Sherman's (1993) defiance theory would have it, a necessary requirement for a return preference to develop; some detainees were simply 'tired' after repeated detention. A Turkish Kurd had lived in a foster home in Greece until the age of fourteen, when he migrated irregularly to Italy, where the police allegedly denied him the opportunity to apply for asylum. As there was little work, he went to France, Belgium, and, eventually, the Netherlands, where he applied for asylum claiming to be from Iraq because he had been told that would increase his chances of obtaining asylum.

> 'I've seen nothing outside [since arriving in Europe]. Just prison. The first time they caught me at the border and kept me for six months. They released me, I went to Norway, got sent back to the Netherlands, was locked up for eleven months. Then I went to Belgium, got sent back, was detained a year. And now it's six months already! I'm so angry. Every day somebody comes to talk. First a lawyer, then a woman, then a man, now you. The people [guards] are nice, but I'm kept for nothing, just for papers. They have no right to detain me. I came for asylum and I have done nothing wrong. But I'm really tired. I've never seen Iraq, but I really want to go to Turkey. I can work there. I watch Turkish TV every day [Turkey was indeed experiencing an economic boom]. But I'm not registered there, and they keep trying to send me to Iraq.'

9.5.2.3 Labour migrants

Deterrent effects at the attitudinal level were stronger among labour migrants than among family and asylum migrants, but the former did not perceive immigration detention as more severe, nor did they perceive repeated detention as more probable. Rather, the differential impact of the detention experience on respondents' migration preferences seemed to be related to both the differential migration projects among the three groups and to different perceptions of the legitimacy of the detention. While most family and asylum migrants had a strong orientation towards a permanent stay, most labour migrants either intended to go to their country of citizenship after having earned a certain amount of money, or lacked a clear plan about how long they would be away but still intended to 'return' eventually. Still others intended to establish themselves in Europe permanently, but were open to work in a different European country. In fact, a significant number of labour migrants had lived elsewhere in Europe. As was mentioned in the quantitative overview, labour migrants were also notably less negative about the legitimacy of immigration detention.

A Nigerian man, who had migrated to work and 'because he had always dreamt about living in Amsterdam', represented a case where latent return intentions became more manifest under the influence of detention. He came with the intention of being away for seven years but had been apprehended after three. In the meantime, he had been doing relatively well sharing a room with a friend and saving money by way of informal jobs via an Amsterdam church. He would not mind continuing that life in Amsterdam were he to be released, but after nine months of detention he was prepared to go to Nigeria; he feared 'going crazy' in detention where he was regularly having 'weird dreams'. Like others who developed a return preference, he accounted for these changes in terms of deterrence, that is, in terms of perceived severity and risk. However, he also indicated that the government did have the right to detain him, although no more than a month, suggesting that the influence of legitimacy may largely operate on a more subconscious level.

In some cases, pre-existing plans to eventually return to one's country of citizenship were brought forward because of a more encompassing and gradual process of deterrence in which repeated detention was one element. A Moroccan man from a middle-class family had immigrated in the 1990s. After being homeless for some time, he had found informal work in horticulture, as well as housing that he shared with other unauthorized immigrants. It had become increasingly difficult for him to work in the greenhouses because of checks by the labour inspectorate. The Dutch policy of discouraging unauthorized residence – which was mainly developed in the 1990s and early 2000s – then seemed to have initiated a process of marginalization and criminalization, which eventually contributed to a still unfulfilled desire to go to Morocco:

> 'When I could no longer work in greenhouses, I started doing irregular jobs for acquaintances, like painting, carpentry work. But I didn't earn enough. I also became addicted to cocaine and committed petty crimes. These were added up in court, and I got 33 months of imprisonment, and was declared an undesirable alien [continued residence as an undesired alien is punishable as a crime against the state]. When I was detained for so long and so frequently, I

> wanted to return. Since then I've been presented to the embassy six times. They know my nationality and identity but cannot do anything [he indicated that the Moroccan authorities do not want to take him back because of his record of offenses]. One time I tried to go back myself but got arrested in Belgium [on my way to Morocco].'

The man was classified into the higher legitimacy group, yet was quite critical about repeated detention, a practice that clearly shows the informal 'incapacitation' function of immigration detention (see Leerkes and Broeders, 2010):

> 'I think that people [like me] should be detained until they can be expelled. And if that doesn't work out, they should find a different solution. People should be able to go themselves or stay here. I can't be deported. They know it, too, and yet they detain me again.'

For geographical reasons, many unauthorized labour migrants initially migrate to Mediterranean EU countries, but a notable number eventually travel to Western Europe. For a number of such respondents, the perceived severity of immigration detention contributed to a desire to go back to their initial destination countries. A Palestinian stated:

> 'As a teenager I went to Libya. My parents had died, so nothing kept me in Gaza. I worked in Libya for ten years before going to Italy, both for work and the experience. After three years I could no longer find work when three friends went here. So, I decided to also take the train up North. I got arrested after spending 1.5 weeks here. The detention conditions are okay, but it's terrible to be locked up. When I'm free again, I want to go back to Italy. The Netherlands is a beautiful country, but the law is horrible….'

A few respondents developed a preference to leave but hoped that they would be away only temporarily. A Moroccan man, who had worked in various informal jobs and had eventually entered into a relationship with a Dutch girl of Moroccan origin, thereby also illustrating how labour migrants may resemble family migrants over time. He found it difficult to be deprived of his liberty and income, and therefore preferred to go to Morocco to arrange his immigration documents there. Should that be impossible, he hoped to go from Morocco to Spain, and reunite with his girlfriend there.[62] He intended to go to Spain

62 The Netherlands requires family migrants to apply for a residence permit in their country of origin. Deportees who are not considered a 'security threat' are not prevented from re-immigrating legally,

directly should the deportation procedure fail. Several of his friends had gone there after having been detained in the Netherlands and claimed that Spain was preferable. He explained:

> 'I had work and we [my girlfriend and I] went to the beach each week. I was happy. But here we are in our cells from 5 pm to 8:15 am. That's almost fifteen hours! It drives me crazy: I've done nothing, why am I here? And I don't get enough food and need to do my own shopping on [an allowance of] 10 euro per week, but that's not enough.'

Like most family and asylum migrants, several labour migrants nonetheless persisted in a preference to stay, even when confronted with prolonged or repeated detention. They usually mentioned that they were afraid to leave 'empty handed': they could not return without bringing a sufficient amount of savings from their earnings. In these cases, detention sometimes seemed to extend rather than shorten migration projects. For example, a Chinese man, who was in his third immigration detention period in eight years, had initially planned to stay in Europe for a few years only. Although his detention experiences had made him believe that 'the Dutch government is really determined to arrest me' – thereby appearing to confirm theoretical assumptions about the effect of being caught on the perceived probability of being recaught – this was insufficient for him to consider returning. 'Every time I'd saved some money, they put me in detention. Every time my life's on track, I get arrested. I've lost everything I had. My planning was not to stay, but now I have to.' A Cameroonian man, who had stopped contacting his family when he found himself unable to send remittances, similarly explained: 'You're keeping me in jail. How can I consider leaving this country without money?'

9.6 To conclude

This chapter has examined whether and how immigration detention – under conditions found in the Netherlands in 2011 – affects the willingness on the part of detainees to leave the territory of the detaining state, and whether eventual influences can be regarded the product of deterrence. The analysis sheds light on two types of 'specific deterrence'; first, the possibility that detainees are pressured into cooperating with the deportation procedure and, second, the possibility that detainees are pressured into leaving the country on their own, should they be released because of a failed deportation procedure. This chapter focused on stated preferences; it was not observed whether respondents were

---

provided that all admission requirements are met.

cooperating with the deportation procedure or whether they actually went to a neighbouring country after a failed deportation procedure (various repeatedly detained individuals did mention that they had done so after earlier detention periods). It should be remarked that an eventual preference on the part of migrants to leave the country of the detaining state, does not automatically translate into 'permanent departure', as the administrative detention outcome also depends on supra-individual factors, including the willingness by receiving states to provide laissez passers (Ellermann, 2008; Leerkes and Kox, 2016). Furthermore, migrants who are pressured into a preference to 'return' may start a new (illegal) migration project after having been repatriated (Brotherton and Barrios, 2011; Cardoso et al., 2016), while those who manage go to a third country may eventually come back to the country where they were detained, such as when former detainees are returned to the 'responsible country' under the Dublin Regulation after having been apprehended elsewhere in Europe.

A *first* main conclusion is that immigration detention seems to be producing limited selective deterrent effects at the attitudinal level. At the time of the interview, seventeen out of 81 respondents expressed a preference to go to their country of citizenship – in some cases in hopes of starting a new (legal or illegal) migration project from there – and in sixteen cases that preference was reported to have been coerced, at least in part, by detention, including repeated detention. Additionally, the number of respondents preferring onward migration increased by seven when previous detention periods are taken into consideration. These results are obtained for a detention regime that is relatively punitive comparatively, especially in the European context given the relatively long maximum and actual detention duration, and the common practice of repeated detention.

As expected, most respondents found the detention quite painful, reflecting both Sykes's (1958) classic 'pains of imprisonment', Crewe's (2011) 'pains of uncertainty and indeterminacy', and what could perhaps be called the 'pain of perceived illegitimacy', that is, the belief that one does not deserve immigration detention – either not at all, or not under conditions that characterized the Dutch detention regime in 2011. Much in line with deterrence theory, respondents appeared to be making a kind of rational decision by weighing the 'costs' of immigration detention against the 'benefits' of a continued stay in the Netherlands or Europe more generally. In most cases, however, the outcome of that comparison turned out to be a persistent preference for continued stay; respondents' interests in continuing their stay in the Netherlands typically outweighed their interests in ending the immigration detention experience – thus indicating strong 'threshold effects'. Deterrent effects were also found to be limited because the detention experience also triggers mechanisms that actually reinforce a preference to stay. Some respondents, who were afraid of the stigma of returning 'empty handed', reasoned that they actually needed to prolong their migration project in order to make up for income that was lost during the detention. Others received advice from other detainees on how to resist deportation or on how to survive without a resident permit more generally (see Campesi, 2015). A low perceived legitimacy of the detention seemed to be reinforcing migrants' preferences to stay as well; while the 'pain of perceived illegitimacy' sometimes added to a desire to leave the territory of the detaining state, so as to end one's exposure to it, it also triggered resistance.

The nature of the interests offsetting the 'costs' of immigration detention varied by migration motive. Respondents classified as family migrants often persisted in a preference to stay due to their family ties and socio-cultural attachment to Dutch society. Asylum migrants emphasized safety concerns and an interest to stay away from their country of citizenship. They were relatively open to going to a different European country but found themselves being tied to the country of the first asylum application because of the Dublin regulation. Respondents classified as labour migrants were more likely to emphasize financial obstacles to return.

A *second* conclusion is that the specific deterrent effects were concentrated among labour migrants. Some of them brought pre-existing return migration plans forward. Others hoped to be able to evade repeated detention by seeking employment elsewhere in Europe, should the deportation procedure fail. On average, migrants classified as labour migrants seemed to have a weaker commitment to continued stay than family and asylum migrants, but they also seemed to consider their detention somewhat more legitimate, which results in the *third* and final main conclusion: while all respondents who developed a preference to leave attributed these attitudinal changes to the perceived severity of the detention or the risk of repeated detention, those developing a preference to 'return' to their country of citizenship were notably less negative about the outcome and process legitimacy of the detention. That observation, which is consistent with defiance theory (Sherman, 1993), suggests that deterrent effects mostly occur if some degree of perceived legitimacy is also present, and that perhaps some degree of compliance would also have occurred had the government used a 'lighter' measure than detention – or that such measures would actually have been more effective, as they can be expected to perform better on perceived process legitimacy. It also suggests that the distinction between forced return and voluntary return is blurred in reality; there may be a measure of (indirect) force in voluntary return, and a trace of voluntariness in forced return. To the extent that perceived severity and risk in the absence of some measure of perceived legitimacy were capable of changing migration preferences, they mostly pressured detainees into a preference for onward illegal migration to a different European country – thus turning them into a kind of 'fugitives' who contribute to a spatial displacement of illegal residence.

In order to get a more complete picture of the operation and effects of immigration detention, future research should try to pay attention to both the detainee *and* the institutional level (Leerkes and Kox, 2016). The decisions that embassies and consulates make on readmission seem to 'dilute' the limited specific deterrent effects at the attitudinal level. As was reported, over two-thirds of the respondents were eventually released because of a failed deportation procedure, including ten of the seventeen respondents who preferred going to their country of citizenship. While more research is urgently needed on how receiving states handle requests by governments in the Global North to provide laissez passers to unauthorized migrants, a perceived legitimacy deficit of deportation and immigration detention on their part – perhaps in addition to critical assessments regarding the fairness of the immigration policies of the Global North more generally – may well be among the reasons for non-cooperation. Another implication of these figures is that most respondents probably stayed in Europe in a worse condition than in which they entered detention, also given the loss of employment that regularly came with it and the health issues that were reported. One would hope that such perverse outcomes create an interest on the part of detaining states to limit the punitive uses of immigration detention, and to find other ways of dealing with the presence of noncitizens who are formally deportable but are difficult to deport in practice.

This chapter can be read as a case study on the social operation of migration law, with a focus on deportation law. It has broader scientific implications for the study of international migration and legal compliance. In a world in which international migration is increasingly being regulated by states, it is crucial to obtain better insight in how immigration regimes, including deportation regimes, codetermine migration and mobility. In migration studies, the structuring influence of 'immigration law in action is undertheorized and underresearched' (see Massey et al., 2005; Massey, 2015). So far, most researchers interested in 'policy effects' have implicitly or explicitly limited themselves to economic ('rational choice') compliance models, and have mostly focused on migration decisions taken in countries of origin, such as by asking whether apprehension risks at the U.S. border influence migration decisions (see for example Cornelius and Salehyan, 2007; Gathmann, 2008; Massey and Riosmena, 2010). Ryo (2013) and others (e.g. Braithwaite, 2010; Van Alphen et al., 2013) have argued that in order to advance our knowledge of contemporary migration, it is essential to incorporate models of legal compliance that also pay attention to (non)compliance on normative grounds. Ryo used a legal compliance framework in order to understand the migration decisions of (potential) migrants in Mexico; we use a similar lens to understand (changes in) migration preferences among deportable migrants. Like Ryo, we find that normative compliance models are important to consider, but we also find that economic models certainly cannot be disregarded. Future research could pay more attention to the complex interrelationship between normative and economic dimensions of compliance, including the possibility that deterrent measures need to be perceived as (somewhat) legitimate in order to be effective, and the tendency of deterrent measures to eventually undercut process legitimacy. While this chapter focuses on migrants, it is also crucial to analyse how professionals working in relevant institutions in the field of immigration law – such as embassy personnel, immigration lawyers, (migration) police, NGOs-structure migration patterns, using a similar lens.

A vast amount of scholarly work has enhanced our knowledge of legal (non)compliance, but little is known on how people give meaning and respond to the laws of foreign governments (see Ryo, 2013) – especially when such laws mostly target them, as is the case with immigration law. Existing models in socio-legal studies are useful starting points, but some claims of the compliance literature do not seem to hold, such as the central claim in criminal justice research that perceived process legitimacy is more influential than perceived outcome legitimacy (see Tyler, 2003). Compared to other fields of law, there is less agreement that the content of immigration law is fair and serves the 'common good'. Using two powerful sociological concepts by James Coleman (1990), one could say that the laws in other fields usually resemble codified 'conjoint norms' where those targeted by the norm also benefit from the norm being observed (say: 'improved public safety'). Immigration laws, by contrast, are more akin to 'disjoint norms', where those targeted by a norm and those benefitting from it constitute different groups. Immigration law benefits a substantial number of residence permit holders and those obtaining citizenship through naturalization, but also is a repressive, protectionist instrument that is designed to reduce migration, and that has the effect of keeping a significant part of the migrants at the bottom of the social hierarchy in a rather vulnerable position – without extending voting rights to them (also see De Genova, 2002; Menjívar and Abrego, 2012). As a consequence, the perceived outcome legitimacy of immigration law is much more contested and variant than is found in other fields of law. The central importance of process legitimacy in criminal justice research may well be due to perceived outcome legitimacy being close to a constant there.

More generally, there is a need for a better understanding of legitimacy issues in immigration law. These need not only be addressed from a formal-legal or normative-philosophical perspective; eventually, we also need to understand how migrants and other relevant actors perceive the outcome and process legitimacy of immigration law in countries of the Global North, how their views are affected by the social structure and cultural factors, and how these may be changing under the influence of globalization and a rise of a global citizenship in countries in the Global South.

10 'I AM SO TIRED OF THE LAW.' UNDERSTANDING THE SHAPING OF UNAUTHORIZED MIGRANTS' LEGAL CONSCIOUSNESS OVER TIME*

ABSTRACT

This chapter addresses the fourth and final sub-question on how the migrants' understandings of, experiences with, and meaning-making processes toward the law are translated into interactions with the law. The chapter describes two legal consciousness processes observed among unauthorized migrants. These processes differ in terms of the migrants' proximity to and expectations from the law, as well as their motivations (or lack thereof) to interact with the law. This understanding helps to determine whether, why, and how unauthorized migrants contest, obey, mobilize, resist, protest, or give up on the law over time. Moreover, these processes offer insights into the constitutive powers and instrumental powerlessness of the law, raising serious questions about the current functioning of the law for unauthorized migrants.

10.1 INTRODUCTION

It's almost 2.30 when the demonstration in front of the office of the Immigration and Naturalization Service [IND] in Amsterdam starts. About 50 unauthorized migrants and supporters are singing and shouting in a megaphone. Their songs vary from 'Remove our fingerprints!' to 'No man, no woman, no human being is illegal' and from 'Down, down IND' to '*Solidarité pour les Sans-Papiers*'. The group consists of mainly African rejected asylum seekers who believe that their asylum claims are unjustly rejected. They request that an IND representative listens to their concerns but, despite the demonstration lasting about an hour, the IND ignores their presence. Marc tells me that it's mostly like this during their demonstrations. Nevertheless, they keep on demonstrating, hoping to be heard by the Dutch authorities. A spokeswoman of the group then starts to read out a declaration to the audience, stating that

* This single authored paper has been submitted to *Law and Society Review*.

> they are refugees who need protection and who shouldn't be subjected to a harsh immigration system (fieldnotes 06/03/2015).

This is an observation of a demonstration by seekers whose legalization claims were rejected and who were ordered to leave the country. As they were unwilling and/or lacked the documents required to return, they decided to unauthorizedly stay in the Netherlands. Consequently, they were excluded from social services and subjected to a comprehensive multi-layered immigration system consisting of a wide range of laws, policies and practices aimed at preventing, controlling and ending unauthorized residence (see also Chapter 4). The rejected asylum seekers considered their subjection to this system as unjustified, as we see in Marc's words: 'That's injustice, you know? It's injustice'. They united in a protest group called 'We Are Here' to collectively step out of the shadows of society and reveal the perceived shortcomings of the law in the Netherlands (see also Hajer and Bröer, 2020).

The We Are Here group demonstrates that unauthorized migrants have political agency. While it has often been assumed that disadvantaged groups such as unauthorized migrants are trapped and obstructed by the law's pervasive authority (Silbey, 2005), these migrants may invoke the law to claim their rights and improve their precarious situation (cf. Calavita, 2005; Eule et al., 2019; Mainwaring, 2016). Previous research shows that unauthorized migrants interact differently with the law. They may, for instance, develop a wide range of strategies to circumvent the law, meaning that they try to avoid being checked, detected or identified by immigration authorities (Broeders and Engbersen, 2007; Ellermann, 2010; Fabini, 2019; Mainwaring, 2016). They may also mobilize the law to improve their situation or claim basic rights (Abrego, 2011; Menjívar and Lakhani, 2016; Schwenken, 2013). Unauthorized migrants may protest the law, either individually or in a collective with other unauthorized migrants, supporters or unions such as the We Are Here group (Haddeland, 2021; Hajer and Bröer, 2020; Nyers, 2006). Examples of such protests include demonstrations (Summers Sandoval, 2008), hunger or thirst strikes (McGregor, 2011), protests in immigration detention centres (Mainwaring, 2016), pro-regularization movements (Laubenthal, 2007) and/or grassroots campaigns (Varsanyi, 2005). Yet not all unauthorized migrants are willing or able to contest the law. Some prefer to comply with it by leaving the country (Leerkes et al., 2017) while the interactions of others are characterized by withdrawal (Eule et al., 2019; Griffiths, 2013).

The differentiated behaviour of unauthorized migrants raises the question of how to understand and explain (changes in) their thoughts on and interactions with the law over time. This question has not yet been answered as most studies focus on a specific interaction with the law, a specific group of unauthorized migrants or a specific moment in time (e.g. Abrego, 2011, 2018, 2019; Haddeland, 2021; Kubal, 2014; Ryo, 2011; Schwenken, 2013). Some studies do provide a rich description of unauthorized migrants' thoughts on or interactions with the law yet without comprehensively explaining the migrants' underlying motivations (cf. Young, 2014). However, a subject-centred study on what unauthorized migrants think and do in relation to the law that provides insights into the migrants underlying motivations for what they think and do may enrich the current academic debate on the power of the law in unauthorized migrants' everyday reality (e.g. Calavita, 1998, 2005; Menjívar and Abrego, 2012; Ryo, 2015). Moreover, such a study may help to develop more ethical, equitable and effective immigration systems (Ryo, 2015, 2017). Finally, such a study may contribute to the current debate on the (hegemonic) force of the law (Levine and Mellema, 2001; Silbey, 2005). Therefore, this chapter draws on ethnographic fieldwork amongst 105 migrants – who (used to) reside unauthorized in the Netherlands – to describe and explain their thoughts on and interactions with the law over time and to provide insights into the power of the law for this specific legal category of people.

The chapter takes legal consciousness as its theoretical starting point. There are several definitions of this socio-legal concept, which has been differently applied (Chua and Engel, 2019; Halliday, 2019; Horák, Lacko and Klocek, 2021; Silbey, 2005). The concept is usually understood as 'the ways in which people experience, understand, and act in relation to law' (Chua and Engel, 2019: 336). It is based on the idea that people might give different meanings to laws, despite these laws being similarly and equally applied (Merry, 1990). The concept moves beyond the idea of legal awareness or knowledge of laws and focuses on understanding and explaining how (disadvantaged) people think about and interact with the law to gain insight in the powers of the law (Chua and Engel, 2019). Although 'the law' has a central role in legal consciousness studies, legal consciousness scholars do not unambiguously define the term and use different operationalizations of it (Halliday, 2019). In this chapter, I move beyond a positivistic notion of the law by using a so-called approach from below (cf. Engel, 1998; Hertogh, 2004). This means that 'the law' covers all the legal norms in society *and* the institutions and practices associated with them (cf. Deflem, 2008). Consciousness refers to what unauthorized migrants both say and do as it may be 'discursively deployed as reflexive consideration about day-to-day activities; it is also tacitly enacted as competent social action' (Ewick and Silbey, 1998: 46).

In what follows, I first elaborate on the legal consciousness concept, the methods and the Dutch regulatory context in which unauthorized migrants' legal consciousness is being shaped. Then, in the results section, I demonstrate that the shaping of unauthorized migrants' legal consciousness cannot be brought back to a single moment in time. Instead, I argue, it should be seen as a fluid, disorderly process in which the migrants' thoughts on and interactions with the law are subject to change under the influence of many legal and non-legal factors. I describe and explain two different types of legal consciousness processes which substantially differ from each other in terms of the migrants' proximity to and expectations from the law as well as their motivations (not) to interact with the law. In both processes, unauthorized migrants may indeed invoke, circumvent, challenge, mobilize, protest and obey the law. Yet, it is dependent of (their stage in) the legal consciousness process if and why they decide to do so and how they motivate their thoughts and interactions. The insights into unauthorized migrants' legal consciousness processes have three major implications as they 1) expose the powers *and* powerlessness of the law in the migration domain, 2) raise severe questions on the current functioning of the law for unauthorized migrants and 3) add to the theoretical debate on the usefulness of the legal consciousness concept. These implications are addressed in the concluding discussion of this chapter in which I advocate for a different use of the law in the migration domain.

10.2 Drawing on legal consciousness

Legal consciousness has long been considered a promising approach through which to empirically examine how law works in people's everyday reality (Cowan, 2004; Ewick and Silbey, 1998, 2020; Hertogh, 2004; Silbey, 2005). Early legal consciousness scholars used the legal consciousness concept as a critical lens to gain insight into how (unequal) power hierarchies were being reproduced by the law (Fritsvold, 2009), as they believed that the 'haves' came out ahead in legal systems (Galanter, 1974). These scholars were therefore mainly concerned with the legal needs of the poor and the law's failure to fulfil these people's needs (Engel, 1998). They explored how ordinary people – as opposed to legal experts, professionals and so-called elites – understood and made sense of the law and legal institutions (Ewick and Silbey, 2020). By shifting their focus from Law *and* Society to Law *in* Society, they examined 'not only how and by whom the law is used, but also when and by whom it is not used' and explored people's motivations for not using the law (Silbey, 2005: 326). As such, these early legal consciousness scholars tried to reveal inequality structures in society and better understand the (hegemonic) force of the law (Ewick and Silbey, 2020; McCann and March, 1995).

The approach of early legal consciousness scholars has also been labelled the 'hegemony' (Chua and Engel, 2019) or 'critical' (Halliday, 2019) legal consciousness research school. This research school differs from other legal consciousness research schools that have come into being in recent decades in terms of research purposes, conceptual operationalization and research methodology (Chua and Engel, 2019; Halliday, 2019; Hertogh, 2018).[63] While early legal consciousness scholars mainly focused on the hegemonic powers of the law, these relatively new legal consciousness research schools

63 Chua and Engel (2019), for instance, distinguish the identity, hegemonic and mobilization school. Halliday (2019) distinguishes a critical approach, an interpretive approach, a comparative cultural approach and a law-in-action approach while Hertogh (2018) urges scholars to shift focus from legal consciousness to legal alienation. These schools are not discussed in depth as the main point is to illustrate that there is no

address the instrumental effects of the law, the impact of the law on one's identity or people's use of legal mobilization strategies (Chua and Engel, 2019). This has resulted in a wide variety in legal consciousness research and brought about a debate on whether the concept is still suited to understanding the (hegemonic) power of the law in society (e.g. Ewick and Silbey, 2020; Silbey, 2005). Susan Silbey (2005), one of the most prominent early legal consciousness scholars, believed it is not. She claimed that the legal consciousness concept had become comprised as its scholars sacrificed 'much of the concept's critical edge and theoretical utility' by solely focusing on the instrumental effects of the law – that is, whether the law inspires or withholds people from acting in certain ways (Silbey, 2005: 324). Scholars were, according to Silbey, too often interested in enhancing the effectiveness of the law while overlooking the law's constitutive aspects – how (the hegemonic force of) law appears in and is constructed by everyday life. She argued that this approach left unanswered the question of why people 'acquiesce to a legal system that, despite its promises of equal treatment, systematically reproduces inequality' (Silbey, 2005: 324). It made her believe that the concept had become part of policy projects instead of a tool to assess the law's hegemonic power, making it time to leave the legal consciousness concept behind.

Yet, the recent revival of legal consciousness studies indicates that many socio-legal scholars still consider it an appealing concept (e.g. Chua and Engel, 2019; Güdük and Desmet, 2022; Halliday, 2019; Horák et al., 2021). Halliday (2019: 872), therefore, argues that early legal consciousness should not hold on to a single correct use of the concept. Instead, he contends, it should be regarded as an adaptable concept that may be differently used and operationalized in order to better understand the role of law in society (see also Chua and Engel, 2019). In this chapter, I make use of the adaptability of the concept. In line with other migration studies (e.g. Güdük and Desmet, 2022; Haddeland, 2021; Schwenken, 2013), I mainly draw upon the hegemony or critical legal consciousness research school, although I do add some elements of other legal consciousness research schools to be better able to understand unauthorized migrants' thoughts on and interactions with the law over time and to gain insights into the power of the law for this specific group in society. This means, more concretely, that I focus on three elements. First, I explore the salience of the law in unauthorized migrants' everyday reality to better understand whether, how and why the law becomes active in their lives and whether this changes over time. After all, the role of the law in one's everyday life cannot be taken for granted (cf. Levine and Mellema, 2001). Second, I focus on unauthorized migrants' thoughts on and interactions with the law, including the underlying motivations for their thoughts and interactions. Third, I examine what the law does for/to unauthorized

monolithic approach in legal consciousness research anymore (but see Chua and Engel, 2019; Halliday, 2019; Hertogh, 2018).

migrants over time and assess the implications for the power of the law in their everyday reality. These three steps enable me to provide insights into unauthorized migrants' legal consciousness over time as well as into the powers of the law for this specific group in society.

10.3 Methods[64]

This chapter is based on multi-sited ethnographic fieldwork amongst 105 migrants who (used to) reside without a legal status in the Netherlands. Ethnographic research is considered the most suited to understanding how ordinary people think and act in relation to the law *and* to explain the power of the law in people's everyday reality (Ewick and Silbey, 1998; Merry, 1990; Nielsen, 2000; Sarat, 1990). Therefore, I followed 45 unauthorized migrants between March 2015 and May 2018. I observed them in their everyday lives and/or during their interaction with controlling institutions; I repeatedly interviewed and/or informally talked to them; and/or we had frequent contact by phone and WhatsApp. Additionally, I interviewed, informally spoke or observed another 60 unauthorized migrants who only wanted to be involved in the research on a limited basis. I included migrants at different locations and at various stages of their unauthorized residency – i.e. hiding from the authorities, just being arrested by the police, living in freedom-restricted (family) locations or staying in immigration detention centres. I contacted the migrants through, *inter alia*, support organizations, controlling institutions and migrant communities. This approach resulted in a heterogenic group of 105 unauthorized migrants from different countries and continents who stayed between almost a year and 38 years (unauthorized) in the Netherlands. The respondents were between eight and 70 years old and differed from each other in terms of age, gender, country of origin, length of stay, migration motive and contacts with the authorities. The respondents were mainly based in the Netherlands but also included migrants who were visited after their (forced) return from the Netherlands to Surinam (10), Nigeria (6) and Guyana (1). The latter migrants were involved in the research to prevent an over-representation of respondents with a negative stance towards the law who are – according to legitimacy theories (e.g. Tyler, 2006; Van den Bos, 2018) – less willing to comply with the law and to leave the country.

During all interactions in the field, unauthorized migrants could – among other things – recall what they did in their everyday lives, their expectations for the future, their understandings of the law and their experiences and interactions with it as well as the law's consequences for them. This resulted in very open conversations on a wide range of topics including the role of the law in their everyday lives. All participant observations and

64 The Methodology section is based on the methods section in the previous chapters.

informal conversations were recorded in extensive fieldnotes, while the interviews were literally transcribed. Data were analysed by using thematic and open coding strategies in Atlas.ti – qualitative data-analysis software (cf. Saldaña, 2016: 235). Both the law and unauthorized migrants were central in the analysis for this chapter (cf. Ewick and Silbey, 2020). I examined whether, how and why the law became active in the migrants' everyday lives,[65] observed how unauthorized migrants think about[66] and interact with the law and tried to explain whether, why and how their thoughts and interactions changed over time to be able to unfold their legal consciousness processes.

10.4 The Dutch immigration system over time

The shaping of unauthorized migrants' legal consciousness should be understood in the context of the legal regulations that come into force once they are unauthorized in the country (e.g. Abrego, 2011; Güdük and Desmet, 2022; Haddeland, 2021; Miežanskienė, 2020). In the Netherlands – where this study is situated – the legal regulations for unauthorized migrants have markedly changed in recent decades, partly under the influence of European developments and legislation. Whereas the authorities used to welcome and tolerate (unauthorized) migrants, they started to problematize the arrival of migrants from the late eighties onwards (Burgers and Engbersen, 1999; Van der Woude, 2022; Van Eijl, 2012). Like other Western countries (Franko, 2020), they repeatedly strengthened their immigration laws, policies and practices (Staring and Van Swaaningen, 2021; Van Eijl, 2012). They created a multi-layered immigration system – which includes laws and policies outside the migration domain – which is being executed by myriad state and non-state actors and stretches out over different geographical locations (see Chapter 4). The system combines strong enforcement interests with extensive enforcement capacities (Leerkes and Van Houte, 2020). While unauthorized residence is not criminalized, the Dutch system is known for the migrants' far-reaching exclusion from society and the state's comprehensive control capacity (e.g. Leerkes and Van Houte, 2020; Staring and Van Swaaningen, 2013, 2021; Van Eijl, 2012). Successive ministers of immigration are said to have used such a system to discourage unauthorized residence and to incite unauthorized migrants to leave the country (e.g. Engbersen, Van San and Leerkes, 2006; Kox, 2010; Staring and Van Swaaningen, 2013; Van Eijl, 2012).

It is not possible to discuss the entire system within the scope of this chapter (but see Kox, 2010; Van Eijl, 2012) but I briefly mention those legal regulations that are supposed

65 I discuss (the role of the lack of a legal status in) unauthorized migrants' everyday lives elsewhere in more detail (Chapters 4 and 6).

66 Unauthorized migrants' thoughts on the immigration system are elsewhere discussed in terms of legitimacy (Chapters 7, 8 and 9).

to have had a severe impact on unauthorized migrants' living conditions in the Netherlands (Van der Leun, 2003; Van Eijl, 2012; Van Meeteren, 2014). One regulation dates from 1991, when unauthorized migrants were no longer eligible to obtain a social-security number (Kox, 2010). These numbers became more important with the introduction of the Compulsory Identification Act in 1994 which, under the threat of a fine, obliged employers to control the residence status of potential employees before hiring them (Kox, 2010). In 1998, the so-called Linking Act was introduced which arranged unauthorized migrants' exclusion from social-security benefits and public services, except for essential healthcare, legal aid and – until the age of 18 – education (Van der Leun, 2003). From then on, unauthorized migrants' access to the formal labour and housing market as well as most public and social-security services was severely complicated (Van der Leun, 2003; Van Meeteren, 2014). Shortly afterwards, these migrants' route to informal markets and services was also hampered by the introduction of the Extended Compulsory Identification Act in 2005 and the increased administrative fines for employers of unauthorized migrants (Van Meeteren, 2014). These measures made it more complicated for migrants to work in the informal economy and earn an independent living while being unauthorized in the country (Kox, 2010; Van Meeteren, 2014; Staring et al., 2022).

The Dutch authorities not only complicated unauthorized migrants' everyday lives in the Netherlands but also tried to encourage their return. Since the early nineties, they have funded various Assisted Voluntary Return (AVR) programmes for unauthorized migrants which consist of logistic support and/or reintegration budgets (Mommers and Velthuis, 2010). These programs were initially offered by the International Organization for Migration (IOM); however, increasing numbers of (non-governmental) organizations have also started to receive AVR funding too as they were assumed to be better able to reach out to unauthorized migrants living underground (see also Chapter 5). Additionally, the authorities established the Repatriation and Departure Service (DT&V) in 2007 to effectuate unauthorized migrants' voluntary *and* forced return processes (Mommers and Velthuis, 2010). After having closed shelter facilities for rejected asylum seekers in 1998 and 2001 (Kox, 2010), the Dutch authorities again started to provide shelter to specific groups of unauthorized migrants in response to protests that arose after the latter's exclusion from them as well as court rulings that obliged them to do so (Pluymen, 2008; Winter et al., 2018). In 2004, for instance, the Dutch authorities opened freedom-restricted shelter facilities for unauthorized migrants who were willing to return to their home country within twelve weeks and, in 2011, offered freedom-restricted family facilities to unauthorized children under 18 and their parents (Winter et al., 2018). In 2014, after another court ruling, temporary Bed, Bath and Bread arrangements were made available for unauthorized migrants who were willing to leave the Netherlands (Mack et al., 2022). However, there are still unauthorized migrants who are *not* eligible for shelter facilities as they do not want to return and/or no longer meet the admission criteria (see also Chapter 5).

Despite its exclusion policies, return programmes and shelter facilities, the Dutch authorities continue struggling to effectuate unauthorized migrants' departure from the Netherlands (Maliepaard et al., 2022). Hoping to increase the effectiveness of the immigration system, they have repeatedly strengthened their control policies and practices (Van Eijl, 2012) – for instance, recurrently extending their opportunities to stop, detain and deport unauthorized migrants (Kox, 2010; Staring and Van Swaaningen, 2013; Van Eijl, 2012). They also expanded the powers of the immigration police with the introduction of the Aliens Act 2000. The police – and other officers – no longer needed 'concrete indications' to stop people and request their identification; 'a reasonable suspicion of unauthorized residence' could suffice (Kox, 2010). Additionally, partly due to current EU legislation, the Dutch authorities increasingly use biometric features such as iris scans, fingerprints and digital facial images to facilitate the detection, identification and deportation of unauthorized migrants (Broeders, 2009). They have also extended the opportunities to detain unauthorized migrants with the purpose of removal (Baudoin et al., 2008), although detention decisions require a more elaborate motivation since the implementation of the EU Return Directive (Klaassen and Rodrigues, 2021). The exclusion and control policies are not always as strictly practiced as proclaimed (Aliverti, 2013) and their effects are moderated by the everyday interactions between border officers and unauthorized migrants (Van der Woude and Van der Leun, 2017). Yet, these do provide the regulatory context in which unauthorized migrants' legal consciousness is being shaped.

10.5 Unauthorized migrants' legal consciousness over time

Like the regulatory context, unauthorized migrants' legal consciousness is dynamic and fluid. Analysis of the research data shows that the shaping of the migrants' legal consciousness cannot be taken back to a single moment in time, as some scholars tend to do (see Abrego, 2011; Hernández, 2010). Instead, as I illustrate later, it should be seen as a fluid, disorderly process that starts in the migrants' home countries and continues en route to and during their stay in the Netherlands. It is subject to change under the influence of many legal and non-legal factors, meaning that they might go back and forth in this process until their residence is (temporarily) legalized, they (forcedly) leave the Netherlands or they die during their unauthorized residence.[67] Here, I distinguish two

67 The shaping of unauthorized migrants' legal consciousness evidently continues to be shaped after their residence is being legalized or once they have left the Netherlands but is not included in this chapter.

legal consciousness processes among unauthorized migrants which substantially differ from each other in terms of the migrants' proximity to and expectations from the law as well as their motivations to (not) interact with the law. I show that these processes are inspired, *inter alia*, by migrants' personal conditions, migration motives, thoughts on the law, future aspirations, social situatedness and economic and social opportunities in home and host countries (see also other studies on migrants' legal consciousness: Abrego, 2008, 2011; Galli, 2019; Gehring, 2013; Güdük and Desmet, 2022; Haddeland, 2021; Kubal, 2014; Kulk and De Hart, 2013; Ryo, 2011, 2013; Schwenken, 2013). Below, I discuss both processes and contribute to the knowledge of the diversity of unauthorized migrants' legal consciousness for which Abrego (2011) calls.

10.5.1 A first legal consciousness process: aspiring better living conditions, staying away from the law

The first legal consciousness process is characterized by unauthorized migrants aspiring to better living conditions and staying away from the law. This process is mainly seen among migrants who originate from countries that are known for their poor social-economic or social-cultural situation such as labour migrants who came to work in the informal economy, family migrants who aimed to reunite with family members and others who lacked perspective in their home country. These respondents aspired to improve their living conditions economically, socially or culturally. As they saw no opportunities to do so in their home country, they migrated to the Netherlands. The Asian Alvin, for instance, tells me that he came to the Netherlands to work in the informal economy: 'That's the reason why most Philippinos are here, especially illegals. They come here for a while because there is no work in the Philippines'. Some respondents turned to transnational networks to arrange their journey while others used a more ad-hoc approach that eventually took them to the Netherlands. These migrants were already informed by public narratives in their home country that they should not turn themselves against the law, as comes to the fore in Alvin's words: 'We are aware of this before we come, you know. When you enter this country, you are already aware of the consequences. "Don't do this, don't go there"'. They realized that interaction with the law could result in their detection and deportation, meaning they mainly reached out to compatriots for housing, work and other needs. This (initially) enabled them to make a living in the Netherlands. They were not concerned with legalizing their residence but were fully occupied with improving their living conditions.

Migrants in this legal consciousness process were initially positive about the law in the Netherlands, which may partly be explained on the basis of their negative experiences with the law in their home and transit countries as well as the positive narratives that (used to) circulate on the Dutch legal system. This also applies to the West African, Arnaud: 'The law in the Netherlands? It is according to the rules'. As elsewhere illustrated in more detail (see Chapters 7 and 8), these respondents recognize the Dutch authorities' right to rule over them. They believe that the Dutch immigration system is necessary to regulate migration into the country, although some believe that the authorities could be more lenient in their admission policies and allow their presence in the country. It is questionable whether these respondents are fully aware of all legal immigration legislation (cf. Hertogh, 2012) and have internalized the dominant ideas and values in Western societies on who deserves to be admitted to a society (cf. Anderson, 2013). Yet, the migrants' thoughts on the law fit what Ewick and Silbey (1998) call a *before the law* stance. This means that people accept the law and generally consider it fair, as it is assumed to bring legally correct and unbiased decisions. This can also be seen in the narrative of Arnaud, whose ideas on the immigration system are positive: 'These [laws] are good. To me, these are good. I have never seen bad decisions of the IND [immigration and naturalization service], of DT&V or COA [the central agency for the reception of asylum seekers]. No, I didn't, never'. While people who are *before the law* are assumed to abide by it and cooperate with the authorities (Ewick and Sibley, 1998; Tyler, 2006), my respondents in this legal consciousness process do not. They feel neither legally nor morally obliged to comply with Dutch law as they prioritize other non-legal considerations over the legal duty to obey the immigration authorities (cf. Black et al., 2004; Koser and Kuschminder, 2015). The Indonesian, Guntur, for instance, says that the Dutch law 'is fair but, if they [Dutch authorities] can, they have to help poor people. (...) In Indonesia, there's no work, no income. (...) That's why I am here'. As he believes that the Dutch authorities neglect to provide migrants from low-perspective countries with regular options to work in the Netherlands, he considers it justified to continue his unauthorized residence and went once more to the Netherlands after his 'voluntary' return from immigration detention.

During their unauthorized residence, these respondents try to stay away from the law. This should be understood in the context of their deportability – that is, the omnipresent awareness of the possibility of being deported from the space of the nation-state (De Genova, 2002: 439). Respondents constantly try to keep the law at a distance by going underground and using different strategies to stay out of sight of the authorities. Guntur explains some of his strategies:

> 'If I see the police, I go the other way. I try to behave normally, to do only good things. So, no fighting, no.... Just normal. That lawyer also says: "You have to do what's normal in the Netherlands. So, if you see a red traffic light, you stop and do not cross. If you're on a footpath, you walk". All that kind of thing. That lawyer explained it all.'

The latter refers to a meeting of a grassroots organization where a lawyer informed him and other unauthorized migrants of their rights and advised them to be 'holier than the pope' to prevent being detected. Other strategies include dressing tidily, behaving confidently, avoiding the company of people who might cause trouble, evading crowded and risky places, learning the language, buying public-transport tickets, regularly changing addresses and/or hiding their (legal) identities. This shows that the law is very salient in these unauthorized migrants' everyday lives as respondents feel disciplinarily pressured by it (cf. Fabini, 2019). They try to stay away from the law, as claiming any rights may result in their deportation. Schwenken (2013) refers to it as a Catch 22 situation, as unauthorized migrants waive their rights and refrain from reporting malpractices experienced on the labour market, declaring (criminal) victimization and using ambulance services to prevent contact with non-immigration authorities.[68] Migrants may also be reluctant to formally marry, register the birth of their children and fulfil internships during high school given the associated risks. This shows that both immigration *and* non-immigration laws shape unauthorized migrants' everyday lives and function as a handicap (cf. Chauvin and Garcés-Mascareñas, 2012). Unauthorized migrants use multiple strategies to work around this handicap. They may uphold their strategies for over thirty years without being detected by the authorities, especially if they are embedded in strong social networks who support them if needed (Staring, Boesveldt and Kox, 2022). Once they have fulfilled their aspirations or have other reasons to do so, they may decide to leave the country. Alvin, for instance, wanted to earn money in the Netherlands to be able open a shop in his home country: 'That's the plan, you know. If I have a small business, then I go back'.

Pragmatically playing the law

Most respondents in this legal consciousness process, however, were sooner or later confronted by the law during traffic controls, at work inspections, in public spaces or on other occasions.[69] This may bring them to the next stage in their legal consciousness process. The respondents' thoughts are usually still *before the law* but they start pragmatically playing the law to fulfil their aspirations in the Netherlands. The migrants' behaviour fits what Ewick and Silbey (1998) call *with the law*, meaning that people use the law as a game or a commodity from which to benefit. Respondents used various strategies

68 The authorities have several 'free in, free out, policies that enable unauthorized migrants, among others, to register the victimization of crime without running the risk of being apprehended for the lack of a legal status, but unauthorized migrants do fear its consequences (see also Timmerman et al., 2020).

69 This has partly to do with the strategies that I used to recruit unauthorized migrants as these were initially solely direct towards unauthorized migrants who had somehow interacted with the immigration authorities. Research among elderly unauthorized migrants shows that these migrants can stay away from the law for many years (Staring, Boesveldt and Kox, 2022).

to do so, depending on their personal situation, opportunities and knowledge of their different opportunities. A few, for instance, mobilized the law to prevent their deportation. Legal mobilization usually refers to people's tendency to 'define their problems as legal ones and take them to some legal regime for help or settlement' (Merry, 2012: 49). Yet, these respondents did not believe they had a legal problem nor did they turn to a legal regime for help. Instead, they mobilized the law in the hope of fulfilling their aspirations in the Netherlands. Ibrahim, for instance, tells me that he was stopped by the police after having been involved in a car accident: 'I applied for asylum. Like others, I had to make up a story. Make it up, you know. I did that.' Ibrahim did not seriously believe he was eligible for asylum but wanted to prolong his residence in the Netherlands given the lack of perspectives in his home country. He succeeded, as the authorities neither granted his asylum nor were able to deport him. However, this strategy may only be used by migrants who originate from countries whose authorities do not/rarely accept the readmission of unauthorized migrants. Otherwise, the migrants' mobilization of the law may be counterproductive as it enforces unauthorized migrants to reveal their identity and nationality, which facilitates the authorities' deportation practices (cf. Leerkes and Kox, 2016).

Some respondents (also) strategically challenged the law by – *inter alia* – hiding their identity, obstructing return meetings, hindering the obtention of travel documents, playing games at the embassy or using scam marriages for legalization. The use of these strategies is partly enabled by the multi-layered organization of the Dutch immigration system in which multiple state and non-state actors have obtained a role. This has increased the reach and opportunities of the immigration authorities, Chapter 4 shows. Yet, it also caused a dependency on (non-state) actors who unauthorized migrants can take advantage of. Ibrahim, for instance, was detained in immigration detention with the purpose of removal. As he still did not want to leave the Netherlands, he started to hamper the obtention of the identity and travel documents that were required for his deportation:

> 'I had talked with that ambassador before and he said: "Yes, if you don't want to return, then we don't give a *laissez passer*". I answer in signs [that he did not want to return], because there were people of the IND behind me, you know. (…) It was just… in five minutes, the meeting was over. And then… Then I went back [to the detention centre] and the only thing they could do was detain me as long as possible as they could not deport me.'

In the end, as planned, Ibrahim could not be deported and was released, meaning that he could continue his unauthorized residence and try to fulfil his aspirations in the Netherlands. This strategy may not be used by respondents who already had a travel document and/or who may easily be deported to their home country. Some of these respondents pretended to comply with the law instead, meaning that they participated in AVR programmes and migrated shortly afterwards to the Netherlands again. The latter has become more complicated, though, with the increasingly restrictive immigration system that requires migrants to have adequate resources and contacts to successfully use this strategy. This means that migrants who use this strategy may end up being stranded in their home country after all.

Complying with the law?

Unauthorized migrants may uphold the use of these game-like strategies for over twenty or thirty years. However, once the law too severely complicates their everyday lives and prevents them from making an independent living, they may move on to the next stage in the legal consciousness process, which consists of migrants leaving the Netherlands. A few respondents who were not able or willing to return decided to try their luck elsewhere in Europe, after which they ended up being unauthorized in the Netherlands again.[70] Those respondents who believed that the conditions in their home country would be better than their unauthorized residence in the Netherlands decided to return like Indra, her husband and their two adult daughters did. This family decided to move back to Surinam after about fifteen years of unauthorized residence in the Netherlands which, as Indra explains, became too problematic for her family. They started to prefer the poor conditions in their home country over their unauthorized residence given all the restrictions they encountered in the Netherlands:

> 'It was the whole sum of things, you know. Age is going to play a role. I thought that if I… if I stayed until my 60th, that is not possible because you cannot earn enough and have no income. And eh, you also think about the kids. They cannot work, they cannot go nowhere. They cannot go to England or Barcelona or something [with school], they can't do anything. And we also got problems with our house and could not solve them like this. (…) Then we thought, let's see whether we can get out of here.'

For most respondents, the decision to return was the outcome of a gradual decision-making process in which they weighed up different factors such as their perspectives, opportunities, social ties, health, financial matters, cultural aspects and shame. For others, the decision to return was the consequence of a specific occurrence such as a family member's death or illness or the expectation that they would be deported. These

70 Based on the so-called Dublin-regulation (EU-Regulation 604/2013), respondents whose unauthorized residence in the Netherlands has been registered run the risk of being deported to the Netherlands once they are caught in another country and the Netherlands is supposed to be responsible for their deportation.

respondents still do not feel legally obliged to comply with the law, which aligns migration studies that show that legal factors usually do not convince unauthorized migrants to return to their home country (see also Black et al., 2004; Koser and Kuschminder, 2015; Leerkes et al., 2017). Instead, (multiple) factors at a personal, household, community and structural level are more compelling in unauthorized migrants' return decisions. This explains why only respondents who believed that their situation in the home country would be better than that in the Netherlands eventually decided to return.

Doubting the justice of the law?

Respondents who do or cannot return while not being deported usually start to doubt the justice of the law in this stage of their legal consciousness process. These respondents argue that the law severely complicates their everyday lives, while the authorities can neither actually enforce it by deporting them nor legalize their residence in the Netherlands. Respondents consider the law's severe impact – combined with its ineffectiveness – unjustified, as explained in Chapter 7 in more detail. The North African, Fazil, is a case in point. He was living and enjoying his 'good life' in the Netherlands and used to say: 'Documents are not important to me, life is!' However, over the years, he has repeatedly been stopped by the authorities and detained in immigration detention with the purpose of removal. He feels respectfully treated by the police and detention officers but starts to believe that 'the law is papers' in the Netherlands: 'Always, always, they ask for my papers! That is the problem for me, that they always ask for papers'. The authorities can neither deport him nor legalize his residence, meaning that he is still unauthorized in the Netherlands without any prospects. He feels like the lack of a legal status is his only identifying characteristic: 'People without papers [a legal status] shouldn't be eh… reduced to the one single article that they don't have papers. They are no article!' He, like others in this legal consciousness process, questions whether this is justified. They want the law to provide a solution for those who cannot be deported. The North African, Badr, who has been unauthorized in the country for almost twenty years, argues: '[the law] does not help while it does harm us. And it does not solve a thing, does not deport people. (…) Really, take care of a solution for us!' These respondents consider the regulations for those who cannot leave the Netherlands through no fault of their own to be no adequate solution (cf. Advisory Council on Migration, 2013).

The above is mainly seen among respondents who cannot be deported and/or whose personal conditions have been changed to such an extent that they believe that they deserve to be in the Netherlands. These respondents start to see legalization as the solution for the problems they experience due to the law. This also applies to Lan, a Chinese woman who arrived in 2007 in the Netherlands to improve her living conditions. She used to live her life away from the law as she did not want to be deported. However, this changed when she gave birth to two children who grew up, went to school and socialized in the

Netherlands. While she does send her children to a weekend school to learn the Chinese language and culture, she cannot prevent her children from feeling Dutch. Her son, for instance, repeatedly asks her: 'Mum, I am Dutch, why do they [DT&V] say that I have to "return"?' Lan used to accept that she was not allowed to stay in the Netherlands but – like her children – she considers it unjustified that her rooted children are forced to leave the country: 'I don't get it. I just don't get the Netherlands'. This is strengthened by her believe that her children would also be unauthorized in China, given the lack of a Hukou (registration in China).[71] The family has been subjected to several return procedures but cannot be deported as the children lack the required documents. Nevertheless, they are not allowed to be in the Netherlands. Given the socialization of her children in the Netherlands and the lack of opportunities to return to China, Lan believes that they are entitled to a residence permit. These changed personal conditions impact on her expectations of the law, as it 'has to give pardon to my children'. Something similar could be seen for other respondents with lengthy (unauthorized) residence, who believed they were undeportable and/or were socialized in the Netherlands (see also Abrego, 2011). These respondents start aspiring to a residence permit and actively turn themselves over to the law to fulfil their new hopes. Their legal consciousness shifts to the second legal consciousness process.

10.5.2 A second legal consciousness process: aspiring to legalization, actively engaging with the law

The second legal consciousness process is characterized by unauthorized migrants aspiring to legalization and therefore actively engaging with the law. It is found among respondents whose legal consciousness shifted from the first to the second process as well as among asylum seekers who fled countries that are known for their insecurity, civil wars, arbitrarily prosecutions and other insecure situations. Despite these respondents' different migration motives, they (eventually) all desire a residence permit in the Netherlands. They do not stay away from the law, as respondents in the first legal consciousness process tend to do. Instead, they actively turn themselves over to the police or immigration authorities to start a legalization procedure. This also applies to the African, Blaise, who fled his home country after his village was attacked by the militia. Blaise was shocked by all the white people he observed upon arrival in the Netherlands. After having spent some time on the streets, he decided to turn to another black man he came across:

71 In principle, children who cannot leave the Netherlands through no fault of their own are not being deported (https://www.dienstterugkeerenvertrek.nl/het-terugkeerproces/bijzondere-omstandigheden/buiten-schuld, accessed 11/09/2023). Yet, in practice, unauthorized migrants believe that the authorities too easily assume that they can return while they believe themselves that they cannot.

> 'That guy asked me: "Are you new here? You have to go to the police. The police can help you". Then I went to the police. I talked to the police and they gave me a train ticket. They said: "Go to the Immigration and Naturalization Service in Rijsbergen [Dutch village]; you may claim asylum over there." So, I took the train and went to Rijsbergen to apply for asylum.'

Being informed by the narratives that circulate in transnational (asylum) communities and their assumed knowledge of asylum and human rights law, these respondents initially expect the law – or the immigration authorities – to grant them a residence permit. The Eastern European, Nikhad, is a case in point: 'We thought that we would get a residence permit, for sure, because we got information letters that stated: "If you have problems with the authorities in your home country, you will get a residence permit"'. Some respondents were, indeed, provided with temporary residence permits that are eventually not prolonged, while the legalization claims of others were directly rejected. The latter applies to the African, Solomon: 'I got rejected, my asylum got rejected. And then I found myself in the streets. (…) I started my life as an illegal man'.

Respondents in this legal consciousness process consider unjustified the immigration authorities' negative decision in their legalization procedure. Initially, they expected the law in the Netherlands to be just as posited by Zabihullah, who fled the Middle East with his wife and son: 'Dutch laws are really good, they are good for security'. However, during their legalization procedures, the respondents' stances towards the law changed. Zabihullah, for instance, does not understand why his family's asylum claim was rejected as his family is, in his view, in severe danger. He argues: 'I've respect for the rules, for all rules here but decisions have to be right!' Zabihullah and other respondents do not consider the decision to reject his legalization claim to be right, either because their lives are assumed to be in danger on return or because they are not deported nor is their residence being legalized. They claim that the human dimension has faded into the background in Dutch legalization procedures, as with advisory councils, NGOs and others (e.g. Advisory Council on Migration, 2022; Amnesty International, 2020; Geertsema et al., 2021). Keon, from Africa, for instance, cries: 'This is no justice; it's no justice!' Hernandez (2010) argues that interactions with the law and experiences with legal services may contribute to a strengthened rights awareness among marginalized groups, whereas I observe the opposite among unauthorized migrants in this legal consciousness process. After their negative encounters with the law and the rejection of their legalization claims, objections and appeals, they no longer know how to make sense of Dutch law. Solomon sighs: 'It is not logical, it is sometimes playing by the law'. These respondents wonder why, in their experience, Dutch law does not provide justice or protection for unauthorized migrants. They question whether human rights even apply to unauthorized migrants in Dutch everyday practice. The respondents' thoughts start to fit with what Ewick and Silbey

(1998) call an *against the law* stance, meaning that these respondents feel caught by the law as they are oppressed by it without having adequate opportunities to go against it.

These feelings of being caught by the law severely impact on their everyday lives. These respondents are constantly occupied with obtaining a residence permit and fulfilling their legalization aspirations, as we see in the words of the elderly Idriss: 'I can't sleep anymore, I think about it [lack of a legal status] all night'. These respondents consider a legal status the key to their life. African Lucas explained to me: 'Wherever you go, (...), they always ask for your legitimation. If you don't have legitimation, you feel psychologically ill as you cannot access anything given the lack of a legal status'. While 'nobody is born with papers', as Marc argues, the law becomes an embedded and emergent feature of their everyday lives that shapes multiple domains of their everyday lives. Given their lack of a legal status and residence permit, these respondents are, for instance, usually (temporarily) housed in freedom-restricted or humanitarian organizations' facilities, embedded in the humanitarian support community and confronted with considerable stress. They put their lives on hold until their residence is legalized, meaning that they cannot work, are reluctant to begin a family and can no longer plan their future. These respondents feel stuck as they are neither allowed to reside in this country given their lack of a legal status nor leave the country. For them, the lack of a legal status is not solely a handicap, as it was for those in the first legal consciousness process. Instead, it is a primary identifying characteristic that overshadows all their others (cf. Engbersen, 2001). As Badr also says: 'It is no life without a legal status, it is just no life. It is very bad'. The law is – to use the renowned words of Sarat (1990) – 'all over' as the Dutch immigration system makes respondents feel that they are in a web-like enclosure from which they cannot escape, while it controls all facets of their everyday lives. This is exhausting, as Arnaud says with a sigh: 'I am so tired of the law. I am so tired to hear about the law'. It severely impacts on their well-being as well as their legal consciousness process.

Seeking justice, exploring different strategies

The respondents in this legal consciousness process may then move on to the next phase in this process whereby they start invoking the law in search for justice. While they believe that the law – and the acts of the immigration authorities in particular – are unjust, they are dependent on it. Keon contends that 'The IND [Immigration and Naturalization Service] has to give me my passport!' The respondents usually start mobilizing the law, which answers Silbey's (2005) question of why people acquiesce to a legal system which, in their view, does not produce justice. The respondents use different legal mobilization strategies, often in collaboration with lawyers and/or NGOs. Depending on their personal situation, opportunities and financial and social resources, they may launch repeated or new asylum claims, apply for regularization schemes, send humanitarian appeals to the authorities, ask to postpone their deportation given their medical condition and/or look for other legal trajectories. The more injustice respondents experience, the more persistent their legal mobilization seems to be. They appear to desperately grasp at all glimmers of hope. Out of despair, they may even redefine and reinterpret the law in such a way that their legal claims are believed to be valid (cf. Coutin, 2000). The latter comes to the fore in the story of Zabihullah, who tells me that he was happily married and taking care of his son. However, when the family received another negative decision from the IND, his wife left the centre with their son and accused Zabihullah of domestic violence. Although Zabihullah was never prosecuted for it, their divorce provided his ex-wife with the opportunity to start a successful legalization procedure as she – as an Afghan Westernized single woman with a child – could not safely be deported. Zabihullah believes that his wife was pressured by her mother to use this strategy and legalize her own residence as the civil servants working at the freedom-restricted shelter facility where the family resided did. These civil servants thought that more Afghan women, out of despair, accused their partners of domestic violence to increase their own legalization chances (fieldnotes 06/22/2016). Respondents in this process may uphold their legal mobilization strategies for years, especially if regularization schemes or changed legal regulations provide them with new hope (cf. Van Zwol Committee, 2019). It is only when they run out of hope, legal opportunities and/or financial and social resources that they feel forced to stop their legal mobilization strategies.

Respondents in this legal consciousness process may also protest against the law in search for justice, especially those who have had such experience in their home country and/or are embedded in communities that initiate them. They believe that they need to step out of the shadows to bring about political change. Hossam, from the Middle East, explained that 'openness is needed. It is important to speak up. If you have rights, you have to fight for your rights and to inform people about your rights'. He has been involved in different protests, as Dutch citizens, in his view, need to know what the law does to unauthorized migrants. Inspired by their (transnational) knowledge, which creates awareness of their rights as well as the perceived violation of them, these respondents participate in protests, demonstrations, tent camps, advocacy campaigns and other forms of political contestation. They protest individually and in collectives. Jaafar, who was part of the We Are Here group, explains: 'It is important that we all participate. We must unite if we want to get heard' (fieldnotes 06/03/2015). Rejected asylum seekers mainly advocate for regularization schemes, visibility and Bed, Bath and Bread arrangements. Other respondents are usually less willing to protest against the law, which may be explained by the low likeability factor that is considered necessary for public action (Hasselberg, 2016), the perceived stigma of being unauthorized (Abrego, 2011) or the fear of detection and deportation by the authorities (Gleeson, 2010). While respondents believe to be within their rights, they have lost their faith in the transformative capacity of the law. They are somewhat sceptical of the outcome of their protests. Marc, for instance, says that 'nothing has changed in these three years of our protests'. Nevertheless, he continues his protests as there is nothing else that he can do while he 'really needs a solution'. Some respondents were successful in their protests and created change which may inspire and empower other migrants to also invoke the law as well as provide false hope for other migrants who are not eligible for such regularization schemes.

Resisting the law

Respondents in this second legal consciousness process may also challenge the law to prevent their deportation. Like respondents in the first legal consciousness process, they hide their identity, obstruct return meetings, hinder the obtention of travel documents and/or play games at the embassy. However, they do not use these strategies for pragmatic reasons, as respondents in the first process tend to do. Instead, they use them given the perceived injustice in the immigration system, meaning that it concerns oppositional acts of resistance – that is, the individualized and covert use of everyday means that arise from implicit disavowal with the state and aims to bring about short-term changes (Scott, 1985). Marc, for instance, explains that he was very upset by the treatment by his case manager at the Repatriation and Departure Service who posed him 'the worst questions' during his immigration detention, solely focusing on Marc's return, without addressing his fears about the war in his home country: 'The way they treat people. Tsss. (…) Then I say: "Fuck the DT&V!"' As Marc considered his treatment unfair, he refused to talk further with his case manager and could not be deported. Eventually, Marc was allocated a new case manager who – in Marc's view – treated him more humanely by discussing his return concerns and off-topics such as World Cup football. Only then was he willing to meet the DT&V again and discuss his return. Marc's behaviour is thus directly inspired by his disavowal with the Dutch immigration system and not a pragmatic interaction with the law aimed at preventing deportation. While the challenging of the law by migrants in the first legal consciousness process is inspired by pragmatism and, in the second process, by the migrants' disavowal of the law, the outcomes of respondents' acts are similar, as migrants in both legal consciousness processes prevent the state from exercising its powers in terms of deportation.

Giving up on the law?

Respondents in this legal consciousness process may mobilize, protest and resist the law for many years – some were still doing so at the end of my fieldwork. Over time, however, their legal consciousness may further evolve. The experienced injustice, the frustrating confrontations with the law and the uncertainty that comes with it make some migrants give up on the law. They lose their faith that it can be used as a tool for social change. They not only believe that the law fails to produce justice but also argue that the law actively and consciously produces injustice to maintain the existing social order, which Fritsvold

(2009) refers to as being *under the law*. Keon, an African respondent whose asylum claims were repeatedly rejected and who is receiving long-term psychiatric treatment, is one example. While discussing the justice of the law, he contends that:

> 'It is a game that the authorities use for some groups of people, to play with these people. But they forget that the people who they are playing the game with are also human beings. Now, these people have no life, they are suffering, they are dying. (...) You cannot use it to play such a game. (...) It's a crime against the humanity!'

However, respondents cannot escape from this game – or the law – and have no escape for it anymore as Sarat (1990) also illustrates for the welfare poor.[72] Keon argues that this may bring about extreme suffering among unauthorized migrants: 'It is a lot of frustration. It is destroying human beings. It is destroying people's mind. Some people can take these difficulties but not everyone can.' As these respondents feel they are being positioned outside the protective sphere of the law, they stop interacting with it. As Keon contends: 'I just have no energy anymore.' For some, this was a reason not/no longer to participate in this study as they lacked the energy to share their stories. Hossam, for instance, texted me at the end of my fieldwork: 'I am really sorry, but I cannot make appointments right now, I am not in the position and the mood to do that now, it is not going well.' Like others, he was exhausted by his lengthy unauthorized residence and the social suffering that came with it. Those who can no longer accept these difficulties may withdraw from society – something seen, in particular, among those without a strong supportive network to rely upon. Others temporarily stop eating or seriously consider suicide if they cannot cope with the situation.

A few respondents eventually start considering return at this stage of their consciousness process. Jaafar, for instance, used to mobilize and protest against the law. However, he feels exhausted and disempowered by the 'psychological games' of the Dutch authorities and the hard living conditions that come with it. He is not sure how much longer he can cope:

> 'Some of my brothers committed suicide. I can't cope with it anymore. (...) I am just thinking about plan b. Maybe to go to another country to get help because the situation on the street is hard for me, I cannot survive on the streets my whole life you know. (...) But eh... this moment it is not safe. But if it were safe, I would like to go back to my original country.'

72 Sarat (1990) uses the term 'welfare poor' to refer to people who receive benefits distributed by governmental entities to support low-income Americans.

His family tells him that he should not return given the insecure conditions in his home country. While Jaafar was still in the Netherlands at the moment of writing this chapter, he had – like a few other respondents – started doubting whether return should not be preferred over prolonging his exhausting situation in the Netherlands. As Nikhad explains: 'It says "voluntary return" but it is not actually "voluntarily". Because if you don't return, you are everyday invited by the DT&V and they threaten you [with deportation]!' While the Dutch authorities prefer to use the term 'independent' over 'voluntary' return because of this, such return decisions might be considered a form of what Carrabine (2004) calls dull compulsion. This means that migrants consider the system unjust but begin to obey the authorities as they can no longer cope with the consequences of the lack of a legal status. Such decisions are – in the words of Tankebe (2009: 1280) – 'founded on feelings of endemic powerlessness and resignation', as they believe that their structural conditions in the Netherlands are unjustified but unalterable and they can no longer cope with them. This is the result of them being completely disempowered by the law's pervasive authority which makes them give up on it.

10.6 To conclude

This chapter has highlighted two legal consciousness processes that I observed among unauthorized migrants in the Netherlands. The law is salient in both processes, albeit differently. In the first process – which is mainly seen among unauthorized migrants who aspire better living conditions – the law functions as a handicap that shapes and complicates the migrants' lives. The migrants in this process are (initially) positive about the law but do not feel legally nor morally obliged to obey it. On the contrary, they try to circumvent it and – if confronted with the law – play around with it to be able to continue their unauthorized residence. Only if the law becomes too much of a handicap *and* the conditions in their home country are preferred over their unauthorized residence migrants will perhaps decide to comply with the law and leave the country. If return is not considered an option, migrants begin to doubt the justice of the law, given its ineffectiveness and obtrusiveness, especially if their personal situation changes. They may start aspiring to legalization after which their legal consciousness shifts to the second process. In this second process – which is mainly found among both unauthorized migrants whose legal consciousness has shifted and rejected asylum seekers – the law is a primary identifying characteristic that overshadows the migrants' other identifying characteristics and severely impacts on their well-being and identity. Respondents in this process feel played with by an unjust law while being dependent on it to improve their position and become a formal member of society. They desperately and sometimes endlessly mobilize, protest and resist the law in search for justice, sometimes upholding their interactions with the law for years.

Over time, though, some end up being disempowered by the law as they can no longer cope with it and may give up by either withdrawing from it or fatalistically accepting its consequences.

The insights into unauthorized migrants' legal consciousness processes have three major implications. First, they expose the powers *and* powerlessness of the law towards unauthorized migrants. The law may be considered powerful given its strong constitutive effects – its indirect effects on the migrants' internal meaning-making processes and behaviour (Levine and Mellema, 2001; Silbey, 2005). The law shapes unauthorized migrants' everyday lives in both legal consciousness processes as the ever-present deportability forces migrants to organize their lives around the law. The law is, in Sarat's (1990) words, 'all over' to unauthorized migrants, which makes dealing with it a pervasive and painful everyday activity for them, especially as the current Dutch regulatory context contributes to the migrants' economic and social marginality (see also Chapters 4 and 6). While respondents in the first process are better capable of dealing with this than those in the second process, the law negatively impacts on the health and social well-being of migrants in both processes. It has an existential impact on them, as their lack of a legal status functions as a handicap or a primary identifying characteristic that shapes – to use Menjívar's words (2006: 1000) – 'who they are, how they relate to others, their participation in local communities, and their continued relationship with their homelands'. The doubts and feelings of inferiority that come with it may cause a 'deeply interiorised mode of being' among unauthorized migrants (De Genova and Peutz, 2010: 14). Some eventually give up on the law. While they used to contribute to sustaining the law's power and reproducing its hegemonic function by using legal structures (cf. Silbey, 2005), they lose their faith in (the transformative power of) the law over time, given the injustice the law apparently produces. For these migrants, the law has absented itself by being inadequately available and offering insufficient protection. This shows that the law not only has strong symbolic powers but also negatively affects unauthorized migrants at the everyday, existential and legal level.

Yet – and this is often neglected in the academic debate on the powers of the law – the law is also powerless if seen through an instrumental lens – that is, if we examine whether the law inspires or deters unauthorized migrants to act in particular ways (cf. Levine and Mellema, 2001). Unauthorized migrants have the agency to prevent the state from exercising its sovereign powers by operating with, negotiating, resisting or even benefiting from the law. While it has become more complicated for unauthorized migrants to effectively resist the law, given the intensified and digitalized forms of surveillance (Broeders and Engbersen, 2007), such migrants may uphold their strategies for many years (Staring et al., 2022). The law does not inspire them to leave the country, as the authorities intend, since unauthorized migrants prioritize non-legal over legal arguments in their gradual return decisions. They usually only want to return when life in the home country is considered equal or better than their unauthorized residence in the Netherlands, when a specific occurrence in the family sphere urges them to do so or when they eventually can no longer cope with the law. The latter is assumed to have a quite limited role in this process (see also Black et al., 2004; Koser and Kuschminder, 2015; Leerkes et al., 2017; Van Wijk, 2008) and the authorities lack coercive measures to realize the departure of those who prefer to continue their unauthorized residence. After all, they cannot indefinitely detain unauthorized migrants nor use unchecked physical force (Bakewell, 2010; Campesi, 2015; Ellermann, 2010). Besides, immigration detention puts just limited pressure unauthorized migrants to leave the Netherlands (see Chapter 9) and only partly results in deportation (Advisory Council on Migration, 2021). As the authorities are dependent on – and bounded by – other actors to put their laws into effect and deport unauthorized migrants (see Chapter 4; Leerkes and Kox, 2016), the Dutch authorities – like other states – struggle to effectuate the departure of unauthorized migrants from the Netherlands (e.g. Leerkes and van Houte, 2020; Maliepaard et al., 2022; Van Zwol Committee, 2019). This makes the law in the migration domain powerful *and* powerless at the same time.

Second, insights into unauthorized migrants' legal consciousness processes raise crucial questions on the current functioning of the law in the migration domain. Both unauthorized migrants' legal consciousness processes show that the law has a central, negative role in their everyday lives. While the law is supposed to protect people, this chapter shows that it does otherwise for unauthorized migrants. The law constructs the migrants' otherness and drives them to the margins of society (cf. Calavita, 1998). Additionally, the law in this domain is said to be inhumane (Aas and Bosworth, 2013), inflict harm (Bhatia, 2020), racialize migrants (Turnbull, Bhatia and Lousley, 2020) and have cumulative injurious and painful effects on the well-being and health of unauthorized migrants (Chapter 6; Menjívar and Abrego, 2012; Menjívar and Lakhani, 2016). Subjection to such laws may mark unauthorized migrants for life (Menjívar, 2006) while it is only partially effective in terms of return. The law may be legally valid but these insights raise the question of whether it is morally acceptable. Menjívar and Abrego (2012) – who focus on the US – believe not. They qualify immigration laws as a form of legal violence given the normalized, cumulatively injurious effects the law generates for unauthorized migrants as well as their social environment. They refer to the immediate social suffering and potential long-term harm that is enabled and amplified by the law. This chapter demonstrates that the law in the Netherlands has similar effects on unauthorized migrants, justifying the conclusion that the law produces legal violence in this country too. I believe that this should be a reason to develop more ethical, equitable and effective immigration systems that align with the aims and core principles of the law.

Third and finally, I believe that this chapter has implications for the current use of the legal consciousness concept. As shown in my theoretical framework, there is an academic debate on the usefulness of the legal consciousness concept given its different purposes, conceptualizations and operationalizations (Chua and Engel, 2019; Halliday, 2019; Hertogh, 2018; Silbey, 2005). I believe this debate to be redundant. This claim aligns with the ideas of Chua and Engel (2019) as well as Halliday (2019) but my argumentation differs. Unlike these authors, I do not think that legal consciousness is an adaptable concept that may be variously used and operationalized with different aims that fit the law and society movement. Instead, I argue that focusing on the powers of the law, as early or 'critical/hegemony' legal consciousness scholars tend to do, also helps to understand how the law impacts on one's identity and legal mobilization strategies, elements that are central in other legal consciousness research schools. This study, for instance, mainly draws on the critical or hegemony legal consciousness research school in order to understand the powers of the law. Yet, the findings also shed light on the mutually constitutive relationship between someone's legal consciousness and their identity (cf. Abrego, 2008) as well as unauthorized migrants' belief in the transforming capacity of the law (cf. Menjívar and Lakhani, 2016) – i.e. those elements that are central in other legal consciousness schools. For me, this calls for a reunion of the different legal consciousness research schools in order to gain a complete picture of the powers of the law as common among early users of the legal consciousness concept. This is, in my view, preferable to the use of an adaptable legal consciousness concept. After all, using a concept for different purposes and with different conceptualizations and operationalization carries the risk of (eventually) blurring the meaning of the concept, which comes at the cost of its strength. This also prevents a clear understanding of what we are talking about and may hollow out a concept, making it lose its explanatory power, as Silbey (2005) also fears. I believe that this is neither beneficent nor necessary to understanding the role of law *in* society and its powers in all its different facets.

11 To conclude: The limits of the law

This book began by examining European nation-states' aim to limit the arrival *and* residence of migrants without a legal status in order to protect their national sovereignty (Bosworth and Guild, 2008; Kaufman, 2015; Koulish and Van der Woude, 2020). These nation-states therefore turn themselves to 'the law' (Anderson, 2013; Calavita, 2005; Dauvergne, 2008; Mainwaring and Walton-Roberts, 2018) – that is, all the legal norms in society *and* the institutions and practices associated with them (cf. Deflem, 2008). In using the law, the European Union (EU) strives for an 'unequivocal commitment to respect and protect the dignity, human rights and fundamental freedoms of all migrants as well as to ensure that migration takes place in a safe, orderly and well-managed way'.[73] Yet the arrival and presence of migrants who lack a legal status has repeatedly been accompanied by disorder and drama. Examples include the death of the Syrian toddler Alan Kurdi and of others who lost their lives on the way to Europe, the migrants' poor reception conditions upon arrival in Europe, the protests by migrants and supporters against the nation-states' restrictive approach towards those lacking a residence permit as well as the suicide of some migrants who could no longer cope with their unauthorized residence. This selection of examples from recent years raises the question of whether and how the law matters to these migrants and what this means for the functioning of the law in this domain.

These latter questions guided this study. I used four sub-questions on how unauthorized migrants 1) understand, 2) experience, 3) give meaning to and 4) interact with 'the law' in their everyday lives in order to describe and explain unauthorized migrants' legal consciousness processes. Insights into the migrants' legal consciousness processes enabled me to find answers to the intriguing puzzle of how law matters to migrants without a legal right to reside on a nation-state's territory and how this is of concern for the law. Throughout this study, the perspective of unauthorized migrants – i.e. those without a legal status who are not allowed to reside within the territorial borders of the nation-state concerned – has been centre stage. The unauthorized migrants' emic perspective in relation to the law is still under-represented in academic debates, as anthropological, ethnographic studies mainly focus on migrants' subsistence strategies and social networks, socio-legal studies only involve a limited focus on unauthorized migrants and the flourishing border criminology discipline pays relatively little attention to the voices of the migrants themselves. Yet, as shown in the introduction of this book, there are moral, instrumental and academic reasons for drawing on the emic perspective of these migrants and giving them a voice in this debate on the functioning of the law in the migration

73 https://ec.europa.eu/commission/presscorner/detail/en/statement_19_6791, accessed 05/14/2023.

domain. This is why I conducted multi-sited ethnographic research with 105 (former) unauthorized migrants between March 2015 and May 2018. I explicitly added a longitudinal dimension to the research in order to add possible changes in the migrants' relationship with the law and to better understand their legal consciousness over time.

In this final chapter of this book I present insights which contribute to the solution of this conundrum of how the law matters to unauthorized migrants as well as its consequences for the functioning of the law. First, I show how the Dutch authorities have created a comprehensive, multi-layered control system to discourage unauthorized residence, a system which unauthorized migrants perceive as 'the law' (Section 11.1). I then illustrate how the law matters to unauthorized migrants by addressing its indirect effects, which exposes the constitutive powers of the law for this specific group in society (Section 11.2). Yet, at the same time, the law is also relatively powerless if seen through an instrumental lens as it does not matter that much to unauthorized migrants. They do not feel legally or morally obliged to obey the law, while the authorities are only partly able to enforce it by deporting unauthorized migrants from the Netherlands (Section 11.3). After this, I point out that the law is not equally power*ful* and power*less* to unauthorized migrants and matters to them in different ways, which should be understood in the context of the patterned diversity among these migrants. By presenting three interrelated, interacting factors that mitigate how the law matters to unauthorized migrants, I add to the academic debate new insights into the diversity in their legal consciousness in a bid to show the differentiated powerful and powerless functioning of the law in the migration domain (Section 11.4). Finally, I show that the law's ability to disempower unauthorized migrants and its inability to end unauthorized residence raise severe legal, moral and instrumental concerns over the authorities' current approach to counteract unauthorized residence (Section 11.5). These concerns call, I argue, for a human-rights-based, empirically legitimate and differentiated approach in the migration domain that is morally right and better suits the core principles of law in society.

11.1 The law as a comprehensive, multi-layered system

The first sub-question of this study addressed unauthorized migrants' understandings of 'the law'. My analysis shows that these migrants understand 'the law' in a context of European nation-states increasingly trying to regulate mobility flows through comprehensive immigration laws, policies and practices, as illustrated in Chapter 2. This also applies to the Netherlands, the country that is central in this book. The Netherlands used to welcome and tolerate the arrival and residence of migrants (Burgers and Engbersen, 1999; Van Eijl, 2012). However, given the increased influx of refugees, a deteriorating labour market and a supposedly changed societal stance towards migrants in the

Netherlands, the authorities started to problematize these latter's arrival and presence from the late 1980s onwards (Burgers and Engbersen, 1999; Van Eijl, 2012). As other European nation-states, they tried to restrict the unauthorized entry of migrants as well as to prevent and end unauthorized residence. They turned to the law as the basis for all collaborative, digital, penal, military and other strategies to govern unauthorized migration and residence (Franko, 2020; Rijken, Staring and Van der Woude, 2022). This includes specific immigration laws as well as labour, social-security, criminal, crimmigration[74] and other laws (Aas and Bosworth, 2013; Bonjour, 2010). The Dutch authorities developed a 'thick enforcement regime' in which they combined strong enforcements interests with extensive enforcement capacities in order to realize the departure of unauthorized migrants from the Netherlands (Leerkes and Van Houte, 2020). This has gradually translated into more restrictive admission policies, increased exclusion from social services, intensified control collaboration, extended voluntary-return programmes and an increased urgency for migration controls (Brouwer, 2020; Engbersen, Van San and Leerkes, 2006; Van Eijl, 2012; Van der Woude, 2020). While there have also been some counter movements in terms of more lenient migration control practices (Staring and Timmerman, 2021), the overall tendency is to discourage unauthorized migration on the basis of the law (Staring and Van Swaaningen, 2021; Van der Woude, 2020).

Unauthorized migrants argue that the efforts of the Dutch authorities to end unauthorized residence have resulted in a comprehensive system of controls that stretches out over a wide range of controlling actors, non-immigration laws and policies, and geographical locations. It is possible to distinguish three interrelated layers within this system, as has been illustrated in Chapter 4. The first layer refers to the whole range of state and non-state actors who have become involved in the control system because of the state's responsibilization processes, meaning that the state seeks to act upon migration 'not in a direct fashion through state agencies (police, courts, prisons, social workers) but, instead, by acting indirectly, seeking to activate action on the part of non-state agencies and organizations' (cf. Garland, 1996: 452). State actors such as the (immigration) police, immigration officers, municipalities and others have become part of this control system, as have non-state actors such as employers, acquaintances, citizens, lawyers, flight captains, landlords, and – as shown in Chapter 5 – humanitarian organizations which have simultaneously become occupied with supporting and controlling unauthorized migrants. The second layer concerns the laws and policies that have gradually been included in the system. This concerns more comprehensive immigration laws, policies and practices as well as labour laws, housing laws and social rights that have mandated the requirement of a legal status for eligibility to the entitlements in these laws. Additionally, the authorities

74 Crimmigration laws refer to the convergence of criminal and immigration laws, which is one of the most rapidly developing fields in law (Stumpf, 2013).

use criminal laws, development aid and civic-integration requirements as instruments to prevent and put an end to unauthorized residence. This means that non-immigration laws are used to control the mobility of the unauthorized migrants in the Netherlands and to add to the comprehensiveness of the control system. The third and final layer refers to the reach of the system in terms of geographical location. The effects of the control system are not bounded by the Dutch territorial borders but are felt at different geographical locations outside the Netherlands, as seen in Chapter 4. These locations extend to the migrants' home and transit countries, as internal control mechanisms that are aimed at preventing or ending unauthorized residence have severe consequences after the migrants' deportation or return. Using these three different layers has brought about a comprehensive, multi-layered immigration system.

The unauthorized migrants' experiences with this system impact on their understandings of the law. While unauthorized migrants do differentiate between the various legal arrangements when discussing their understandings of the law, they tend to believe that many encounters with the law and legal authorities are (eventually) centred on or reduced to them not having a legal status. They see themselves as confronted with a wide range of legally embedded limitations, control mechanisms and exclusionary practices because they lack a legal status. This latter also has multiple limitations in terms of the migrants generating an adequate income, arranging housing as well as accessing health care or other rights. They additionally experience being asked for their legal documents when they are, *inter alia*, involved in a traffic incident, want to marry, need to report victimization or exploitation, want to register their children in primary school, are stopped in the street, etc. The lack of a legal status initially seems irrelevant for unauthorized migrants' commonplace activities as well as their encounters with the law. Yet, the migrants' everyday experiences turn out otherwise, as their legal status has become important in all their commonplace activities as well as their encounters with the law. This fits with De Genova's idea that the law creates unauthorized migrants' 'deportability' – i.e. the legal production of the migrants' omnipresent possibility of being detected by the authorities and deported from the space of the nation-state (De Genova, 2002: 439). As illustrated in Chapters 4 and 6, dealing with the lack of a legal status is consequently superimposed on unauthorized migrants' everyday reality, making the law a very salient and pervasive part of their everyday lives (cf. Coutin, 2000: 40; see also De Genova, 2002). As unauthorized migrants construct a legal consciousness on the basis of their everyday encounters and experiences with the law (cf. Sarat, 1990), this is reflected in their understandings of it.

So, the answer to the first sub-question on how unauthorized migrants understand 'the law' in their everyday lives would be that they understand 'the law' as a system of controls that first produces their unauthorized residence and then reduces them to lacking a legal status which, for some, outweighs all other aspects of their everyday being. Consequently, the law resembles a web-like enclosure for unauthorized migrants from which they cannot escape, even as it controls all facets of their everyday lives. Yet, as illustrated later, there is a difference in how unauthorized migrants experience and deal with this situation as well as how it affects them.

11.2 The law as a powerful force

Looking at unauthorized migrants' experiences of, thoughts on and interactions with the law over time – the themes that were central in sub-questions 2, 3 and 4 of this study – shows that the law seriously matters to unauthorized migrants given its constitutive effects; these are the law's indirect effects on the migrants' internal meaning-making processes and behaviour (cf. Levine and Mellema, 2001; Silbey, 2005). The reason for this is that unauthorized migrants' everyday lives are shaped by their lack of a legal status and the legal reality that comes with it. The law plays a central role in their exclusion, marginalization, identity and mobility as it produces their 'illegality' and brings accompanying limitations. The law is, to use the well-known words of Sarat (1990), 'all over' for unauthorized migrants, which makes dealing with it a pervasive and painful everyday activity for them. The law not only has a strong symbolic function, as Calavita (1998) illustrates; it also creates strong indirect, constitutive effects that are felt at five different levels.

First, the law severely shapes unauthorized migrants' everyday lives. While it has often been argued that the law is constructed in the everyday (e.g. Ewick and Silbey, 1998; Silbey, 2005), the law also constructs unauthorized migrants' everyday. It creates unauthorized migrants' exclusion from society and puts up a myriad of barriers, which forces these migrants to organize their lives around the law. They cannot organize their everyday lives as they would prefer, as the law prohibits them, *inter alia*, from accessing both formal and informal markets given the identity checks which employers and landlords are obliged to undertake and the controls by the inspectorate and the police (see also Staring, Boesveldt and Kox, 2022; Van Meeteren, 2013). Unauthorized migrants (eventually) become aware of these limitations, meaning that they know that they will need to be creative to earn an (adequate) income and live independently. They are – as Van der Leun (2003) calls it – looking for loopholes in the law to circumvent all these limitations. They feel the disciplinary pressure imposed by the law and use – as shown in several chapters of this book – multiple strategies to circumvent the law and prevent detection, detention and deportation. Previous research also showed that the limitations and risks that accompany unauthorized residence encourage the use of a wide range of subsistence strategies by unauthorized migrants in the Netherlands to maintain their unauthorized residence (e.g. Burgers and Engbersen, 1999; Kox, 2010; Staring, 2001; Staring and Aarts, 2010; Staring et al., 2022; Van der Leun, 2003; Van Meeteren, 2014). This usually results in difficult living conditions, as illustrated throughout this book. Whereas some unauthorized migrants succeed in their efforts with the support of members of their social networks, others become dependent of professionals, compatriots and friends and/or marginalize over time. The impact of the law impacts differently on the unauthorized migrants' everyday lives, but all are somehow affected by the law at this level. Consequently, they all experience some form of deprivation that negatively affects their quality of their lives – what is called 'the pains of being unauthorized' in Chapter 6.

Second, the law has a more existential impact on unauthorized migrants as it affects their self-understanding. Their subjection to the law and the pain it causes hurt and frustrate many respondents in the extreme and constitute a severe attack on their personality, self-esteem and security, as illustrated in Chapter 6. Unauthorized migrants question who they are, what they are worth and where they are heading. This should be understood in the context of the current organization of the state's migration management strategies that produce hierarchies of citizenship by filtering who is allowed to enter and reside in a country meanwhile excluding unwanted others (Aas, 2011; Newman, 2006). Unauthorized migrants are in the latter category of so-called unwanted others, a category that is based on pre-set, non-personal criteria such as a person's race, ethnicity, geographical origin and welfare level (Calavita, 1998; Franko, 2020). Yet the filtering and exclusion – and especially the 'otherness' that the law constructs (Calavita, 1998) – clearly affect the migrants' self-worth. Whereas these migrants believe themselves to be refugees, asylum seekers or good, law-abiding citizens or parents who deserve the chance to make a living in the Netherlands, the state calls them 'illegal'. Being labelled 'illegal' and being subjected to exclusion and controls makes some migrants feel like unwanted, second-class citizens, especially as they have fewer rights and opportunities in comparison with those with a legal status. They are usually aware of the social construction of their 'illegality'. Nevertheless, the doubts and feelings of inferiority that come with it may cause a 'deeply interiorised mode of being' among them (De Genova and Peutz, 2010: 14). They feel punished by the law and consider it unfair, which strengthens the pain of perceived illegitimacy that I addressed in Chapters 6 and 9. It does not really affect the migrants' ideas of right and wrong – as can be seen in Chapters 7, 8 and 9 – but it does produce labels that negatively affect unauthorized migrants' identity and self-esteem. They believe that even animals seem to have more rights than they do. The law as such shapes who they are and what they can be. Menjívar (2006) argues that such experiences may mark unauthorized migrants for life.

Third, the law indirectly permeates unauthorized migrants' social lives. Sarat and Kearns (1993) argue that the law may dominate people's understanding of themselves as well as their relationships with others, the principal categories of social life. This can also be seen among unauthorized migrants, as the law indirectly governs their (intimate) social relationships. As shown above, the lack of a legal status may cause feelings of inferiority among unauthorized migrants, which affects how they relate to and behave towards others. They may, for instance, subordinate themselves to others or exceed their personal boundaries in response to their dependence on others for housing, living allowances or access to work or medical healthcare; all this may deprive them of healthy and secure living conditions, as Chapter 6 shows. Furthermore, their relationships may be characterized by a fear of betrayal as the lack of a legal status and the vulnerability that comes with it bring about deep-seated mistrust, even of humanitarian organizations, as shown in Chapter 5. Additionally, unauthorized migrants may stay away from relationships altogether. Some feel deprived of their social mobility as the lack of a legal status may prevent them from starting intimate relationships and/or families, as Chapter 6 shows. For unauthorized migrants, the lack of a legal status may shape – to use the words of Menjivar (2006: 1000) – 'who they are, how they relate to others, their participation in local communities, and their continued relationship with their homelands'. It may destroy relationships, create despair and bring about behavioural changes (cf. Menjívar and Lakhani, 2016). While some unauthorized migrants are blessed with strong social relationships and rich social lives, others stay away from it all together given the social complexities that accompany the lack of a legal status. The latter results in loneliness and grief for these migrants, which severely affects their well-being, as illustrated below.

Fourth, the law's effects can be seen indirectly in the legal domain. As shown in Chapters 7, 8 and 9 of this book, unauthorized migrants question the empirical legitimacy of the law in the Netherlands as, in their view, fundamental values such as their security, the best interests of their children, human dignity, effectiveness and proportionality are inadequately respected by the Dutch authorities. Consequently, they consider the law to be illegitimate, which comes at the cost of their consent to it. This may also contribute to the delegitimation of the powers of the authorities. Unauthorized migrants – especially those who aspire to legalization – do (initially) turn themselves over to the law to seek justice, as illustrated in Chapter 10. Given their dependency on the law, they have no other option than to use legal structures to improve their situation, meaning that they reproduce the hegemonic function of the law and contribute to the sustaining of the law's power (cf. Silbey, 2005). Yet, over time, some unauthorized migrants give up on the law as, they believe, it actively produces injustice. They lose their faith in the transformative power of the law, as they observe that the law is all over for them. The law seriously (and negatively) affects the different domains of their lives and has also absented itself by being inadequately available and offering insufficient protection to unauthorized migrants. Migrants blame the authorities for this and lose their trust in them, which carries severe risks for society in the long term, as illustrated in Chapters 7 and 8. After all, a system of power that is chronically unable to meet the interests of the subordinate members of society is subject to power erosion (Beetham, 1991: 209), which has consequences for the attitudes and behaviour of these subordinate groups and may impact on the state's ability to secure cooperation from them (Beetham, 1991; Bottoms and Tankebe, 2012). The withdrawal of consent may eventually result in the delegitimation of the power-holder according to Beetham (1991), meaning that the powers of the immigration authorities become subject to erosion and a large-scale state of turbulence may arise.

Fifth and finally, the law may seriously affect unauthorized migrants' well-being. It creates what I have called the 'pains of being unauthorized' – that is, the suffering that results from the legal reality that is superimposed on these migrants by the legal system that nation-states use to limit unauthorized residence (see Chapter 6). Others label the consequences of the law for unauthorized migrants 'social suffering' – in other words, the whole assemblage of problems that result from – in this context – the immigration system that the authorities have developed to end unauthorized residence (e.g. Drothbohm and Hasselberg, 2015; Schultz, 2021). Regardless of the label, the suffering may be considered as the result of living in a painful, enduring state of deportability that is accompanied by many limitations and severe hardship. The difficult material and immaterial living conditions that are typical of unauthorized residence cause serious distress for those without a legal status, especially those who are underage and who find themselves, through no fault of their own, in this situation. It causes feelings of fear, anxiety and frustration, particularly after long-term unauthorized residence (Staring et al., 2022). Earlier studies show that being (long-term) unauthorized in a country may negatively affect unauthorized migrants' health and cause physical and psychological complaints (Hintjens, Siegmann and Staring, 2020; Martinez et al., 2013; Scherder, van Os and Zijlstra, 2018), which the unauthorized migrants in this study also report. While unauthorized migrants are entitled to any necessary medical healthcare, they experience difficulties in claiming it in everyday practice, which complicates them finding some relief in their situation and improving their well-being. Consequently, their pain can persist – or worsen – over time, causing them to follow a downward spiral in terms of well-being.

Thus, the answers to the second, third and fourth sub-questions on how unauthorized migrants experience, give meaning to and interact with the law demonstrate that the law seriously matters to them on an everyday, existential, social, legal and well-being level. While there are differences among unauthorized migrants in how and how severely the law matters to them, its constitutive effects seem to – indirectly – affect all migrants at some point, making the law a powerful force in their everyday lives. Unauthorized migrants are assumed to be able to resist these powers by leaving the nation-state's territory. Yet, this is not that straight-forward in reality as they may have several reasons for being unwilling to return – or even incapable of returning – and may be deported back to the Netherlands if they move to another European country. This means that they continue to be subjected to the strong constitutive powers of the law during their unauthorized residence.

11.3 The law's powerlessness

Looking at unauthorized migrants' experiences with, thoughts on and interactions with the law shows that they are not solely trapped and obstructed by the law's powerful, pervasive authority. On the contrary, unauthorized migrants are subordinated to the law but not subservient to it. As shown throughout this book, they have the agency to prevent the state from exercising its sovereign powers by operating along with, negotiating, resisting or even benefiting from the law. Some, for instance, successfully circumvent the law by using multiple strategies and finding creative loopholes that enable them to stay out of sight of the authorities. Others – repeatedly and sometimes endlessly – mobilize the law to legalize their residence and/or postpone their deportation. They may also, pragmatically or in desperation, contest the law once they are confronted with it, either to limit the law's consequences in terms of deportation or to seek justice. Furthermore, unauthorized migrants protest against the law, go on demonstrations and use other strategies to contest its powers. They use a wide range of – legal and extra-legal – structures to fight the law, which enable them to continue their unauthorized residence in the Netherlands. While it has become more complicated for unauthorized migrants to effectively resist a state's controlling policies given the intense and digitalized forms of surveillance (Broeders and Engbersen, 2007; Van Meeteren, 2014), they may maintain their strategies for many years and even decades (see also Staring et al., 2022). Whereas the law may be considered power*ful* in constitutive terms, it is also power*less* if seen through an instrumental lens – i.e. when researchers examine whether the law inspires or deters unauthorized migrants to act in particular ways.

The law, for instance, barely inspires unauthorized migrants to leave the country nor deters them from continuing their unauthorized residence in the Netherlands, which are among its aims in fact. Unauthorized migrants are seriously affected by the constitutive powers of the law, as shown in the previous section. However, they usually weigh up the different factors at a personal, household, community and structural level when deciding upon return and tend to prioritize non-legal over legal factors in these gradual, return decision-making processes. They only decide to return when life in the home country is (eventually) considered equal or better than the unauthorized residence in the Netherlands (see also Black et al., 2004; Koser and Kuschminder, 2015; Leerkes, van Os and Boersema, 2017), when a specific occurrence in the family sphere urges them to do so (cf. Van Wijk, 2008) or when they eventually, fatalistically, accept the law's consequences. While Assisted Voluntary Return (AVR) programmes and reintegration budgets may influence unauthorized migrants' decisions to return up to a point, the impact of the law or of specific policy interventions on unauthorized migrants' return decisions is generally considered limited (Black et al., 2004; Koser and Kuschminder, 2015; Leerkes et al., 2017). This study shows that it takes a long time before such an impact comes about. One of the reasons for this limited impact is that migrants do not feel legally nor morally obliged to obey the law, which may be explained based on the perceived illegitimacy of a law that triggers defiance rather than compliance, as demonstrated in Chapters 9 and 10. Even the last resort of immigration detention only puts limited pressure on unauthorized migrants to leave the Netherlands – and then only if these migrants attribute some level of empirical legitimacy to it, as suggested in Chapter 9. This shows that the law does not matter that much to unauthorized migrants as far as their return decisions are concerned, making it relatively instrumentally powerless.

Additionally, the Dutch authorities encounter numerous barriers that prevent them from successfully enforcing the law and deporting unauthorized migrants from the country (Maliepaard et al., 2022; Van Houte and Leerkes, 2019), which further adds to the powerlessness of the law. The authorities have repeatedly tried to overcome these barriers in order to increase the effectiveness of their deportation practices (Advisory Council on Migration, 2021; Van Zwol Committee, 2019). Yet, despite their best efforts, they keep on encountering a wide range of limitations that prevent them from effectuating unauthorized migrants' deportation. These barriers vary from the migrants' home countries' reluctance to provide the travel documents that are required for the migrants' deportation, to the unauthorized migrants' unwillingness to arrange such documents; from the authorities' dependence on other actors for the migrants' deportation, to a lack of adequate collaboration and information in the state's deportation process; and from a lack of priority for the deportation in intra-national negotiations, to all kind of organizational matters (e.g. Advisory Council on Migration, 2021; DT&V, 2023; Leerkes and Kox, 2016; Maliepaard et al., 2022). These barriers negatively impact on the state's return and deportation figures. These figures are usually based on the caseload of the Dutch Repatriation and Departure Service, meaning that unauthorized migrants living out of sight of the authorities are not included in these rates. While these rates may be incomplete in terms of the unauthorized population in the Netherlands, they are the only figures available. They show that about 46 percent of unauthorized migrants in the caseload of the DT&V were deported in 2019 (Ministry of Justice and Security, 2020), which includes 50 percent of the unauthorized migrants in immigration detention who were deported from the centre (Advisory Council on Migration, 2020).[75] Others – so-called undeportable migrants – may have either independently left the Netherlands, successfully legalized their residence or decided to continue their unauthorized residence in the Netherlands. The authorities lack the coercive measures to realize their departure as they cannot indefinitely

75 The Advisory Committee on Migration argues that around 90 percent of immigration detainees with a Dublin claim are sent back to the European country that is responsible for their deportation. I did not include this number in the figures, though, as it is unsure whether the migrants concerned will be deported and leave the EU.

detain unauthorized migrants or use unchecked physical force (Campesi, 2015; Ellermann, 2010).

So, looking at how unauthorized migrants experience, give meaning to and interact with the law shows not only that the law seriously matters to them but also does not matter that much in terms of the migrants' return. Other non-legal factors are more compelling in their return decisions, which negatively impacts on the effectiveness of the law. This contributes to the instrumental powerlessness of the law as the Dutch authorities – like other European nation-states – keep on struggling to effectuate the departure of unauthorized migrants from the Netherlands (e.g. Leerkes and Van Houte, 2020; Maliepaard et al., 2022; Van Zwol Committee, 2019).

11.4 Understanding the powerful and powerless functioning of the law

The previous sections provided insights into both the powerful and the powerless functioning of the law. These insights are part of the answer to the central question that guided this study – that is, how the law matters to unauthorized migrants and what this means for the functioning of the law in the migration domain. Yet, as shown throughout this book, the law matters in different ways to unauthorized migrants. It is not equally power*ful* and power*less* to them. This should, in my view, be understood in the context of the diversity among unauthorized migrants. These latter are often referred to as if they were one common group but whose members substantially differ from each other in terms of countries of origin, ethnicities, migration motives, incorporation strategies, social embeddedness and aspirations (Staring et al., 2022; Vertovec, 2007). These differences result in the migrants having a wide variety of social positions, relations and opportunities in society (Burgers and Engbersen, 1999; Vertovec, 2007; 2019). Moreover, the differences produce diverse relationships with the law (see also Abrego, 2011; Gehring, 2013; Güdük and Desmet, 2022; Kubal, 2014; Virdi, 2013). Some unauthorized migrants, for instance, experience relatively little pain in being unauthorized in their everyday lives, as Chapter 6 demonstrates, whereas others are completely mentally and physically broken due their lack of a legal status; yet others are somewhere in between these two poles. Moreover, as shown in Chapters 7 to 9, some migrants are seriously affected by the perceived illegitimacy of the law in the migration domain, whereas others tend to accept the Dutch state's use of restrictive migration-management strategies or to only question the empirical legitimacy of some specific aspects of it. Furthermore, as is revealed in Chapter 10, some unauthorized migrants succeed in keeping out of sight of the law in their everyday lives while others are constantly interacting with it to legalize their residence in the Netherlands. This results in different legal consciousness processes which have been discussed in depth in Chapter 10.

Insights into (the evolution of) these different legal consciousness processes could help to better understand the powerful and powerless functioning of the law in the migration domain. However, to date, adequate insights into this diversity are lacking, which makes Abrego (2011) call for more research on this topic. Güdük and Desmet (2022) followed up on this call. They conducted a literature review on (authorized and unauthorized) migrants' legal consciousness and grouped all factors that are supposed to shape it into four categories. Their first category includes migrants' individual characteristics such as their legal status, migration histories, arrival experiences, legal and language knowledge, age, gender, class and health, all of which inform someone's legal consciousness (see also Abrego, 2008, 2011; Galli, 2019; Gehring, 2013; Kubal, 2014; Schwenken, 2013; Virdi, 2013). Their second category covers all relational aspects including the (transnational) social context in which migrants' legal consciousness is shaped as well as the migrants' social contacts, transnational spaces, collective public narratives and/or reports of internationals organizations, which can impact on a person's thoughts on the law (see also Gehring, 2013: 1037; Haddeland, 2021; Kulk and De Hart, 2013; Schwenken, 2013). Their third category addresses cultural dynamics – i.e. the migrants' experiences with the law in their home countries as well as their cultural backgrounds, which may have an impact on their perceptions of the law in their destination country (see also Güdük and Desmet, 2022; Kubal, 2013). Finally, their fourth category refers to the law itself and includes all public policies and discourses. Mieżanskienė (2020) considers this latter category to be key in explaining (unauthorized) migrants' legal consciousness.

This categorization helps us to understand under which influences unauthorized migrants' legal consciousness comes about. However, in my view, the factors in the four categories are not sufficient to enable an understanding of the diversity in unauthorized migrants' legal consciousness processes (over time). They provide, for instance, too little insight into the variety and fluidity of unauthorized migrants' legal consciousness processes whereas the variety and fluidity of legal consciousness are generally acknowledged (e.g. Hertogh, 2018; Merry, 1990; Sarat, 1990). Additionally, these factors fail to explain how and why the legal consciousness of some unauthorized migrants evolves over time while that of others does not or does so differently. Furthermore, these factors are inadequate in helping us to understand why the migrants have such different relationships with the law, despite them being situated in a similar legal context. This means that further insights into (the working of) these factors in the evolvement of unauthorized migrants' legal consciousness processes are needed to better understand both the power*ful* and the power*less* functioning of the law in the migration domain. In what follows, I add some new insights into the academic debate on the differentiation in unauthorized migrants' legal consciousness processes. Drawing upon previous migration studies on the latter's living conditions (e.g. Burgers and Engbersen, 1999; Staring, 2001; Staring et al., 2022; Van Meeteren, 2014) as well as Güdük and Desmet's (2022) categorization, I present three interrelated, interacting factors that mitigate unauthorized migrants' relationships with the law over time: 1) unauthorized migrants' previous migration experiences, including their migration motives, 2) their social embeddedness and 3) their future aspirations. These factors deserve further exploration as, based on them, different groups of unauthorized migrants emerge who go through quite varied legal consciousness processes. This concluding section is not the place to present a typology of migrants or their legal consciousness processes, meaning that I limit myself to a brief description of these factors and tentatively describe how these mitigate unauthorized migrants' legal consciousness over time and shed light on the consequences for the functioning of the law in the migration domain.

11.4.1 Unauthorized migrants' previous migration experiences

The first factor – the migrants' previous migration experiences – includes their reasons for leaving their home country, their migration journeys to the Netherlands as well as their experiences upon arrival (see also Abrego, 2008, 2011; Gehring, 2013). This builds on the first category that Güdük and Desmet (2022) distinguish. I believe that this category deserves more refinement, as unauthorized migrants' have different migration experiences that variously impact on their expectations of and interactions with the law. These thus differently shape their subsistence strategies as well as their legal consciousness processes (cf. Abrego, 2011). Although I am aware that the migrants' (retrospective reflections on their) migration experiences are multifaceted and versatile, I roughly observe three types of migration experience among my respondents, which shape their legal consciousness and impact on the effects of the law experienced. This tripartite categorization needs further exploration but already helps us to understand the variety in the legal consciousness processes of unauthorized migrants who are situated in a similar legal context.

I encountered, for instance, unauthorized labour migrants and so-called 'adventurers' who (initially temporarily) left their home country for socio-economic or socio-cultural motives (see also Staring et al., 2022). These migrants wanted to improve their own and their families' living conditions, which made them decide to try their luck elsewhere. Some – usually unauthorized labour migrants – could go relatively easily to the Netherlands given their falsified documents, specifically lenient visa requirements or other accessible migration pathways. Others – commonly adventurers – had fewer options to legally migrate to the Netherlands, meaning that they were dependent on lengthy, hazardous and expensive journeys into Europe before they ended up in the destination country. Given the migration narratives that circulate in their home countries as well as their transnational legal knowledge, these migrants were usually aware that they would not be eligible for a residence permit (cf. Schwenken, 2013). They expected that any interaction with the law could bring about detection, detention and deportation. Therefore, they tried to stay away from the law from the moment they entered the Netherlands, meaning that their legal consciousness was being characterized by a search for better living conditions and the effort to stay away from the law, as we saw in Chapter 10. By turning to their social networks (see below), these respondents could (initially) access the informal economy and make an independent living. The migrants' previous migration experiences and the attitude they engendered severely limited the effects of the constitutive powers of the law on these migrants.

The labour migrants' and adventurers' experiences and interactions with the law contrast with those of rejected asylum seekers. These latter claim that they left their home country out of fear of prosecution or security. They used different routes to travel into Europe. Immediately on arrival in their destination country, they turned themselves in to the law in order to claim asylum. Being inspired by collective public narratives or reports by international organizations (cf. Schwenken, 2013), they expected to be granted residence rights, especially as they thought that the law in the Netherlands was fair in comparison with that in their home country. Their legal consciousness was characterized by active engagement with the law, given their wish for a residence permit. Yet, their asylum claims were being rejected by the authorities, something which the asylum seekers did not understand. They were usually quite upset about not being granted asylum and being subjected to the state's comprehensive immigration system, as this – combined with being unauthorized – caused them severe pain and made the law constitutively more powerful to them. This also inspired their further interactions with the law in terms of legal mobilization, resistance and demonstrations, as I outlined in Chapter 10. These rejected asylum seekers initially believed that the law would offer them a solution to their problems and kept on attempting to obtain it.

11.4.2 Unauthorized migrants' social embeddedness

The second factor – unauthorized migrants' social embeddedness – helps us to understand whether, when and how unauthorized migrants' legal consciousness evolves during the course of their unauthorized residence. Their social embeddedness refers to the characteristics of and the migrants' position in their social networks (Burgers and Engbersen, 1999). These networks are usually categorized based on the type of ties that exist between the migrants and their social contacts, the support which migrants may mobilize from their social contacts as well as the degree of solidarity and reciprocity that accompanies the support (Staring and Kox, 2022). Earlier research has convincingly shown that the migrants' social embeddedness affects their journeys, arrival processes and subsistence strategies during their unauthorized residence (e.g. Burgers and Engbersen,

1999; Engbersen et al., 2002; Staring, 2001). I believe that the migrants' differentiated social embeddedness also helps to understand the evolvement of their legal consciousness over time, given its impact on their opportunities to generate support from their social networks, their ability to circumvent the law during their unauthorized residence as well as their capacity to deal with the law's constitutive powers. This affects the migrants' relationships with the law, which fits in the second, relational category that Güdük and Desmet (2022) distinguish. It also aligns with the current trend in which relational legal consciousness has taken on greater importance, meaning that an individual's thoughts and interactions with the law are understood in their wider social context (Chua and Engel, 2019).

Some migrants are, for instance, strongly embedded in transnational social networks consisting of family, friends and compatriots who are based both in their home and in their destination country. Migrants may use their networks to find housing, jobs and other needs while not having to provide anything in return. This enables these migrants – usually unauthorized labour migrants – to make an independent living and to prevent marginalization during their unauthorized residence. It also helps them to circumvent the law on an everyday basis and then successfully play with it once confronted with it. While unauthorized residence is never easy, migrants with such a strong transnational social embeddedness may maintain their position for a long time (see also Staring et al., 2022). The migrants' social networks thus have an intermediate function to limit the law's salience on an everyday basis, which means that the migrants are less touched by the constitutive and instrumental effects of the law. Their legal consciousness, then, barely evolves over time, changing mainly only if the migrants' personal conditions alter or when they are confronted with the law, as outlined in Chapter 10. Such migrants may start to consider returning to their home country, at least if life over there is considered better than in the Netherlands (perhaps they might again remigrate at a later stage to the Netherlands). It shows that migrants are less affected by the law and less willing to end their unauthorized residence as long as they can successfully maintain their subsistence strategies.

Yet not all unauthorized migrants are embedded in such strong social networks. The networks of some migrants are less extended, characterized by less solidarity or impeded by more (monetary) reciprocity, partly because these networks are built after the migrants' arrival in the Netherlands. Migrants who are embedded in such networks – often adventurers – are less capable of generating support from their social network, receive less comprehensive solidarity or are expected to offer a reciprocal service (see also Staring et al., 2022). This negatively affects the migrants' access to formal and informal markets, although race might also have something to do with it. This complicates making an independent living and circumventing the law during the migrants' unauthorized residence. Additionally, these migrants receive less emotional support from their networks. The migrants' weaker social embeddedness increases the risks of marginalization and confrontation with the law over time, which contributes to the perceived pain of being unauthorized. It makes the law more salient on an everyday basis, which strengthens its constitutive effects. At the same time, the law is also powerless as these migrants do not return. They are usually less willing to return than unauthorized labour migrants, partly because they realize that they cannot make such a hazardous, expensive journey to the Netherlands again. The authorities also fail to deport them, especially as these migrants mainly originate from countries without readmission agreements with the Dutch authorities. As return is not considered an option and deportation has failed, these migrants find themselves in a marginalized and frustrating situation. It makes them start aspiring to legalization, which – as shown in Chapter 10 – contributes to a shift in their legal consciousness. They often fall back on humanitarian organizations for unauthorized migrants which may help them to explore their legalization (and return) opportunities. From then on, these migrants no longer stay away from the law but start actively engaging with it in order to fulfil their legalization aspirations.

Finally, there are unauthorized migrants whose legal consciousness is characterized by active engagement with the law from the moment of their arrival in the Netherlands. These migrants – usually asylum seekers – mainly have contacts with professionals and volunteers in the asylum community as well as other asylum seekers whom they got to know during their asylum procedures. These professionals may provide costless comprehensive solidarity in terms of shelter, living allowances, legal aid and medical assistance for a select period of time, provided that the respondents (continuously) meet the selection criteria. Yet, this support is mainly aimed at legalizing their residence or finding another sustainable solution for them. If there is no further likelihood of such a solution, migrants may lose their support, as I illustrated in Chapter 5. When this happens, the rejected asylum seekers' lives become more complicated and the law becomes even more salient on an everyday basis. These migrants are very severely affected by the constitutive powers of the law while they are, at the same time, extremely reluctant to return to their home country. Their social embeddedness initially helps them to deal with the law; however, this changes over time if the support decreases and the impact of their negative legal experiences increases. While they keep on relying on their social networks, this becomes more complicated, which severely impacts on their well-being. Their legal consciousness continues to evolve over time, as illustrated in Chapter 10, until they can no longer cope with the lack of a legal status. At this point, they may (fatalistically) decide to return. This shows that the migrants' social embeddedness affects their relationship with the law and impacts on the (faster) evolvement of their legal consciousness.

11.4.3 *Unauthorized migrants' aspirations*

Finally, the third factor – unauthorized migrants' aspirations – also helps us to understand unauthorized migrants' interactions with and thoughts on the law over time and to explain the evolving of the migrants' legal consciousness. According to Van Meeteren (2014), the term 'aspirations' refers to the migrants' present-day goals and future ambitions, whereas the migrants' previous migration experiences refer to their past, meaning that their initial migration aims and their aspirations do not necessarily align. She distinguishes three types of aspiration: 1) the investment aspiration, which refers to unauthorized migrants' wish to make money during their residence abroad in order to successfully return to the country of origin and kickstart their life again, 2) the settlement aspiration, which entails looking for personal gain during the period of residence abroad regardless of the legal status and 3) the legalization aspiration, which involves the migrants' aim to obtain residence rights in the destination country. Van Meeteren (2014) shows that unauthorized migrants' aspirations impact on their material living conditions, leisure time, social contacts, transnational activities and dreams. I believe that migrants' aspirations also help to explain unauthorized migrants' relationships with the law, as their aspirations impact on whether and how they reach out to the law, what they expect from it and what they decide to do in relation to it. Their aspirations thus help to explain how unauthorized migrants' legal consciousness evolves over time, which supplements the individual dimension of the categorization of Güdük and Desmet (2022).

Unauthorized migrants with investment aspirations – usually unauthorized labour migrants – use their unauthorized residence to improve their living conditions once they return to their home country. This requires avoiding the law and working as much as possible in order to be able to send remittances to their home country and prepare for their eventual return. Migrants with such aspirations try to uphold these strategies as long as possible – usually quite successfully – especially given their strong social embeddedness (see also Staring et al., 2022). Over time, some may decide to leave the Netherlands if they believe that they have fulfilled – or will not be able to fulfil – their aspirations. Then, life in the home country is considered better than life in the Netherlands, meaning that the law does have an indirect instrumental effect on them. It is also possible, however, that their aspirations change under the influence of evolving personal conditions such as the birth and socialization of children in the Netherlands, lengthy residence in the country or other conditions that make them more willing to stay in the country. Then they may either develop settlement or legalization aspirations, which contributes to a shift in their legal consciousness, as described in Chapter 10. They no longer try to invest in their unauthorized residence but aim to stay in the Netherlands and might even start reaching out to the law to fulfil their aspirations.

Unauthorized migrants with settlement aspirations – usually adventurers – initially want to reside in the Netherlands and improve their lives there, regardless of their legal status. Like those with investment aspirations, they start to work as much as necessary in order to facilitate their unauthorized residence. However, this is more complicated for them given their less-strong social embeddedness in comparison with labour migrants. As soon as their lives become too complicated, given their increased dependency or marginalization or given their frustrating experiences with a perceived ineffective law, they start to aspire to legalization. They no longer avoid the law as they used to do but start to actively engage with it in order to obtain residence rights, which fits with the second legal consciousness process discussed in Chapter 10. They are then more often confronted with the constitutive powers of the law although the latter remains powerless to, as it does not inspire them to return to their home country.

Finally, some unauthorized migrants – including rejected asylum seekers – aspire to legalization from the moment of their arrival in the Netherlands. These migrants usually directly turn themselves over to the law and continue doing so during their unauthorized residence. Despite the multiple rejections and their negative experiences with the law, they keep on aspiring to legalization and turning to the law, usually with the assistance of their social networks. Over time, though, they are increasingly affected by the constitutive effects of the law and may no longer be able to cope with them, making them eventually give up on the law. Nevertheless, only a few of them eventually decided to fatalistically accept the law's consequences and return, which exposes the powerlessness of the law yet again.

I believe that these three factors – which add further differentiation to Güdük and Desmet's (2022) categorization – help to explain whether, how and when unauthorized migrants' legal consciousness evolves over time, while the legal consciousness of others does not or does so differently. While individual factors such as age, ethnicity, legal history and deportation opportunities impact on migrants' experiences with the law as well, these three factors provide more insights into the variety and fluidity of unauthorized migrants' legal consciousness processes. What is more, these help us to understand the unauthorized migrants' different relationships with the law despite them being situated in a similar legal context. I believe that follow-up research is needed on these factors, especially as they help to better understand the differentiated powerful and powerless functioning of the law in the migration domain.

11.5 Legal, moral and instrumental limits of the law

This brings me to the end of this book, which has shown that the Dutch authorities have created a comprehensive, multi-layered system to discourage unauthorized residence, a system which impacts on unauthorized migrants' understandings of the law as it first produces their unauthorized residence and then reduces them to people lacking a legal status. The latter is a pervasive and painful part of their lives which, for some, outweighs all other aspects of their everyday being, making the law 'all over' in their lives. This shows that the law seriously matters to unauthorized migrants – which answers my central research question. Regarding the consequences for the functioning of the law, it can be said that the law has powerful constitutive effects on an everyday, existential, social, legal and well-being level. At the same time, the law is powerless if seen through an instrumental lens, as it does not convince unauthorized migrants to leave the country, while the authorities lack the power to actually enforce it in terms of deportation. Yet, the law is not equally power*ful* and power*less* to unauthorized migrants and matters in different ways to them. Insights into unauthorized migrants' legal consciousness processes and how these evolve over time help us to better understand the differentiated powerful and powerless functionings of the law in the migration domain. This book has presented three interrelated, interacting factors that mitigate unauthorized migrants' relationships with the law over time – the migrants' previous migration experiences, their social embeddedness and their future aspirations. These factors – which differ between unauthorized migrants and may change over time – impact on the migrants' expectations of and interactions with the law as well as their opportunities to circumvent it. They explain why the law greatly matters to some and less to others, although all unauthorized migrants are somehow affected by it. More research is needed on these explanatory factors and how these impact on unauthorized migrants' relationships with the law – or perhaps a more grounded and less pragmatic analysis of the data of this study – if we are to better understand how unauthorized migrants' previous migration experiences, social embeddedness, aspirations and perhaps other factors impact on their legal consciousness processes and what this means for the functioning of the law. Such a study or analysis may help to present a typology of unauthorized migrants' legal consciousness processes and to provide greater insight into what the law does to whom and under which conditions. These insights may be used to develop more ethical, equitable and effective immigration systems that better suit the differentiation among unauthorized migrants (see also Ryo, 2017).

I believe that a different immigration system is needed as the authorities' current use of the law to counteract unauthorized residence has, I would argue, some severe legal, moral and instrumental limits. First, I would like to point to the legal limits of the current use of the law towards unauthorized migrants. Unauthorized migrants have human rights like everyone else, which may not be restricted just because they lack the legal right to reside on a nation-state's territory.[76] Nation-states like the Netherlands are bound to respect these rights for everyone who resides within their jurisdiction or effective control on the basis of international human rights law.[77] This means that they must respect everyone's human rights by refraining from any violations of them, protect them by preventing any violations by others and fulfil migrants' human rights by taking positive measures that facilitate the migrants' enjoyment of human rights (Karp, 2020). The Dutch authorities have formally laid down human rights in Dutch immigration legislation, as we have seen in several chapters of this book. Yet, the question arises as to whether they do, in fact, respect, protect and fulfil their human rights obligations towards unauthorized migrants in everyday practice. Unauthorized migrants believe that they have been accorded the injustice they experience which – in their view – has been produced by the law, as demonstrated in Chapters 7 to 10. Lawyers, legal scholars and humanitarian organizations also question whether the Dutch authorities adequately protect unauthorized migrants' human rights (e.g. Amnesty International, 2018a, 2018b, 2020; Cornelisse, 2011; De Nationale Ombudsman, 2020; Geertsema et al., 2021; Klaassen et al., 2020; Rodrigues, 2016). Paragraph 120 of the Dutch Constitution states that legal courts may not test whether laws and treaties are in conflict with the Constitution. Besides, Dutch courts are supposed to back the authorities in immigration cases (Geertsema et al., 2021). Yet, the Dutch authorities have been held legally accountable for violations of unauthorized migrants' human rights in some court rulings. These obliged them, *inter alia*, to provide shelter to unauthorized minors, to offer Bed, Bath and Bread arrangements and to adjust certain admission procedures based on income requirements. While these legal obligations have somewhat improved the conditions for unauthorized migrants, the adjustments seem insufficient to undo all the injustice experienced by them and in fact take away legal experts' concerns over the Dutch state's use of the law towards unauthorized migrants. This means that the current use of the law towards unauthorized migrants still raises legal concerns.

Second, even if the law in the migration domain is considered legally valid by courts, the current use of it with unauthorized migrants has severe moral limits. As has been shown above, the law is supposed to protect people and safeguard their human rights in order to protect their dignity, regardless of their legal status. This book has shown that the law currently causes serious suffering among unauthorized migrants on an everyday, existential, social, legal and well-being level. It creates problems that the Dutch authorities try to prevent for others in the Netherlands (Staring et al., 2022). As in other legal contexts (Canning, 2018; Menjívar and Abrego, 2012), the law structurally – and I believe intentionally, as can be seen in Chapter 6 – harms unauthorized migrants. It allows and

76 https://www.ohchr.org/en/migration, accessed 08/07/2023.
77 Ibid.

(actively) produces instances of physical, economic and emotional harm to unauthorized migrants and their families which affects their everyday lives. Menjívar and Abrego (2012) refer to these harms as 'legal violence'. This qualification – which is based on studies in the US – seems to fit the situation in the Netherlands too, given the cumulative injurious and painful effects that the law creates for unauthorized migrants situated in this country. This is not what the law is supposed to do. Tamanaha (2001: 241) argues that 'every application of law or action in the name of law that increases human misery must be carefully scrutinized, regardless of whether it does or does not mirror society or enhance social order, and must stand up to a test of rightness'. The law – including what nation-states do with it – must be right in order to withstand this test. While we may discuss what is 'right', I believe that it is safe to say that the law actively – and consciously – producing suffering, injustice and harm for unauthorized migrants to make them leave the country, cannot be considered right. On the contrary, it is immoral, even though this is what currently happens in the Netherlands. Several scholars argue that states should be held responsible for the law's consequences (e.g. Menjívar and Abrego, 2012). Soliman (2021: 236), for instance, writes that states may perhaps not be held legally accountable for potential human-rights violations but that this does not mean that their responsibility cannot be scrutinized. I agree with Soliman as, in my view, the current use of the law towards unauthorized migrants has fallen to a morally lower level and can no longer be justified.

Third, the current use of the law concerning unauthorized migrants is characterized by severe instrumental limits. While a state should just do what is supposed to be right from a legal and moral point of view, the current ineffectiveness of the law in the migration domain provides an extra argument for revising the current approach towards unauthorized migrants. As has been shown throughout this book, the law only limitedly incites unauthorized migrants to leave the country, as non-legal factors are more important than legal factors in unauthorized migrants' decision-making processes regarding return (Black et al., 2004; Koser and Kuschminder, 2015; Leerkes et al., 2017; Van Wijk, 2008). The law may even trigger unauthorized migrants to mobilize, contest and resist the law given the experienced empirical illegitimacy (see also Breuls, 2022). Furthermore, unauthorized migrants are too occupied with complex subsistence strategies to seriously consider and organize their return processes during their unauthorized residence (Pro Facto, 2018). Additionally, the authorities can only partly enforce the law given the limitations they encounter in deporting unauthorized migrants, as has been shown above (Maliepaard et al., 2022; Van Houte and Leerkes, 2019). These facets negatively affect the law's effectiveness. Moreover, they can incur severe risks for society, as illustrated in Chapter 6. Some unauthorized migrants are driven underground into the clandestine circuit, which prevents them from seeking healthcare and reporting victimization or exploitation to the authorities (cf. Engbersen et al., 2006; Hintjens et al., 2020; Timmerman, Leerkes and Staring, 2019). This may not only put them in a vulnerable position but may also contribute to the migrants' immobility, as shown in Chapter 4. This is even more useless for those who do, in the end, obtain a residence permit, though sometimes after lengthy delays and desperate resistance to their first rejection (Van Zwol Committee, 2019).[78] This current approach is thus not only ineffective but it also incurs high costs for both unauthorized migrants and society.

11.5.1 *Towards a human-rights-based, empirically legitimate and differentiated approach*

These legal, moral and instrumental limits of the law call, in my view, for a different legal approach towards unauthorized migrants – a human-rights-based, empirically legitimate and differentiated approach that is grounded in academic insights. It should no longer be accepted that the solution to unauthorized residence is mainly sought through discouraging those who lack a legal status from residing in the territory (see also Staring et al., 2022), especially as the authorities are obliged to take care of unauthorized migrants whose deportation fails (Rodrigues, 2016). Since the law has produced unauthorized residence and the problems for unauthorized migrants as well as the authorities associated therewith, I believe that it is the law that is the instrument for solving the problems of unauthorized migrants (despite local authorities often trying to provide a solution for the problems the migrants encounter). If we do not look for a different approach and if we allow the human rights of certain groups of people to be curtailed, our liberal democracy might turn into a dictatorship by the majority. I believe that this is neither desirable nor acceptable. I believe that the insights from this study may be used to develop an immigration system that fully respects and safeguards the human rights and dignity of unauthorized migrants as well as the moral principles of the law. Additionally, these may contribute to a system that is less confusing and better suits the differentiation between unauthorized migrants (see also Ryo, 2017). I use the last section of this book to unfold my arguments for another approach.

First, I believe that a human-rights-based approach is needed to overcome the current legal and moral limits of the law in the migration domain. Human rights are formally included in Dutch immigration laws but the unauthorized migrants' experiences, as well as the aforementioned concerns of legal experts, imply that these migrants' human rights are not adequately respected in either policy or practice. Yet, I believe that respect for the

78 The percentage of successful repeated asylum claims, for instance, varied between 35 percent in 2014 and 18 percent in 2017 (Van Zwol Committee 2019: 48). This percentage does not include residence permits on other grounds (regularization schemes, medical residence permit or Dutch children), meaning that the number of asylum seekers who legalized their residence may be higher in practice. Around 29 percent of the migrants residing at freedom-restricted family locations eventually obtained a residence permit and 30 percent of those living in the Netherlands have been able to temporarily postpone their deportation while 13 percent returned from these locations to their home country (Van Zwol Committee, 2019: 50).

migrants' human rights is needed for a legally valid and morally right use of the law. After all, rules cannot justify themselves simply by being rules. These have to be justified in terms of the prevailing beliefs and values in society. Otherwise, the powerful can enjoy no moral authority for the exercise of their power, whatever its legal validity (Beetham, 1991). While people's views on the necessary link between law and morality may differ and while people may have different thoughts on what is morally right, it is commonly accepted that the law needs to be legally valid *and* morally right (e.g. Beetham, 1991; Dworkin, 1977; Radbruch, 1945 in Taekema, Gaakeer and Loth, 2020). This is where human rights come in, as they provide the moral principles that need to be respected for the justification of the law (e.g. Dworkin, 1977; Radbruch, 1945 in Taekema et al., 2020). If a law does not meet human-rights criteria, it cannot enjoy moral authority or be legally valid (*Ibid.*). This book has shown that the current approach towards unauthorized migrants is not human-rights-based in everyday practice, which comes at the cost of both its legally validity and its moral justification. I believe that this calls for a different approach that does better justice to these moral principles. Regardless of whether this approach is more or less restrictive towards unauthorized migrants, it should respect, protect and fulfil their human rights in theory *and* in practice.

Second, I believe that a new approach should be considered empirically legitimate by those subjected to it – unauthorized migrants. Evidently, the law should be established democratically and within the rule of law to assure its normative legitimacy. However, the law's empirical legitimacy is also of importance as there are several reasons why there is more to be expected from laws that are considered empirically legitimate and morally right by those individuals whose behaviour the authorities seek to regulate. Laws that are empirically legitimate and morally right contribute to a just society (cf. Tyler and Darley, 2000). These recognize a person's basic humanity, cause less suffering and harm, and limit personal distress among those who are subjected to the authorities' power (cf. Ryo, 2017). Empirically legitimate laws improve the quality of the authorities' execution of power and increase their moral authority (Beetham, 1991; Jackson et al., 2015). Such laws also foster public acceptance, limit resistance and enhance order in society (cf. Beetham, 1991; Coicaud, 2002; Van den Bos, 2018), which contributes to the viability of institutions in the long term (Beetham, 1991; Jackson et al., 2015). In addition, such laws are supposed to be more effective as empirically legitimate laws usually bring better results in terms of law-abiding behaviour and cooperation with legal authorities than do instrumentalist laws based on social control and rational choice (cf. Bottoms and Tankebe, 2012; Tyler, 2006; Tyler and Jackson, 2013). This reduces the governments' need for and costs of monitoring and enforcement (cf. Levi, Sacks and Tyler, 2009). For these and other reasons, authorities should govern based upon the consent of those whom they govern (cf. Tyler, 2006: 277). Authorities including unauthorized migrants' empirical legitimacy perceptions – meaning respecting the substantive values that are important to the migrants – helps to overcome the legal, moral and instrumental limits of the current use of the law towards unauthorized migrants. That is why I call for an approach that is considered empirically legitimate by those subjected to it.

Third, I believe that a differentiated approach towards unauthorized migrants may help to overcome the current instrumental limits of the law. While the principle of equality is a human right that should be respected at all times, it is possible to develop different laws within the immigration system that meet the needs of the differentiated groups of unauthorized migrants. After all, this study has shown that unauthorized migrants not only have different expectations of the law but also differently interact with it (over time) given their varying migration experiences, social embeddedness and aspirations. Unauthorized labour migrants, for instance, are usually willing to return if they have accomplished their investment aspirations, meaning that circular labour-migration opportunities could prevent or put an end to their unauthorized residence (see also Sie Dhian Ho et al., 2021). Furthermore, adventurers who have been repeatedly detained for the purpose of removal without being deported from the Netherlands should be offered an opportunity for legalization if the authorities fail to end their unauthorized residence as current policies for those who cannot leave the Netherlands through no fault of their own are insufficient (Advisory Council on Migration, 2013). Additionally, asylum seekers should be differently involved and treated in their asylum claims since they are less willing to leave the Netherlands because they believe that substantive values have not been respected during their legalization process, which makes them desperately and endlessly mobilize the law (see also Staring et al., 2022; Van Berckel Smit, 2022). A differentiated approach towards unauthorized migrants should be better adjusted to the migrants' reality to increase its instrumental effects (see also Engbersen et al., 2006).

The above raises the question what a human rights-based, empirically legitimate and differentiated use of the law towards unauthorized migrants entails. It is outside the scope of this study to suggest a completely different legal approach, but I do want to use this opportunity to briefly mention some ideas that would be beneficial to the current approach. As shown before, the authorities have included human rights in their immigration laws, which implies that they consider this to be an important element as well. Yet, these rights are not included in all laws, resulting in unauthorized migrants' large-scale exclusion from society, repeated immigration detentions that cumulatively exceed the eighteen months, health concerns and severe suffering. These non-human-rights-driven laws need to be replaced by laws that do respect migrants' rights. Additionally, it should ensure that migrants' human rights are adequately protected in everyday practice. This implies that a possible solution lies at the policy and executive level, meaning that the focus of the implementation and execution of current laws in everyday practice should be less on restriction and more on human rights. This seems to fit the wishes of some officers working in the migration domain who ask for more political lenience as they see themselves confronted with complex, painful casefiles in which they are struggling to come to decisions that adequately respect human values given the politically inspired legal framework they are bounded by (DT&V, 2023; IND, 2022). There needs to be more legal guarantees for unauthorized migrants to ensure that they can claim their human rights, especially as courts cannot test the laws themselves but only have a marginal review opportunity in migration cases and would appear to back the Dutch authorities in their legal rulings (Geertsema et al., 2021). If the protection at a national level fails, a to-be-established legal entity – e.g. a human-rights institute for people with a vulnerable legal status – that focuses on the protection of unauthorized migrants' human rights should be able to force states to undo any injustices and prevent further violations of the migrants' rights. This should be a hard law to ensure that the migrants' human rights can be guaranteed in everyday practice.

To conclude; I believe that centralizing human rights in the use of the law towards unauthorized migrants would do more justice to the human-right treaties that have been ratified by the Dutch authorities. I am aware that such an empirically legitimate approach goes against the current trends in the migration domain at national and European levels, which are still dominated by greater restriction, exclusion and collaboration. Yet dehumanisation is neither necessary nor sufficient for an effective returns policy (Kuschminder and Dubow, 2022). Given the intense suffering, injustice and harm that the law currently inflicts on unauthorized migrants, the creation of a human-rights-based, empirically legitimate and differentiated law towards unauthorized migrants seems the only right thing to do.

References

Aarrass B (2021) *Mensenrechten en migratierecht. Mensrenrechtennormen als grond voor toelating en verblijf.* The Hague: Boom juridisch.

Aas K (2007) Analysing a world in motion: Global flows meet criminology of the other. *Theoretical Criminology* 11(2): 283–303.

Aas K (2011) 'Crimmigrant' bodies and bona fide travellers: Surveillance, citizenship and global governance. *Theoretical Criminology* 15(3): 331–346.

Aas KF (2014) Bordered penality: Precarious membership and abnormal justice. *Punishment & Society* 16(5): 520–541.

Aas KF and Bosworth M (eds) (2013) *The Borders of Punishment: Citizenship, Crime Control, and Social Exclusion.* Oxford: Oxford University Press.

Abizadeh A (2010) Democratic theory and border coercion. *Political Theory* 35(1): 37–65.

Abrego LJ (2008) Legitimacy, social identity, and the mobilization of law: The effects of Assembly Bill 540 on undocumented students in California. *Law & Social Inquiry* 33(3): 709–734.

Abrego LJ (2011) Legal consciousness of undocumented Latinos: Fear and stigma as barriers to claims-making for first- and 1.5-generation immigrants. *Law & Society Review* 45(2): 337–370.

Abrego L (2015) Immigration law and immigrants' lived experiences. In: Sarat A and Ewick P (eds) *The Handbook of Law & Society.* Chichester: Wiley, pp. 258–273.

Abrego LJ (2018) Renewed optimism and spatial mobility: Legal consciousness of Latino Deferred Action for Childhood Arrivals recipients and their families in Los Angeles. *Ethnicities* 18(2): 192–207.

Abrego LJ (2019) Relational legal consciousness of US citizenship: Privilege, responsibility, guilt, and love in Latino mixed-status families. *Law & Society Review* 53(3): 641–670.

Advisory Council on Migration (2013a) *Vreemdelingenbewaring of een Lichter Middel?* The Hague: Advisory Committee for Migration Affairs.

Advisory Council on Migration (2013b) *Waar een wil is, maar geen weg. Advies over de toepassing van het beleid voor vreemdelingen die buiten hun schuld niet zelfstandig uit Nederland kunnen vertrekken.* The Hague: Advisory Committee for Migration Affairs.

Advisory Council on Migration (2018) *Verslag Vooronderzoek Bed, Bad, Brood.* The Hague: Advisory Council on Migration.

Advisory Council on Migration (2021) *Samen Werken aan Terugkeer. Advies over Effectiviteit en Zorgvuldigheid van Vreemdelingenbewaring.* The Hague: Advisory Council on Migration.

Advisory Council on Migration (2022) *Naar een Gelijker Speelveld bij Vaststelling Nationaliteit en Identiteit van Migranten.* The Hague: Advisory Council on Migration.

Advisory Council on Migration (2023) *In Nederland verblijvende kinderen zonder verblijfsvergunning. Rondetafelgesprek Tweede Kamer 12 april 2023*. The Hague: Advisory Council on Migration.

Albrecht HJ (2002) Fortress Europe? Controlling illegal immigration. *European Journal of Crime, Criminal Law and Criminal Justice* 10(1): 1–22.

Aliverti A (2012) Making people criminal: The role of the criminal law in immigration enforcement. *Theoretical Criminology* 16(4): 417–434.

Aliverti A (2013) *Crimes of Mobility*. Abingdon: Routledge.

Aliverti A (2015) Enlisting the public in the policing of immigration. *British Journal of Criminology* 55(2): 215–230.

Aliverti A, Milivojevic S and Weber L (2019) Tracing imprints of the border in the territorial, justice and welfare domains: A multi-site ethnography. *The Howard Journal of Crime and Justice* 58(2): 240–259.

Alpes MJ (2011) *Bushfalling: How Young Cameroonians Dare to Migrate*. Amsterdam: University of Amsterdam, PhD thesis.

Ambrosini M (2018) *Irregular Immigration in Southern Europe: Actors, Dynamics and Governance*. Cham: Palgrave Macmillan.

Ambrosini M and Van der Leun J (2015) Implementing human rights: Civil society and migration policies. *Journal of Immigrant and Refugee Studies* 13(2): 103–115.

Amnesty International (2009) *Jailed without Justice: Immigration Detention in the USA*. New York: Amnesty International.

Amnesty International (2011) *Vreemdelingendetentie in Nederland: Het moet en kan anders. Alternatieven voor Vreemdelingendetentie*. Amsterdam: Amnesty International.

Amnesty International (2018a) *Het recht op vrijheid. Vreemdelingendetentie: het ultimum remedium-Beginsel*. Amsterdam: Amnesty International.

Amnesty International (2018b) *Geen cellen en handboeien! Het beginsel van minimale beperkingen in het regime vreemdelingendetentie*. Amsterdam: Amnesty International.

Amnesty International (2020) *Bewijsnood. Wanneer Nationaliteit en Identiteit Ongeloofwaardig Worden Bevonden*. Amsterdam: Amnesty International.

Anderson B (2013) *Us and Them? The Dangerous Politics of Immigration Control*. Oxford: Oxford University Press.

Andersson R (2014) Time and the migrant other: European border controls and the temporal economics of illegality. *American Anthropologist* 116(4): 795–809.

Ansems L (2021) *Procedural Justice on Trial: A Critical Test of Perceived Procedural Justice from the Perspective of Criminal Defendants*. Utrecht: Utrecht University, PhD thesis.

Arendt H (1976) *Eichmann in Jerusalem. A Report on the Banality of Evil*. Dallas: Penguin.

Ataç I, Rygiel K and Stierl M (2016) Introduction. The contentious politics of refugee and migrant protest and solidarity movements: Remaking citizenship from the margins. *Citizenship Studies* 20(5): 527–544.

Aulsebrook G, Gruber N and Pawson M (2021) Pushbacks on the Balkan route: A hallmark of EU border externalisation. *Forced Migration Review* 68: 13–15.

Bäärnhielm S, Laban K, Schouler-Ocak M, Rousseau C and Kirmayer LJ (2017) Mental health for refugees, asylum seekers and displaced persons: A call for a humanitarian agenda. *Transcultural Psychiatry* 54(5–6): 565–574.

Bakewell O (2010) Some reflections on structure and agency in migration theory. *Journal of Ethnic and Migration Studies* 36(10): 1689–1708.

Baldaccini A (2009) The return and removal of irregular migrants under EU law: An analysis of the returns directive. *European Journal of Migration and Law* 11(1): 1–17.

Baldwin-Edwards M (2008) Towards a theory of illegal migration: Historical and structural components. *Third World Quarterly* 29(7): 1449–1459.

Balibar E (2002) *Politics and the Other Scene*. London: Verso.

Barbero I (2012) Expanding acts of citizenship: The struggles of *Sinpapeles* migrants. *Social & Legal Studies* 21(4): 529–547.

Barker V (2012) Global mobility and penal order: Criminalizing migration, a view from Europe. *Sociology Compass* 6(2): 113–121.

Barnes J (2022) Torturous journeys: Cruelty, international law, and pushbacks and pullbacks over the Mediterranean Sea. *Review of International Studies* 48(3): 441–460.

Bauder H (2014) Why we should use the term 'illegalized' refugee or immigrant: A commentary. *International Journal of Refugee Law* 26(3): 327–332.

Baudoin B, van de Burgt B and van Kalmthout A (2008) *Vrijheidsontneming van vreemdelingen*. The Hague: SDU.

Becker H (1967) Whose side are we on? *Social Problems* 14(3): 239–247.

Becket K and Evans H (2015) Crimmigration at the local level: Criminal justice processes in the shadow of deportation. *Law & Society Review* 49(1): 241–277.

Beetham D (1991) *The Legitimation of Power*. Atlantic Highlands, NJ: Humanities Press International (Issues in political theory).

Beetham D (1993) In defence of legitimacy. *Political Studies* 41(3): 488–491.

Beetham D (2013) Revisiting legitimacy, twenty years on. In: Tankebe J and Liebling A (eds) *Legitimacy and Criminal Justice: An International Exploration*. Oxford: Oxford University Press, pp. 19–36.

Beijersbergen K and Dirkzwager A (2015) Procedural justice, anger, and prisoners' misconduct: A longitudinal study. *Criminal Justice and Behavior* 42(2): 196–218.

Benseddik A and Bijl M (2004) *Onzichtbaar achter glas: onderzoek naar de bijdrage van illegalen in de glastuinbouw van het Westland*. The Hague: Stek.

Besters M and Brom FW (2010) 'Greedy' information technology: The digitalization of the European migration policy. *European Journal of Migration and Law* 12(4): 455–470.

Bhatia M (2014) Researching 'bogus' asylum seekers, 'illegal' migrants and 'crimmigrants'. In: Lumsden K and Winter A (eds) *Reflexivity in Criminological Research: Experiences with the Powerful and the Powerless*. London: Palgrave Macmillan, pp. 162–177.

Bhatia M (2020) The permission to be cruel: Street-level bureaucrats and harms against people seeking asylum. *Critical Criminology* 28: 277–292.

Bialasiewicz L (2012) Off-shoring and out-sourcing the borders of Europe: Libya and EU border work in the Mediterranean. *Geopolitics* 17(4): 843–866.

Billet C (2010) EC readmission agreements: A prime instrument of the external dimension of the EU's fight against irregular immigration. An assessment after ten years of practice. *European Journal of Migration and Law* 12(1): 45–79.

Bircan T and Korkmaz EE (2021) Big data for whose sake? Governing migration through artificial intelligence. *Humanities and Social Sciences Communications* 8(1): 1–5.

Black R and Gent S (2006) Sustainable return in post-conflict contexts. *International Migration* 44(1): 15–38.

Black R, Koser K, Munk K, Atfield G, D'Onofrio L and Tiemoko R (2004) *Understanding Voluntary Return*. London: Home Office.

Bloch A (2014) Living in fear: Rejected asylum seekers living as irregular migrants in England. *Journal of Ethnic and Migration Studies* 40(10): 1507–1525.

Bloch A and Chimienti M (2012) Irregular migration in a globalizing world. In: Bloch A and Chimienti M (eds) *Irregular Migrants: Policy, Politics, Motives and Everyday Lives*. London: Routledge, pp. 1–15.

Blumer H (1969) *Symbolic Interactionism. Perspective and Method*. Berkely CA: University of California Press.

Boekhoorn P and Speller T (2006) *Vreemdelingenpolitie in transitie. Een nadere verkenning van het operationeel vreemdelingentoezicht*. Nijmegen: BBSO.

Bonjour S (2010) Between integration provision and selection mechanisms: Party politics, judicial constraints, and the making of French and Dutch policies of civic integration abroad. *European Journal of Migration and Law* 12(3): 299–318.

Boone M and Kox M (2012) What works for irregular migrants in the Netherlands? *European Journal of Probation* 4(3): 54–68.

Boone M and Kox M (2023) Reconceptualizing empirical legitimacy for situations of severely conflicting social interests. *Utrecht Law Review* 19(2): 13–25.

Borrelli LM and Andreetta S (2019) Introduction: Governing migration through paperwork. *Journal of Legal Anthropology* 3(2): 1–9.

Bosniak L (2006) *The Citizen and the Alien: Dilemmas of Contemporary Membership*. New Jersey: Princeton University Press.

Bosworth M (2008) Border Control and the Limits of the Sovereign State. *Social & Legal Studies* 17(2): 199–215.

Bosworth M (2011) Subjectivity and identity in detention: Punishment and society in a global age. *Theoretical Criminology* 16(2): 123–140.

Bosworth M (2013) Can immigration detention centres be legitimate? Understanding confinement in a global world. In: Aas KF and Bosworth M (eds) *The Borders of Punishment: Migration, Citizenship, and Social Exclusion*. Oxford: Oxford University Press, pp. 149–165.

Bosworth M (2014) *Inside Immigration Detention*. Oxford: Oxford University Press.

Bosworth LM (2017) Mary Bosworth on border criminology, *Social Science Bites Podcast*, 6 January.

Bosworth M (2019) Immigration detention, punishment and the transformation of justice. *Social & Legal Studies* 28(1): 81–99.

Bosworth M and Guild M (2008) Governing through migration control: Security and citizenship in Britain. *British Journal of Criminology* 48(6): 703–719.

Bosworth M, Franko K and Pickering S (2018) Punishment, globalization and migration control: 'Get them the hell out of here'. *Punishment & Society* 20(1): 34–53.

Bosworth M, Parmar A and Vázquez Y (eds) (2018) *Race, Criminal Justice, and Migration Control: Enforcing the Boundaries of Belonging*. Oxford: Oxford University Press.

Bottoms A and Tankebe J (2012) Beyond procedural justice: A dialogic approach to legitimacy in criminal justice. *Journal of Criminal Law & Criminology* 102(1): 119–179.

Bouter H (2013) *Giving Shelter. The Logics and Likelihood of Irregular Migrants Receiving Shelter from Nongovernmental Organizations in the Netherlands*. Nijmegen: Radboud University, unpublished Master's dissertation.

Bowling B (2013) Epilogue. The borders of punishment: Towards a criminology of mobility. In: Aas KF and Bosworth M (eds) *The Borders of Punishment: Citizenship, Crime Control, and Social Exclusion*. Oxford: Oxford University Press, pp. 291–306.

Bowling B and Westenra S (2020) 'A really hostile environment': Adiaphorization, global policing and the crimmigration control system. *Theoretical Criminology* 24(2): 163–183.

Braithwaite V (2010) *Compliance with Migration Law: Report for the Department of Immigration and Citizenship*. Canberra: DIAC.

Brandariz JA (2021) An expanded analytical gaze on penal power: Border criminology and punitiveness. *International Journal for Crime, Justice and Social Democracy* 10(2): 99–112.

Brandariz JA and Fernández-Bessa C (2020) A changing and multi-scalar EU borderscape: The expansion of asylum and the normalisation of the deportation of EU and EFTA citizens. *International Journal for Crime, Justice and Social Democracy* 9(3): 21–33.

Breuls L (2022) *Vreemdelingendetentie in de Lage Landen. Een Etnografisch Onderzoek naar Uitvoeringspraktijken van Vreemdelingendetentie in België en in Nederland.* The Hague: Boom criminologie.

Brochmann G (1999) The mechanisms of control. In: Brochmann G and Hammar T (eds) *Mechanisms of Immigration Control: A Comparative Analysis of European Regulation Policies.* New York: Routledge, pp. 21–28.

Broeders D (2007) The new digital borders of Europe. EU databases and the surveillance of irregular migrants. *International Sociology* 22: 71–92.

Broeders D (2009) *Breaking Down Anonymity. Digital Surveillance on Irregular Migrants in Germany and the Netherlands.* Amsterdam: Amsterdam University Press.

Broeders D and Engbersen G (2007) The fight against illegal migration: Identification policies and immigrants' counterstrategies. *American Behavioral Scientist* 50(12): 1592–1609.

Brotherton DC (2019) Studying the gang through critical ethnography. Online at: https://academicworks.cuny.edu/cgi/viewcontent.cgi?article=1606&context=gc_pubs.

Brotherton DC and Barrios L (2011) *Banished to the Homeland: Dominican Deportees and their Stories of Exile.* New York: Columbia University Press.

Brouwer J (2018) *Family Matters: A Study into the Factors Hampering Voluntary Return of Migrants Residing at Family Locations.* The Hague: International Organization for Migration.

Brouwer J (2020) *Detection, Detention, Deportation: Criminal Justice and Migration Control through the Lens of Crimmigration.* The Hague: Eleven.

Burgers J and Engbersen G (1999) *De Ongekende Stad I: Illegale Vreemdelingen in Rotterdam.* Amsterdam: Boom.

Busser A, Oosterhuis R and Strik T (2019) Vreemdelingendetentie II. Gronden getoetst aan wetsvoorstel en aan Europees en Internationaal Recht. *Asiel- en Migrantenrecht* 10(9): 372–381.

Calavita K (1998) Immigration, law, and marginalization in a global economy: Notes from Spain. *Law & Society Review* 32(3): 529–566.

Calavita K (2005) *Immigrants at the Margins: Law, Race, and Exclusion in Southern Europe.* Cambridge: Cambridge University Press.

Campesi G (2015) Hindering the deportation machine: An ethnography of power and resistance in immigration detention. *Punishment & Society* 17(4): 427–453.

Canning V (2018) Zemiology at the border. In: Boukli A and Kotze J (eds) *Zemiology: Reconnecting Crime and Social Harm.* Cham: Palgrave Macmillan, pp. 183–201.

Cantat C and Feischmidt M (2019) Conclusion. Civil involvement in refugee protection: Reconfiguring humanitarianism and solidarity in Europe. In: Feischmidt M, Pries L and Cantat C (eds) *Refugee Protection and Civil Society in Europe.* Cham: Palgrave Macmillan, pp. 379–399.

Cardoso J, Randle Hamilton E, Rodrigues N, Eschbach K and Hagan J (2016) Deporting fathers: Involuntary transnational families and intent to remigrate among Salvadoran deportees. *International Migration Review* 50(1): 197–230.

Carling J (2007) Migration control and migrant fatalities at the Spanish-African borders. *International Migration Review* 41(2): 316–343.

Carling J, Erdal MB and Ezzati R (2014) Beyond the insider–outsider divide in migration research. *Migration Studies* 2(1): 36–54.

Carrabine E (2004) *Power, Discourse, and Resistance: A Genealogy of the Strangeways Prison Riot*. Aldershot: Ashgate.

Carrera S, Allsopp J and Vosyliūtė L (2018) Policing the mobility society: The effects of EU anti-migrant smuggling policies on humanitarianism. *International Journal of Migration and Border Studies* 4(3): 236–276.

Carrera S, Guild E, Aliverti A, Allsopp J, Manieri MG and Levoy M (2016) *Fit for Purpose? The Facilitation Directive and the Criminalisation of Humanitarian Assistance to Irregular Migrants. Report Commissioned by the Policy Department for Citizens' Rights and Constitutional Affairs*. Brussels: European Parliament.

Casas-Cortes M, Cobarrubias S, de Genova N, Garelli G, Grappi G and Heller C (2015) New keywords: Migration and borders. *Cultural Studies* 29(1): 55–87.

Cassarino JP (2009) The co-operation on readmission and enforced return in the African-European context. In: OECD/Sahel and West Africa Club (eds) *Regional Challenges of West African Migration: African and European Perspectives*. Paris: OECD, pp. 49–72.

Castaneda H (2007) *Paradoxes of Providing Aid: NGOs, Medicine, and Undocumented Migration in Berlin, Germany*. Tucson: University of Arizona Graduate College, PhD thesis.

Castillo Goncalves D (2020) Distinctive ethical challenges in qualitative research with migrant children. *Qualitative Research Journal* 20(3): 293–303.

Chacón J (2009) Managing migration through crime. *Columbia Law Review Sidebar* 109: 138–148.

Charmaz K (2006) *Constructing Grounded Theory: A Practical Guide through Qualitative Analysis*. London: Sage.

Chauvin S and Garcés-Mascareñas B (2012) Beyond informal citizenship: The new moral economy of migrant illegality. *International Political Sociology* 6(3): 241–259.

Chavez L (1998) *Shadowed Lives: Undocumented Immigrants in American Society*. Orlando: Harcourt Brace (2nd edition).

Chua LJ and Engel DM (2019) Legal consciousness reconsidered. *Annual Review of Law and Social Science* 15: 335–353.

Cleton L (2022) *Deporting Children: Policy Framing, Legitimation and Intersectional Boundary Work*. Antwerp: University of Antwerp, PhD thesis.

Cleton L and Chauvin S (2020) Performing freedom in the Dutch deportation regime: Bureaucratic persuasion and the enforcement of 'voluntary return'. *Journal of Ethnic and Migration Studies* 46(1): 297–313.

Coicaud JM (2002) *Legitimacy and Politics: A Contribution to the Study of Political Right and Political Responsibility*. Cambridge: Cambridge University Press.

Coleman J (1990) *Foundations of Social Theory*. Cambridge, MA: The Belknap Press of Harvard.

Commission Zeevalking (1991) *Commissie Binnenlands Vreemdelingentoezicht: Eindrapport*. The Hague: Commission Zeevalking.

Cornelisse G (2010) *Immigration Detention and Human Rights: Rethinking Territorial Sovereignty*. Leiden and Boston: M Nijhoff.

Cornelisse GN (2011) A new articulation of human rights, or why the European Court of Human Rights should think beyond Westphalian sovereignty. In: O'Keefe R and Tams CJ (eds) *Are Human Rights for Migrants?* Abingdon/New York: Routledge, pp. 99–119.

Cornelius W and Salehyan I (2007) Does border enforcement deter unauthorized immigration? The case of Mexican migration to the United States of America. *Regulation & Governance* 1(2): 139–153.

Côté-Boucher K, Infantino F and Salter MB (2014) Border security as practice: An agenda for research. *Security Dialogue* 45(3): 195–208.

Coutin SB (2000) *Legalizing Moves: Salvadoran Immigrants' Struggle for U.S. Residency*. Ann Arbor: University of Michigan Press.

Cowan D (2004) Legal consciousness: Some observations. *Modern Law Review* 67(6): 928–958.

Cox A (2011) Doing the programme or doing me? The pains of youth imprisonment. *Punishment & Society* 13(5): 592–610.

Crewe B (2011) Depth, weight, tightness: Revisiting the pains of imprisonment. *Punishment & Society* 13(5): 509–529.

Cullen PP (2009) Irish pro-migrant nongovernmental organizations and the politics of immigration. *VOLUNTAS* 20(2): 99–128.

Cuttitta P (2018) Delocalization, humanitarianism, and human rights: The Mediterranean border between exclusion and inclusion. *Antipode* 50(3): 783–803.

Cuttitta P and Last T (eds) (2020) *Border Deaths: Causes, Dynamics and Consequences of Migration-Related Mortality*. Amsterdam: Amsterdam University Press.

Cvajner M and Sciortino G (2010) Theorizing irregular migration: The control of spatial mobility in differentiated societies. *European Journal of Social Theory* 13(3): 389–404.

Dauvergne C (2008) *Making People Illegal: What Globalization Means for Migration and Law*. Cambridge: Cambridge University Press.

De Backer M, Felten P, Kirndörfer E, Kox M and Finlay R (2022) 'Their lives are even more on hold now': Migrants' experiences of waiting and immobility during the COVID-19 pandemic. *Social & Cultural Geography* 24(10): 1846–1862.

DeBono D (2013) 'Less than human': The detention of irregular immigrants in Malta. *Race & Class* 55(1): 60–81.

Decorte T and Zaitch D (eds) (2009) *Kwalitatieve Methoden en Technieken in de Criminologie*. Leuven: Acco Uitgeverij.

Deflem M (2008) *Sociology of Law*. Cambridge: Cambridge University Press.

De Genova N (2002) Migrant 'illegality' and deportability in everyday life. *Annual Review of Anthropology* 31: 419–447.

De Genova N (2013) 'We are of the connections': Migration, methodological nationalism, and militant research. *Postcolonial Studies* 16(3): 250–258.

De Genova N and Peutz N (eds) (2010) *The Deportation Regime: Sovereignty, Space, and Freedom of Movement*. Durham: Duke University Press.

De Gier N, Kox M, Boone M and Vanderveen G (2020) 'Ik Verblijf in een Gevangenis, Daar is Niets Moreels Aan'. Ervaren Procedurele Rechtvaardigheid bij Binnenkomst in Vreemdelingenbewaring. *Crimmigratie & Recht* 4(2): 101–120.

De Giorgi A (2010) Immigration control, post-Fordism, and less eligibility: A materialist critique of the criminalization of immigration across Europe. *Punishment & Society* 12(2): 147–167.

De Haan M (2018) *'Verwend, verwaand, verwesterd': Duurzaamheid van het Nederlandse terugkeerbeleid in de ogen van de terugkeerder.* Rotterdam: Erasmus Universiteit Rotterdam: Master's dissertation.

De Hart B (2003) Onbezonnen vrouwen. Gemengde relaties in het nationaliteitsrecht en het vreemdelingenrecht. *Nemesis* 3: 54–61.

De Hart B and Besselsen E (2021) 'Everything went according to the rules'. Female citizen sponsors' legal consciousness, intimate citizenship and family migration law. *Identities: Global Studies in Culture and Power* 28(1): 37–55.

Dekkers T (2019) *Mobility, Control and Technology in Border Areas: Discretion and Decision-Making in the Information Age*. Leiden: University of Leiden, PhD thesis.

De Lange T (2007) *Staat, markt en migrant. De regulering van arbeidsmigratie naar Nederland 1945-2006*. The Hague: Boom Juridische uitgevers.

De Nationale Ombudsman (2020) *Grenzen aan vreemdelingenbewaring. Een onderzoek naar de uitvoering van vreemdelingenbewaring*. The Hague: De Nationale Ombudsman.

Diepenhorst D (2012) *Praktische maatregelen tegen illegale migratie in Nederland*. Rijswijk: European Migration Network.

Di Molfetta E and Brouwer J (2019) Unravelling the 'crimmigration knot': Penal subjectivities, punishment and the censure machine. *Criminology & Criminal Justice* 20(3): 302–318.

Dingeman-Cerda MK and Coutin SB (2012) The ruptures of return: Deportation's confounding effects. In: Kubrin CE, Atz MS and Martinez R Jr (eds) *Punishing Immigrants: Policy, Politics and Injustice*. New York: New York University Press, pp. 113–137.

Donato KM and Armenta A (2011) What we know about unauthorized migration. *Annual Review of Sociology* 37: 529–543.

Doomernik J and Jandl M (eds) (2008) *Modes of Migration Regulation and Control in Europe*. Amsterdam: Amsterdam University Press.

Dourleijn E and Dagevos J (2011) *Vluchtelingengroepen in Nederland. Over de integratie van Afghaanse, Iraakse, Iraanse en Somalische migranten*. The Hague: Sociaal en Cultureel Planbureau.

Drotbohm H and Hasselberg I (2015) Deportation, anxiety, justice: New ethnographic perspectives. *Journal of Ethnic and Migration Studies* 41(4): 551–562.

DT&V (2023) *De stand van de uitvoering 2023*. The Hague: DT&V.

Durnescu I (2011) Pains of probation: Effective practice and human rights. *International Journal of Offender Therapy and Comparative Criminology* 55(4): 530–545.

Düvell F (2006) Irregular migration: A global, historical and economic perspective. In: Düvell F (ed.) *Illegal Immigration in Europe: Beyond Control?* London: Palgrave Macmillan, pp. 14–39.

Düvell F (2008) Clandestine migration in Europe. *Social Science Information* 47(4): 479–497.

Düvell F, Triandafyllidou A and Vollmer B (2010) Ethical issues in irregular migration research in Europe. *Population, Space and Place* 16(3): 227–239.

Dworkin R (1977) *Taking Rights Seriously*. London: Duckworth.

Ellermann A (2006) Street-level democracy: How immigration bureaucrats manage public opposition. *West European Politics* 29(2): 293–309.

Ellermann A (2008) The limits of unilateral migration control: Deportation and interstate cooperation. *Government and Opposition* 43(2): 168–189.

Ellermann A (2010) Undocumented migrants and resistance in the liberal state. *Politics and Society* 38(3): 408–429.

Ellermann A and Goenaga A (2019) Discrimination and policies of immigrant selection in liberal states. *Politics & Society* 47(1): 87–116.

Engbersen G (2001) The unanticipated consequences of panopticon Europe: Residence strategies of illegal immigrants. In: Guiraudon V and Joppke C (eds) *Controlling a New Migration World*. London: Routledge, pp. 222–246.

Engbersen G, Staring R, van der Leun J, de Boom J, van der Heijden P and Cruijff M (2002) *Illegale Vreemdelingen in Nederland. Omvang, Overkomst, Verblijf en Uitzetting*. Rotterdam: Erasmus University Rotterdam/Risbo.

Engbersen G, van San M and Leerkes A (2006) A room with a view: Irregular immigrants in the legal capital of the world. *Ethnography* 7(2): 209–242.

Engel D (1998) How does law matter in the constitution of legal consciousness? In: Garth BG and Sarat A (eds) *How Does Law Matter?* Evanston: Northwest University Press, pp. 109–144.

Ericson RV and Haggerty KD (eds) (2006) *The New Politics of Surveillance and Visibility.* Toronto: University of Toronto Press.

Espenshade TJ (1995) Unauthorized immigration to the United States. *Annual Review of Sociology* 21(1): 195–216.

Eule TG, Borrelli LM, Lindberg A and Wyss A (2019) *Migrants Before the Law. Contested Migration Control in Europe.* Cham: Springer International.

Evers J (2015) *Kwalitatieve Analyse: Kunst en Kunde.* Amsterdam: Boom Lemma uitgevers.

Ewick P and Silbey SS (1992) Conformity, contestation, and resistance: An account of legal consciousness. *New England Law Review* 26(3): 731–749.

Ewick P and Silbey SS (1998) *The Common Place of Law. Stories from Everyday Life.* Chicago: University of Chicago Press.

Ewick P and Silbey SS (2020) Looking for hegemony in all the wrong places: Critique, context and collectivities in studies of legal consciousness. In: Priban J (ed.) *Research Handbook on the Sociology of Law.* Cheltenham: Edward Elgar, pp. 163–176.

Fabini G (2017) Managing illegality at the internal border: Governing through 'differential inclusion'in Italy. *European Journal of Criminology* 14(1): 46–62.

Fabini G (2019) Internal bordering in the context of undeportability: Border performances in Italy. *Theoretical Criminology* 23(2): 175–193.

Fallon R (2005) Legitimacy and the constitution. *Harvard Law Review* 118(6): 1789–1853.

Fassin D (2011) *Humanitarian Reason: The Moral History of the Present.* Berkeley, CA: University of California Press.

Feischmidt M, Pries L and Cantat C (2019) *Refugee Protection and Civil Society in Europe.* Cham: Palgrave Macmillan.

Fekete L (2009) Europe: Crimes of solidarity. *Race & Class* 50(4): 83–97.

Ferrell J (2018) Criminological ethnography: Living and knowing. In: Rice SK and Maltz MD (eds) *Doing Ethnography in Criminology: Discovery Through Fieldwork.* Cham: Springer International, pp. 147–161.

Finotelli C and Sciortino G (2013) Through the gates of the fortress: European visa policies and the limits of immigration control. *Perspectives on European Politics and Society* 14(1): 80–101.

FitzGerald D (2012) A comparativist manifesto for international migration studies. *Ethnic and Racial Studies* 35(10): 1725–1740.

FitzGerald D (2020) Remote control of migration: Theorising territoriality, shared coercion, and deterrence, *Journal of Ethnic and Migration Studies* 46(1): 4–22.

Fitz-Gibbon K (2014) Overcoming barriers in the criminal justice system: Examining the value and challenges of interviewing legal practitioners. In: Lumsden K and Winter A (eds) *Reflexivity in Criminological Research: Experiences with the Powerful and the Powerless*. London: Palgrave Macmillan, pp. 247–258.

Fleischmann L (2019) Making volunteering with refugees governable: The contested role of 'civil society' in the German welcome culture. *Social Inclusion* 7(2): 64–73.

Franko K (2020) *The Crimmigrant Other: Migration and Penal Power*. London: Routledge.

Fraser N (1999) Social justice in the age of identity politics: Redistribution, recognition, and participation. *Culture and Economy after the Cultural Turn* 1: 25–52.

Fraser N (2005) Reframing justice in a globalizing world. *New Left Review* 36 https://newleftreview.org/issues/ii36/articles/nancy-fraser-reframing-justice-in-a-globalizing-world.

Frelick B, Kysel IM and Podkul J (2016) The impact of externalization of migration controls on the rights of asylum seekers and other migrants. *Journal on Migration and Human Security* 4(4): 190–220.

Fritsvold ED (2009) Under the law: Legal consciousness and radical environmental activism. *Law & Social Inquiry* 34(4): 799–824.

Galanter M (1974) Why the haves come out ahead: Speculations on the limits of legal change. *Law & Society Review* 9(1): 95–160.

Galli C (2019) The ambivalent US context of reception and the dichotomous legal consciousness of unaccompanied minors. *Social Problems* 67(4): 763–781.

Gammeltoft-Hansen T and Sørensen NN (eds) (2013) *The Migration Industry and the Commercialization of International Migration*. London: Routledge.

García-Villega M (2003) Symbolic power without violence? Critical comments on legal consciousness studies. *International Journal for the Semiotics of Law* 16: 363–393.

Garelli G and Tazzioli M (2018) The humanitarian war against migrant smugglers at sea. *Antipode* 50(3): 685–703.

Garkisch M, Heidingsfelder J and Beckmann M (2017) Third sector organizations and migration: A systematic literature review on the contribution of third sector organizations in view of flight, migration and refugee crises. *VOLUNTAS* 28(5): 1839–1880.

Garland D (1996) The limits of the sovereign state. *British Journal of Criminology* 36(4): 445–471.

Garland D (2001) *The Culture of Control. Crime and Social Order in Contemporary Society*. Chicago: University of Chicago Press.

Gathmann C (2008) Effects of enforcement on illegal markets: Evidence from migrant smuggling along the southwestern border. *Journal of Public Economics* 92(10–11): 1926–1941.

Geertsema K, Groenendijk C, Grütters C, Minderhoud P, Nissen E, Strik T, Terlouw A and Zwaan K (2021) Ongezien Onrecht in het Vreemdelingenrecht. *Nederlands Juristenblad* 96(14): 1046–1053.

Geertz C (1973) *The Interpretation of Cultures*. New York: Basic Books.

Gehring A (2013) Seeking access to long-term care: Legal consciousness of Dutch retirement migrants on the Costa Blanca. *Oñati Socio-Legal Series* 3(6): 1023–1040.

Geiger M and Pécoud A (eds) (2013) *Disciplining the Transnational Mobility of People*. London: Palgrave Macmillan.

Genç F, Heck G and Hess S (2018) The multilayered migration regime in Turkey: Contested regionalization, deceleration and legal precarization. *Journal of Borderlands Studies* 34(4): 489–508.

Gerard A and Weber L (2019) 'Humanitarian borderwork': Identifying tensions between humanitarianism and securitization for government contracted NGOs working with adult and unaccompanied minor asylum seekers in Australia. *Theoretical Criminology* 23(2): 266–285.

Gilboy JA (1997) Implications of third-party involvement in enforcement: The INS, illegal travelers, and international airlines. *Law & Society Review* 31(3): 505–530.

Glaser BG and Strauss AL ([1967] 2006) *The Discovery of Grounded Theory: Strategies for Qualitative Research*. New Brunswick: Aldine Transaction.

Gleeson S (2010) Labour rights for all? The role of undocumented immigrant status for worker claims making. *Law & Social Inquiry* 35(3): 561–602.

Glick Schiller N and Salazar NB (2013) Regimes of mobility across the globe. *Journal of Ethnic and Migration Studies* 39(2): 183–200.

Goffman E (1961) *Asylums. Essays on the Social Situation of Mental Patients and Other Inmates*. New York: Anchor Books.

Griffiths M (2013) Living with uncertainty: Indefinite immigration detention. *Journal of Legal Anthropology* 1(3): 263–286.

Groenendijk K and den Heijer M (2022) Verblijfsrechten voor Surinaamse Oud-Nederlanders. *Nederlands JuristenBlad*, 1 December 2022. https://www.njb.nl/blogs/verblijfsrechten-voor-surinaamse-oud-nederlanders/.

Güdük A and Desmet E (2022) Legal consciousness and migration: Towards a research agenda. *International Journal of Law in Context* 18(2): 213–228.

Guild E (2004) Who is an irregular migrant? In: Bogusz B, Cholewinski R, Cygan A and Szyszczak E (eds) *Irregular Migration and Human Rights: Theoretical, European and International Perspectives*. Leiden: Brill Nijhoff, pp. 3–28.

Guild E (2009) *Security and Migration in the 21st Century*. Cambridge: Polity Press.

Guiraudon V and Joppke C (eds) (2001) *Controlling a New Migration World*. London: Routledge.

Guiraudon V and Lahav G (2000) A reappraisal of the state sovereignty debate: The case of migration control. *Comparative Political Studies* 33(2): 163–195.

Gülzau F (2021) A 'new normal' for the Schengen area. When, where and why member states reintroduce temporary border controls? *Journal of Borderlands Studies*. Epub ahead of print https://doi.org/10.1080/08865655.2021.1996260.

Haddeland HB (2021) 'Victims not wrongdoers': The legal consciousness of rejected asylum seekers in Norway. *Journal of Law and Society* 48(4): 645–668.

Hadjimatheou K and Lynch DJ (2018) UK anti-slavery policy at the border: Humanitarian opportunism and the challenge of victim consent to assistance. *European Journal of Criminology* 17(5): 678–698.

Hajer M and Bröer C (2020) We are here! Claim-making and claim-placing of undocumented migrants in Amsterdam. *European Journal of Cultural and Political Sociology* 7(4): 431–451.

Halliday S (2019) After hegemony: The varieties of legal consciousness research. *Social & Legal Studies* 28(6): 859–878.

Halliday S and Morgan B (2013) I fought the law and the law won? Legal consciousness and the critical imagination. *Current Legal Problems* 66(1): 1–32.

Hammersley M (2013) *What is Qualitative Research?* London: Bloomsbury Academic.

Hannah-Moffat K and Lynch M (2012) Theorizing punishment's boundaries: An introduction. *Theoretical Criminology* 16(2): 119–121.

Hannah-Moffat K and Maurutto P (2012) Shifting and targeted forms of penal governance: Bail, punishment and specialized courts. *Theoretical Criminology* 16(2): 201–219.

Hannerz U (2003) Being there... and there... and there! Reflections on multi-site ethnography. *Ethnography* 4(2): 201–216.

Harkin D (2015) Police legitimacy, ideology and qualitative methods: A critique of Procedural Justice Theory. *Criminology and Criminal Justice* 15(5): 594–612.

Hasselberg I (2014) Coerced to leave: Punishment and the surveillance of foreign national offenders in the UK. *Surveillance & Society* 12(4): 471–484.

Hasselberg I (2016) *Enduring Uncertainty. Deportation, Punishment and Everyday Life.* New York: Berghan.

Hayes D (2015) The impact of supervision on the pains of community penalties in England and Wales: An exploratory study. *European Journal of Probation* 7(2): 85–102.

Hayes D (2018) Proximity, pain, and state punishment. *Punishment & Society* 20(2): 235–254.

Heck G and Hess S (2017) Tracing the effects of the EU-Turkey deal. *Movements. Journal for Critical Migration and Border Regime Studies* 3(2): 35–56.

Hernández D (2010) 'I'm gonna call my lawyer': Shifting legal consciousness at the intersection of inequality. *Studies in Law, Politics and Society* 51: 95–121.

Hertogh M (2004) A 'European' conception of legal consciousness: Rediscovering Eugen Ehrlich. *Journal of Law and Society* 31(4): 457–481.

Hertogh M (2012) Mind the (new) gap. A selective survey of current law and society research in the Netherlands. *International Journal of Law in Context* 8(1): 137–153.

Hertogh M (2018) *Nobody's Law: Legal Consciousness and Legal Alienation in Everyday Life*. London: Palgrave Macmillan.

Hiah J (2019) *Having a Chinese Job. A Study on Interdependencies, Vulnerabilities and Opportunities within Migrant Businesses in Romania and the Netherlands*. Rotterdam: Erasmus University Rotterdam, PhD thesis.

Hiah J and Staring R (2016) 'But the Dutch would call it exploitation'. Crimmigration and the moral economy of the Chinese catering industry in the Netherlands. *Crime, Law and Social Change* 66(1): 83–100.

Hinds L and Murphy K (2007) Public satisfaction with police: Using procedural justice to improve police legitimacy. *Australian and New Zealand Journal of Criminology* 40(1): 27–42.

Hinsch W (2010) Justice, legitimacy, and constitutional rights. *Critical Review of International Social and Political Philosophy* 13(1): 39–54.

Hintjens HM, Siegmann KA and Staring R (2020) Seeking health below the radar: Undocumented people's access to healthcare in two Dutch cities. *Social Science and Medicine* 248: 1–10.

Horák F, Lacko D, and Klocek A (2021) Legal consciousness: A systematic review of its conceptualization and measurement methods. *Anuario de Psicología Jurídica* 31(1): 9–34.

Hough M, Jackson J and Bradford B (2013) Legitimacy, trust and compliance: An empirical test of procedural justice theory using the European Social Survey. In: Tankebe J and Liebling A (eds) *Legitimacy and Criminal Justice: An International Exploration*. Oxford: Oxford University Press, pp. 326–352.

IND (2022) *De Stand van de Uitvoering*. The Hague: Immigration and Naturalisation Service.

Jackson J and Bradford B (2019) Blurring the distinction between empirical and normative legitimacy? A methodological commentary on 'police legitimacy and citizen cooperation in China'. *Asian Journal of Criminology* 14(4): 265–289.

Jackson J, Bradford B, Hough M, Myhill A, Quinton P and Tyler TR (2012) Why do people comply with the law? Legitimacy and the influence of legal institutions. *British Journal of Criminology* 52(6): 1051–1071.

Jackson J, Hough M, Bradford B and Kuha J (2015) Empirical legitimacy as two connected psychological states. In: Mesko G and Tankebe J (eds) *Trust and Legitimacy in Criminal Justice*. London: Springer, pp. 137–160.

James MR (2021) Democratic legitimacy and coercively enforced borders: Assessing the argument of Arash Abizadeh. *Ethics, Politics and Society* 4(1): 1–22.

Jesuit Refugee Service (2010) *Becoming Vulnerable in Detention, Civil Society Report on the Detention of Vulnerable Asylum Seekers and Irregular Migrants in the European Union*. Brussels: JRS-Europe.

Joppke C (1999) How immigration is changing citizenship: A comparative view. *Ethnic and Racial Studies* 22(4): 629–652.

Kalhan A (2010) Rethinking immigration detention. *Columbia Law Review* 110(1): 42–58.

Kalir B (2019) Repressive compassion: Deportation caseworkers furnishing an emotional comfort zone in encounters with illegalized migrants. *PoLAR* 42(1): 68–84.

Kalir B and Wissink L (2016) The deportation continuum: Convergences between state agents and NGO workers in the Dutch deportation field. *Citizenship Studies* 20(1): 34–59.

Karp DJ (2020) What is the responsibility to respect human rights? Reconsidering the 'respect, protect, and fulfil' framework. *International Theory* 12(1): 83–108.

Kaufman E (2015) *Punish and Expel: Border Control, Nationalism and the New Purpose of the Prison*. Oxford: Oxford University Press.

Kennedy D (1980) Toward an historical understanding of legal consciousness: The case of classical legal thought in America 1850–1940. *Research in Law & Society* 3: 3–24.

Khosravi S (2009) Sweden: Detention and deportation of asylum seekers. *Race & Class* 50(4): 38–56.

Khosravi S (ed.) (2018) *After Deportation: Ethnographic Perspectives*. Cham: Palgrave Macmillan.

King R (2018) Context-based qualitative research and multi-sited migration studies in Europe. In: Zapata-Barrero R and Yalaz E (eds) *Qualitative Research in European Migration Studies*. Cham: Springer Open, pp. 35–56.

Klaassen M and Rodrigues P (2021) *Interpretatie en implementatie van de Terugkeerrichtlijn*. The Hague: WODC.

Klaassen M, Rap S, Rodrigues P and Liefaard T (2020) *Safeguarding Children's Rights in Immigration Law*. Cambridge: Intersentia.

Koppes S (2017) *Valse Hoop of Bittere Noodzaak? Opvang van Mensen zonder Verblijfsrecht*. Amsterdam: Amnesty International/LOS Foundation.

Koser K and Kuschminder K (2015) *Comparative Research on the Assisted Voluntary Return and Reintegration of Migrants*. Geneva: International Organization for Migration.

Koslowski R (2002) Immigration, border control and aging societies in the European Union. *The Brown Journal of World Affairs* 8(2): 169–180.

Koulish R and van der Woude M (eds) (2020) *Crimmigrant Nations: Resurgent Nationalism and the Closing of Borders*. New York: Fordham University Press.

Kourachanis N (2018) Asylum seekers, hotspot approach and anti-social policy responses in Greece (2015–2017). *Journal of International Migration and Integration* 19: 1153–1167.

Kox M (2007) De menswaardigheid van de vrijheidsontneming van vreemdelingen in Nederland. *Proces* 2007(5): 186–193.

Kox M (2010) *Het Leven Gaat Door. Een Onderzoek naar de Effecten van het Illegalenbeleid op het Leven van Uitgeprocedeerde Asielzoekers in Utrecht.* Utrecht: Stichting LOS.

Kox M (2011) *Leaving Detention... A Study on the Influence of Immigration Detention on Migrants' Decision-Making Processes Regarding Return.* The Hague: International Organization for Migration.

Kox M and Staring R (2020) 'If you don't have documents or a legal procedure, you are out!' Making humanitarian organizations partner in migration control. *European Journal of Criminology* 19(5): 974–993.

Kox M and Staring R (2021) 'I call it a system': Unauthorized migrants' understandings of the long reach of Dutch internal migration controls. *International Journal for Crime, Justice and Social Democracy* 10(3): 87–100.

Kox M, De Ridder S, Vanhouche A-S, Boone MM and Beyens K (2014) Detentiebeleving van strafrechtelijk gedetineerden zonder verblijfsrecht. *Tijdschrift voor Criminologie* 56(2): 31–47.

Kox M, Boone M and Staring R (2020) The pains of being unauthorized in the Netherlands. *Punishment and Society* 22(4): 534–552.

Kreichauf R (2023) Governing migration through small towns: Dispersal and the production of spaces of transit. *International Journal of Urban and Regional Research* 47(3): 349–367.

Kromhout M, Kloppenburg R and Doorn LV (2015) Kinderen Buiten Beeld. De Leefsituatie van Ongedocumenteerde Kinderen in Nederland. *Journal of Social Intervention: Theory and Practice* 24(1): 4–23.

Kubal A (2013) Conceptualizing semi-legality in migration research. *Law & Society Review* 47(3): 555–587.

Kubal A (2014) Struggles against subjection. Implications of criminalization of migration for migrants' everyday lives in Europe. *Crime, Law & Social Change* 62: 91–111.

Kulk F and de Hart B (2013) Mixed couples and Islamic family law in Egypt: Legal consciousness in transnational social space. *Oñati Socio-Legal Series* 3(6): 1057–1069.

Kunz R (2013) Governing international migration through partnership. *Third World Quarterly* 34(7): 1227–1246.

Kuschminder K and Dubow T (2022) Moral exclusion, dehumanisation, and continued resistance to return: Experiences of refused Afghan asylum seekers in the Netherlands. *Geopolitics* 28(3): 1057–1078.

Laban CJ (2017) Suicidal behaviour among asylum seekers in the Netherlands: Prevalence, background and prevention. *European Psychiatry* 41(S1): S24–S24.

Lahav G (1998) Immigration and the state: The devaluation and privatisation of immigration control in the EU. *Journal of Ethnic and Migration Studies* 24(4): 675–694.

Larruina RL (2023) *The Winding Road to Meaningful Integration: A Ten-Year Multi-Perspective Approach to Unravelling Refugee Reception and Integration in the Netherlands.* Amsterdam: University of Amsterdam, PhD thesis.

Laubenthal B (2007) The emergence of pro-regularization movements in Western Europe. *International Migration* 45(3): 101–133.

Lavenax S (2006) Shifting up and out: The foreign policy of European immigration control. *West European Politics* 29(2): 329–350.

Leerkes A (2016a) Managing migration through legitimacy? Alternatives to the criminalisation of unauthorized migration. In: Carrera S and Guild E (eds) *Irregular Migration, Trafficking, and Smuggling of Human Beings: Policy Dilemmas in the EU.* Brussels: Centre for European Policy Studies, pp. 24–32.

Leerkes A (2016b) 'Back to the poorhouse? Social protection and social control of unauthorized immigrants in the shadow of the welfare state. *Journal of European Social Policy* 26(2): 140–154.

Leerkes A and Broeders D (2010) A case of mixed motives? Formal and informal functions of administrative immigration detention. *British Journal of Criminology* 50(5): 830–850.

Leerkes A and Kox M (2016) Pressured into deportation? Detainees' unwillingness to 'return' and the moderating influence of international relations. In: Epps D, Lamphear G and Furman R (eds) *Detaining the Immigrant Other. Global and Transnational* issues. New York: Oxford University Press, pp.15–26.

Leerkes A and Kox MH (2017) Pressured into a preference to leave? A study on the 'specific' deterrent effects and perceived legitimacy of immigration detention. *Law & Society Review* 51(4): 895–929.

Leerkes A and Kulu-Glasgow I (2011) Playing hard(er) to get: The state, international couples, and the income requirement. *European Journal of Migration and Law* 13(1): 95–121.

Leerkes A and van Houte M (2020) Beyond the deportation regime: Differential state interests and capacities in dealing with (non-)deportability in Europe. *Citizenship Studies* 24(3): 319–338.

Leerkes A, Varsanyi A and Engbersen G (2012) Local limits to migration control: Practices of selective migration policing in a restrictive national policy context. *Police Quarterly* 15(4): 446–475.

Leerkes A, van Os R and Boersema E (2017) What drives 'soft deportation'? Understanding the rise in Assisted Voluntary Return among rejected asylum seekers in the Netherlands. *Population, Space & Place* 23(8): e2059.

Legomsky S (2007) Learning to live with unequal justice: Asylum and the limits to consistency. *Stanford Law Review* 60(2): 413–474.

Levi M, Sacks A and Tyler T (2009) Conceptualizing legitimacy, measuring legitimating beliefs. *American Behavioral Scientist* 53(3): 354–375.

Levine K and Mellema V (2001) Strategizing the street: How law matters in the lives of women in the street-level drum economy. *Law & Social Inquiry* 26(1): 169–207.

Liebling A (2001) Whose side are we on? Theory, practice and allegiances in prisons research. *British Journal of Criminology* 41(3): 472–484.

Liefaard T (2020) Preface: Children on the move are children in the first place. In: Klaassen M, Rap S, Rodrigues P and Liefaard T (eds) *Safeguarding Children's Rights in Immigration Law*. Cambridge: Intersentia, pp. v–xii.

Lietaert I, Derluyn I and Broekaert E (2013) Returnees' perspectives on their re-migration processes. *International Migration* 52(5): 144–158.

López-Sala A and Barbero I (2019) Solidarity under siege: The crimmigration of activism(s) and protest against border control in Spain. *European Journal of Criminology* 18(5): 678–694.

LOS Foundation (2014) *Hulpverlening aan Uitgeprocedeerde Asielzoekers in 2013*. Utrecht: LOS Foundation.

Lucassen L and van Houtum H (2016) *Voorbij Fort Europa: een nieuwe visie op migratie*. Amsterdam: Atlas Contact.

Lumsden K and Winter A (eds) (2014) *Reflexivity in Criminological Research: Experiences with the Powerful and the Powerless*. London: Palgrave Macmillan.

Lyon D (2007) Surveillance, security and social sorting: Emerging research priorities. *International Criminal Justice Review* 17(3): 161–170.

Mack A, Buimer L, Rog J, Witvliet M and Pluijm M (2022) *Eindevaluatie Landelijke Vreemdelingenvoorziening*. The Hague: WODC.

Maillet P, Mountz A and Williams K (2017) Researching migration and enforcement in obscured places: Practical, ethical and methodological challenges to fieldwork. *Social & Cultural Geography* 18(7): 927–950.

Mainwaring C (2012) Constructing a crisis: The role of immigration detention in Malta. *Population Place & Space* 18(6): 687–700.

Mainwaring C (2016) Migrant agency: Negotiating borders and migration controls. *Migration Studies* 4(3): 289–308.

Mainwaring C and Walton-Roberts M (2018) Governing migration from the margins. *Social & Legal Studies* 27(2): 131–141.

Maliepaard M, Meer M, Leerkes A and Ramdin M (2022) *Intergovernmental Relations and Return, Part 1: Measuring Enforced Return to Europe*. The Hague: WODC.

Marshall AM and Barclay S (2003) In their own words: How ordinary people construct the legal world. *Law & Social Inquiry* 28(3): 617–628.

Martin L (2012) 'Catch and remove': Detention, deterrence, and discipline in US noncitizen family detention practice. *Geopolitics* 17(2): 312–334.

Martinez O, Wu E, Sandfort T, Dodge B, Carballo-Dieguez A, Pinto R, Rhodes S, Moya E and Chavez-Baray S (2013) Evaluating the impact of immigration policies on health status among undocumented immigrants: A systematic review. *Journal of Immigrant and Minority Health* 17(3): 947–970.

Massey D (2015) A missing element in migration theories. *Migration Letters* 12(3): 279–299.

Massey D and Riosmena F (2010) Undocumented migration from Latin America in an era of rising U.S. enforcement. *Annals of the American Academy of Political and Social Science* 630(1): 137–161.

Massey DS, Arango J, Hugo G, Kouaouci A, Pellegrino A and Taylor JE (1998) *Worlds in Motion: Understanding International Migration at the End of the Millennium*. Oxford: Clarendon Press.

Mathiesen T (2006) *Prison on Trial*. Winchester: Waterside Press (3rd English edition).

Matsueda R, Kreager D and Huizinga D (2006) Deterring delinquents: A rational choice model of theft and violence. *American Sociological Review* 71(1): 95–122.

McCann MW and March T (1995) Law and everyday forms of resistance: Socio-political assessment. *Studies in Law, Politics, and Society* 15: 207–236.

McDowell M and Wonders N (2010) Keeping migrants in their place: Technologies of control and racialized public space in Arizona. *Social Justice* 36(2): 54–72.

McGregor J (2011) Contestations and consequences of deportability: Hunger strikes and the political agency of non-citizens. *Citizenship Studies* 15(5): 597–611.

Meijer R and Righton N (2023) Coalitie grotendeels akkoord over asielpakket, maar kabinet wankelt door hoogoplopende ruzie over gezinshereniging. *De Volkskrant*, 6 July 2023.

Menjívar C (2006) Liminal legality: Salvadoran and Guatemalan immigrants' lives in the United States. *American Journal of Sociology* 111(4): 999–1037.

Menjívar C and Abrego L (2012) Legal violence: Immigration law and the lives of Central American immigrants. *American Journal of Sociology* 117: 1380–1421.

Menjívar C and Lakhani SM (2016) Transformative effects of immigration law: Immigrants' personal and social metamorphoses through regularization. *American Journal of Sociology* 121(6): 1818–1855.

Menz G (2009) The neoliberalized state and migration control: The rise of private actors in the enforcement and design of migration policy. *Journal of Contemporary Central and Eastern Europe* 17(3): 315–332.

Merry SE (1990) *Getting Justice and Getting Even. Legal Consciousness among Working-Class Americans*. Chicago: University of Chicago Press.

Merry SE (2012) What is legal culture? An anthropological perspective. *Journal of Comparative Law* 5: 40–58.

Meuleman R, Lubbers M and Kraaykamp G (2016) Opinions on migration in a European perspective: Trends and differences. In: Boelhouwer J, Kraaykamp G and Stoop I (eds) *Trust, Life, Satisfaction and Opinions on Immigration in 15 European Countries*. The Hague: The Netherlands Institute for Social Research, pp. 32–55.

Mezey N (2001) Out of the ordinary: Law, power, culture, and the commonplace. *Law & Social Inquiry* 26(1): 145–167.

Micinski NR (2022) *Delegating Responsibility: International Cooperation on Migration in the European Union*. Ann Arbor: University of Michigan Press.

Miežanskienė R (2020) Exploring tendencies in migrants' legal consciousness research and uncovering factors for socio-legal integration. *European Integration Studies* 14(1): 26–38.

Ministry of Justice and Security (2020) *Rapportage Vreemdelingenketen Jan-Dec 2019*. The Hague: Ministry of Justice and Security.

Mitsilegas V (2013) The changing landscape of the criminalisation of migration in Europe: The protective function of European Union law. In: Guia MK, van der Woude M and van der Leun J (eds) *Social Control and Justice: Crimmigration in the Age of Fear*. The Hague: Eleven International, pp. 87–114.

Mommers C and Velthuis E (2010) *Leaving the Netherlands: Twenty Years of Voluntary Return Policy in the Netherlands (1989–2009)*. The Hague: International Organization for Migration.

Mortelmans D (2009) Het kwalitatief onderzoeksdesign. In: Decorte T and Zaitch D (eds) *Kwalitatieve Methoden en Technieken in de Criminologie*. Leuven: Acco Uitgeverij, pp. 73–118.

Namey E, Guest G and Thairu L (2008) Data reduction techniques for large qualitative data sets. In: Guest G and MacQueen K (eds) *Handbook for Team-Based Qualitative Research*. Lanham: Altamira Press, pp. 137–162.

Newman D (2006) The lines that continue to separate us: Borders in our 'borderless' world. *Progress in Human Geography* 30(2): 143–161.

Nicholls W (2013) Fragmenting citizenship: Dynamics of cooperation and conflict in France's immigrant rights movement. *Ethnic and Racial Studies* 36(4): 611–631.

Nielsen LB (2000) Situating legal consciousness: Experiences and attitudes of ordinary citizens about law and street harassment. *Law & Society Review* 34(4): 1055–1090.

Noaks L and Wincup E (2004) *Criminological Research. Understanding Qualitative Methods*. London: Sage.

Noyon L, Ansems L, Riesthuis T and Tinnevelt R (2023) Legitimacy of institutions for conflict resolution: An introduction. *Utrecht Law Review* 19(2): 1–12.

Nyers P (2006) The accidental citizen: Acts of sovereignty and (un)making citizenship. *Economy and Society* 35(1): 22–41.

Obdeijn HLM and Schrover M (2008) *Komen en gaan. Immigratie en emigratie in Nederland vanaf 1550*. Amsterdam: Bert Bakker.

Paasi A (2011) Borders, theory and the challenge of relational thinking. *Political Geography* 30: 62–63.

Pakes F and Holt K (2017) Crimmigration and the prison: Comparing trends in prison policy and practice in England and Wales and Norway. *European Journal of Criminology* 14(1): 63–77.

Pallister-Wilkins P (2015) The humanitarian politics of European border policing: Frontex and border police in Evros. *International Political Sociology* 9(1): 53–69.

Pallister-Wilkins P (2017a) Humanitarian rescue/sovereign capture and the policing of possible responses to violent borders. *Global Policy* 8(1): 19–24.

Pallister-Wilkins P (2017b) The tensions of the Ceuta and Melilla border fences. In: Gaibazzi P, Dünnwald S and Bellagamba A (eds) *EurAfrican Borders and Migration Management: Political Cultures, Contested Space, and Ordinary Lives*. Basingstoke: Palgrave Macmillan, pp. 63–81.

Pallister-Wilkins P (2018) Hotspots and the geographies of humanitarianism. *Environment and Planning D: Society and Space* 38(6): 991–1008.

Passel J and Cohn D (2016) *Overall Number of U.S. Unauthorized Immigrants Holds Steady since 2009. Decline in Share from Mexico Mostly Offset by Growth from Asia, Central America and Sub-Saharan Africa*. Washington, DC: Pew Hispanic Centre.

Peeperkorn M (2023) Een akkoord met Tunesië moet blauwdruk worden voor EU-migratiebeleid. *De Volkskrant*, 29 June 2023.

Peutz N (2010) 'Criminal alien' deportees in Somaliland: An ethnography of removal. In: De Genova N and Peutz N (eds) *The Deportation Regime: Sovereignty, Space, and Freedom of Movement*. Durham: Duke University Press, pp. 371–409.

Pham H (2007) The private enforcement of immigration laws. *Georgetown Law Journal* 96(3): 777–826.

Pickering S and Weber L (2006) *Borders, Mobility and Technologies of Control*. New York: Springer.

Pickering S and Weber L (2014) New deterrence scripts in Australia's rejuvenated offshore detention regime for asylum seekers. *Law & Social Inquiry* 39(4): 1006–1026.

Pickering S, Bosworth M and Aas KF (2015) The criminology of mobility. In: Pickering S and Ham J (eds) *The Routledge Handbook on Crime and International Migration*. London: Routledge, pp. 382–395.

Picozza F (2017) Dubliners: Unthinking displacement, illegality, and refugeeness within Europe's geographies of asylum. In: De Genova N (ed.) *The Borders of 'Europe'. Autonomy of Migration, Tactics of Bordering*. Durham/London: Duke University Press, pp. 233–354.

Piquero A and Pogarsky G (2002) Beyond Stafford and Warr's reconceptualization of deterrence: Personal and vicarious experiences, impulsivity, and offending behavior. *Journal of Research in Crime and Delinquency* 39(2): 153–186.

Pluymen MH (2008) *Niet toelaten betekent uitsluiten. Een rechtssociologisch onderzoek naar de rechtvaardiging en praktijk van uitsluiting van vreemdelingen van voorzieningen*. The Hague: Boom Juridische uitgeverij.

Portes A (1978) Toward a structural analysis of illegal (undocumented) immigration. *International Migration Review* 12(4): 469–484.

Poulton E (2014) Having the balls: Reflections on doing gendered research with football hooligans. In: Lumsden K and Winter A (eds) *Reflexivity in Criminological Research: Experiences with the Powerful and the Powerless*. London: Palgrave Macmillan, pp. 77–89.

Pound R (1910) Law in books and law in action. *American Law Review* 44(1): 12–36.

Pratt A (2005) *Securing Borders: Detention and Deportation in Canada*. Vancouver/Toronto: UBC Press.

Pro Facto (2018) *Onderdak en Opvang door Rijk en Gemeenten van Vertrekplichtige Vreemdelingen en de Invloed daarvan op Terugkeer*. Groningen: Pro Facto.

Radburn M and Stott C (2019) The social psychological processes of 'procedural justice': Concepts, critiques and opportunities. *Criminology and Criminal Justice* 19(4): 421–438.

Rap S (2020) The right to information of (un)accompanied refugee children: Improving refugee children's legal position, fundamental rights' implementation and emotional well-being in the Netherlands. *International Journal of Children's Rights* 28(2): 322–351.

Rijken C, Staring R and van der Woude M (2022) Governing through migration control. *Tijdschrift voor Criminologie* 64(3): 235–250.

Roberts JV and Plesničar MM (2015) Sentencing, legitimacy, and public opinion. In: Meško G and Tankebe J (eds) *Trust and Legitimacy in Criminal Justice: European Perspectives*. Cham: Springer, pp. 33–51.

Rodrigues P (2016) *Zorgen voor Uitgeprocedeerde Vreemdelingen*. Leiden: Universiteit Leiden.

Rose G (1997) Situating knowledges: Positionality, reflexivities and other tactics. *Progress in Human Geography* 21(3): 305–320.

Rothe DL (2010) Book review: Tom Tyler (ed.) Legitimacy and Criminal Justice: International Perspectives. *International Criminal Justice Review* 20(4): 449–450.

Rusinovic K, van der Leun J, Chessa T, Weltevrede A and Engbersen G (2002) *Nieuwe Vangnetten in de Samenleving. Over Problemen en Dilemma's in de Opvang van Kwetsbare Groepen*. Rotterdam: Risbo.

Ryo E (2011) *Becoming Illegal: Modelling Rationality and Morality of Unauthorized Migrants*. Stanford: Stanford University, PhD thesis.

Ryo E (2013) Deciding to cross norms and economics of unauthorized migration. *American Sociological Review* 78: 574–603.

Ryo E (2015) Less enforcement, more compliance: Rethinking unauthorized migration. *UCLA Law Review* 62(3): 622–671.

Ryo E (2016) Detained: A study of immigration bond hearings. *Law & Society Review* 50(1): 117–153.

Ryo E (2017) The promise of a subject-centred approach to understanding immigration noncompliance. *Journal on Migration and Human Security* 5(2): 285–296.

Saldaña JM (2016) *The Coding Manual for Qualitative Researchers*. Los Angeles: Sage.

Sarat A (1990) '… The law is all over': Power, resistance and the legal consciousness of the welfare poor. *Yale Journal of Law & the Humanities* 2(2): 343–379.

Sarat A and Kearns T (1993) Beyond the great divide. In: Sarat A and Kearns T (eds) *Law in Everyday Life*. Ann Arbor: University of Michigan Press, pp. 21–61.

Scholten S (2014) *Privatisation of Immigration Control? A Socio-Legal Study on the Role of Private Transport Companies in the Netherlands and the United Kingdom*. Leiden: Brill Nijhoff.

Scherder E, van Os C and Zijlstra E (2018) *Schaderisico bij uitzetting langdurig verblijvende kinderen. Een multidisciplinaire wetenschappelijke onderbouwing*. Groningen: University of Groningen.

Schultz SU (2021) 'The adventure is not easy': The discretionary politics of social suffering and agency in post-deportation narratives in Southern Mali. *International Journal for Crime, Justice and Social Democracy* 10(3): 101–114.

Schuster L and Majidi N (2013) What happens post-deportation? The experience of deported Afghans. *Migration Studies* 1(2): 221–240.

Schwenken H (2013) 'The EU should talk to Germany': Transnational legal consciousness as a rights claiming tool among undocumented migrants. *International Migration* 51(6): 132–145.

Scott JC (1985) *Weapons of the Weak: Everyday Forms of Resistance*. London: Yale University Press.

Scott R (2008) Approaching adulthood: The maturing of institutional theory. *Theory and Society* 37(5): 427–442.

Servaas L (2019) *'Terugkeer op maat?' Een onderzoek naar de terugkeer van onrechtmatig verblijvende Indonesische migranten*. Rotterdam: Erasmus Universiteit, Master's dissertation.

Shammas VL (2014) The pains of freedom: Assessing the ambiguity of Scandinavian penal exceptionalism on Norway's prison island. *Punishment & Society* 16(1): 104–123.

Sherman L (1993) Defiance, deterrence, and irrelevance: A theory of the criminal sanction. *Journal of Research in Crime and Delinquency* 30(4): 445–473.

Sie Dhian Ho M, van Heukelingen N, van de Weem N, van Mulligen A and Lepla R (2021) *Gedeeld Belang bij Circulaire Migratie: Naar Duurzame Partnerschappen*. The Hague: Netherlands Institute of International Relations 'Clingendael'.

Siegel D (2008) Veldwerk online: Mensensmokkel vanuit het perspectief van de gesmokkelde migrant. *Tijdschrift voor Criminologie* 50(4): 406–412.

Sigona N (2018) The contested politics of naming in Europe's 'refugee crisis'. *Ethnic and Racial Studies* 41(3): 456–460.

Silbey SS (2005) After legal consciousness. *Annual Review of Law and Social Science* 1(1): 323–368.

Sinatti G (2019) Humanitarianism as politics: Civil support initiatives for migrants in Milan's Hub. *Social Inclusion* 7(2): 139–148.

Sitkin L (2014) Coordinating internal immigration control in the UK. *International Journal of Migration and Border Studies* 1(1): 39–56.

Smith H (2015) Shocking images of drowned Syrian boy show tragic plight of refugees. *The Guardian*, 2 September 2015. https://www.theguardian.com/world/2015/sep/02/shocking-image-of-drowned-syrian-boy-shows-tragic-plight-of-refugees.

Snel E, Bilgili Ö and Staring R (2020) Migration trajectories and transnational support within and beyond Europe. *Journal of Ethnic and Migration Studies* 47(14): 3209–3225.

Social Inclusion (2019) Special Issue 7(2): The European refugee controversy: Civil solidarity, cultural imaginaries and political change. https://www.cogitatiopress.com/socialinclusion/issue/view/107.

Soliman F (2021) States of exception, human rights, and social harm: Towards a border zemiology. *Theoretical Criminology* 25(2): 228–248.

Squire V (2017) Governing migration through death in Europe and the US: Identification, burial and the crisis of modern humanism. *European Journal of International Relations* 23(3): 513–532.

Staring R (1998) Scenes from a fake marriage: Notes on the flip-side of embeddedness. In: Koser K and Lutz H (eds) *The New Migration in Europe. Social Constructions and Social Realities*. London: Springer, pp. 224–241.

Staring R (2001) *Reizen Onder Regie: Het Migratieproces van Illegale Turken in Nederland.* Amsterdam: Het Spinhuis.

Staring R (2014) Lezing wake detentiecentrum Rotterdam. https://repub.eur.nl/pub/77353/.

Staring R and Aarts J (2010*) Jong en Illegaal in Nederland. Een Beschrijvende Studie naar de Komst en het Verblijf van Onrechtmatig Verblijvende (Voormalige) Alleenstaande Minderjarige Vreemdelingen en hun Visie op de Toekomst.* The Hague: Boom Juridische uitgevers.

Staring RHJM and Kox MH (2016) Safe havens voor onrechtmatig in Nederland verblijvende vreemdelingen. Veiligheid en het toezicht op irreguliere migratie via hulpverleningsinstanties. *Tijdschrift over Cultuur en Criminaliteit* 6(3): 71–90.

Staring R and Kox M (2020) *Hulp bij terugkeer. Vice Versa 4.0 van Stichting ROS nader bekeken.* Rotterdam: Erasmus University Rotterdam/Stichting ROS (internal report).

Staring R and Kox M (2022) Re-socializing migrant networks: Moving beyond dominant migrant-network approaches. In: van Liempt I, Schapendonk J and Campos-Delgado A (eds) *Research Handbook on Migration.* Cheltenham: Edward Elgar, pp. 140–151.

Staring RHJM and Kroese J (1991) Een kwestie van vertrouwen: Daderonderzoek in gevangenissen. *Justitiële Verkenningen* 17(9): 112–140.

Staring R and Timmerman R (2021) The Crimmigration trend in the Netherlands: Some critical reflections. *Crimmigratie & Recht* 5(1): 60–73.

Staring R and van Swaaningen R (2013) Irreguliere migratie en illegaal verblijf: Beleid, conflicten en contradicties. *Tijdschrift over Cultuur and Criminaliteit* 3(1): 3–14.

Staring R and van Swaaningen R (2021) Borders, mobilities, and governance in transnational perspective. In: Pontell HN (ed.) *Oxford Research Encyclopedia of Criminology and Criminal Justice.* Oxford: Oxford University Press.

Staring R, Alves d'Almeida J, Noya S and van Schijndel M (2012*) Ondersteuning bij Zelfstandige Terugkeer.* The Hague: Boom/Lemma.

Staring R, Boesveldt N and Kox M (2022) *Vechten met het Leven: Een kwalitatief onderzoek onder ongedocumenteerde oudere migranten in Nederland.* The Hague: Boom criminologie.

Statham P and Geddes E (2006) Elites and the 'organised public': Who drives British immigration politics and in which direction? *West European Politics* 29(2): 248–269.

Stel N (2021) Uncertainty, exhaustion, and abandonment beyond South/North divides: Governing forced migration through strategic ambiguity. *Political Geography* 88(23): 102391.

Stichting LOS (2011) *Eindrapportage: Migrantengroepen en Ongedocumenteerde Hulpvragers.* Utrecht: Stichting LOS.

Strauss A and Corbin J (1998) *Basics of qualitative research: Techniques and procedures for developing grounded theory (2nd ed.)*. Thousand Oaks, CA: Sage Publications Inc.

Stronks M (2014) Na Twintig Jaar Verblijf ben je Veilig. *Asiel & Migrantenrecht* 10: 423–427.

Stumpf J (2006) The Crimmigration crisis: Immigrants, crime, and sovereign power. *American University Law Review* 56(2): 367–419.

Stumpf J (2013) The process is the punishment in crimmigration law. In: Aas KF and Bosworth M (eds) (2013) *The Borders of Punishment: Citizenship, Crime Control, and Social Exclusion*. Oxford: Oxford University Press, pp. 58–75.

Summers Sandoval Jr TF (2008) Disobedient bodies: Racialization, resistance, and the mass (re)articulation of the Mexican immigrant body. *American Behavioral Scientist* 52(4): 580–597.

Sun I, Li L, Wu Y and Hu R (2018) Police legitimacy and citizen Cooperation in China: Testing an alternative model. *Asian Journal of Criminology* 13: 275–291.

Sunshine J and Tyler TR (2003a) The role of procedural justice and legitimacy in shaping public support for policing. *Law & Society Review* 37(3): 513–548.

Sunshine J and Tyler TR (2003b) Moral solidarity, identification with the community, and the importance of procedural justice: The police as prototypical representatives of a group's moral values. *Social Psychology Quarterly* 66(2): 153–165.

SVMA and VAJN (2021) *Ongehoord Onrecht in het Vreemdelingenrecht*. The Hague: SVMA and VAJN.

Sykes G (1958) *The Society of Captives. A Study of a Maximum Security Prison*. Princeton: Princeton University Press.

Taekema S, Gaakeer J and Loth M (2020) *Recht in context. Een inleiding tot rechtswetenschap (zesde druk)*. The Hague: Boom juridisch.

Tamanaha B (2001) *A General Jurisprudence of Law and Society*. Oxford: Oxford University Press.

Tankebe J (2009) Public cooperation with the police in Ghana: Does procedural fairness matter? *Criminology* 47(4): 1265–1293.

Tankebe J (2013) Viewing things differently: The dimensions of public perceptions of police legitimacy. *Criminology* 51(1): 103–135.

Tankebe J and Liebling A (2013) Legitimacy and criminal justice: An introduction. In: Tankebe J and Liebling A (eds) *Legitimacy and Criminal Justice: An International Exploration*. Oxford: Oxford University Press, pp. 1–6.

Terlouw AB (2013) Fundamentele rechten van niet rechtmatig in Nederland verblijvende vreemdelingen. Een fata morgana. *Rechtsgeleerd Magazijn THEMIS* 1: 9–19.

Terlouw A and Groenendijk C (2009) *Tussen Onafhankelijkheid en Hiërarchie. De Relatie Tussen Vreemdelingenrechters en de Raad van State 2001-2007*. The Hague: Sdu Uitgevers.

Thielemann E and Armstrong C (2013) Understanding European asylum cooperation under the Schengen/Dublin system: A public goods framework. *European Security* 22(2): 148–164.

Timmerman R (2018) *European Borderscapes and the Illegali(ized) Migrant: Undeportability and Repeated Detention in the Dutch Migration Control Field.* Utrecht: Utrecht University, unpublished Master's dissertation.

Timmerman R, Leerkes A and Staring R (2019) *Safe Reporting of Crime for Migrants with Irregular Status in the Netherlands.* Oxford: University of Oxford, COMPAS.

Timmerman RI, Leerkes A, Staring R and Delvino N (2020) 'Free in, free out': Exploring Dutch firewall protections for irregular migrant victims of crime. *European Journal of Migration and Law* 22(3): 427–455.

Tomczak P and Thompson D (2019) Inclusionary control? Theorizing the effects of penal voluntary organizations' work. *Theoretical Criminology* 23(1): 4–24.

Triandafyllidou A (ed.) (2010) *Irregular Migration in Europe.* Aldershot: Ashgate.

Trubek DM (1984) Where the action is: Critical legal studies and empiricism. *Stanford Law Review* 36(2): 575–622.

Turnbull S and Hasselberg I (2017) From prison to detention: The carceral trajectories of foreign-national prisoners in the United Kingdom. *Punishment & Society* 19(2): 135–154.

Turnbull S, Bhatia M and Lousley G (2020) Editors' Introduction. *Critical Criminology* 28(2): 169–173.

Tyler TR (1988) What is procedural justice? Criteria used by citizens to assess the fairness of legal Procedures. *Law & Society Review* 22(1): 103–135.

Tyler T (2003) Procedural justice, legitimacy, and the effective rule of law. *Crime and Justice* 30: 283–357.

Tyler TR (1990) *Why People Obey the Law.* Princeton: Princeton University Press.

Tyler TR and Darley JM (2000) Building a law-abiding society: Taking public views about morality and the legitimacy of legal authorities into account when formulating substantive law. *Hofstra Law Review* 28(3): 707–740.

Tyler T and Huo YJ (2002) *Trust in the Law: Encouraging Public Cooperation with the Police and Courts.* New York: Russell Sage Foundation.

Tyler T and Jackson J (2013) Future challenges in the study of legitimacy and criminal justice. In: Tankebe J and Liebling A (eds) *Legitimacy and Criminal Justice: An International Exploration.* Oxford: Oxford University Press, pp. 84–105.

Tyler T, Schulhofer S and Huq A (2010) Legitimacy and deterrence effects in counterterrorism policing: A study of Muslim Americans. *Law & Society Review* 44(2): 365–401.

Ugelvik T (2014) Paternal pains of imprisonment: Incarcerated fathers, ethnic minority masculinity and resistance narratives. *Punishment & Society* 16(2): 152–168.

Ugelvik T and Damsa D (2018) The pains of crimmigration imprisonment: Perspectives from a Norwegian all-foreign prison. *British Journal of Criminology* 58(5): 1025–1043.

United Nations High Commissioner for Refugees (1999) *UNHCR's Guidelines on Applicable Criteria and Standards Relating to the Detention of Asylum seekers*. New York: UNHCR.

Van Alphen B, Molleman T, Leerkes A and van den Hoek J (2013) *Van Bejegening tot Vertrek. Een Onderzoek Naar de Werking van Vreemdelingenbewaring*. The Hague: Boom Lemma.

Van Amersfoort H (1999) International migration and civil rights: The dilemmas of migration control in an age of globalisation. In: Brochmann G and Hammar T (eds) *Mechanisms of Immigration Control: A Comparative Analysis of European Regulation Policies*. New York: Routledge, pp. 73–88.

Van Berckel Smit J (2022) *Juridische Verkenning van het recht op voorzieningen en verblijf voor oudere ongedocumenteerden*. The Hague: Boom juridisch.

Van den Bos K (2018) *Why People Radicalize: How Unfairness Judgments are Used to Fuel Radical Beliefs, Extremist Behaviors, and Terrorism*. Oxford: Oxford University Press.

Van den Bos K, Vermunt R and Wilke HAM (1997) Procedural and distributive justice: What is fair depends more on what comes first than what comes next. *Journal of Personality and Social Psychology* 72(1): 95–104.

Van der Heijden P, Cruyf M, Engbersen G and van Gils G (2020) *Schattingen onrechtmatig in Nederland verblijvende vreemdelingen 2017–2018*. The Hague: WODC.

Van der Leun J (2003) *Looking for Loopholes. Processes of Incorporation of Illegal Immigrants in the Netherlands*. Amsterdam: Amsterdam University Press.

Van der Leun JP (2010) *Crimmigratie*. Apeldoorn/Antwerpen: Maklu Uitgevers, inaugural lecture.

Van der Leun J and Bouter H (2015) Gimme shelter: Inclusion and exclusion of irregular immigrants in Dutch civil society. *Journal of Immigrant and Refugee Studies* 13(2): 135–155.

Van der Leun J and van der Woude M (2011) Ethnic profiling in the Netherlands? A reflection on expanding preventive powers, ethnic profiling and a changing social and political context. *Policing and Society* 21(4): 444–455.

Van der Leun JP and van der Woude MAH (2013) Ethnic profiling in the Netherlands? A reflection on expanding preventive powers, ethnic profiling and a changing social and political context. In: Weber L and Bowling B (eds) *Stop and Search: Police Power in Global Context*. London: Routledge, pp. 92–103.

Van der Welle I and Odé A (2009) *Omvang Gemeentelijke Noodopvang aan Uitgeprocedeerde Asielzoekers*. Amsterdam: Regioplan.

Van der Woude MAH (2016) *Chain Reactions in Criminal Justice: Discretion and the Necessity of Interdisciplinary Research*. The Hague: Eleven International.

Van der Woude M (2020) Euroskepticism, nationalism, and the securitization of migration in the Netherlands. In: Koulish R and van der Woude M (eds) *Crimmigrant Nations: Resurgent Nationalism and the Closing of Borders*. New York: Fordham University Press, pp. 227–248.

Van der Woude MAH (2022) Criminology of the borderlands. In: Nelken D and Hamilton C (eds) *Research Handbook of Comparative Criminal Justice*. Cheltenham: Edward Elgar, pp. 207–224.

Van der Woude MAH and Brouwer J (2017) Searching for 'illegal' junk in the trunk: Underlying intentions of (cr)immigration controls in Schengen's internal border areas. *New Criminal Law Review* 20(1): 157–179.

Van der Woude M and Staring R (2021) Transforming borders and the discretionary politics of migration control [Guest editorial to a special issue]. *International Journal for Crime, Justice and Social Democracy* 10(3): i–viii.

Van der Woude M and van der Leun J (2017) Crimmigration checks in the internal border areas of the EU: Finding the discretion that matters. *European Journal of Criminology* 14(1): 27–45.

Van der Woude M, van der Leun J and Nijland JA (2014) Crimmigration in the Netherlands. *Law & Social Inquiry* 39(3): 560–579.

Van der Woude MAH, Dekkers T and Brouwer J (2015) Over crimmigratie en discretionair beslissen binnen het Mobiel Toezicht Veiligheid…of Vreemdelingen…of Veiligheid? *Tijdschrift voor Veiligheid* 14(2): 19–35.

Van der Woude MAH, Brouwer J and Dekkers TJM (2016) *Beslissen in grensgebieden: Een onderzoek naar het Mobiel Toezicht Veiligheid zoals uitgevoerd door de Koninklijke Marechaussee*. The Hague: Boom criminologie.

Van der Woude M, van der Leun J and Nijland J (2014) Crimmigration in the Netherlands. *Law and Social Inquiry* 39(3): 560–579.

Vandevoordt R (2017) Between humanitarian assistance and migration management: On civil actors' role in voluntary return from Belgium. *Journal of Ethnic and Migration Studies* 43(11): 1907–1922.

Vandevoordt R and Verschraegen G (2019a) Subversive humanitarianism and its challenges: Notes on the political ambiguities of civil refugee support. In: Feischmidt M, Pries L and Cantat C (eds) *Refugee Protection and Civil Society in Europe*. Cham: Palgrave Macmillan, pp. 101–128.

Vandevoordt R and Verschraegen G (2019b) The European refugee controversy: Civil solidarity, cultural imaginaries and political change. *Social Inclusion* 7(2): 48–52.

Van Eijl C (2012) *Tussenland. Illegaal in Nederland 1945–2000*. Hilversum: Uitgeverij Verloren.

Van Houte M and Leerkes AS (2019) *Dealing with (Non-)Deportability. A Comparative Policy Analysis of the Post-entry Migration Enforcement Regimes of Western European Countries*. Rotterdam/Maastricht: Erasmus University Rotterdam/Maastricht University.

Van Houte M, Siegel M and Davids T (2014) Return to Afghanistan: Migration as reinforcement of socio-economic stratification. *Population, Space & Place* 21(8): 692–703.

Van Houte M, Leerkes A, Slipper A and Breuls L (2021) Globalised citizenship and the perceived legitimacy of immigration control: Narratives and acts of resistance in immigration detention. *Migration Studies* 9(3): 1269–1291.

Van Kalmthout A (2004) *Terugkeermogelijkheden van Vreemdelingen in de Vreemdelingenbewaring*. Nijmegen: Wolf Legal Publishers.

Van Liempt I and Bilger V (2018) Methodological and ethical dilemmas in research among smuggled migrants. In: Zapata-Barrero R and Yalaz E (eds) *Qualitative Research in European Migration Studies*. Cham: Springer Open, pp. 269–285.

Vanobberghen R, Louckx F, Devroey D and Vandevoorde J (2020) Five years later: The impact of a hunger strike on undocumented migrant workers in Brussels. *Journal of Immigrant and Minority Health* 22: 392–398.

Van Meeteren M (2013) Illegale migranten en informele arbeid in België en Nederland. *Cahiers Politiestudies* 29(4): 51–70.

Van Meeteren M (2014) *Irregular Migrants in Belgium and the Netherlands: Aspirations and Incorporation*. Amsterdam: Amsterdam University Press.

Van Schijndel C and van Gemmert N (2012) *Vreemdelingenbewaring in Getal 2007–2011*. The Hague: Custodial Institutions Agency.

Van Wijk J (2008) *Reaching Out to the Unknown: Native Counselling and the Decision-Making Process of Irregular Migrants and Rejected Asylum Seekers on Voluntary Return*. The Hague: International Organization for Migration.

Van Zwol Committee (2019) *Rapport Onderzoekscommissie Langdurig verblijvende vreemdelingen zonder bestendig verblijfsrecht*. The Hague: Van Zwol Committee.

Varsanyi MW (2005) The paradox of contemporary immigrant political mobilization: Organized labor, undocumented migrants, and electoral participation in Los Angeles. *Antipode* 37(4): 775–795.

Vavouli N (2022) *Immigration and Privacy in the Law of the European Union: The Case of Information Systems*. Leiden: Brill Nijhoff.

Verbaten H (2022) 25 jaar terugkeerbeleid: Frappez toujours. *Justitiële Verkenningen* 48(2): 10–21.

Vertovec S (2007) Super-diversity and its implications. *Ethnic and Racial Studies* 30(6): 1024–1054.

Vertovec S (2019) Talking around super-diversity. *Ethnic and Racial Studies* 42(1): 125–139.

Vervliet M, Rousseau C, Broekaert E and Derluyn I (2015) Multilayered Ethics in Research Involving Unaccompanied Refugee Minors. *Journal of Refugee Studies* 28(4): 468–485.

Virdi PK (2013) Barriers to Canadian justice: Immigrant Sikh women and izzat. *South Asian Diaspora* 5(1): 107–122.

Vollmer BA (2011) Policy discourses on irregular migration in the EU. 'Number games' and 'political games'. *European Journal of Migration and Law* 13(3): 317–339.

Vreemdelingenvisie (2022) https://www.vreemdelingenvisie.nl/vreemdelingenvisie/2022/04/knopen-doorhakteam.

Walsh JP (2014) Watchful citizens: Immigration control, surveillance and societal participation. *Social & Legal Studies* 23(2): 237–259.

Walsh J (2020) Report and deport: Public vigilance and migration policing in Australia. *Theoretical Criminology* 24(2): 276–295.

Walters W (2011) Foucault and frontiers: Notes on the humanitarian border. In: Broeckling U, Krasmann S and Lemke T (eds) *Governmentality: Current Issues and Future Challenges.* New York: Routledge, pp. 138–164.

Walters W (2018) Aviation as deportation infrastructure: Airports, planes, and expulsion. *Journal of Ethnic and Migration Studies* 44(16): 2796–2817.

Walzer M (1983) *Spheres of Justice.* New York: Basic Books.

Warr J (2016) The deprivation of certitude, legitimacy and hope: Foreign national prisoners and the pains of imprisonment. *Criminology & Criminal Justice* 16(3): 301–318.

Webber F (2011) How voluntary are voluntary returns? *Race & Class* 52(4): 98–107.

Webber F (2012) Borderline justice. *Race & Class* 54(2): 39–54.

Weber L (2006) The shifting frontiers of migration control. In Pickering S and Weber L (eds) *Borders, Mobility and Technologies of Control.* Dordrecht: Springer, pp. 21–44.

Weber L (2013) *Policing Non-Citizens.* New York: Routledge.

Weber M (2017) Economy and society: An outline of interpretive sociology. Organized groups (an excerpt). *Journal of Economic Sociology* 18(1): 13–27.

Weber L and Bowling B (2008) Valiant beggars and global vagabonds: Select, eject, immobilize. *Theoretical Criminology* 12(3): 355–375.

Welch M (2012) The sonics of crimmigration in Australia: Wall of noise and quiet manoeuvring. *The British Journal of Criminology* 52(2): 324–334.

Westerink H (2000) Wetenschappers roken illegalen uit. *De Fabel van de Illegaal,* 38/39. https://www.doorbraak.eu/gebladerte/10641f38.htm.

Wilsher D (2012) *Immigration Detention: Law, History, Politics.* Cambridge: Cambridge University Press.

Wilson JQ (1993) The moral sense. *American Political Science Review* 87(1): 1–11.

Wincup E (2017) *Criminological Research: Understanding Qualitative Methods.* London: Sage.

Winter H, Bex-Reimert VM, Geertsema B and Krol E (2018) *Onderdak en Opvang door Rijk en Gemeenten van Vertrekplichtige Vreemdelingen en de Invloed Daarvan op Terugkeer.* Groningen: Pro Facto.

Wonders NA (2017) Sitting on the fence – Spain's delicate balance: Bordering, multiscalar challenges, and crimmigration. *European Journal of Criminology* 14(1): 7–26.

Wyss A (2022) *Navigating the European Migration Regime: Male Migrants, Interrupted Journeys and Precarious Lives.* Bristol: Bristol University Press.

Young KM (2014) Everyone knows the game: Legal consciousness in the Hawaiian cockfight. *Law & Society Review* 48(3): 499–530.

Zaitch D, Mortelmans D and Decorte T (2009) Participerende observatie in de criminologie. In: Decorte T and Zaitch D (eds) *Kwalitatieve Methoden en Technieken in de Criminologie.* Leuven: Acco Uitgeverij, pp. 57–310.

Zedner L (2016) Penal subversions: When is a punishment not punishment, who decides and on what grounds? *Theoretical Criminology* 20(1): 3–20.

Župarić-Iljić D and Valenta M (2019) Opportunistic humanitarianism and securitization discomfort along the Balkan Corridor: The Croatian experience. In: Feischmidt M, Pries L and Cantat C (eds) *Refugee Protection and Civil Society in Europe.* Cham: Palgrave Macmillan, pp. 129–160.

www.ingramcontent.com/pod-product-compliance
Lightning Source LLC
Chambersburg PA
CBHW080938240926
51849CB00004BA/494
* 9 7 8 9 0 4 7 3 0 2 0 9 4 *